International Studies

of the

Committee on International Relations

University of Notre Dame

International Studies

The Catholic Church in World Affairs
Edited by Waldemar Gurian and M. A. Fitzsimons

Diplomacy in a Whirlpool: Hungary between Nazi Germany and the Soviet Union
Stephen Kertesz

Soviet Imperialism: Its Origins and Tactics
Edited by Waldemar Gurian

Panslavism: Its History and Ideology
Hans Kohn

The Foreign Policy of the British Labour Government: 1945-51
M. A. Fitzsimons

Bolshevism: An Introduction to Soviet Communism
Waldemar Gurian

Christian Democracy in Italy and France
Mario Einaudi and François Goguel

Europe Between Democracy and Anarchy
Ferdinand A. Hermens

The Soviet Union: Background, Ideology, Reality
Edited by Waldemar Gurian (Out of Print)

In Preparation

The Social Ethic of German Protestantism: 1848-1933
W. O. Shanahan

THE CATHOLIC CHURCH
IN WORLD AFFAIRS

THE CATHOLIC CHURCH IN WORLD AFFAIRS

Edited by

Waldemar Gurian

and

M. A. Fitzsimons

UNIVERSITY OF NOTRE DAME PRESS

Notre Dame, Indiana

IMPRIMI POTEST:
  Theodore J. Mehling, C.S.C.
    Provincial

NIHIL OBSTAT:
  Leo R. Ward, C.S.C.
    Censor Deputatus

IMPRIMATUR:
  ✠ John F. Noll, D.D.
    Archbishop-Bishop of Fort Wayne

April 15, 1954

Library of Congress

Catalog Card Number

53-7351

To

FATHER JOHN J. CAVANAUGH, C.S.C.

President of the University of Notre Dame
1946-1952

Whose vision made possible
the work of the
Committee on International Relations

PREFACE

The purpose of this volume is to present an account of the Catholic Church in the contemporary world. This has inevitably meant a description of the unity and variety of the present life of the Church. The fact of variety will not surprise Catholics but should bewilder those who see in the Church a monolithic centralization universally fostering totalitarianism. Actually the various chapters of this book, in spite of all differences of approach, reiterate Father Murray's restatement of the traditional conception of two perfect societies, the Church and the state. From this it follows that the Church is anti-totalitarian. Other general points would include the Church's defense of reason and of human and social rights as well as the Church's subordination of all nationalist aspirations to the claims of the human community.

The editors, then, welcomed diversity. They did not seek to impose any unnecessary external uniformity. On such a question as democracy the positions of the contributors range from the philosophical affirmation of democracy in the essay of Yves Simon to the very critical views of Calvo Serer.

The volume is not designed as a directory or reference book. The editors have rejected the temptation to be comprehensive at the almost inevitable cost of diffuseness. The first part of the volume consists of systematic or general accounts of typical situations, major problems and activities of the Church in the middle of the twentieth century. The latter half of the volume consists of studies of particular countries or a particular area.

Omissions were unavoidable. The rapid flux of events compel us to leave unmentioned the sad case of "the deposition" and confinement of Cardinal Wyszynski. Nevertheless, we hope that our volume will enable the reader to look with insight upon the life of the Church today.

Waldemar Gurian
M. A. Fitzsimons

Notre Dame, Indiana

TABLE OF CONTENTS

INTRODUCTION

by Waldemar Gurian

The Catholic Church of the nineteenth century lived in the shadow of the French Revolution. Although the revolutionary attempt to replace traditional religion by a purely secular cult and morality failed, and the realist Napoleon made a concordat with Pius VII, the Church even after her restoration in the public life of France was regarded and criticized as inseparably connected with the pre-revolutionary regime and its feudal order. She was contemptuously characterized in the famous phrase of the Protestant theologian and sociologist Ernst Troeltsch as an impressive ruin surviving from the middle ages. When the great historian, Leopold von Ranke published his *History of the Popes* in the eighteen-thirties he remarked that the time was favorable for writing about the Roman pontiffs, for the Papacy belonged to the past. There were, of course, romantic writers and Catholic converts, such as John Henry Newman, whose intellectual greatness could not be denied. But they were judged to be exceptions, as paradoxical opponents of the trend of the times, as men who without sufficient reason despaired of the present, and were full of strange aesthetic or sentimental longings for buried ages.

The Church seemed to be incompatible with science and its belief in evolution and biblical criticism—as well as with the liberties of modern society. This lack of understanding of the modern world was allegedly proved by the condemnation of Lamennais, who had vainly tried to emancipate the Church from the fettering alliance with the throne, and particularly by the *Syllabus of Errors* of Pius IX. The fate of the Papal State, annexed by the kingdom of Italy, that product of modern, active liberal nationalism, was regarded as symbolic. The Church still had her roots in the masses, as the outcome of Bismarck's *Kulturkampf* and the popularity of

1

the doctrine of papal infallibility (interpreted as a declaration of war against modern enlightened society) showed. But the intellectual elites were against the Church; even when they did not directly reject or fanatically attack her, they looked upon her with condescension and dislike as a purely historical institution or with some antipathy and anger as basing her power on the prejudices and passions of half-literate emotional masses.

What a change has taken place since those days when, in spite of the warnings and misgivings of a few great men such as Kierkegaard and Burckhardt, belief in progress, and in an enlightened and therefore peaceful society prevailed. Crises and struggles, if they were accepted as undeniable realities, were then seen only as the means of the selection of the best, as instruments for the survival of the fittest. The return of French intellectuals to the Church, the English conversions are today no longer seen as isolated, exceptional events. Now they appear as characteristic of a new atmosphere in society, as the early manifestations of a new epoch. Secularist liberalism, which saw the Church as a purely historical institution (though perhaps a socially useful one) is still alive, but is on the defensive. The nineteenth century belief in the triumphant march of science, putting positive truth in the place of allegedly out-dated dogmas, is no longer self-evident for the intellectual avantgarde, although such belief survives (in somewhat sophisticated forms) among social scientists who pretend that they will be or are able to supplement the control of nature by control of society. Since the Pontificate of Leo XIII the utterances of the Popes, once regarded as anachronistic reactionary claims and taken seriously only in order to reject them emphatically, have received increasing recognition as wise pronouncements containing teachings and ideas from which our time has much to learn. Even those who do not recognize Papal religious authority praise the Popes as social leaders, as guides to peace. It is, of course, true that in the United States, which has fortunately escaped the tragic experiences that shake the foundations of social and individual life, secularism and a vague humanitarian progressive liberalism have retained more strength than in Europe, and old anti-Catholic prejudices continue in some circles, though expressed mostly in a cautious and polite form. In some American circles, however, Catholics are still regarded as having no true education, as belonging to illiterate pressure groups, as clinging to inherited irrational traditions, and as supporting primitive mass mentality.

Although there are these survivals of the secularized world of the nineteenth century and others who consider the modern influence of religion and particularly the Catholic Church to be only the failure of modern nerve, who hail Bertrand Russell as a great philosopher and courageous destroyer of prejudices, the general atmosphere has changed. The secularist world is on the defensive; it has lost its self-assurance, for it is no longer certain that it has the future on its side. The twentieth century is not only the century of nihilistic despair and bitter disappointment; it is also a period of longing for faith and certitude beyond the ups and downs of social and political struggles. The Catholic Church is taken seriously even by many who reject her claim to be the Church founded by Christ, but look upon her as a force working for psychological certitude.

On the other hand, secularism has survived. But it has assumed, when it exercises great active influence, a violent, and pseudo-religious character. It claims to have the key not only to the understanding of history, but also to the knowledge of the future. After the paroxysm and hysteria of the French Revolution with its cult of reason, secularism had in general taken a respectable form; trying to appear as tolerant, opposing only intolerance embodied allegedly in the Catholic Church. But today, in Communism, it shows an absolutely intolerant character. Communism is a belief (in the guise of the "science" and the only "rational philosophy") in the self-sufficiency of a perfect society here on earth and in the possibility, even the necessity to achieve it by social engineering, which includes violence, calculated violence and cynical amoral maneuvering. And Communism threatens not only the Church (which according to it must disappear, since it is an organization based on ignorance and prejudices and destined to be overcome by the progressive reorganization of society) but it also endangers liberal secular society. This society is condemned as the product of an individualist and sceptical relativism, corresponding to the anarchy of free competition and doomed by the perfect planning of the future based on *one* true theory and one practice corresponding to it. And, of course, the Communist leaders claim to have *the* truth and therefore to be able to determine all practice and all behavior of individuals and groups.

Communism is one of the pseudo-religious heresies of our time. In the twentieth century heresies appear not in the form of theolog-

3

ical doctrines, but as explanations of history and social development. The enemies of revealed religion are the adherents of political religions. Communism, as determined by the USSR, still belongs to the nineteenth century insofar as it pretends to an exclusive claim to being scientific and reasonable. Its atheism openly tries to replace God by self-sufficient man who, when he has been educated and has erected after many struggles and reversals the perfect society, will be satisfied with his earthy reality. Then he will not need to escape from a sad life by creating God; in Communist thought God is only a product of a backwardness which will disappear as soon as progress is achieved and man knows what is his and society's true nature.

But there are other forms of socio-political pseudo-religions in the twentieth century, and their basic element is the emphasis upon myth. Racialist pseudo-philosophy, which substitutes biology for economics and puts the racial elites and their biological superiority in the destiny-laden role of the proletariat, the class destined according to Marxian Communism to create the classless perfect society, is a less characteristic element. The decisive factor is the emphasis upon myth as the expression of the vital irrational forces which shape history. Whereas Marxian Communism is openly atheistic, the totalitarian myth subordinates God and Church to itself, tries to utilize them—and thus, of course, denying them, as Pope Pius XI pointed out in his Encyclical against Nazism—as means for strengthening the power of the racial elite, that is, of those who are the bearers of the myth. For their purposes the racialist elites use those inferior men who are unable to grasp the myth, who continue to take seriously the traditional religious terminology and who naively conclude that the myth of the twentieth century is pro-religious since it fights its competitor, communist atheism.

What is common to both basic forms of the political religions of the twentieth century, is their immanentism. Only *this* world, the socio-political reality of this world matters and exists as the ultimate reality. The one form (Communism) denies openly all transcendence; the other (racialism) tries to utilize the transcendence as an important psychological force which is meaningful only in the service of those destined to exercise power. The twentieth century, the century of world wars involving gigantic total mobilizations and propaganda campaigns, which cause beliefs to appear to be ideologies for power-political purposes, has replaced the relativism and optimistic belief in scientific progress and in a purely natural humanitarianism, and replaces revealed religion, which it regards as dated and irrational, by the ruthless power urge of elites. They claim to be the spirit, the avantgarde, the revolutionary consciousness of the peoples and masses; ruthless wars and conflicts are accepted either as the inevitable means for the establishment of the perfect future or simply as expressions of heroic and tragic human nature. Man is an intelligent beast of prey, as Spengler has said, and there is no meaning beyond domination, the fulfillment of one's given fate, which results either in power or destruction.

What is the position of the Church among these forces of the twentieth century? In the nineteenth century the enemies were first the heirs of the French Revolution and utilitarian enlightenment which could not accept the Church as a free and independent society with her own dignity because they knew only one sovereign society, that of the will of the people and one happiness, that of pleasures; they were inclined to believe that the Church as an anti-social force was doomed to disappear before the victorious laicist purely utilitarian rational morality and civic natural religion. Further, the Church was threatened by various forms of belief in the omnipotence of the state and its bureaucracy; the government claimed to control and determine all social and all religious groups; and the bureaucracy allied with more or less progressive liberals often tried to streamline and modernize Church life and organization.

The Church reacted against these encroachments of the omnipotent state through appeals to liberty and to the masses, whose influence in politics increased with the extension of the right to vote. Churchmen also became the advocates of those who felt themselves to be unjustly and inhumanly treated by an economic-social system in which the individual worker was only an object of the law of demand and supply. The same Pope who had condemned the erroneous ultra-optimistic democratic utopianism of Lamennais praised the American system to Tsar Nicholas I, when that representative of an omnipotent state with an all permeating and controlling power visited him. On that occasion the Pope praised the American system because the Church there enjoyed as a social group all liberties unhampered by the state. After aggressive secularism had experienced a new revival in the French fight against religious congregations and for a hostile separation between Church and State at the beginning of the twentieth century, it lost its

5

violence. In France men had grown too sceptical to have even anti-clerical beliefs; and in Germany the support of the powerful, practically Catholic political organization, the Center party, was necessary for the government. Finally anti-Catholic prejudices inherited from the Protestant past had steadily lost their strength. The Church could now live in the liberal secularized world without an anti-Catholic public religion or general atmosphere. She could even develop her activities—among intellectuals as well as among the masses—building up systems of education, surrounding the parish with organizations, she participated in various ways corresponding to traditions, in national life, sometimes as the national historical religion, sometimes as a moral force, sometimes protected by concordats, sometimes relying on public opinion and constitutional liberties.

This world was perhaps too quiet—harmless and peaceful. It has collapsed in many large areas of the globe and in others is threatened by the social and political earthquakes resulting from the totalitarian political religions which the world wars transformed from sects into powerful organized forces. First there was the communistic one; then came, beginning as reaction against Communism, the Fascist—Nazi variety; this reaction seemed to win out with the successes of Mussolini and particularly Hitler; but then the Communists came back, having been forced to fight on the side of the liberal-democratic world against the most dangerous enemy of the moment. Their defensive soon became an offensive; Hitler's defeat was the beginning of the Cold War between the West under the leadership of the United States and the Soviet World.

Today, the world situation is obviously very serious for the Church, even for all religion. Atheist doctrine officially dominates large parts of the world. Traditional Christian social order and institutions are destroyed; and the Church not only has lost her property and social standing but all her liberties. She is subjected to a wide and fettering control by a state whose rulers believe that religion must and will disappear and who for the time being tolerate some Church life only for purely power-political, tactical reasons. Attempts are made to eliminate Church leadership loyal to the Papal authority, to mobilize nationalism against the Church, to discredit her as the ally of Capitalism, and Wall Street, and most important of all, to replace her belief by the totalitarian doctrine. But there is more than visible persecution going on in the Communist world. Christianity is destined to be destroyed not only by creating martyrs, for instance, by putting Cardinal Mindszenty in jail—but by changing the whole of public life and education in such a way that religion becomes a museum piece, an anachronistic survival without vitality.

This explains why the Church fights Communism. Communism is a political secularized religion which puts self-sufficient society and its man-made organization in the place of God and Redemption. Communism has renewed on a large scale, with systematic policies, and with shrewd calculations, the attempt of the enlightenment of the eighteenth century and its culmination in the French Revolution to make the Church superfluous, to wipe out the "infamous institution" (to quote Voltaire) and going farther, to abolish even natural religion, all belief in God. The deification of man and his productive power is the essence of Communism, and therefore, its threat can be fully understood only by the Church; the various forms of secularism cannot discover the roots of its evil nature, the belief that in erecting the classless society, where man will be his own master and where the slavish acceptance of God as the master of men will have died out as the result of social transformation and social engineering, men will be as God.

Therefore, the war of the Church against Communism is not conducted in order to defend a particular secular order though Communist utopianism and misunderstanding of the nature of man and society result in threats to and destruction of natural reasonable institutions as for instance the family or human rights. But the defense of the natural world, corresponding to a truly human order, is the consequence of the Church's rejection of Communism as one of the forces trying to oppose the City of God with the City of Man, the divine City with the forces of the devil.

The twentieth century with its cruelties, its unspeakable brutalities and pitiless, coolly-calculated inhumanities has undermined a tendency to overestimate culture and civilization. More and more voices denounce the optimistic, somewhat harmless belief in the unity and harmony of religion and culture. There is an opposite tendency emerging in the twentieth century—not among the masses and unsuspecting average citizens who have not yet grasped the fact that utilitarian civilization is not able to overcome the crisis at the foundations of society. Religion is seen by many children of the twentieth century as the denial of all harmonious, civilizing human tendencies, which justify the peaceful life of society and minimize everything tragic. But the Church is not the Church of such theological existentialists, who despise reason and science and delight in the prospect of everyone going to hell. She lives under the necessity of understanding the average man, who does not aspire to be a hero or a saint, who likes to live in peace and some comfort and without the constant threat of imminent catastrophes and of difficulties for which apparently there are no solutions.

What a change in comparison with the nineteenth century! At that time the Church was accused of being too pessimistic, allegedly defying science and civilization; today she is often accused of being too optimistic, of believing in a harmonious order of life, of being too progressive and too liberal. At the same time the Church is accused of siding with all forms of anti-communism, even those which are totalitarian, of being anti-communist only for the sake of her alliance with an order which favors her comfortable and secure existence, of not fighting for the universal cause of men, but for her own benefit and vested interests. For some the Church is too liberal-progressive, for others too authoritarian-conservative, too happy that twentieth century political religions have helped to discredit liberal secularism.

But the Church is neither liberal nor conservative. She is a child of particular times, but not inseparably married to any of them. She has to teach and bring salvation to all periods of history with their changing social order and atmosphere. She is not just the Church of the nineteenth or the twentieth century; though she participates in all centuries, she is not bound to any of them. She is the embodiment of history and tradition, just because she knows their changes, developments and adaptations to new needs. There is *one* Church, the Church founded by Christ with her visible organization, her hierarchy, her doctrinal authority, her means of salvation, the universal and Catholic Church sent for all times and all peoples—but there are many Catholicisms, that is, forms of historical and social existence for Catholics and Catholic groups. The Catholicism typical of the twentieth century is not the Catholicism which optimistically believes that the activity of the Church is primarily determined by her utilization of liberties. These liberties are given by a truly tolerant society with true religious freedom. This freedom does not mean a particular philosophy or theology, for example, indifferentism, but the factual acceptance of the existence of several religious bodies in the same civic and political community.

8

Surely much of the Catholicism of the nineteenth century survives powerfully and impressively today; it has great and admirable merits. But another type of Catholicism is becoming more characteristic today—though existing in minorities, and not yet affecting the general atmosphere, the average life. It is the Catholicism which emphasizes everything that separates religion from the features of average life accessible to normal common sense. This Catholicism emphasizes revelation, stressing not what is common—from the point of view of natural society, to all religious groups, but what is specific to the Catholic Church, dogma, liturgy, monastic life, contemplation. Such emphasis may be seen as a reaction against the general secularization of life, which, in the United States, is closely connected with the history and humanization of Puritan groups. Sometimes it assumes paradoxical forms. The Church is seen only as the Church of great sinners; only they can be converted, touched by grace, only their affairs can end in sanctity, whereas the orderly average man, who observes the rules, is the man beyond redemption, the hypocrite, whose soul is lost in the world with its comfortable and unheroic-average life. There may be also some excessive zeal to denounce all social action, to withdraw in contemplation beyond time and space forgetting that true contemplation nurtures true action. The sentence of the great mystic Eckhart, is forgotten today, "Even if I exist in the highest state of contemplation and a poor man asks me for food, I must give him a bowl of soup." The anti-activist approach often overlooks the fact that escape from the world may mean abandonment of the world to the devil.

The Catholicism of the twentieth century has lost the defensive apologetic attitude of the nineteenth century. It is aware of the insufficiency of secularism. Sometimes this awareness is exaggerated and there follows a tendency to reject or neglect science and reason, to see religion simply as something anti-secular and anti-human. But it can be stated that with all its one-sidedness and extreme features, characteristic of a time of crisis in which traditions are shaken but in which new stable ones have not yet developed, — the Catholicism of today is a proof of the vitality and the eternal youth of the Church. It shows that the Church is the institution which survives. She has survived the rise of liberal secularism, utilized its positive features and possibilities and she will survive the crisis of the twentieth century, produced by the dangers introduced into our time by a pseudo-religious secularism. This secularism is at the same time

the heir and deadly enemy of that belief in *this* world which among
many non-Communists has lost its original self-confidence and its
assurance of having a universal mission. What the nineteenth century did not foresee has happened today: it is the mission of Catholics to defend the true values of secular civilization and of its liberties against secularist pseudo-religions. The true faith, presupposing
nature and reason, opposes the scientifically or vitalistically formulated myth, which would destroy the variety and complexity of
human existence and force it into the harness of man-made totalitarian doctrine and its absolute domination. The Catholicism of
today is able to defend secular civilization because the Church
rejects its deification and therefore is aware of its true human character. Just because a Catholic understands its limits and shortcomings without falling into absolute despair, he can defend this world
against those who threaten it by absolute denial or by deifying
acceptance.

I

On the Structure of the Church-State Problem

by *John Courtney Murray, S.J.*

Throughout history the Church-State problem has always retained the same general structure, and the efforts of the Church toward its solution have always been guided by the same set of general principles. At the same time the problem has exhibited differences in the manner of its position, in consequence of the various historical forces operative in particular ages and situations. And these specific differences have contributed to alter the emphases placed by the Church upon one or other element within her body of unchanging principles. In turn these varying emphases have given different orientations to the action of the Church. The general purpose of this paper is to illustrate these four propositions.

I

From the standpoint of the Church the effort has constantly been to achieve and maintain, in terms of social fact as well as in terms of idea, a manner of social organization based on the traditional doctrine of a juridical and social dualism characterized by a primacy of the spiritual over the political. The effort has met opposition from the tendency, seemingly inherent in the reality of the State, towards an organization of society governed by a juridical and social monism marked by a primacy of the political over the spiritual. The history of Church-State relationships has been basically a record of the clash between these two contrary tendencies, and a record of the measure of success that each has alternately achieved.

The clash has been ineluctable. It has often been remarked that the essential political effect of Christianity was to destroy the classical view of society as a single homogeneous structure within which the political power, however institutionalized, stood forth as the principal representative of society both in its religious and in its political aspects. The new Christian view was based on a radical distinction between the sacred and the secular: "Two there are, august Emperor, by which this world is ruled on title of original and sovereign right—the consecrated authority of the priests and the royal power." In the emphatic word, "two," in this celebrated sentence of Gelasius I, lay the virtualities of a great revolution. The family of mankind under the Christian dispensation is to be organized in two societies, under two laws, emanating from two authorities. The two are not societies, laws and authorities in a univocal sense, but only in an analogous sense, by reason of a radical diversity in origin, end, and means to their respective ends. The two are irreducible one to the other, as grace is irreducible to nature and nature to grace. At the same time the two are not simply incommensurable, much less antinomous; they are related to each other as nature to grace and grace to nature. And the essential condition of their harmonious relation is the maintenance of the primacy of the spiritual—the primacy of the spiritual power over the temporal power, of the ecclesiastical society over the secular society, of the law of the Gospel over the human law.

This dualism of Church and State has created one of the permanent nodes of that pervasive tension introduced into the whole of human life by the Christian fact, the advent of Christ the King, the promulgation of the New Law and the supernatural statute of the Church. The dualism is not natural; indeed its establishment involved a certain dislocation of the natural order, a diminution of the stature and scope which the political power would have possessed in another, purely natural dispensation. This is why the tension produced by the dualism has constantly shown a tendency to dissolve into some manner of monism. The tendency is inherent in one of the poles of the tension, the State. As the political expression of human reason, the State seems to share that tendency, inherent in reason, which has been the origin of all heresy—the tendency to subsume all things under itself and reduce all things to itself, to fashion a unitary rational order, and to close this order against whatever would resist rationalization. Moreover, this tendency to rationalize—in this case, to politicize—all aspects of the life of man, which is inherent in the State as reason, seems to be strengthened by the fact that the State is likewise power. Of itself power undertakes to impose order; therefore it tends to effect a unification. And in its drive toward political unity, which is the bulwark of power as well as its reason for being, the State seeks to subordinate to itself and to its task all the forces that make for social cohesion, notably that most powerful cohesive force, religion.

This tendency toward a juridical and social monism has been historically visible even in states that bore the name of Christian. It appeared at the very moment when the Christian dualistic view first gained historical recognition, in the empire of Constantine. The Byzantine empire showed the monistic tendency in full tide. And it was part of the dynamism of the national states during the era of royal and confessional absolutism. In these instances the effort was in greater or lesser degree to reduce the Church to the State. But the tendency was likewise visible in another form in the medieval Christian commonwealth. It appeared not so much in social fact (the Christian dualism maintained itself in terms of fact), as in social theory—in those theories of hierocratic stamp which exhibited a will to reduce the State to the Church, largely under the influence of a principle which derived from reason rather than from revelation, *Duo principia ponere nefas est.*

The tendency has manifested itself more strikingly than ever in the modern state. And the reasons are not far to seek. First, the power of the modern bureaucratic state outmatches anything known in the most absolute of past monarchies, in the breadth of its scope and in the means at hand for the enforcement of its will. Again, all of modern politics has been dominated by the monist concept of the indivisibility of sovereignty. Finally, a new idea, unknown to medieval times, has increasingly entered political history—the idea that the state is not simply an executive agency for limited purposes, to be directed by the organized moral conscience of society, but a moral end in itself, an entity with its own self-determined spiritual substance, the embodiment of an ethos, the vehicle of an ideology— a secularist ideology—which purports to be the basic and sufficient principle of national and social unity.

It is easy to see why this tendency towards a juridical and social monism has been the Church's permanent enemy. Its chief vice lies in the fact that it more or less completely transforms the *res sacra* into a *res politica*. It can do this in two ways. One movement can be against that suprapolitical *res sacra* which is the Church herself— her faith, her unity, her administration. The effort here is so to build the Church into the structure of the legal and political order as to make her *instrumentum regni*, a simple adjunct of political sovereignty, subordinate to its purpose. Another movement, more common in modern times, goes against the intrapolitical *res sacra*, the *res sacra in temporalibus*. This concept embraces all those things which have their roots within the temporal order of human life and are a part of it, at the same time that, in their finality or in their Christian mode of existence, they transcend the purposes of the political order. Perhaps the chief example is the institution of the family—the marriage contract itself, and the relationship of husband and wife, parent and child. Here the effort is to politicize these sacred things in the temporal order by bringing them under the single undivided jurisdiction of the state. They are totally enclosed within the political order, and, as the political order itself is made a closed order, these sacred things are set beyond the reach of the spiritual authority of the Church.

In either event, whether the Church be included within the political order or excluded from it, the result is the same: a profanation of the sacred takes place. The order of primacies is inverted. The inviolable distinction between the sacred and the secular is subverted. The result may indeed be a unification; it is ordinarily in the name of the "integrity" of the political order that the process of politicization of the sacred goes forward. But the unity created is a false unity, achieved at the expense of right order. What happens is a reduction of Gelasius' "two" to "one," not an organization of the two, under respect for their distinction, into a true unity of order.

Moreover, the further fatal consequence of this subversion of the right order between the sacred and the secular is the destruction or diminution of the spiritual freedom of man. The common man instinctively knows this. He knows, as by natural inclination, that no man can be free if nothing be sacred from the power of the state. In the name of its own freedom the human spirit spontaneously resists the reduction of all human life to political terms and the total enclosure within the state of all that the spirit, human and divine, creates upon earth. In this sense the divine mission of the Church, which is to preserve the distinction between the sacred and the secular (and, if you will, to furnish this distinction with an armature of power), constitutes a polarization of a natural human tendency.

It is a primal mission of the Church to preserve her own being in all its sacredness against any profanation by enclosure within the state. It is likewise her mission to preserve the original sacrednesses inherent in human social life from complete politicization by the secular power. But her discharge of this twofold function in regard of the temporal order has a far-reaching consequence even in what concerns the earthly destiny of man. It is in effect an espousal of the spiritual freedom of mankind and a patronage of that unity of order which is the complement and condition of freedom. It is inherent in the mission of the Church that she be the patron of both freedom and order, as it is inherent in the nature of things that both freedom and order should need effective patronage. (The latter idea is uncommon today, when it is still widely supposed that only freedom needs patronage, and order is expected somehow automatically to result.) Any movement towards a monistic manner of social organization is inimical to freedom by the same token that it is destructive of order. For this reason the secular effort of the Church to install and strengthen a structure of juridical and social dualism in human society has been an effective patronage of the twin principles upon which a free and orderly society depends.

II

One may discern in almost any historical phase of Church-State relations the same general problematic created by the clash, more or less resounding, between the opposing assertions: "Two there are . . ." and: "One there is. . . ." But the historical dynamism behind the latter assertion has varied. To speak only of modern times, this dynamism in the seventeenth and eighteenth centuries was the royal absolutism that found its theories in Widdrington, Barclay and James I. In the nineteenth century it was French republicanism—the whole complex of forces that went under the name of the Revolution. In the twentieth century it is a new revolutionary dynamism, totalitarianism, either in its finished and complete Soviet form or in its inchoative form, the totalitarianizing tendency inherent in the contemporary idolatry of the democratic process.

All of these movements have looked, or still look, to the realization in social fact of the same idea: "One there is. . . ." But each sought this same objective in its own way and under invocations of different names. Royal absolutism made its monistic pretenses in the name of the divine right of kings; French republicanism, in the name of the sovereignty of the people, as the social projection of the absolutely autonomous sovereignty of reason; Soviet totalitarianism, in the name of the class destined to sovereignty, and its organ, the party, whose function is to be the servant and ally of the materialist forces of history. The contemporary totalitarianizing democrat urges his new monism in the name of something less clear. He urges a monism, not so much of the political order itself, as of a political technique, the democratic process, the formal processes of freedom, which tend to be for him the single substantial constituent of a democratic social order. His proposition is that all issues of the intellectual and moral, as well as of the formally political, order are to be regarded as, or resolved into, political issues, and settled by the omnicompetent political technique of majority vote. On the surface the monism is one of process, but the underlying idea is a monism of power: "One there is whereby this world is ruled, the power in the people, above and beyond and beside which there is no other power." The inspiration of the idea is still a rationalism, a secularist mystique of individual freedom, softened—or, if you will, clouded—by a vague moral idealism that regards the power in the people, in distinction from all other powers, as ultimately and inevitably beneficent in its exercise. And this optimistic rationalism is further buttressed and given a still more rosy hue by a hearty confidence in the expanding achievements of science as reason's chosen instrument for whatever salvation man may aspire to.

There are therefore differences in the historical dynamisms which urge the enthronement of that monism of power whose formula is anti-Gelasian: "One there is. . . ." And these differences make a difference to the Church and alter the accent of her utterances and the lines of her action. She does indeed always fight under the same banner on which is emblazoned the pregnant device of Gelasius: "Two there are. . . ." And the stake in the struggle is always the same—the freedom of the Church to dispense the sacred things— in brief, the Word and the sacraments—committed to her charge; and the freedom of the human spirit as anchored to the inviolability from political profanation of the sacred things in the temporal order.

Moreover, the Church always fights against the same hostile flag, whether it be unfurled by the Emperor Anastasius, by Marshal Stalin, by some tweedy, pipe-smoking professor, or by some hot-eyed, ink-stained journalist.

On the other hand, the Church must conduct the struggle on the historical plane against concrete historical forces in their specific modality. The weapons are words, of course, but the argument itself is no mere verbal one. Nor has the Church's part in it been confined to the utterance of transtemporal truths couched in formulas long finished in their language. If the metaphor be admissible, the contest is fought out, as it were, between social organisms, each of which grapples with the other where it stands at the moment and counters hold with hold. This historical character of the conflict makes it necessary that the Church should have a strategy as well as a goal, an idea of how principles may at the moment be applied as well as a grasp of the permanent principles themselves.

In general it may be said that the strategy of the Church is to seek in terms of legal and social institutions such an application of her principles, under vital adaptation of them to political circumstance, as will effectively counter the current monism and the specific dynamism behind it (whatever it may concretely be), and effectively insure the operative existence on the historical plane of her own doctrine and all its implications: "Two there are. . . ." It must be noted that the relation between Church and State is not an abstract relation and cannot be. Its purpose is dynamic, to be fulfilled in the temporal order. The end in view is a certain management of society, the exertion of a spiritual influence on that living action which is public order, the imparting of a moral direction to the total political movement. Therefore the Church-State relation has to assume concrete and operative form in institutions. The institutions may be symbolic, as in the case of the medieval consecration of the Emperor or the ceremony of investiture in the royal or ducal *Eigenkirche*. Or they may be customary, as in the case of certain rights of the medieval papacy within the Empire. Or they may be formally legal, as in the case of the Concordats of modern times, or the legal institution of "establishment," or the constitutional guarantee of parity or freedom of religion.

This fact—that the Church-State relation, though governed by unchanging principles, must assume concrete institutional form— has two consequences of considerable importance. First, it inevitably subjects the Church-State relation, as far as its concrete forms are concerned, to the law of historical change. For all the divinely established character of the Church herself, the actual relation between Church and State, especially in its legal forms, is a matter of human institutions. And all human institutions, even those which embody some permanent idea, are in some sense historically conditioned. Their fashioning, though inspired by idea and principle, is likewise affected by contingent fact. In our present case, political contingencies play their determining role. For instance, the appearance of the institution of the *Eigenkirche* in the Frankish kingdom was related to the political development of the Frankish kingdom itself and its disappearance was in considerable part consequent upon the rise of the Empire. The modern Concordat or the formally legal establishment of Catholicism as the religion of the state were likewise consequent upon political developments—the rise of the nation-state, the rationalization of public law concomitant on the centralization of public power, the peculiar political position of the king in the absolutist era (his status as the single and only channel through which the spiritual authority of the Pope could reach the people or even the bishops), the later legal phenomenon of the written constitution, etc.

Since they are historically conditioned, human institutions—even necessary human institutions—cannot hope for total immobile permanence. The Faustian cry to the fleeting moment (*Verweile doch, du bist so schön!*) is unreal and therefore hopeless. The point is clear, say, from the history of the two necessary institutions of the family and of private property. As an idea, private property is a dictate of the natural law; but the institutionalizations of the idea in our era of finance capitalism differ widely from those prevalent under feudal regimes. So, too, the modalities of the husband-wife, and parent-child, relation exhibited in today's family, even when it is properly Christian, are not those which obtained between Abraham and Sara, or between the nineteenth-century Bavarian *paterfamilias* and his brood. To this law of historical development and change the institutional expressions of the Church-State relation constitute, on the evidence of history, no exception. If anything about history is certain, it is that history knows no unchangeably "ideal" institutional realization of any idea. What one hopes for in history is that ideas themselves should stay alive and present, and succeed in paying the price of life and presence, which is a vital adaptation to what, around them, is present and alive.

There is therefore a second consequence. The principles governing the Church-State relation are not of the strategic order but of the order of truth; they are not dependent for their truth upon the contingencies of history. But the strategy of the Church does reckon with such contingencies. It revolves upon institutions—such institutions as, in certain circumstances of space and time and political fact, may represent an effective incarnation of principle. And this fact involves the risk of a lag behind history, whose movement, for better or for worse, is continuous, unlagging. The Church undertakes to be the protagonist of truth, not simply in the unclouded air of disembodied principle but on the dusty plane of earthly history, where the truth must somehow, so to speak, take institutional flesh before it can avail to save. The Church is therefore obliged to be the protagonist of those currently existent institutions which embody or support the truth, however contingently, however defectively. The truth in our present case—indeed perhaps in every case—is something to be done and not merely said. And its doing depends on certain forms of action—those organized forms of actions which are called institutions.

One may readily see how this manner of concrete historical engagement in the cause of truth involves a risk. The risk is that, in the course of defending the truth, one may defend certain institutional expressions of it upon which the passage of time and the process of historical change have already passed sentence, with whatever measure of justice or injustice (and the measure is usually mixed). In defending her own inherent rights the Church has been obliged also to defend certain historic rights which accrued to them; but this is to risk claiming as historic right what may no longer be rightful because its historic basis has dissolved in the flux of time. So Pius VI claimed from the King of Naples the annual white mule, finely caparisoned, as the symbol of feudal faith; the trouble was that the relation of vassalage no longer existed. So too Boniface VIII asserted a concrete relation with Philip the Fair that was, in the historical context, unreal and unrealizable. France was no longer a fief of the Holy See but a new political phenomenon, an autonomous territorial kingdom; and Philip himself was a new political portent, the King of a nation-state, *imperator in regno suo*. At this distance it is clear that in the Bull *Unam Sanctam* Boniface VIII was contending for a conception of Christian society that, however noble in idea, was not then actually viable, if indeed it ever had been. For a variety of reasons that need not concern us here, the concept of "one society, two swords" could have only literary, not political, existence. Temporal society had changed, as had its swordsman and its sword. The Bernardine and Victorine and Aegidian theologoumenon would still persist as a theme in the texts of canonists for more than two centuries, until even the canonists relinquished it. (In the end, to adapt Santayana's phrase, they did not refute it, but quietly bade it goodbye.) But long before this negative literary farewell history had left it behind.

This risk of a lag behind history is always taken by every conservative force; and the Church is frankly such. The risk is fully worthwhile; indeed it is as necessary as conservatism itself. (It might be added that it is also necessary that not everyone should be conservative; otherwise how would there be any gains of progress for the conservatives to protect and consolidate?) To avert the dangers of the risk the Church relies upon her thinkers. She looks to them to prepare the positions to which she herself can retire or advance. Their function is to do a double work of reflection; first, on the tradition, to understand it in its purity; and second, on the movement of history, to discern the rational from the irrational in its progress, the workings of the Holy Spirit from the human dialectic of egoism and error. Upon the intelligence and integrity of this work of reflection depends the possibility of suggesting what manner of presentation and vital adaptation of traditional principle is required in order to maintain the Church in that position of presence to the age which is the condition of her saving mission. When the *studium* fails to fulfill its function, the *magisterium* in the normal course of providence falls off in its effectiveness. If, for instance, Boniface VIII had sought light elsewhere than in Giles of Rome, there might have been no tragedy of Anagni—who knows? And as it was part of the tragedy of Pius IX that he was not surrounded by men of learning and wisdom, so it was part of the glory of Leo XIII that his own high intelligence found stimulus and support in the stirrings of great thought that marked the latter quarter of the nineteenth century.

III

The foregoing has been concerned with the general Church-State problematic—the essential sameness of the general structure, and the alterations of its contours that historical forces induce, alterations that in turn create crises of thought, upon whose successful resolution depends the efficacy of the Church's effort to apply those principles which make for freedom and order in society. The point now is to indicate the alteration in the problematic that has taken place since the nineteenth century gave way to the twentieth. The description will be simplified, perhaps oversimplified. Yet the method of simplicity is one followed by the Church herself in her concern for basic issues, which are always simple.

The nineteenth-century enemy was the ancient one—a social and juridical monism. But it took the form of a false theory of freedom that was destructive of order, notably of that element of order which is the freedom of the Church. The theory was false because its premise was the rationalism of the Enlightenment in all its uni-dimensionality. The theory was operative because it found a political expression in French republicanism. And its operation was powerful because behind it was all the emotional dynamism of the Revolution.

Its most spectacular and sustained purpose was the destruction of an old order characterized by a high measure of authoritarianism; conspicuous in it were the differing but potent authorities of the Church, the monarchy, and the privileged social classes. In the political order one of the chosen weapons for the destruction of the old order was "the modern liberties." In their historical appearance and their concrete functioning they possessed a special dissolving force by reason of their special and conscious inspiration—the rationalist theory of the absolutely autonomous freedom of human reason as the single architect of all order. This monistic concept of a closed rational order then found political expression in the concept of a closed order wherein "the sovereign people" acting through the forms of freedom was to be the single sovereign, juridically omnipotent.

No one, of course, will deny that there was much in the old historical order that needed to be destroyed. The trouble was that in the course of its destruction a principle essential to the concept of order itself was likewise destroyed—the freedom of the Church and the inviolability of the *res sacra* from profanation by transfer into the domain of the *res politica*. The history of this process need not be recounted in detail; it ran from the Civil Constitution of the Clergy of July, 1790, through the educational reforms associated with the name of Jules Ferry, to the climactic Law of Separation of 1905. The goal of the whole process was a monism of power within the state, under reduction of the Church to the status of a corporation of private law regulated by governmental statute. Against her old enemy in this new modality the Church directed a threefold action—diplomatic, magisterial, and intellectual or theological.

The diplomatic effort looked to the restoration or maintenance of whatever measure of the *status quo ante* could be restored or maintained, through the technique of legal stabilization of Church-State relations by the instrumentality of Concordats. The direction of the effort was traditional—to rescue as far as possible the freedom of the Church, and to protect the distinction of jurisdictions based on the distinction of the sacred and the political. With the tragic vicissitudes of this diplomatic effort we need not concern ourselves here.

The more basic effort of the Church was magisterial. It consisted of an absolute, total and uncompromising protest against the infringement of her freedom and the politicization of her sacred things; it likewise consisted of an equally absolute opposition to the idea behind the state monism that was destroying true freedom and right order—the rationalist idea of "freedom." This absolute opposition was pitched on the high plane of truth, primarily the ancient truth: "Two there are. . . ." But then what may be called the "law of overflow" began to operate. The doctrinal defense of the freedom of the Church and the inviolability of the sacred, which are essential to the concept of right order, carried over with greater or less emphasis to a defense of the institutions which had furnished an armature for these principles in the old historical order—an armature that was not perfect but was certainly more protective than the subsequent nakedness. In other words, upon the basic doctrinal conflict between two ideas which stood in pure opposition to each other ("Two there are . . ." and "One there is . . ."), there was built another conflict whose terms were not so pure, between the institutions of the old "Union of Throne and Altar" and the institutions of the new "separation of Church and State," as these latter grew with successive pieces of legislation.

These two conflicts—call them the doctrinal and the historical—were not readily distinguishable at the time of their turbulent raging, when the injuriousness of the "separation" served to cloud

22

from view the ambiguousness of the prior "union," which had been brought into being as much, or more, by forces inherent in royal absolutism as by ideas inherent in Catholic tradition. In any event, at our distance in time these two conflicts can and should be distinguished.

The law of overflow operated also in another respect. The absolute doctrinal opposition to the rationalist premises of "the modern liberties" carried over, again with greater or less emphasis, to a disapproval of these "modern liberties" as political institutions (the more so in that these institutions in their concrete intent and functioning were more than means of management of the political order; they were also engines of war against traditional religion). In other words, the primary doctrinal conflict between opposing philosophies of freedom found echo on the more properly historical plane in a conflict between opposing institutional methods for the conduct of political affairs—the method of authority characteristic of the old regime and the method of freedom characteristic of the new regime. Again these two conflicts are now distinguishable and should be distinguished.

The magisterial action of the Church was therefore pure in itself, confined to the plane of principle, but its overflow on the historical plane revealed some ambiguity. One need not greatly regret the ambiguity. At a time when the process of politicizing all human life was beginning to accelerate its pace the Church did a great service, not least to her ancient human cause of freedom and order in society, by resolving, even with a measure of ruthlessness, issues falsely presented as purely political into issues moral and theological, and by solving these issues in their proper terms. Perhaps the greatest danger at the time was lest the issues themselves be obscured.

The third action of the Church, which may be called intellectual or theological, was of a somewhat later growth and of a more tentative nature. It was an effort to find some intellectual basis for at least a *modus vivendi* with the new order which, whether one liked it or not, had come to stay. This was no easy task, especially in view of the radical vice of the new order, its roots in a false philosophy of men and society, the *Liberalismo* which the Spaniard calls *pecado,* as indeed it is. The best that could be done at the time to reach this *modus vivendi* was the casting up of the distinction between "thesis" and "hypothesis."

The distinction had one great merit at the time. On the one

hand, it registered the Church's opposition to the new "Liberal state" in its concrete theory, dynamism, and actual religious and social effects. On the other hand it recognized that this new manner of state was "there," and had to be lived in, willy nilly. As a polemic statement the thesis-hypothesis disjunction was adequate; but it had the disadvantage common to all polemic statements. Even apart from its lack of venerable antecedents in traditional vocabulary, it lacked universality. No one has ever demonstrated its applicability to the greatest, fundamentally most sound, and historically most fruitful political experiment of modern times, the United States of America, whose inspiration was not Continental Liberalism, but the older liberal tradition of Western politics. Moreover, even in the area for which the thesis-hypothesis theory was devised, Western Continental Europe, it could be only temporarily valid, valid for the duration of the specific polemic state of affairs characteristic of the nineteenth century.

In that age the Church was espousing the cause of order against a false "freedom" that threatened it; and by inevitable, if perhaps unhappy historical consequence, this espousal of the cause of order as a structured idea shaded over into an approval of the old historical order-by-authority and a disapproval of the new order-by-freedom. The thesis-hypothesis disjunction was born of this controversy and used as a weapon in it. It is therefore not surprising that the disjunction should contain not only an affirmation of the abstract structural principles of order but also and implicitly an approval of the concrete political and legal institutions of the old historical order; that it should contain not only a denial of the pseudo-principle of the new historical order but also a disapproval of its free institutions. These complex implications of the thesis-hypothesis disjunction were inevitable by reason of the role it had to play in a controversy in which the doctrinal and the historical were mixed, and questions of principle were replaced by questions of institutions. The thesis could not fail to imply some espousal of the method of authority in political affairs, just as the hypothesis could not fail to imply some rejection of the method of freedom. The result was inconvenient, if necessary; for in this sense both thesis and hypothesis verge in their implications toward some diminution of the cardinal principle that is the heart of the ancient Gelasian doctrine, the freedom of the Church and her transcendence to all political forms. Actually, this principle first began to receive its proper stress in modern times with Leo XIII, whose major, if not wholly successful, effort was to reduce the ambiguities in the Church-State controversy and posit it singly on its proper doctrinal basis. It is significant that Leo XIII nowhere uses the thesis-hypothesis disjunction. The core of his doctrine was his emphatic and reiterated and developed statement of the Gelasian dualism: "Two there are. . . . "

If we turn now to the twentieth century, we can see a significant alteration of the Church-State problematic. The old enemy is still abroad, but in a new and more threatening form. The old situation in which the idea of right order was endangered by a false theory of freedom has largely given way to a new situation in which the true idea of freedom is endangered by a false theory of order. In some diminished measure the new threat is latent in the enormously powerful and positive, centralized, bureaucratic, social-service and social-welfare state that has succeeded the negative, laissez-faire, "umpire" state of nineteenth-century theory, and that now makes increasingly extensive and onerous claims upon the individual and the family unit. The new threat loomed blatantly in the Nazi regime. But it exists in its finished form in Communism, as an ideology and as a power-system. Here is the new Enemy, capitalized, in whose shadow all other dangers pale.

The movement of the enemy is towards a monism of power in a tighter and more complete sense than history has ever known. The goal is a new kind of order, and the chosen instrument for its attainment is the police-power of the state exercised with devastating thoroughness in all areas of human life, even of human thought. Within this order freedom perishes at its roots and in all the forms that it has traditionally assumed—the freedom of the Church, the freedom of sacred things from profanation at the hands of political power, the freedom of association that is the condition of political freedom to share in the direction of the res publica, and even the freedom of the human mind itself to search for truth and embrace it when found.

Continental Liberalism had distorted and disorganized the structured concept of freedom by exaggerating beyond bounds its rational component. But the concept still retained at least one saving note that rescued its root from withering away; freedom was still regarded as the endowment of the human personality. But within the Communist order the idea of freedom is not merely distorted; it perishes altogether, because it is made, no longer the endowment of

25

the individual, but the exclusive prerogative of the state (or of the party which is in effect the state). And even as such, freedom is in theory no more than a successful servitude to the materialist historical dialectic.

The new order and its principle, totalitarian state power, are radically false to a depth and extent not matched by the principle of the old Liberalist order that Communism seems to destroy. The premises of the new order—the Marxist concept of man and history, as completed by the Leninist-Stalinist concept of power as totalitarian and imperialist, are vicious to a degree far beyond the vices of the rationalism of the Enlightenment. The latter represented a decadence of the liberal tradition whose origins are Greek and Roman, Germanic and Christian. But Communism completely subverts and overthrows the liberal tradition in its essence, and marks a reversion to a paganism, marked by a reabsorption of man into the processes of nature and history, that is darker than the paganism of pre-Christian times; for it is not the darkness before a dawn, but a night falling upon a day that knew its brightnesses.

Moreover, the fact is that in striking at the essence of the liberal tradition Communism strikes at the condition upon which the existence of Christianity in this world as an organized society seems, humanly speaking, to depend. This is the crucial fact that seems today to have received indisputable proof. Today the spiritual freedom of the Church seems everywhere linked to the political freedom of the people and to that limitation of governmental power by the right of the human person which is of the essence of the liberal tradition, entrenched in it by its long alliance with the Christian tradition. Under the conditions created by the decadence of the liberal tradition into Liberalism Christianity could at least live. But the experience of Communist-dominated lands seems to have demonstrated that Christianity cannot long hope even to live in this world, if the liberal tradition that was its secular support is altogether cancelled out of history.

In this present situation the strategy of the Church has undergone important alterations in consequence of new and necessary doctrinal emphases. Against the old enemy in his new form the Church again deploys a threefold action—a magisterial, an intellectual or theological, and a third action, not now diplomatic but social.

The old diplomatic effort looked to the enforcement upon government of some manner of Christian attitude and orientation; it sought the alliance of the rulers of the Church with the rulers of the state in the legal organization of society. The new social action looks rather to the people, and seeks an alliance between the spiritual authority of the Church and a regenerated people in effecting the restoration of a civilization somehow Christian in all its institutions, not only legal but political, economic, and social. This new social action affirms both a fact and a principle—the fact that the focus of power in societies where the elements of right order still endure has shifted to the people, and the principle that so it ought to be. Insofar as the diplomatic action of the Church still continues, it is subordinate to this social action. The new orientation began with Leo XIII, who firmly shifted the terms of the major problem from the limited ones, "Church and State," to the broader one, "Church and human society."

The magisterial action of the Church still looks to its traditional objective—the assertion of the freedom of the Church, and the maintenance of a total opposition to the ideas and forces that would destroy or diminish this freedom. This means at the moment a total opposition to the new order in all its falseness, its perversion of the concept of freedom and its exaltation of totalitarian power as the single agent of order. But the law of overflow still operates. The doctrinal affirmation of the freedom of the Church and the doctrinal rejection of totalitarianism carries over on the historical plane to a defense of those human institutions of religious, civil, and political freedom with which in the contemporary situation the cause of the Church's freedom is historically linked. These institutions do in fact provide the necessary armature for the protection of the freedom of the sacred.

Similarly, the Church's opposition to the current monism of state power and her newly accented affirmation of the ancient Gelasian dualism carry over to a new affirmation of the political dualism of society and government which, as Watkins has pointed out, was born of the dualism of Church and State and became the most important structural rib of the liberal tradition. The cardinal assertion of the new order is that the power is singly in government and functional to purposes upon which the party-in-power alone decides. Against this assertion the Church affirms with new insistence, not possible in the days of a rationalist "sovereignty of the people," the principle which was foundational in the medieval Christian commonwealth, was obscured during the era of royal absolutism, and falsified by the Enlightenment—the principle that the power is in government by consent of the people, that government indeed has the power, but as an executive agency subject to another "power," the spiritual and moral power inherent in the organized conscience of society, the people, whereby the purposes and actions of government are to be judged, directed and corrected.

Thus the logic of the new affirmation of the old dualism of Church and State and of society and government, as made in this unique historical juncture, moves an inevitable step farther to an affirmation of the method of freedom within society. This is the method presently necessary for the preservation and effective operation of the traditional dualisms. The conscience of society, mediating the demands of the natural law and the law of the Gospel, is the natural immanent, active principle of resistance to the movement of government towards a monism of power. Therefore the conscience of society must be enabled to articulate its demands and enforce them. And in a day of danger to the dignity of man in his political dimension it is fitting as well as necessary that he should be empowered to voice the demands of his spiritual dignity through those effective channels of utterance and of political change which are the ordered set of free institutions now known as "democratic."

If then one must condense into a phrase the general orientation of the Church's action today, the phrase might be: "A free Church amid a free people." The formula has very different resonances than the slogan of the Risorgimento: "A free Church in a free State." The latter hid the juridical and social monism that was the rationalist program; the former is pregnant of the juridical and social dualism that has been the traditional Christian program.

The third action of the Church is of the intellectual order. Actually, it is a prolongation of Leo XIII's great effort toward *concordia,* the ending of the long alienation between the Church and human society and its modern dynamisms. This action is evident in the efforts being made by Christian thinkers to re-examine the concept of democracy, its history, its true philosophical origins, its debt to the ethos of the Gospel, its institutions, etc. As long as the energies of the Church were absorbed in protest against the monistic, and at bottom absolutist, "democracy" that issued from the Revolution, it was not possible to undertake this more positive and constructive work of political thought. One cannot, for instance, imagine Pius XII's 1944 Christmas Allocution being delivered by

Leo XIII. Again, though one may find in Leo XIII a developed theory of political authority, one will find no comparably full theory of citizenship, no adequate analysis of the great concept that was newly taking shape in the nineteenth century, the concept of "the people" in their total relation to government. In Leo XIII the "good citizen" is still pretty much the "good subject," the man who obeys the laws. There is little recognition of other functions of citizenship than obedience to lawful authority. The preoccupation of Leo XIII was in fact with the bases of authority in a world in which they were dissolving, not with the functions of freedom in the body politic—the contemporary preoccupation in a world in which the threat is to the freedom of the body politic.

This effort of political thought has been stimulated by the twentieth-century totalitarian experience, which has set the democratic development in a new light. The problem now is not to stop this development in favor of a return to authoritarian methods, but rather to save it from being stopped by a ruthless totalitarianism. It is not, of course, a question of the Church making a belated peace with the rationalism of the Enlightenment. The invitation to do this, proffered to Pius IX, was rejected in the Syllabus; and the rejection is as uncompromising today as ever. But it is a question of disengaging the concept of democracy as a political system from its rationalist premises and of purifying it of its monistic ethos. It is a question of constructing a positive theory of the method of freedom in society, under appeal to principles embedded in the body of Christian truth and in the experience of Christian political history. Many of these principles will need development, since their expression and institutionalization may have been only inchoative; so, for instance, the basic medieval distinction, lost in the absolutist era (and not quite recovered even by Leo XIII) between "society" and "state" or government.

It is a question of showing that the "modern freedoms" as political institutions are as capable of projection from right as from wrong premises, and that this is true also of freedom of religion as a political principle, resting on a sound political theory of the limitations of governmental power, implying a disallowance of legal establishments in the post-Reformation sense, but not implying (as in Continental Liberalism) any "atheism of the state," any denial of the social obligation of worship, any false "separation" of religion and society (or education), any restriction of the freedom of the

Church within society, any pseudo-neutrality of government towards the interests of religion, any monistic, "closed" concept of the political order, any destructive secularization of the political process.

One intellectual problem therefore centers about the theory of democratic society and of government by the people (as well as of and for the people). There ensues another problem—that of the relation of the Church to the state in its democratic form, as structured in accord with the complex principle of the freedom of the people. This problem too is speculative, not polemic. Its starting point is not the simple recognition that the democratic state is "there" in sheer point of brute fact, but rather the sincere acknowledgment that this political form is good in demonstrable point of sound principle. One need not acknowledge it to be perfect in theory, much less in practice; it is enough to say that it is good, and relatively perfectible, in dependence on the kind of human persons, the quality of "the people" who live in it and make it work.

Reflection on the problem of the relation between the Church and the democratic state, as this political form appears in today's historical perspectives, cannot be short-circuited by any peremptory statement that the problem is already solved—in terms of the thesis-hypothesis disjunction. The fact is that this nineteenth-century distinction is no longer particularly useful. It reflects a different state of the question, and it was part of an effort that was polemic, not positive. Like the theory of "the two swords," it has had its moment in history. There are, of course, elements of truth in it; they must be saved, by all means, and it is not difficult to save them. But for the rest, it is, as again in the case of the "two-swords" theory, a matter not so much of refuting this nineteenth-century thesis. Concretely, it is not a question of openly allying the Church with democracy as the old French Right allied the Church with monarchy. Nor is it allowable, in an excess of polemical zeal against the current myth about the incompatibility of Catholicism with democracy, to attempt to show some native kinship between the two, after the fashion of the liberal Protestant who claims democracy as the political expression of his religious faith. Again, it is not a question of condemning past or present realizations of the confessional state, or of setting up a counter-ideal or even an alternate ideal to this pseudo-ideal of an earlier era.

The approach to the present problem must be from more serene and solidly established viewpoints. There is, first, the fact of the relativity of all concrete political forms, which forbids the incorporation of any of them into what would purpose to be a trans-temporal statement of the doctrine of the Church. Secondly, the supreme commanding viewpoint is furnished by the cardinal principle that has emerged with increasing clarity in these latter generations of turbulent political change—the principle of the transcendence of the Church to all political forms, as the consequence and condition of her freedom. Even in her institutional, historical aspect the Church is of a radically distinct order of social reality than the state; therefore an essential part of the problem is to preserve this radical distinction. When it is obscured, the primacy of the spiritual is by the same token damaged; the Church is inevitably drawn down to the level of the temporal. Obviously, the transcendence of the Church to the state does not mean their "separation" in the sense of Continental Liberalism. But it does forbid their "union" in the sense of the *ancien régime*.

Indeed the term "union" tends to be misleading, as the term "separation" tends to be meaningless (there is no such univocal thing as "separation"). The true word is "relation." But it must be understood that the relation is not of the order of being, as when one "incomplete substance" is ordered to another to form a subsistent *unum per se;* here is the limp in the traditional "body-and-soul" metaphor. The relation does not somehow draw the state into the Church as part of its structure, as aspect of itself, an instrument for its specific purposes; this was the defect in the medieval idea. Nor does the relation somehow draw the Church into the state as part of its legal order, a constitutent of its political unity, a support of its government; this was the erroneous idea of absolutism, in both its royal and its popular forms. The relation of Church and State is not constitutive of the being of either or of a third being somehow distinct from both. The relation is in the order of action. It implies a dynamic relatedness of distinct purposes and of distinct lines of action toward these purposes, under respect of their proper hierarchy. Leo XIII had, and incessantly repeated, the essential word, *concordia,* a harmony of actions, a co-operation that respects the integrity of both operative principles and of their specific operations, at the same time that it collineates both operations towards one common, complex, hierarchically structured end and good, which is the perfection of man in the distinct but related orders of nature and grace.

31

As a matter of method, it would seem that the present problem of Church and State could be most fruitfully discussed under conscious abstraction from those categories (e.g., "union" vs. "separation") into which the discussion settled during the nineteenth century. Actually, the first step in the intellectual task of the moment is a *ressourcement* (to use the convenient French word). The whole tradition needs to be reviewed, not simply that segment of it which tends to dominate the ordinary manual *de jure publico,* whose separate existence as a treatise dates from the nineteenth century and reflects its anxieties. If this *ressourcement* is properly theological, not directed to polemic or apologetic purposes, and if it is informed by a sense for the relativities of history and of the political forms that history brings forth, one might expect that it would serve to accomplish a vitally important work of discernment—the discernment of unchanging principles from their variant applications, the discernment of the permanent purposes of the Church in her relation to the state from the contingent means of achieving these purposes that were relative to political and social circumstance. In the light of this work of discernment it would then be possible to elaborate a unitary theory of the Church-State relation that would be fixed enough to do justice to the absolute exigencies of principle and also flexible enough to take account of the contingencies of changing political situations.

II

Papal Diplomacy: Its Organization and Way of Acting

by Edward L. Heston, C.S.C.

It is a commonplace that the Pope is the supreme visible Head of the Roman Catholic Church. His authority stretches out to the most farflung corners of the earth, and some four hundred millions of the earth's inhabitants look to him for sure guidance in the belief and practice of their religion. The Church that he rules is a spiritual society. Her purpose is essentially supernatural, namely, to be the divinely established normal means of salvation for all mankind. Consequently, the main essential means she employs to achieve the realization of this purpose are likewise spiritual and supernatural. These means are summed up in the transmission of divine grace through the administration of the Sacraments and the faithful preaching of the Word of God.

Nevertheless, divine though his mission be, the Pope is subject to all the limitations imposed on human powers by the laws of nature. Before the evident physical impossibility of maintaining contact with all the members of the Church, or even with the hierarchy of all the countries in which members of the Church are found, he follows the principles of sound administration, and appoints various representatives throughout the world to safeguard and to promote the interests of the Church. Some of these representatives are officially accredited to the governments of the countries where they reside. Others are vested with purely ecclesiastical authority, to deal with the Catholic hierarchy of different countries. Thus it is that the Holy Father is represented throughout the world by apostolic nuncios, apostolic internuncios, and apostolic delegates.

It is not surprising, consequently, that in its treatment of the organization of the Holy See, the Code of Canon Law, which is the official legislation for the Catholic Church, devotes several canons to the representatives of the Sovereign Pontiff. The Code dedicates a special chapter to this important subject, and formulates succinct canons on the legates *a latere* of the Holy Father (canon 267), as well as on bishops holding the title of apostolic legate because of the one-time historical importance of their respective sees. Canons 267-270 specify the nature of the offices of apostolic nuncio and internuncio, and also that of apostolic delegate, and determine the powers pertaining to each.

The place thus accorded papal diplomacy in the official law of the Church indicates clearly that, although its specific purpose is to represent the Sovereign Pontiff before civil governments, papal diplomacy is but another phase of the activity of the Church, as imposed on the Vicar of Christ in the exercise of his supreme apostolic authority. Diplomatic activity thus emerges as an altogether normal phenomenon in the government of the Church.

It should be remarked, however, that there is a clear-cut distinction between the strictly spiritual mission of the Church and the diplomatic activities which aim to facilitate the fulfilment of this mission. When he speaks *ex cathedra,* or officially, on a point of faith or morals affecting the entire Church, the Sovereign Pontiff enjoys the prerogative of personal infallibility. His diplomatic activities are not protected by this special divine safeguard. Hence the faithful are not bound to accept or to approve such activities unquestioningly, as they would be obliged for instance to accept a dogmatic definition. By the simple fact of their eminent position and reliable sources of information, the Holy Father and his advisers have a clearer and more comprehensive view of the international situation than is available to any private individual, however expert. Hence the Holy See is entitled to the benefit of the doubt in points which may be open to question. This, however, does not interfere with the basic right of the individual to hold a prudent opinion of his own on the advisability or opportuneness of a particular diplomatic démarche.

I. *The Fact of Papal Legation*

A rapid glance at the historical aspects of the present subject establishes the fact that the activity now called diplomacy has been found in the Church from the earliest centuries. The historians of

34

papal diplomacy tell us that the present-day cadre of the diplomatic service of the Vatican was set up no earlier than 1560. They point to the sending of the first permanent apostolic nuncio to Vienna in 1500, and trace the appointment of the first apostolic delegate to 1762, when a prelate was despatched from Rome to Syria, to study questions arising from differences in liturgical rites and other problems. But long before any such permanent missions were established, representatives of the Pope were found at the courts of princes.

As early as the fifth century, the papacy was represented at the imperial court of Constantinople by officials known as *apocrisiarii*. One of their number was the ecclesiastic who became Sovereign Pontiff and is now known as Pope St. Gregory the Great. The office of these *apocrisiarii* was to supervise the handling of those religious affairs which were of mutual interest both to the internal life of the Church and to the proper government of the Roman Empire. Official relationships were subsequently maintained with emperors, kings, feudal princes, and other temporal lords throughout the Middle Ages and the first years of the Renaissance. Eventually, following along the lines of the general tendency of European international life, the Holy See set up a system of continued relationships with civil states. When the diplomatic activities of the different states became an internationally recognized institution, they were provided with specific juridical norms by the treaties of Westphalia (1648), and the diplomacy of the Holy See has formed part of this international structure down to the present day.[1]

It should be borne in mind that mutual diplomatic relations between the Holy See and civil governments do not contribute solely to the benefit of the Vatican. The exchange of diplomatic representatives is also of great advantage to the various nations with which such relationships are maintained. This explains why not a few countries which are officially and traditionally non-Catholic (such

---

[1] The official list of the countries maintaining diplomatic relations with the Vatican in 1951 as given in the *Annuario Pontificio,* the official Vatican yearbook, is as follows: Argentine, Austria, Belgium, Bolivia, Brazil, Chile, China, Columbia, Costa Rica, Cuba, Czechoslovakia, Ecuador, Egypt, Eire, El Salvador, Finland, France, Germany, Great Britain, Guatemala, Haiti, Honduras, Hungary, India, Indonesia, Italy, Japan, Jugoslavia, Lebanon, Liberia, Lithuania, Monaco (Principality of), The Netherlands, Nicaragua, The Knights of Malta (by long-standing privilege), Panama, Paraguay, Peru, Philippine Republic, Poland, Portugal, Rumania, San Marino, Santo Domingo, Spain, Uruguay, and Venezuela. Just recently the Vatican announced the establishment of diplomatic relations with Pakistan.

as China, Egypt, India, and Japan among others) have established diplomatic relations with the Vatican in recent years. From 1940 until 1950 the President of the United States was represented at the Vatican by a personal representative with the rank of ambassador. This element of prestige, the maintaining of official relations with the Holy See, is also discerned in the noteworthy fact that not even the Iron Curtain countries have seen fit to break off officially the relationships which were in existence before their communist-controlled governments came to power.

Even a cursory glance at the list of countries represented at the Vatican, many of which have constitutionally established state religions (Great Britain, Egypt, India, Finland, etc.), is sufficient indication that the establishment of diplomatic relations with the Holy See does not in any way imply automatically union of Church and state.

II. *The Right of Papal Legation*

Fifteen centuries of continuous diplomatic activity on the part of the Holy See are evidently much more than the mere outgrowth of the physical impossibility of personal contact with the Catholic world at large. Such a striking phenomenon finds its foundation in a basic right inherent in the very constitution of the Church. By virtue of her divine foundation, the Church is a perfect society. We say "perfect society," not as if implying that the Church is not susceptible of improvement in accidentals, but we refer to her as a perfect society in the juridical sense, that is to say, a society possessing within her own structure all the essential means needed for the realization of her special purpose. In this sense a perfect society is distinguished from an "imperfect" society, such as the family, an individual city, a state belonging to a federal union, since societies such as these need the indispensable assistance and cooperation of societies higher than themselves. There are only two juridically perfect societies: the Church and the state, the former in the spiritual order, and the latter in the order of material welfare and prosperity.

As the only perfect society in the spiritual order, the Church directs all her efforts towards the attainment of a strictly spiritual goal. As far as the attainment of this spiritual goal is concerned, the Church is entirely self-sufficient, and is thus dependent on no other society, no matter what its nature or power. Because of the innate pre-eminence of the spiritual world of which she is the guardian, and by her very inner constitution, the Church is, in the international world, a unit whose nature and end endow her with a strict right to be heard and to be provided with the freedom necessary for the fulfillment of her God-given mission.

In addition, the Sovereign Pontiff enjoys over all the members of the Church a primacy of order, honor, and real jurisdiction. He is thus empowered to intervene in the Church, directly or indirectly, in order to assure the attainment of the goal of the Church for each and all its members. Since this right of intervention is safeguarded particularly through the maintaining of diplomatic relations with civil governments, the diplomatic activity of the Church is rooted in the primacy of jurisdiction which was conferred on the Prince of the Apostles by Christ, and which has been continued down to our own times in the person of Peter's successors in the papacy.

The Holy See has re-affirmed this basic truth on many occasions, when it was questioned, and even denied, by the actions of civil governments. On April 15, 1885, Cardinal Jacobini, then Secretary of State under Pope Leo XIII, undertook to rectify certain erroneous principles published in the Spanish newspaper *Siglo futuro*. In the course of his refutation of an error which aimed to deny the right of the Holy See to send representatives into different countries, the Cardinal declared: "If, because of his primacy, the Roman Pontiff enjoys full and supreme power over the universal Church, and if he is entitled to exercise this power immediately and directly, it follows that he may also send his legates or representatives wherever he chooses, and may entrust to them the exercise of his own power in any measure he may see fit to designate."

Similarly, in 1880, Leo XIII protested vigorously when the apostolic nuncio was expelled from Belgium. In his formal denunciation of the injury and injustice thus inflicted on the Holy See, the Pope stated: "Since the Roman Pontiff has the right, particularly in distant countries and, with still greater reason, in Catholic countries, to have individuals who will represent him in his absence, We demand of the guilty parties an accounting for their violation of this right. This We do with all the more insistence, because the basis of this right is all the more august, proceeding as it does from the universal authority conferred by that primacy which the Sovereign Pontiff has received from God over the entire Church." Leo XIII then quoted Pius VI, who, in 1790, on the occasion of certain protests against the erection of an apostolic nunciature in Munich, had asserted unequivocally and in detail the right of the Holy See in terms which Leo XIII borrowed almost textually. Pius VI's defense of the rights of the Holy See concluded with a clear statement that the right of the Vatican to diplomatic representation was established by "the intrinsic power and nature of the primacy, the rights and prerogatives flowing therefrom, and the constant practice of the Church since the earliest centuries."

Hence it is clear that the right of diplomatic representation is not conferred on the Church by the goodwill of the individual nations. It is true that, according to the provisions of international law, no diplomatic representative can be sent to any country without the previous agreement of the authorities of the interested country. But such agreement does not confer a right. It simply recognizes an existing right and renders its exercise possible.

Neither is this right of diplomatic representation the consequence of territorial independence. Possession of an independent territory is an external, though entirely accidental, expression of sovereignty. Even during the years in which the Holy See did not enjoy actual territorial sovereignty, many nations continued to recognize the diplomatic rights of the Vatican by naming ambassadors and ministers as their representatives to the court of the Sovereign Pontiff. This was an indirect, but none the less convincing, demonstration that the rights of the Church in international life flow essentially from her intrinsic nature as a supreme spiritual society.

In addition to this internal argument, if we may call it such, there is a further consideration, drawn from extrinsic circumstances. In the intricate workings of modern national and international government, the world is confronted with a situation which was for centuries unknown. A rapidly growing tide of secularism and laicism has gradually but surely swept spiritual considerations from the national and international scene. The result has been that most governments, at least in practice, have forgotten, first of all, that there is anything else of importance in human life beyond purely material happiness and welfare. Secondly, in their efforts to achieve such happiness and welfare as they have thought possible and have set up as an ideal, they have consistently forgotten that there is such a thing as the basic moral law, and that no happiness or welfare can be worthy of the name, unless it both springs from and ultimately leads to the observance of that fundamental moral law of human nature which we call the "natural law." The result has been a frightening confirmation of St. Paul's grim warning that "the wages of sin is death."

Now, like the Church in the spiritual and supernatural order, the state is a perfect society in the natural and material order, self-sufficient and independent in its own particular order. But the natural and the material do not constitute the integral whole of human life. They represent only part of that marvelous dual composition of the spiritual and the material which we admire in human nature. And just as spiritual things are essentially and necessarily superior to material realities, so also, the natural and material order of human life must be regarded as a means to the achievement of that higher and nobler order which consists in man's supernatural destiny. Experience has demonstrated that civil governments not infrequently tend to become exclusive in the exercise of their undeniable rights and duties in the ordering of human life. The Church, consequently, must have within her reach some means whereby she may remind civil governments of the indispensable role of spiritual values in individual, national, and international life.

The necessity of cooperation between Church and State becomes all the more evident when we recall that the same men and women are members of both these societies. The civic activities of Catholics as citizens are governed by the State; their moral lives as Catholics are directed by the Church. The two orders are indeed distinct, but it is a principle of sound philosophy that distinction does not necessarily imply separation. Such great realities as marriage, education, social activities, charitable and other cultural works, have both civic and religious aspects. Both Church and state have full power to make laws and to see to their enforcement, each in its own respective field. The Church, as a public and perfect society, is endowed with such inalienable prerogatives as the right of assembly, the right to preach, and the right to pursue her goal for the salvation of mankind. The state has the right to take whatever steps are required to see to the realization of its own legitimate aims.

Now the state can undertake the discharge of its own divinely imposed duties, either in a spirit of respect for the Church and her mission, or in a spirit of callous lack of concern for spiritual values, if indeed this negative approach does not degenerate at times into downright persecution. The Church can carry out her mission without the State, through the use of her exclusively spiritual means

39

of action. The Church does not, of course, deny the purifying and strengthening value of persecution. She bows her head in reverent emotion as she recalls the sagas of heroism and courage with which countless sons and daughters have honored her in the past and are still honoring her today in those countries which are being ground under the heel of atheistic communism for their refusal to obey men in the things that are of God.

But, all this notwithstanding, persecution is not the normal way of life for the Church. The mission of the Church is accomplished much more naturally and efficaciously, and is greatly facilitated when harmonious cooperation between Church and state on a diplomatic level places at the disposal of each the prestige and the power of the other in the realization of what is, basically for both of them, one common purpose: the *full* and *complete* happiness and welfare of their subjects.

The diplomatic activity of the Vatican thus aims to create or to deepen an atmosphere of friendly collaboration with different nations. This international juridical bond may serve to snuff out the early beginnings of hostility or persecution, inspire social and educational legislation based on Christian principles, and make it easier for all citizens to work together toward their heavenly goal. The voice of an apostolic nuncio, speaking in the name and with the authority of the Roman Pontiff, may resound before a government as the thundering voice of conscience, like John the Baptist before the throne of a lustful Herod. Recent events in Poland, Hungary, Rumania, Czechoslovakia and other countries have made it clear that the silencing of a nuncio through expulsion is but an immediate prelude to persecution. History is witness that persecution of religion in any country marks a period of national degradation, in which the nation loses the respect of other countries in the world family of nations, and is doomed to witness the gradual weakening, if not the complete ruin, of its whole internal structure.

From the preceding remarks it will be seen that the diplomatic activity of the Holy See is vested with a special spiritual character. With the devious ways of the diplomacy of power politics it has nothing in common but the name. Vatican diplomacy, by its very nature, is basically spiritual and sacerdotal. It does not aim at political power, material advantage, or the defense of the interests of any particular group. Its goal is the salvation of souls, and to this end it directs its activity in order to safeguard in individual nations the preaching of the Gospel, the administration of the Sacraments, and the education of youth. At times, as is only natural, this calls for the protection of material and financial interests. But such interests are not at stake in themselves. They enter into the picture only because they are the necessary human means of attaining a supra-human goal. The Church must deal with any government animated by even a spark of goodwill, even when the basic motives of this government are patently insincere and selfish. With her eyes on a spiritual aim, the Church can answer with the forceful words attributed to Pius XI in reply to a critic who took him to task for negotiating concordats with Mussolini and Hitler: "To save a soul, I would treat with the devil himself!"

III. *The Organization of Papal Diplomacy*

Representatives of the Holy See are divided into four categories: (1) legates *a latere;* (2) apostolic nuncios; (3) apostolic internuncios; (4) apostolic delegates. This is the enumeration found in canons 266-270 of the Code of Canon Law. For all practical purposes, however, the diplomatic activity of the Sovereign Pontiff is exercised directly and officially through his nuncios and internuncios, and indirectly and unofficially through his apostolic delegates. The appointment of legates *a latere* to represent the Pope personally as though they came *from his very side* (which is the meaning of the Latin phrase *a latere*), has only a temporary character, such as on the occasion of national and international Eucharistic Congresses, centenaries of unusual importance, and the like. The office of legate *a latere* involves more religious and liturgical prestige than strict diplomatic activity.

Apostolic nuncios

Apostolic nuncios are the real ambassadors of the Holy See. They are the officially accredited representatives of the Sovereign Pontiff in the countries to which they are assigned, and their presence and activity in those countries are governed by the norms of international law regulating diplomatic representatives in general. Prescinding from the varying lengths of time spent by individual incumbents, the office of apostolic nuncio has a permanent character, in the same way as the diplomatic recognition of which it is normally the outward expression.

Apostolic nuncios have a twofold task, the one strictly spiritual, and the other diplomatic or political. Canon 276, 1, of the Code of Canon Law describes their duties well when it declares that permanent legates of the Holy See are to foster good relationships with the governments to which they are accredited, watch over the state of the dioceses in the territories assigned to them, and make reports thereon to the Pope.

Besides these prerogatives, which belong to their office by its very nature, apostolic nuncios are usually granted special powers, according to the circumstances of the respective countries where they reside. They are usually empowered to grant certain dispensations which would ordinarily be reserved to the Holy See itself. The extent of such powers varies with the distance of the country from Rome, and with the demands of particular situations. During the recent world conflict, apostolic nuncios and other representatives of the Vatican throughout the world were granted unusually ample powers, in order that the work of the Church might not be unduly hampered by the complications inseparable from world war. In addition, their office enabled them to carry on other helpful works. Among these, the Vatican Information Service for the exchange of messages to and from prisoners of war and civilian internees, as well as among civilians in various countries, was responsible for untold happiness in countless families, both Catholic and non-Catholic, and provided a neutral and efficient channel for the transmission of millions of war-time messages. Such activity would have been impossible without the goodwill and cooperation of the governments with which the Vatican had to deal in order to secure the required authorization for this activity and to be assured of the collaboration of government officials and agencies.

Apostolic nuncios share in all the privileges accorded by international law and the respective governments to the members of the diplomatic corps to which they belong. By virtue of a long standing custom explicitly confirmed by the Congress of Vienna on June 9, 1815, the apostolic nuncio, irrespective of his personal seniority, takes precedence over all other diplomatic agents of the same rank, and is the Dean of the diplomatic corps accredited to the government to which he is assigned.

Apostolic internuncios

For all practical purposes there is no important difference between the office of apostolic internuncio and that of apostolic nuncio.

Historically speaking, some discussion can be raised regarding the genuine origin and meaning of the term. As a matter of fact, it was not until May 8, 1916, that a special directive from the Vatican Secretariat of State provided authoritative information on the present-day meaning of the term. According to this clarification, papal diplomatic agents who were not nuncios would henceforth be known as "internuncios" rather than as "envoys extraordinary," which term was to be regarded as more applicable to lay representatives. If a conclusion may be based on procedure in the past, it might be said that the establishment of an apostolic internunciature is oftentimes the first step in the setting up of full diplomatic representation between the Holy See and a particular government, the erection of a nunciature coming after a fuller spirit of understanding has been achieved. Thus it was that the present apostolic nunciature in Brazil was preceded by an apostolic internunciature over a period of years. At the present time, for example, the Vatican has internunciatures in China, Holland, India, Indonesia, and Pakistan, to mention only a few. Prior to World War II, internunciatures were also maintained in several of the Baltic countries, but were suspended when these countries were engulfed by the Soviet invasion.

Apostolic delegates

If from the office of apostolic nuncio or internuncio we subtract all diplomatic representation before the government of the country, we have a clear picture of the office of the apostolic delegate. These representatives of the Sovereign Pontiff have no official standing in the diplomatic corps of the country to which they are assigned, nor do they deal directly with the governments of these countries. They attend only to matters of ecclesiastical jurisdiction. Whereas apostolic nuncios and internuncios represent the Vatican before the civil government of a given country, apostolic delegates represent the Holy Father before the hierarchy and the faithful of that country. The duties of apostolic delegates are strictly ecclesiastical in character and, barring special powers granted to them by the Pope, they consist solely in the task of keeping watch over the government and the progress of the Church in the country, and in providing reports and suggestions for the Holy Father. Without specific authorization from the Sovereign Pontiff—and this principle is applicable also to nuncios and internuncios—they have no power to intervene directly in the administration of the dioceses of the country by the individual bishops. Their reports are drawn up at stated times and aim to provide for the Pope and his aides in Rome as complete a picture as possible of the status of the Church in the country where they reside. Such reports are examined by the officials and consultors of the respective Sacred Congregations in Rome, and afford them invaluable assistance in formulating norms for the government of the Church in various countries.

As a rule, apostolic delegates are sent to countries where the number of Catholics is small, such as in countries served largely by the Oriental Church; to localities where the Church is still officially in a missionary stage, like Australia and the colonial possessions of the different countries in Africa, and so on; or, lastly, to countries which, notwithstanding their large number of Catholics or their state of progress, nevertheless make no provision for official recognition of the Church as a member of the international community. This is the case with the United States.

Inasmuch as apostolic delegates are entrusted with a mission which is purely internal to the Church, no previous consent of the civil government of the country is necessary for their appointment. Nevertheless, as a matter of courtesy and prudence, and in order to forestall possible misunderstandings and difficulties, the Holy See not infrequently sounds out the government authorities before actually proceeding to erect an apostolic delegation within the territory.

Apostolic nuncios, internuncios, and delegates are, traditionally, titular archbishops, that is to say, archbishops without residential sees, taking their "title" from one or other of the many defunct sees in the Orient and elsewhere. Many of the more important nunciatures and delegations have in the past been regarded as leading directly to elevation to the Sacred College of the Cardinals. Thus, for instance, all the prelates who have held the office of apostolic delegate in the United States were eventually recalled to Rome and honored with the Red Hat.

To avoid embarrassing situations in case of worldwide conflict, and to obviate the possibility of papal representatives being classified in a country as enemy aliens, Pope Pius XII decreed on July 6, 1940, that the official personnel of all apostolic nunciatures, internunciatures, and delegations, would, for the duration of their office, and irrespective of their nationality as individuals, be accorded Vatican City citizenship.

Dependence of Vatican Diplomats on the Holy See

All apostolic nuncios and internuncios depend directly on the Vatican Secretariat of State and, more particularly, on the Sacred Congregation for Extraordinary Ecclesiastical Affairs. This Sacred Congregation is a unit of the Secretariat of State of His Holiness, and is always presided over by the Cardinal Secretary of State. It corresponds to the State Department of our own government.

Since apostolic delegations have only an ecclesiastical mission, their immediate superior is the Cardinal in charge of the Sacred Congregation dealing with the affairs of the various countries to which the apostolic delegates are sent. Thus, some apostolic delegations are immediately responsible to the Sacred Consistorial Congregation, which handles business pertaining to nations in which the government of the Church is permanently established and functions in conformity with the common and general law of the Church. The countries under the Sacred Consistorial Congregation are Canada, Great Britain, Mexico, and the United States.

Other apostolic delegations are under the supervision of the Sacred Congregation for the Propagation of the Faith, which is the Vatican office responsible for the world-wide missionary activity of the Church. These apostolic delegations are found in Albania, Australia, Belgian Congo, British East and West Africa, French Africa, Indo-china, Japan, Korea, New Zealand, Oceania, and South Africa.

Lastly, a small number of apostolic delegations report to the Sacred Congregation for the Oriental Church, which handles the special problems arising from the liturgical and disciplinary differences existing between the Roman Church and the churches of the Orient. Thus, the Sacred Congregation for the Oriental Church supervises the apostolic delegations in Bulgaria, Ethiopia, Greece, Iran, Iraq, Jerusalem and Palestine (including Jordania and Cyprus), Syria, and Turkey. As in the case of some apostolic nunciatures and internunciatures, circumstances have prevented certain of these officially existing apostolic delegations from being occupied by actual incumbents.

The Training of Vatican Diplomats

There exists in Rome a special institution which serves as a training school for the formation of candidates for the Vatican Diplomatic Service. This institution is known as the *Pontifical Ecclesi-*

astical Academy, and only recently celebrated the two hundred and fiftieth anniversary of its foundation. In this academy, promising young ecclesiastics from various nations are provided with the special technical formation required to constitute a successful diplomat. The course of studies includes the securing of a doctorate in canon law, as well as the study of the various phases of diplomatic style and activity. It always includes a period of apprenticeship served in one or other of the offices of the Vatican Secretariat of State. The usual practice of the Vatican is to transfer its young diplomats rather frequently, to provide them with a broader and richer background of experience, and their period of training in the "home office" is sometimes supplemented by a turn of duty in the Secretariat of State even some years after they have been actually put to work in the different diplomatic posts. The majority of the ecclesiastics who are eventually appointed as nuncios, internuncios, and apostolic delegates, have spent long years of technical training in the different phases of Vatican diplomacy both at home and abroad.

Illustrious names connected with the Pontifical Academy in recent years include those of Pope Leo XIII and his Secretary of State, Cardinal Rampolla; Cardinal Merry del Val, former President of the Academy and later Secretary of State under Blessed Pius X; Monsignor Giacomo della Chiesa, professor of diplomatic style, who later became Pope Benedict XV, and Cardinal Luigi Maglione. From 1900 to 1914 the professor of ecclesiastical diplomacy was Monsignor Eugenio Pacelli, now gloriously reigning as Pope Pius XII.

IV. *The Procedure of Vatican Diplomacy*

We have already remarked that the diplomatic activity of the Holy See bears a distinctly spiritual and priestly stamp. This is a natural consequence of its essentially spiritual aim. Its purpose is not political aggrandizement in the international world, but simple assurance that the Church will have the freedom of action necessary to enable it to carry on its work of expanding and consolidating the Kingdom of Christ. The Vatican diplomat is first and foremost a priest; as an archbishop he is endowed with the fullness of priestly powers. Yet he does not spend his life preaching the Word of God and administering the Sacraments. His task is to make it possible for his fellow-priests and bishops to engage in this divinely imposed work of saving souls.

From this it should not be concluded that the Church is blind to the human side of its diplomatic activity, or that it counts presumptuously only on the assistance of divine grace. Whether they be nuncios or delegates, the representatives of the Sovereign Pontiff must deal with men, sometimes with political figures whose outlook is not particularly distinguished for spiritual emphasis. In such cases, the representative of the papacy must bring into play all his natural and acquired human gifts, in order to win the goodwill of those in whose power it is either to assist him or to hamper him in his efforts to facilitate the proper functioning of the Church.

It would be folly to assume that Vatican diplomacy has never made mistakes or that all Vatican diplomats have been saints. In an institution which goes back some fifteen centuries, it would be astounding, to say the least, if some individuals had not been more politicians than priests, and had not succumbed to many of the human temptations which beset even those engaged in a basically spiritual mission.

Without casting aspersions on the past, we might recall that among others, recent Vatican Secretaries of State like Cardinal Rampolla, under Leo XIII, and Cardinal Merry del Val, under Blessed Pius X, have been well known for the depth and the genuineness of their spiritual mentality. The present Holy Father, who has spent practically the whole of the fifty years of his priestly life in diplomatic work at home or abroad, is a most outstanding example of that perfect embodiment of the saintly priest and the skilful diplomat which is the ideal for every representative of the Sovereign Pontiff. Men such as he, along with many others in the history of papal diplomacy, are living proofs that this activity of the Holy See is but one further aspect of the Church's tireless efforts to make itself all things to all men, in order that the prayer of Christ may be fulfilled and that all men may know the Father and, knowing Him, may love Him and come to full and endless possession and enjoyment of Him in heaven.

III

The Popes and Peace in the Twentieth Century

by Monsignor Harry Koenig

The twentieth century opened with the solemn and impressive ceremonies of Holy Year, and on that occasion Pope Leo XIII exhorted all the pilgrims to pray "for peace and concord among Christian princes."[1] Prayers were necessary at that time because two fierce but widely separated wars were raging. Between the British and the Boers from the Transvaal and Orange Free State a bitter conflict had arisen. Resenting the ominous threat of British imperialism in South Africa, the hardy Dutch Boers were struggling to maintain their independence and their way of life. In China a secret society, Iho Ch'üan, commonly known as the Boxers, had fomented a revolution to expel all foreigners from their land.

Sanguinary and lamentable as these hostilities were, they were nothing more than shadows compared to the depressing pall and gloom which clouded the European scene. In response to an inspired suggestion from Czar Nicholas II of Russia an International Peace Conference assembled at the Hague on May 18, 1899, under the auspices of Queen Wilhelmina of the Netherlands. During its deliberations, which lasted until July 29, many excellent resolutions were passed regarding disarmament, the peaceful adjustment of international differences and the establishment of a permanent court of arbitration.

Writing to the Vatican, Queen Wilhelmina urged Leo XIII to lend his valuable moral support to the conference. In the most forthright language the pope replied: "We consider that it comes especially within Our province not only to lend Our moral support

---

[1] Bull *Properante ad Exitum* in *American Ecclesiastical Review*, Vol. XXI, 70.

to such enterprises, but to cooperate actively in them, for the object in question is supremely noble in its nature and intimately bound up with Our August Ministry, which, through the Divine Founder of the Church, and in virtue of traditions of many secular instances, has been invested with the highest possible mission, that of being a mediator for peace. In fact, the authority of the Supreme Pontiff goes beyond the boundaries of nations; it embraces all people, to the end of federating them in the true peace of the Gospel. His action to promote the general good of humanity rises above the special interests which the chiefs of the various States have in view, and, better than any one else, his authority knows how to incline toward concord peoples of diverse nature and character. History itself bears witness to all that has been done, by the influence of Our Predecessors, to soften the inexorable laws of war, to arrest bloody conflicts when controversies have arisen between princes, to terminate peacefully even the most acute differences between nations, to vindicate courageously the rights of the weak against the pretensions of the strong. Even unto Us, notwithstanding the abnormal condition to which We are at present reduced, it has been given to put an end to grave differences between great nations such as Germany and Spain, and this very day We hope to be able soon to establish concord between two nations of South America which have submitted their controversy to Our arbitration."[2]

In this letter the pope refers to his office as mediator between Germany and Spain over the Caroline Islands in 1885. Spain had discovered these islands but never colonized them. Vitally aware of their strategic importance in the Pacific, Germany claimed them and thus antagonized the Spaniards. Threats of war were fulminated by both sides. Although the *Kulturkampf* had seriously strained relations between Germany and the Vatican, the German emperor recommended that Leo XIII arbitrate the delicate question of the Caroline Islands. Shrewdly the pope offered his services as mediator rather than as arbitrator and his proposals amicably settled the dispute. In his efforts to arbitrate the treaty quarrel between Haiti and Santo Domingo he was not so successful, but at least these two nations recognized the peace-making functions of the Holy See.

Leo XIII did not conceal his grave disappointment at being excluded from the Hague Conference through the machinations of

---

[2] Letter *Nous Ne Pouvons* in *Principles for Peace*, pp. 99-100.

the Italian government. The Vatican had more than moral support to offer; it wished effectually to cooperate with all efforts to establish international peace. While the Hague Conference was unable to effect any general limitations of armaments, it did dissipate some of the suspicion, apprehension and skepticism that had paralyzed international relations before it assembled. To Leo XIII, however, it was only too clear that if the results of this conference and of future treaties were to have any lasting value, they must be anchored on the solid foundation of Christian virtue. In his encyclical *Tametsi* he emphasized this point: "How little that kind of virtue which despises faith avails in the end, and what sort of fruit it brings forth, we see only too plainly. Why is it that with so much zeal displayed for establishing and augmenting the commonwealth, nations still have to labor and yet in so many and such important matters fare worse and worse every day? They say indeed that civil society is self-dependent, that it can go on happily without the protection of Christian institutions, that by its own unaided energies it can reach its goal. Hence, they prefer to have public affairs conducted on a secular basis, so that in civil discipline and public life there are always fewer and fewer traces discernible of the old religious spirit. They do not see what they are doing. Take away the supremacy of God, Who judges right and wrong; and law necessarily loses its paramount authority, while at the same time justice is undermined, these two being the strongest and most essential bonds of social union. In the same way, when the hope and expectation of immortality are gone, it is only human to seek greedily after perishable things, and everyone will try, in proportion to his power, to clutch a larger share of them. Hence spring jealousies, envies, hatreds; the most iniquitous plots to overthrow all power and mad schemes of universal ruin are formed. There is no peace abroad, nor security at home, and social life is made hideous by crime."[3]

Despite this prophetic papal warning secularism continued to spread and nations blindly spurned the only principles that could guarantee the peace. Dreading war they continued to prepare for it, and the armed peace which prevailed was almost more nerve-wracking than war itself. Seeing the inevitable result of these mistaken policies Leo warned the world in 1902 on the occasion of his silver jubilee as pope: "This lamentable confusion in the realm of

---

[3] *Principles for Peace,* p. 104.

ideas has produced restlessness among the people, outbreaks and the general spirit of rebellion. From these have sprung the frequent popular agitations and disorders of our times which are only the preludes of much more terrible disorders in the future."[4] Future events were amply to demonstrate the truth of his words.

Historians are fond of contrasting the temperaments, careers and policies of Leo XIII and of his successor, Pius X. An aristocrat, scholar and poet, Leo XIII had raised the prestige of the papacy to new heights by his diplomatic finesse and by his brilliant and enlightening encyclicals on such diverse subjects as scholastic philosophy, socialism, communism, the origin of civil power, the Christian constitution of states, human liberty, the condition of the working man, church and state, and Christian democracy. Pius X, on the other hand, was the son of a postman, had been a parish priest, Bishop of Mantua, Patriarch of Venice and was better known for his sanctity than for his learning or diplomatic acumen. His main efforts were directed toward the internal reform of the Church and in the matter of diplomatic relations he experienced serious difficulties, especially with France and Portugal. But when it came to peace and the means for preserving it, Leo XIII and Pius X saw eye to eye and had only one policy.

Following in his predecessor's footsteps Pius X employed the mediation of his nuncios, Msgr. Giulio Tonti and Alessandro Bavona, to help settle the boundary dispute between Brazil, Peru and Bolivia.[5] The Fifteenth World Peace Conference held at Milan in 1906 received his hearty approval[6] and a vigorous letter of commendation was sent to the Carnegie Endowment for International Peace on the occasion of its foundation.[7] The Holy Father besought all Catholics in Mexico, where revolution was devastating the countryside, to support the Niagara Falls Conference in which Argentina, Brazil and Chile were trying to mediate the controversy between the United States and Mexico.[8]

Notwithstanding his many pleas, the armament race continued. The assassination at Sarajevo of the Archduke Francis Ferdinand of

---

[4] Letter *Pervenuti* in *Principles for Peace*, p. 107.
[5] *Principles for Peace*, p. 113 and Müller, *Das Friedenswerk der Kirche in den Letzten drei Jahrhunderten*, pp. 49, 60.
[6] *Principles for Peace*, p. 120.
[7] *Ibid.*, pp. 122-123.
[8] *Ibid.*, p. 123 and Schlarman, *Mexico: A Land of Volcanoes*, pp. 447-448.

Austria was the spark that threatened to ignite the powder in the arsenals. Pius X instructed his nuncios in the different European capitals to do everything in their power to stave off the impending conflict but, alas, the zero hour had arrived. By the first week in August Germany and Austria-Hungary were at war with Russia, France, Great Britain, Belgium, Serbia and Montenegro.

This crushing blow rent the saintly pontiff's soul with grief. Convinced of the complete futility of all merely human means he addressed himself on August 2, 1914 to the Catholics of the whole world: "We deeply feel and realize that Our fatherly charity and Our Apostolic Ministry demand of Us that We direct men's minds upward to Him from Whom alone help can come, to Christ, the Prince of Peace, and man's all-powerful Mediator with God. Therefore, We do exhort the Catholics of the whole world to turn, full of confidence, to His throne of grace and mercy, and let the clergy lead the way by their example and by appointing special prayers in their respective parishes, under the orders of the bishops, that God may be moved to pity and may remove as soon as possible the disastrous torch of war and inspire the supreme rulers of the nations with thoughts of peace and not of affliction."[9]

Frequently it has been stated that the Austrian Ambassador at the opening of the war begged Pius X to bless the armies of the Central Powers and that the pope sternly replied: "I bless peace, not war." For this response no documentary evidence has been found; but as the Italians so aptly say, *se non è vero, è ben trovato*.

On June 2, 1914, Pius X commenced his eightieth year in apparently good health. The ominous threats of war, however, were a constant worry to him. When the armies actually began to march, he lost heart. On August 17 a slight attack of bronchitis confined him to bed, but it caused no alarm either to the doctors or to the papal household. By the following evening the bronchitis had developed into pneumonia and the pontiff was sinking rapidly. Two days later he was dead—not of pneumonia but of a broken heart— one of the first victims of the war he had tried so strenuously to avert.

Standing before the shrine of Our Lady of Lourdes in the Vatican Gardens, Pius X turned to his chaplain one day and sighed: "I

---

[9] *Principles for Peace*, p. 125.

pity my successor."[10] Few men indeed have ever ascended Peter's throne under more trying circumstances than Giacomo della Chiesa, Cardinal Archbishop of Bologna, who chose the name of Benedict XV. Small and undistinguished in appearance but with a finely trained diplomatic mind, he began his apostolic labors by summoning all Christians to pray Almighty God to enlighten rulers that they might initiate councils of peace. His first encyclical showed him in the role of an Old Testament prophet lamenting the sad state of the world, analyzing the evils which had provoked the war, and proposing means for establishing peace.

From the first days of his pontificate three cardinal principles guided his policy. He proposed: first, to maintain an absolute impartiality towards all belligerents; secondly, to do the utmost good to all without distinctions of persons, nationality or religion; thirdly, to make every effort to bring the belligerents to discuss their war aims so that they might reach a peaceful agreement.

So scrupulously neutral was the pope that each side accused him of favoring the other. The French, in particular, made a spectacle of themselves by their slanderous insinuations.[11] On June 22, 1915, M. Latapie, a correspondent of the French newspaper, *Liberté,* published what purported to be an interview with Benedict XV, placing the blame for the war upon England and exonerating Germany.[12] This journalist actually had an audience with the pontiff, but Benedict XV publicly denounced the published account as representing neither his thoughts nor his words.[13] What disappointed the Holy See was not so much the clumsy and irresponsible attempts of the calumniators as the fact that vast numbers of Catholics in the warring nations pathetically believed these ridiculous charges.[14] Vatican neutrality did not hinder Benedict XV from denouncing injustices by whatsoever nation they had been committed. But it was not necessary nor proper to entangle papal authority in the disputes between the belligerents. Not on the special interests

---

[10] Merry del Val, *Memories of Pius X,* p. 22.

[11] See the letters of Benedict XV and Cardinal Gasparri to the Cardinal Archbishops of Paris and Lyons in *Principles for Peace,* pp. 146-147.

[12] Rope, *Benedict XV, Pope of Peace,* pp. 85-87.

[13] *Principles for Peace,* pp. 177-178.

[14] *Ibid.,* p. 257.

which divided the belligerents but on the common faith which united them was his attention focused.[15]

Like the Divine Master whose vicar he was, Benedict XV gave a luminous example to the warring nations by his abundant charity and tireless solicitude for the wounded, suffering and persecuted war victims. The conflict was only weeks old when he wrote to the Archbishop of Cologne asking Christian charity for French prisoners.[16] Shortly thereafter Cardinal Gasparri suggested a truce for Christmas day but this was "a project that met with sympathy 'in principle' from Great Britain, Belgium and Germany, but refusal from France and from Russia."[17] To priests in all countries instructions were sent to seek the spiritual and material welfare of all war prisoners, to urge them to write home, and, if through sickness or illiteracy they were unable, to undertake this correspondence themselves.[18] Benedict pleaded with the belligerents to exchange wounded war prisoners[19] and certain classes of interned civilians.[20] At his insistence the Swiss government agreed to hospitalize sick prisoners from both camps.[21] From the meager Vatican funds generous sums were sent for relief in Belgium, Poland, France, Luxembourg, Lithuania, Armenia, Syria, Lebanon and for German prisoners in Russia. No attempt was made to earmark this money for Catholics because papal charity recognized no boundaries of faith, race or nationality.

Wars do not generate peace; only violence, hatreds and prejudice result therefrom. With this in mind Benedict addressed his cardinals on December 6, 1915: "To prepare the way for peace . . . a peace that is just, lasting and not profitable to only one of the fighting parties, the way which can truly lead to a happy result is that which has already been tried and found good in similar circumstances . . . that in an exchange of ideas, directly or indirectly, there should be definitely and clearly put forward and duly weighed with good will and serene conscience, the aspirations of each one, eliminating all that is unjust and impossible and taking account of all that is just and possible, with any arrangement and compensa-

---

15 *Ibid.,* p. 152.
16 *Ibid.,* p. 130.
17 Rope, *Benedict, XV, Pope of Peace,* p. 70.
18 *Principles for Peace,* pp. 143-144.
19 *Ibid.,* p. 145.
20 *Ibid.,* p. 150.
21 *Ibid.,* p. 168.

tion that may be needful. Naturally, as is the case in all human controversies which are settled by the contending parties themselves, it is absolutely necessary that on one side and the other of the belligerents there should be concession on one point and renunciation of some hoped-for gain; and each should make such concessions willingly, even if it entail some sacrifice."[22] Compromise is what the pope here advocates, not appeasement. But neither side was in any mood to compromise. A year and a half later the war had reached such a stalemate that the papal nuncios in the different capitals thought a negotiated peace to be a distinct possibility. After having carefully explored their views, Benedict on August 1, 1917, proposed the following articles to serve as a basis for peace:

1. Substitution of the moral force of right for the material force of arms.
2. The simultaneous and reciprocal diminution of armaments.
3. In place of armies the institution of arbitration, with sanctions against the state which should refuse either to submit international questions to arbitration or to accept its decisions.
4. Common rights over the sea.
5. An entire and reciprocal condonation of war damages with certain adjustments to be made if necessary.
6. On the part of Germany a total evacuation of Belgium and France; on the part of the other belligerent powers, a restoration of the German colonies.
7. Territorial questions between Italy and Austria, between Germany and France, in Armenia and Balkan States and Poland to be settled in a conciliatory spirit by the belligerents.[23]

The papal nuncio to Bavaria, Archbishop Eugenio Pacelli, had been tactfully negotiating these points with the German Chancellor, Bethmann-Hollweg; but when Generals Hindenburg and Ludendorff got wind of what was in the offing, they succeeded in having their tool, Georg Michaelis, appointed Chancellor. Germany then refused to negotiate; and the Allies replied through Lansing, American Secretary of State, that they could not trust the German military regime.[24]

---

[22] *Principles for Peace*, p. 191.
[23] *Ibid.*, pp. 229-232.
[24] Müller, *Das Friedenswerk der Kirche*, pp. 468-470.

One has only to compare dispassionately Benedict's proposals for a just peace with the vindictive reparations of the Versailles Treaty to realize what a boon it would have been to have negotiated peace in 1917. How much human blood would have been saved, how much vengeance would have been dissipated if only Peter's voice had been heard! The world never seems to learn that total victory and total surrender seldom, if ever, bring a just and lasting peace.

Overwhelming as was his disappointment with the belligerents' refusal to adopt his proposals, Benedict did not lose heart. In fact, confidence and trust in Divine Providence have always been and continue to be leading characteristics of the papal peace program. Those pessimists who in peace bewail the inevitability of war and in war deplore the impossibility of peace—and too many Catholics are numbered among them—can find no justification for their despair and gloom in papal writings.

After the Armistice of 1918 Benedict promised the statesmen gathered at Versailles not only the prayers of Catholics but also his "firm resolve to secure to the just deliberations of the world congress the support of Our influence among the faithful."[25] But the virtue of justice did not distinguish the deliberations of the Versailles Conference, and of one flagrant injustice the pope did not hesitate to proclaim "that the actual conditions of Austria are absolutely intolerable, as they take away from an entire nation the possibility of getting the means of existence."[26]

No one was better acquainted with the shortcomings of the Covenant for the League of Nations than Benedict; yet in his encyclical on Peace and Reconstruction he wrote: "It is much to be desired that all states, putting aside mutual suspicion, should unite in one league, or rather a sort of family of peoples, calculated both to maintain their own independence and safeguard the order of human society. What specially, amongst other reasons, calls for such an association of nations, is the need generally recognized of making every effort to abolish or reduce the enormous burden of military expenditures which states can no longer bear."[27]

---

[25] *Principles for Peace*, p. 263.

[26] *Principles for Peace*, p. 305.

[27] *Ibid.*, p. 290.

Armaments and compulsory military service[28] were, in Benedict's mind, the twin evils responsible for modern wars. Their elimination would be the guarantee for future peace. One of Benedict's last acts was to send his blessing to the Washington Disarmament Conference.[29] But the Washington delegates with their secularistic illusions failed to understand what Benedict so admirably stated when he wrote that "men can of their own power throw the whole world into disorder and destroy everything; but they cannot rebuild again and set things in order unless God helps them."[30]

The slender, frail Benedict XV was succeeded by the stocky, sturdy Pius XI. The new pope was the strange combination of librarian and mountain climber, scholar and nuncio, administrator and apostle. Addressing the cardinals who had just elected him, he made the program for his pontificate clear from the very outset when he told them in carefully chosen words: "Pius is a name of peace, and so, desirous of consecrating my efforts to the work of pacification as did my predecessor, Benedict XV, I choose the name of Pius."[31] After a moment's hesitation he continued: "I want to add one word. In the presence of the Sacred College I affirm my purpose of safeguarding and defending all the rights of the Church and the prerogatives of the Holy See. But at the same time I want my first blessing to go out, as a pledge of that peace for which humanity is longing, not merely to Rome and to Italy, but to the whole Church and the whole world. I will therefore give it from the outer balcony of St. Peter's."[32] By this act a precedent of more than fifty years' standing was shattered for since the pontificate of Leo XIII the popes had given their blessing only within St. Peter's basilica. Thus Pius XI asserted that independence of soul which was so integral a part of his character and at the same time demonstrated to all nations his determination to devote all his energies to world peace. In the same spirit he chose for the motto of his reign: "The Peace of Christ in the Kingdom of Christ."[33]

---

[28] "For more than a century conscription has been the real cause of a multitude of evils afflicting society, for which a simultaneous and reciprocal suppression of it will be the true remedy." *Principles for Peace*, p. 239; see also pp. 235-236.

[29] *Principles for Peace*, p. 317.

[30] *Ibid.*, p. 245.

[31] Binchy, *Church and State in Fascist Italy*, p. 78.

[32] *Ibid.*, p. 78.

[33] *Principles for Peace*, p. 331.

In his first encyclical one truth he found inescapable: "Since the close of the Great War individuals, the different classes of society, the nations of the earth have not found true peace. . . . Since the selfsame sad conditions continue to exist in the world today which were the object of constant and almost heartbreaking preoccupation on the part of Our respected Predecessor, Benedict XV, naturally We have come to make his thoughts and his solutions of those problems Our own."[34] Pius XI did not inaugurate a new peace policy, he enlarged and clarified what had been accomplished by his predecessors. Those Catholics who maintained that it was not necessary to follow papal policy on international relations he condemned unequivocally.[35]

When, shortly after his coronation, the Genoa Peace Conference assembled, it received his blessing and encouragement. Recognition of Soviet Russia was on the conference's agenda; and Pius insisted that full liberty of conscience be guaranteed for all citizens, Russians or otherwise, and secondly that private and public exercise of religion and worship be guaranteed in Russia.[36] Experience had acquainted the pope with Communism for, as nuncio to Poland, he had remained at his post when the Red Army was hammering at Warsaw's gates. For the Russian people he had only sympathy and admiration; and when the plague and famine swept their country in 1924, he sent relief worth millions of dollars. But at the very same time he denounced the errors of Communism.[37]

When international disputes arise, they can be settled by war or by negotiation which in practice means compromise. The popes have consistently recommended negotiation. This is not the same as appeasement. In appeasement the weaker nation succumbs to the inexorable demands of the stronger. In compromise both sides negotiate, modify their demands, make concessions to each other so that a mutual agreement can be reached. This is what the papacy has always preached as preferable to war and as a substitute for war.

For more than fifty years there had been a dispute between the Holy See and Italy known as the Roman Question. It dated back to 1870 when the troops of King Victor Emmanuel II seized Rome

---

[34] *Ibid.*, p. 333.
[35] *Ibid.*, p. 351.
[36] *Ibid.*, p. 324.
[37] *Ibid.*, p. 371.

and the Papal States from Pius IX. Against this unprovoked and unjust invasion of his territory Pius IX protested vehemently. He and his successors remained prisoners in the Vatican refusing to recognize the conquest of Rome. In the ensuing years the Italian Government had been petty in many ways, especially in the subtle maneuvers and secret treaties which kept the Holy See from attending the Hague and the Versailles Conferences.

The Roman Question was embarrassing both to Italy and the Holy See, and it caused the Italian people no end of anxieties. To settle it required genuine concessions on both sides. Attempts were made after the armistice while Benedict was still reigning; but they came to naught when the Italian Prime Minister, Orlando, was removed.[38] Under Pius XI negotiations were resumed in 1926, and for two years every aspect of this thorny problem was explored. Finally on February 11, 1929, the Holy See and Italy signed the Lateran Treaty, which finally and irrevocably solved the Roman Question. The dominating force behind this treaty was the personal will of Pius XI. On the very day the treaty was signed he told the parish priests of Rome: "Principally, not to say solely and wholly, it was through Our responsibility—a heavy and terrifying responsibility truly enough—that the whole thing came to pass and will for the future work. . . . We can truthfully say that there is not a line, not an expression of the accords in question, that has not been during thirty months, the special object of Our study, Our meditation, and still more of Our prayer."[39]

Upon the Holy See the Lateran Treaty imposed tremendous sacrifices—too great in the opinion of many influential Roman prelates—but Pius XI was above all else a realist and he knew that peace cannot be achieved except by mutual concessions. Therefore when the popes preach the necessity of honest and sincere negotiations, history already has before it a perfect example of what they mean.

With admirable wisdom the Lateran Treaty stated the Vatican's position in the field of international relations: "With regard to the sovereignty pertaining to it in the field of international relations, the Holy See declares that it wishes to remain and will always remain, extraneous to all temporal disputes between nations, and to

---

[38] Kelley, *The Bishop Jots It Down*, pp. 261-276.
[39] Hughes, *Pope Pius the Eleventh*, p. 195.

international congresses convoked for the setlement of such disputes, unless the contending parties make a joint appeal to its mission of peace; nevertheless, it reserves the right in every case to exercise its moral and spiritual power."[40] To this day the popes have continued to emphasize and clarify the moral issues in the problems underlying war and peace.

The same year that witnessed the signing of the Lateran Pact also saw the beginning of the great depression. This economic collapse increased international tensions. The popes have always been aware that wars have economic and social, as well as political, causes. In no small part national rivalries are due to an unrestrained yearning for a larger share in the world's economic wealth. Political demagogues, such as Hitler, Mussolini and Stalin, enkindled selfish nationalism in the people by promising to readjust international economic inequalities. Pius XI faced a virulent type of nationalism not only in the Fascism of Mussolini and the National Socialism of Hitler, but also in the atheistic Communism of Stalin. For while it may be true that Communism as philosophically expounded by Marx is by its nature international, yet Soviet Communism in its practical policies as pursued by Joseph Stalin is as definitely Russian as Nazism was German.

These three men were dictators; they represented the totalitarian state. They despised Christian morality and scorned the benefits and freedoms of the democracies. If their doctrines were allowed to spread, not only was Christianity doomed but another world war was inevitable. It is to the glory of Pius XI that he recognized these evils for what they actually were and that he had the fortitude to denounce them publicly. Read the encyclicals *"Non Abbiamo Bisogno"*[41] against Fascism, *"Mit Brennender Sorge"*[42] against Nazism, *"Divini Redemptoris"*[43] against Communism, and you cannot fail to be impressed by the profound knowledge Pius XI had of these modern heresies and by the indomitable courage with which he opposed the dictators. When other nations were engaged in appeasement, Pius spoke plainly: "It shall not be said of Us, in the words of an ancient historian, that We have forgotten the real names of things. No, by the grace

---

40 *Principles for Peace,* p. 383.
41 *Ibid.,* pp. 446-448.
42 *Ibid.,* pp. 498-510.
43 *Ibid.,* pp. 510-535.

of God, We have not forgotten the true names; We shall call things by their real names."[44] He called Fascism "a true and real pagan worship of the State,"[5] he ridiculed the Nazi "myth of blood and race,"[46] and warned Catholics that "Communism is intrinsically wrong and no one who would save Christian civilization may collaborate with it in any undertaking whatsoever."[47]

In 1936 Pius XI suffered a severe heart attack and for some time the doctors despaired of his life. By force of his strong will he kept on working and offered his own suffering for peace.[48] He never recovered his health and, as the totalitarian nations prepared for war, at least twice more he offered himself as a holocaust for the salvation and peace of the world.[49] He had summoned the bishops of Italy to Rome to attend the ceremonies commemorating the tenth anniversary of the Lateran Treaty when illness struck again. The speech he had prepared for the occasion was reported to have been a stern reprobation of totalitarianism, especially as it was being practised in Italy. It is pathetic to read how he pleaded with his doctors to keep him alive until he delivered his *Nunc dimittis*. But the doctors were unsuccessful and the speech has never been published.

When the cardinals assembled in conclave after the funeral of Pius XI, their chief resolution was to demonstrate their solidarity behind the vigorous policies of the deceased pope. It took them but one day to elect his most intimate associate, Cardinal Pacelli, who for nearly ten years had been Secretary of State. In physical appearance, in training, in personality the new pope was a decided contrast to his predecessor, the master whom he had served so faithfully. Tall, spare, almost gaunt, he was schooled and experienced mainly in the fields of law and diplomacy. His predilection for law and diplomacy cannot be overemphasized because they, together with his profound faith in God and in the Catholic Church, are the key to an understanding of his pontificate and of his peace program. Take as an example the word "juridical," which is hardly ever used by the other popes but which occurs frequently

---

44 *Ibid.*, p. 539.
45 *Ibid.*, p. 447.
46 *Ibid.*, p. 502.
47 *Ibid.*, p. 530.
48 *Ibid.*, p. 496.
49 *Ibid.*, pp. 548, 551.

in his letters and addresses. He speaks often of the juridical order, juridical system, juridical relations, juridical norms. And at great length he explains the importance and meaning of the natural, moral, human, international, divine laws and their relation to peace.

Secondly, where Pius XI was blunt and direct, Pius XII habitually employs the refined courtesies of diplomacy even in delivering rebukes. This was especially apparent in the dispute between the Vatican and Mussolini over Italian Catholic Action. Relations between the Holy See and Italy were at their worst when Pius XI died. The speech which he had prepared for the tenth anniversary of the Lateran Treaty was cautiously filed away, and Pius XII strove hard to repair the breach. The new pontiff saw correctly that the problems of international peace were the most urgent and important issues facing the Church, and he endeavored to wean Mussolini and Italy away from Hitler by agreeing to minor changes in Catholic Action. For a while his policy appeared successful in that Italy remained out of war despite her close alliance with Germany. But when the panzer divisions rolled over France and Nazi victory seemed assured, Mussolini defied the pope, popular sentiment and the king by forcing Italy into the conflict.

The task confronting Pius XII upon his election was as formidable and appalling as any pope has ever faced. Like a deadly contagion war was in the air, the nations were paralyzed with fear of what was to come. Divine Providence, however, had wonderfully prepared Pius XII for his mission of peace. His family name— Pacelli—stood for peace; his coat of arms bore the device *"opus justitiae pax"*—"peace is the work of justice"; during World War I he had been nuncio to Bavaria and had initiated the delicate maneuvers for a negotiated peace; while Secretary of State he had witnessed the rise of the dictators and the totalitarian states. His information on the world situation was accurate, detailed, up-to-date. United to this comprehensive knowledge of international affairs was a heart that loved God ardently and loved men of all nations, races and religions with that intensity which only a convinced Christian can experience.

Night and day his nuncios in the different capitals labored to discover some solution to the threat of war. When the showdown finally came between Germany and Poland over Danzig and the Polish Corridor, the pope broadcast this plea to those in power and to their peoples: "The danger is imminent but there is yet time.

Nothing is lost with peace; all may be lost with war. Let men return to mutual understanding! Let them begin negotiations anew, conferring with good will and with respect for reciprocal rights. Then will they find that to sincere and conscientious negotiations an honorable solution is never precluded."[50] The consequences of modern war are impossible to foresee. When the conflict begins, no one knows how it will end. It is likely to exhaust the victor as well as the vanquished. The real issues are never settled by the war itself; they are solved afterwards by negotiation. Instead of having negotiations follow war, isn't it more reasonable to negotiate before millions are victimized on the battlefields? The answer, of course, is an emphatic "yes"; but there are not a few who maintained in 1939, as they maintain today, that it is impossible to trust the opponent.

Pius XII had every reason to mistrust Hitler and the Nazis. They had broken almost every article of the Concordat solemnly ratified in 1933, and their defiance of Christianity was as blatant as it was unrelenting. They had made a mockery of Munich; and yet on August 31, 1939, hours before the German army invaded Poland, the pope besought the German and Polish Governments to continue conversations, to avoid any incident whatsoever and to abstain from any measure that might aggravate the present tension.[51] The Holy Father loved Poland, a Catholic country faithful to the Holy See, and he amply demonstrated his affection for the Polish people; yet as a diplomat he knew that Danzig and the Polish Corridor were open to some negotiation.

But negotiations collapsed and war was the inevitable consequence. The Poles were seriously disappointed when Pius XII did not publicly denounce the German aggression against their country. Perhaps (and this is my own interpretation) the pope believed that the war could be localized and that a settlement could still be reached by negotiation. All was quiet on both fronts when Pius announced his five point program for a just and honorable peace in his Christmas address of 1939. The fundamental postulates were:

1. An assurance for all nations, great or small, powerful or weak, of their right to life and independence.
2. A mutually agreed, organic and progressive disarmament, spiritual as well as material.

---

[50] *Ibid.*, p. 585.
[51] *Principles for Peace,* p. 586.

3. The erection of some juridical institution to guarantee the loyal and faithful fulfillment of treaties and to revise and correct these treaties in case of recognized needs.
4. The real needs and just demands of nations, of populations and of racial minorities must receive prompt attention.
5. Peoples and their governments must submit willingly to the influence of religion which alone can give life, authority and binding force to the dead letter of international agreements.[52]

The press and public opinion enthusiastically welcomed these five points as a concrete program for undertaking peace. Because they covered more ground, they were not as specific as those proposed by Benedict XV in 1917. Tragically the belligerent powers were not at that time as interested in negotiations as they were in 1917, and the so-called "phony" war continued. The invasion of Holland, Belgium and Luxembourg on May 10, 1940, convinced Pius XII that the die was cast and that diplomatic efforts for peace would no longer be of any avail. Consequently, the Vatican immediately dispatched messages of sympathy to the sovereigns of the three invaded countries.[53] The wider the conflict spread, the more remote peace became. The pope struggled to keep Italy out of the war; but, as we have already noted, Mussolini wanted Fascism to have a share in what he was certain would be a German triumph.

Acutely aware of the Holy See's excellent diplomatic contacts, President Roosevelt sent Myron Taylor in February, 1940, as his personal ambassador to Pius XII. Between the United States and the Vatican relations were cordial, and the pope was pleased that the United States remained neutral, even if acting as an arsenal for the democracies.

With the German attack upon Russia and the Japanese bombing of Pearl Harbor the war spread virtually to the entire world. At no time did the military situation offer any practical possibilities for a negotiated peace. But the pope continued to write, speak and pray for peace. On Easter Sunday, 1941, he declared: "We have left nothing undone or untried in order to forestall or shorten the conflict, to humanize the methods of war, to alleviate suffering and

---

[52] *Ibid.*, pp. 636-638.
[53] *Ibid.*, pp. 668-669.

to bring assistance and comfort to the victims of war. We have not hesitated to indicate in unmistakably clear terms the necessary principles and sentiments which must constitute the determining basis of a future peace that will assure the sincere and loyal consent of all people."[54] These principles for peace Pius XII explained on numerous occasions, especially in his Christmas messages. In this short sketch it is impossible to give a philosophical analysis of his complete thinking on this subject. In general we may say that his speeches elaborated upon the five points announced in his first Christmas address. In two particulars he advanced the teaching of his predecessors. First, he approved the use of "force" by an international organization in the settlement of disputes.[55] Hitherto the sanctions countenanced by the popes were restricted to the economic sphere. During Mussolini's Ethiopian venture experience proved that economic sanctions would not prevent war. Secondly, he took the unprecedented step of giving his approval to democracy as a form of government in his Christmas message of 1944. Totalitarianism and dictatorships were condemned, and he spoke of the future as belonging to democracy.[56] In this same message he commended the proposals of the Dumbarton Oaks Conference for the erection of an international organization. He said: "The decisions already published by international commissions permit one to conclude that an essential point in any future international arrangement would be the formation of an organ for the maintenance of peace, of an organ invested by common consent with supreme power to whose office it would also pertain to smother in its germinal state any threat of isolated or collective aggression. No one could hail this development with greater joy than he who has long upheld the principle that the idea of war as an apt and proportionate means of solving international conflicts is now out of date."[57]

The United Nations Organization as constituted by the San Francisco Conference in June, 1945, fell far short of what Pius XII had envisioned. The security council with the permanent members having veto powers was a compromise that invited future

---

[54] *Ibid.*, 712.

[55] Address on the Fifth Anniversary of the War, *Catholic Mind*, Vol. 42, 586. See also Koenig, "Dumbarton Oaks," *Catholic Digest*, Vol. 9, Jan. 1945, 4-5.

[56] *Catholic Mind*, Vol. 43, 66-77.

[57] *Ibid.*, Vol. 43, 73.

trouble. Not having been invited to San Francisco, and adhering strictly to the letter of the Lateran Treaty, the Holy See offered no criticism of the new international organization. It waited to see how the United Nations would function.

Soon after the San Francisco Conference the war against Japan came to a sudden conclusion. Overjoyed at the cessation of hostilities, the Holy Father counseled all to work earnestly for peace. Certain agreements, made at Teheran, Yalta and Potsdam—some of them secret and only to be revealed much later—prejudiced the peace. Many concessions had been made to the Soviet Union; but Stalin, not content with these advantages, demanded more. Additional Soviet demands aroused suspicion in the democracies; failure of the democratic nations to grant all Soviet demands awakened suspicion in Russia. The pope described the situation accurately on Christmas, 1946, when he said: "Alas, differences of opinion, mutual distrust and suspicion, the doubtful value, in fact and in justice, of not a few decisions already taken or still to be taken, have made uncertain and fragile the strength and vitality of compromises and solutions based on force or political prestige, which leave deep down in many hearts disillusion or discontent."[58]

This disillusion gave birth to what has been known as the cold war. An iron curtain slowly descended upon Russia and her satellites, disrupting communications and depriving the West of current information on conditions in Eastern Europe. Very likely American possession of the atomic bomb was the only reason that kept the cold war from developing into armed hostilities. Pius XII recognized the latent dangers of the cold war. In the Vatican newspaper, *L'Osservatore Romano,* the editor, Count Della Torre, wrote an editorial on June 14, 1947, entitled: "Is War Inevitable?" It is a long, involved editorial, difficult to summarize; but the question discussed is whether war between Soviet Russia and the West is inevitable because of the different ideologies of Communism and democracy. The editor's answer states that Soviet Russia is not an ideology which has evolved into a state but a state that has adopted an ideology. Hence, for Soviet Russia her existence is primary, her ideology secondary. As long as Russia believes that war will not benefit her existence as a state, she will not fight. Therefore, if

---

[58] *Ibid.,* Vol. 45, 68.

the West demonstrates to the Russians that war cannot profit the Soviet Union, war can be avoided.

An editorial in *L'Osservatore Romano* assuredly does not carry the authority of a papal address. But Count Della Torre had already in February written on this same perplexing subject in the periodical *Vita e Pensiero,* and his article had provoked widespread discussion. It is almost inconceivable that he would have broached the same topic in the Vatican newspaper unless he had consulted the proper authorities. Moreover, in the pope's Christmas address of 1947 there are several sections difficult to understand except in the light of the Della Torre editorial. An analysis of this address would unduly lengthen this paper; consider only these two sentences: "If the frank words We utter during today's celebration know no boundaries, they refer only to doctrines denying faith in God and Christ, and certainly not to nations or groups of nations who are the victims of these doctrines. For these latter the Church ever cherishes the same constant love."[59] Here Pius XII clearly distinguishes between doctrines and nations. The doctrine in question throughout the address is Communism, and the nations are Soviet Russia and her satellites.

The Church has consistently condemned Communism as a pernicious doctrine and Pius XII had warned all Christians of its dangers. Yet the pope foresees the devastating results of a third world war, and as a diplomat he believes that negotiations with Russia are still possible. These negotiations will bear fruit only if the democracies present a united front to Russia. As recently as Christmas 1950, the pope said: "Because We have at heart the good of all nations, We believe that the close union of all peoples who are masters of their own destiny and who are united by sentiments of reciprocal trust and mutual assistance, is the sole means of the defence of peace and the best guarantee of its re-establishment."[60] If these words spoken in December, 1950, do not give papal approval to the North Atlantic Treaty Organization, what then do they mean? This same address closes with the solemn warning of 1939: "Nothing is lost by peace, everything can be lost by war."

According to my reading of the recent papal pronouncements,

---

[59] *Ibid.,* Vol. 46, 75.
[60] *The Tablet* (London), Vol. 196, 578.

the attitude of Pius XII in the current crisis can be briefly stated as follows. The pope distinguishes between Communism and Soviet Russia. His diplomatic mind understands that, even though the Soviet Union may be vanquished in a third world war, Communism will remain because Communism is an ideology and ideologies are not overcome by wars. In fact, the frightful ruins and economic chaos caused by a third world war may accelerate the growth of Communism. The appropriate way to dissipate Communism is not to hurl atomic bombs against it but to allow the dynamic energies of Christian faith and love to motivate every action of our lives and to practice Christian social principles which counteract the evils on which Communism thrives. The diplomat in Pius XII also believes that while we oppose Communist ideology with Christian ideology, the democracies by their own military defenses must demonstrate to Soviet Russia that aggression will not pay. Once the masters of the Kremlin are really convinced of this fact, the cold war can be solved without appeasement, by a method recommended by all the popes. That method is the negotiated peace.

IV

Democracy and the Catholic Church

by Oskar Bauhofer

It is a fact paradoxical in appearance only that the Church
Militant should be richer in political experience, and perhaps in
political wisdom, than any historic worldly power, although that
experience and this wisdom form no part of the Deposit of Faith
entrusted to her by her Divine Founder. This assertion is less
astonishing if one recalls the simple fact that the present reigning
Holy Father, Pope Pius XII, is the 259th rightful occupant of the
Petrine See. When Jesus said: "Render to Caesar the things that
are Caesar's," He did not simply use a metaphorical expression
connoting the duties that go with citizenship, anywhere and in any
time. The utterance directly referred to the supreme political power
in the Mediterranean world of that age. The coin produced by His
interlocutors showed the image and name of Caesar. Christianity,
that is, the Catholic Church, had its origin in a world very different
from ours, the Church being in fact (speaking of corporate bodies)
the only link extant between our age and that of antiquity. As
Macaulay said over a hundred years ago: "No other institution [i.e.,
beside the Catholic Church] is left standing which carries the mind
back to the times when the smoke of sacrifice rose from the Pantheon, and when camelopards and tigers bounded in the Flavian
amphitheater."

The Church, in the course of her history of nearly two millen-
nia, has witnessed the tumultuous procession of empires and kingdoms and nations; she has mingled with all of them, neither espousing some, nor rejecting or despising others. The same holds true in
regard to the various modes of organization of the body politic, of
which she has seen samples of practically every conceivable type;

69

here again, she has no exclusive preferences. Her titles, as the One Holy Catholic and Apostolic Church, are in essence ecumenical and perpetual, that is, all-embracing in space and in time, reaching out to the ends of the earth, and carrying her to the end of times. Being thus an eminently missionary enterprise, the Church — in her individual members, in her established hierarchy, with the profession of her faith, with the public office of her cult—is called, and is resolved, to live in such divers earthly mansions (of the political order) as human reason, the will of man, and the contingencies of history may set up. In pursuance of her divine commission and constitution, she disregards distinctions of race, nationality, language, or political regime.

It is true that *democracy*, too, has entered into the orbit of the Church, as one among other possible and legitimate forms of organization of political society. What, then, is the attitude of the Catholic Church towards democracy, i.e. towards that form of the government of a people, which is exercised 'by the people, and for the people'?

It has sometimes been argued that Catholicism, because of the hierarchical principle underlying it, stands in close analogy and affinity to the principle of monarchical autocracy within the political realm. This view has had some weight in controversies of the past, both in the political and in the doctrinal field, and is advanced today in particular by people who hold that democracy is a direct offspring of Protestantism. This view, in stressing the primacy of the Pope, suspects the Catholic Church of being 'monarchical' in her genius, autocratic in her government, and monarchist in her political sympathies. This is equivalent to saying that the Church is prejudiced against, and hostile to democracy by a sort of congenital disposition. The argument is of interest not so much for what it insinuates or positively asserts, but for the very common fallacy upon which it is based. The fallacy consists in the inadvertent use of conceptions drawn from political phenomena for explaining and understanding a phenomenon wholly unique, such as is the Church. The basis for such a 'comparison,' and for the construing of such an affinity between Catholicism and the institution of monarchy, is simply an external semblance.

It is not very difficult to perceive that the government of the Church is in no way organized along lines suggested by considerations, and corresponding to principles, that may be valid in the po-

70

litical realm. The hierarchical structure of the Catholic Church is not the counterpart of any political system; nor is the papal primacy a pattern, or a copy, of an autocratic monarchy. The reason for this is as simple as it is conclusive. The hierarchical groundwork of the Church is (according to Catholic belief) not man-made, but is based on direct divine institution and commission, with the Pope as the living Vicar of Christ, unerring in his mission as the appointed Teacher of the Universal Church. Nothing even remotely resembling any of these things could be said of the institution of monarchy, or, in fact, of any of the classical forms of secular government. The point of the argument here, and one that will be granted even by a non-Catholic, is that, since these things are what they claim to be, *jure divino,* that is, since they are divinely established according to Catholic teaching, they admit of *no alternative.* On the other hand, it is of the very essence of the temporal power to have, in theory as well as in fact, alternative forms of realizations, each perfectly legitimate in itself. To be sure, then, all similes taken from political terminology are utterly misleading when applied to the Church, and offer no clue either for understanding the life principle of the Church or for explaining and judging her relationship to different political systems.

The Christian and the Citizen are, in real life, one and the same person. That is to say, the Christian, who is also a citizen, responds to a double claim of allegiance. In the Christian view, and in accordance with the express teaching of the Church, to render to God the things that are God's does not detract in any way from rendering to Caesar the things that are due to Caesar. The coexistence, within human society, of the two orders, religious and political, and the acceptance on the part of every Christian of the two rules are made possible just because these are different in nature and origin and yet at the same time complementary, for the sum total of Man's being is not merely the aggregate of material things. The two halves of the saying of Christ make one whole. The religious and the political order are connected by a subtle, though unbreakable link, which is the ordinance of God. The words of St. Paul sum up the formal teaching of the Catholic Church in regard to these matters—"There exists no authority except from God" (Romans, XIII, 1).

Since man is born a social being, and his sociability is part and parcel of his innermost constitution, the life of human society requires a coordinating principle and basic rule directing the wills of men towards the common good. The force and sanction of this rule cannot rest on mere convention. The principle of political power has its source and origin in the Will and Providence of God; it is not bound up with any one definite political form but is directly present in all of them. Conversely, the various political forms (for instance, monarchy, or democracy) are a matter of choice with each nation: the peoples are free to adopt such a form of government and political constitution as best suits their political temperament, or their traditions and status of civilization. Each form of government, once established, is a concrete embodiment of that principle of political power which is supra-human in origin and force and in any of its specific realizations is therefore binding upon the consciences of men. The preference given by a people to a form of constitution and political institutions has always a strong element of contingency in it, but it partakes of that power which God meant to imprint upon the ordering of the political community.

Since the Church herself is no mere moral and intangible entity but a visible body clearly defined and hierarchically organized (notwithstanding her profoundly spiritual and mystical character), the Catholic Church and the State or political community really form two distinct societies, each *perfect* in its own realm. Neither depends on the other for the fulfillment of its own aims, those of the Church being essentially spiritual, those of the body politic, secular. The temporal power, whatever its particular form, does not derive its *authority*—and a true authority it is, as the Church would always insist—from any ecclesiastical delegation, empirical or ideal. Authority is a phenomenon inherent in, and inseparable from, the very notion of society, be it ecclesiastical or secular; nor is that authority (according to the teaching of the Church) merely a sociological phenomenon expressing a general agreement of those composing the social body.

On the other hand, it is equally clear that the Catholic Church can never consent to being regarded, or, in fact, to being administered, as a mere state dependency, say, for instance, as a departmental branch of a country's administration. Every sort of political absolutism has tried hard, and still tries hard, to impose such a scheme upon the Church, or at least upon the national church constituency, clergy and layman. This has often been an issue of life and death for the

Catholic Church. To conform to, or acquiesce in, such a scheme would be tantamount to renouncing the true nature and task of the Church. It would imply that the Church's *authority* is ultimately derived from, and at the same time is inevitably eclipsed by, the temporal power, and that the Church may act and move only as entitled and directed by the State.

This scheme makes the spiritual order, in theory as well as in fact, an annex and radiation of political sovereignty, and tends gradually, as history amply shows, to swallow up the former into the latter. It does not then, in regard to the fundamental issue, make any real difference whether the scheme is handled by a 'Most Christian and Catholic King,' or by a non-Catholic power, suppressing, or tolerating, the Roman Catholic Church at its pleasure and on its own terms, or by an openly hostile, say professedly atheistic, regime. The famous "Liberties of the Gallican Church" imposed by the French absolute Monarchy were in fact but a glittering serfdom, and an early stage of that "civil religion" advocated by Rousseau, which in turn may develop at any moment (and in fact did so during the French Revolution) into an aggressive official Atheism. There have been 'pious' as well as impious editions of Caesaropapism; yet the underlying principle is the same with both, inasmuch as it implies an overruling and consequent effacement of the spiritual by the secular order. The Catholic Church, in refusing to sanction the principle, though at times a factual submission may have been wrested from her, has not only vindicated the sanctity of the spiritual order for which the Church stands and of which she is the visible historic embodiment, but has also been a champion of liberty and of the dignity of the human personality over against the sinister designs and ostentation of the totalitarian *Leviathan*.

Secular power has oftentimes taken a cruel revenge upon the Church for that refusal, by decrying it as insubordination, and vilifying it as a plot for clerical dominion, and by disfranchising the Church in her institutions, and harassing her in her activities. As a matter of fact, the Church has suffered, as well as profited, from monarchical no less than from democratic governments. The Church is faced, in her dealings with the temporal power, not with the abstract principles of monarchy or democracy, but with political entities, each moved by varied and concrete impulses. Legislation is, as a rule, at least as important as is the basic constitution, in shaping and determining the relations between Church and state.

73

A country's legislation is the actual interpreter of the Constitution and brings out what in the judgment of successive generations is its real meaning as applied to the problems of the day. The difficulties and handicaps the Church may encounter do not arise from the basic principle of monarchy or of democracy, as the case may be, but from the spirit, sympathetic and helpful, or hostile and egotistical, that animates a nation or its representatives and the exponents of public opinion towards the Church. The Third French Republic with the avowed purpose of crippling and leaving derelict the Catholic Church enacted a series of laws that elicited this moral censure from the noble and generous mind of Leo XIII: "The State only recognized the Church when it is its pleasure to persecute her." The censure sums up the experiences of a long and sad chapter of Church history, experience of many ages and in every section of the globe, irrespective of the basic political structure and form of government.

The Church draws a clear line between things spiritual and temporal, as well as between the respective authority and legal competence of Church and state. There are of course matters that are of equal interest and consequence both from the point of view of the Church and of the state, so called 'mixed matters' in ecclesiastical language, such as the institution of marriage, or the religious education of children. Within modern society these mixed matters have, most unfortunately but perhaps inevitably, come to be issues of conflict and division, rather than of composition and mutual understanding, between the spiritual and the secular authorities. The concordance of the civil laws with the requirements of Catholic doctrine and morals can hardly be expected except in countries with an unbroken Catholic tradition and a homogeneous Catholic population. Today the opponents of what may be called the Catholic solution of these 'mixed' matters are not only (or even principally) the adherents of Protestantism, but the considerable numbers of nominal Christians, or avowed non-Christians, who form a portion of the population in every country of the present world.

Since the autonomy of the temporal power is fully and unreservedly recognized by the Church, the body politic ought in its turn carefully to respect, and formally guarantee, the autonomy and freedom of the Church. This is a question of equity, and of political wisdom, if not of strict justice. The Church has an absolute moral claim to this. The bare fact of her existence, of her majestic historical and spiritual greatness, apart from her unique (but not undisputed) message and mission, suffices to justify such an expectation. The religious controversies of the Reformation banished the Catholic Church for centuries from the public scene of many a country. Today, however, the question of religion is no longer a matter left to political decision, and to constabulary action. Christianity, of which Catholicism, to say the least, is the most venerable, and most comprehensive historic embodiment, cannot be outgrown, unless it be by Bolshevism, which is a satanic attempt to uproot Western civilization from its Christian foundations and reduce it to its purely technical ingredients and functions. Why should any state moulded on the Western pattern hesitate to give the Catholic Church her due?

Yet, there have been hesitancies, and greater difficulties, up to this day. This fact is not sufficiently explained by referring to the religious disunion at the beginning of our modern era and its effects on the political and social field. What, then, is the reason for this reluctance on the part of the modern state (speaking of the Old World now) to deal with the Church equitably? The answer is to be sought in what we may call modern political philosophy. The Catholic Church is not a creature of state power, while, on the other hand, and with the partial exception of the Huguenot Church in France, all the early Protestant churches have come into existence under full state control, and in the legal form of a national establishment. The Catholic Church, then, by her mere existence, has acted as a constant reminder that state power is not everything— a truth that came to sound most unpleasant to kings, and parliaments, when they began to think of the power of the state as something that could be limited and assuaged only by itself. The Catholic Church was a check to an excessive and uncontrolled state power, and a challenge to its exorbitant claims and attributions.

It is this double fact that has made the Catholic Church the one serious hindrance to an overstated conception of *Sovereignty* typical of modern political thinking. Because it is a moral enmity, not an armed one, it seems all the more exasperating. The state feels its presumption of omnipotence to be effectively questioned by the Church; and a presumption questioned is a presumption defied. A reading of Thomas Hobbes' *Leviathan* (1651), or J. J. Rousseau's *The Social Contract* (1762), will immediately explain why both writers hate the Roman Catholic Church so profoundly. It is not because they are Protestants, but because they realize that the Catholic faith is absolutely incompatible with the scheme of an absolutist regime which they both advocate, though with Hobbes it is monarchical (or parliamentary) in form, and with Rousseau, republican. And both Hobbes and Rousseau were not mere doctrinaires, far away from real life: the former, *ex post facto*, developed into a full-grown legal theory the (Tudor and) Stuart despotism, and the latter wrote, without of course knowing it, the quasi-official guide-book for the French Revolution.

The beginning of the modern era, as a matter of fact, marks a profound change in the relationship between Church and state. The medieval system, i.e. the organization of society, had rested on the uniformity of the faith professed, and on the true universality of the Catholic Church, not disputed by any rival sectarian body; or, to put it somewhat differently, it had rested on the unquestioned public significance of the Christian creed. The Church and the state were two distinct organisms, each with functions of its own, but the two coincided in their basis, namely, in society, which was homogeneously Catholic. The temporal power was not 'secular' in the modern sense of the word, standing aloof from all religious implications and attributions. Its objective was to take care of the secular business of society which it knew to be only part of man's business and destiny. No fundamental divergence of views could arise as to the reciprocal concordance, and repartition of rights, between the spiritual and the temporal power, since the two parties were of one mind on the main point, namely, the absolute truth and the universal validity of the Catholic religion.

The medieval formula on the basic relation between the spiritual and the secular order had been perfect in a way, and on its own ground, but it presupposed clearly that spiritual unity which is a signal feature of medieval society, and unique in history. The Reformation broke this spiritual unity, of which the Catholic Church and faith had been at once the symbol and the warrant, and there appeared on the historical scene competing religious bodies not in communion, nor of the same faith, with the Church of Rome. The disruption of the Christian society was a final one (speaking in terms of historical experience only), and of the most far-reaching consequences. It is one of the characteristic marks of the modern age and of modern society, that the uniformity of faith, that is, of the Catholic faith professed by the preceding age, has disappeared as a social phenomenon, and that the universality of the Catholic Church (taking 'universality' not as a theological but a sociological term) has utterly broken down.

The controversies, religious and political, of the age of the Reformation (and the Catholic Reform) which rent the social body in many countries, have ultimately favored the setting up of a system of practical and legal tolerance for a variety of organized religious bodies, either alongside with, or without, an established church. Modern society is spiritually pluralistic, that is, lacking a basic spiritual unity of public import, such as was found in the Catholic faith in the Middle Ages. The medieval system had admitted of no tolerance (as a public policy) to dissenting religious bodies, not because the Church was 'intolerant', but because a heretical movement was, using the term in no metaphorical sense, a plainly revolutionary event, breaking up the very foundations of the *Societas Christiana*. And when tolerance first came to be considered as a possible practical scheme, it was not a virtue, but a stratagem devised to meet the crucial situation of continuous civil warfare, strife, and unrest in the entire social body.

It is clear that it is not now in the power of either the Church or the state to reverse the course of history, or even simply to ignore the spiritual 'pluralism' of modern society. This is not moral abdication, on the part of the Church. The Catholic Church continues to hold up to the modern mind the guiding principles of a truly Christian Society,—not in a romantic conservatism, as seduced by memories and claims of a past age, but in an essentially missionary spirit. Of course, she does not give up lightly positions which she has held by immemorial usage, say in a country predominantly Catholic, simply because this suits some theory on church and state current among a handful of lawyers and politicians; she is prepared to fight where it is a question of legal titles, or of adverse legislation, or of arbitrary administrative measures. But in very many instances, in many countries, the case was decided long ago, and now the Church has to make the best of it. There are few countries in Continental Europe that are still open to a sort of formal co-partnership and avowed moral solidarity between Church and state. Even in those, as elsewhere, the Church must rely mainly on other ways and means that may not be very satisfactory in themselves but provide a working arrangement whereby the Church can assert her presence and secure her free development, in the midst of public indifference and maybe of adverse public opinion.

From being a party directly involved in the earlier struggle of contending religious creeds and ecclesiastical bodies, the secular power has become an impartial protector of the freedom of conscience, and of the free exercise of any organized religion. In legal theory religious convictions are a matter of private judgment left to the individual; the Church is looked on as an association of people who happen to profess identical religious convictions for the joint furtherance of their collective ideals, and differing in no way from other religious bodies, while in a few countries she enjoys a predominance mainly on historical and factual grounds. The Church may, on the whole, be free from state interference and state control, as a consequence of the legal fiction of the Church being an association. Another consequence is that the law of the Church and the organization of her inner life have no force or significance outside her pale.

The modern state is built on the formal presumption of its total self-sufficiency. This does not preclude some sort of 'recognition' of the Church, but then, to be consistent with the basic theory, such recognition, whatever its legal form or practical effect, is construed as an act of sovereign will on the part of the temporal power, and is a pledge subject to revision and revocation. 'A free Church in a free state' was the ambiguous gospel, and more often the unequivocal war cry, of 19th century liberalism. Nevertheless, under the present Western system the Church is on the whole given a fair chance to act upon the social body (and, through this medium, upon the state itself), through channels open to all. This, practically, is the status of the Catholic Church in most countries of Western Europe today.

It is a status where acquired rights and the rule of prescription, generally speaking, count for little and, yet, where the Church can, and must, show her full measure. It is a freedom at once precarious, and precious. Precarious, because it remains at the discretion of the temporal power and finds no active promoter in the latter; and precious, too, just because the Church is thrown back upon her own spiritual and moral resources, and on the vigor, the inspiration and devotion of her members, clergy and layman alike; —free to conquer the world. The freedom, such as the Church enjoys in practically all parts of the Western world, is, then, not a flawless gain and advantage, nor is it pure loss; it constitutes a weakness, as well as a strength. At any rate, this freedom is the 'talent' put into the hands of the Church with which in the main she has to trade and work in the modern world.

Democracy has for generations been in the ascendancy with Western nations. This in itself, however, is no conclusive evidence that it represents the triumph of human reason and is, or will be, the culminating achievement of mankind. There is a lesson in the historical fact that the institution of Popular Government has been often facilitated, or even been made inevitable, not so much by its own potential merits as by the abuse and corruption of other forms of government it ultimately replaced. It should be remembered that every system of government has its proper merits, and a partial superiority over others, as well as its structural weaknesses and imperfections, which may be said to be the reverse side of its specific excellencies. Every political regime remains vulnerable, not only from without but from within, and on its own ground. There is the technical apparatus of a regime, which is one thing, and there is the 'spirit' operating it, the moral attitude behind it, which is quite another. For example, the 'rule of the majority' represents the technical aspect of the principle of popular government, which cannot be made to work otherwise than upon a majority basis; but the intrinsic value of this practical scheme remains ambiguous when it is considered merely in its technical qualification, that is on the merit of the 'larger number.'

Popular government, in the eyes of the Catholic Church, is not a panacea, nor something in the nature of a gospel truth; it is *one* —not *the one*—possible and legitimate way of achieving the ends of all secular government. But, to be sure, the question of democracy is not only a theoretical and 'political' problem, it also presents an eminently moral aspect. Can anyone believe that the Catholic Church is lacking in sympathy and understanding for the noble aspirations voiced in the universal quest for democratic self-government, or that she is deaf to the profound yearnings of men and women of every tongue and race after a life fuller and more in tune with the dignity of man, when the world has witnessed the great desolation of totalitarianism? This is the true moral inspiration, and the historic justification, of this generation's crusade for democracy, a crusade that has had its great victories as well as its great defeats, and of which the final balance is not yet struck, as the battle is still being waged in many parts of the world.

79

It is inevitable, it is just and praiseworthy, that the peoples should endeavor to take on themselves the responsibility for the ordering of the political community when they have been utterly betrayed, or are in danger of being betrayed, by self-styled leaders and irresponsible cliques whose philosophy implies, and advertises, the abjuration of all Christian and Occidental standards. Pope Pius XII has paid an eloquent tribute to these hopes of mankind in his Broadcast Message, *Benignitas,* of Christmas, 1944. And the Holy Father insisted that human liberty and the dignity of the human person, which are the cornerstones of democracy, are most secure on Christian grounds, that is, when resting on the Christian message of man's adoption through the sacrifice of the Son of God. We might well ask then whether modern democracy is really aware of its Christian endowment, and conscious of its significance for democracy itself. The question is, we believe, of more than academic interest.

What, then, does democracy owe to the Catholic Church? Another aspect presents itself to us when we consider both the Church and democracy as spiritual phenomena, each a body of spiritual and moral forces. Life forces may have the power to call forth life. Might not the Church, being such a life force, have had an eminent part in the origin and growth of democracy,—not in its technicalities so much as in the moral qualities that are its indispensable human prerequisite and foundation? Might not the Church, in holding up to mankind the image and measure of man, contribute some of those essentials the forsaking of which threatens every community, social or political, with degeneration or dissolution?

One does not need to be a professing Christian and a Catholic to be a statesman or to have sound political notions. The political instinct is a part of man's natural equipment, and the foundations of political science and philosophy have been laid in pre-Christian antiquity. Thus, for example, democracy, both as a theoretical proposition and as a practical issue, was known to, and explored by, the Greeks, from whom we borrowed the term. But Greek and Roman antiquity was unable to master permanently and successfully its social and political problems. Its most brilliant times were a respite from the remorseless action of a quasi-omnipotent state, or had been lived in its very shadow. The history of the Roman Empire, from Augustan days, was but the long-drawn-out agony of human liberty. The decline and breakdown of the Graeco-Roman

Civilization is due in a large measure to the failure of the ancients to delineate in a clear and relevant manner the boundary lines between state power and the individual.

The fundamental question of politics is, as we can see perhaps with a particular and impressive clearness on looking back upon pre-Christian antiquity, a moral and spiritual problem; namely, the problem of the nature of man. To be sure, that lofty truth, stated in the American Declaration of Independence and held by it to be self-evident, that all men 'are endowed by their Creator with certain inalienable rights', and that among these are 'life, liberty, and the pursuit of happiness', is as such not out of reach of enlightened human reason unaided by divine revelation, but though glimpses may have been caught of this truth, its practical application in the Graeco-Roman world excluded the masses of the slaves, and its significance was wavering or was set at naught by the reality of the state. It is profoundly significant that a political community not sheltered by that spiritual atmosphere which embraces the fundamental notions and virtues of the Christian religion should be almost powerless to avoid the traps of its own clever inventions.

And now it is of paramount interest to us to see that when, at the close of the Middle Ages, the European mind rediscovered the alluring glories of pagan Antiquity and began shaping (in part) its own destinies upon that mold, a situation very similar to that just referred to evolved. The political thinkers and the secular rulers of the Age of the Renaissance (and later), in Italy, in France, in England, joined hands to deduce and justify from the new-fangled notion of Sovereignty the 'supreme' authority and illimited power of the State. It might of course make all the difference in the world to the prevailing form of government whether this sovereign power was vested in the person of the King (and popularly known as the 'Divine Right of Kings'), or, at first hypothetically, and later on in fact, in a Parliament, or, lastly, and in a more abstract formula, in the 'Nation.' But it made hardly any difference at all in the kind of rule. All of them were in like manner absolute, formally and materially. They were, to put it in modern language, 'constitutional' in the sense only of defining the person or body that was to exercise, or was possessed of, sovereignty, but they were non-'constitutional' inasmuch as they did not impose constitutional restrictions upon the exercise of that sovereign power.

In the Middle Ages, what was considered supreme was law,

81

natural and divine. Law was the bridle, fraenum, put on the arbitrariness of royal power. "If justice, if the observation of the law be banished," said Saint Augustine in the *City of God* (IV, ch. 4), "what are kingdoms but great robbers or bands of robbers?" Medieval society from the 12th century onward had seen the growth of a number of democratic institutions. Communal self-government of the Italian and Transalpine cities, the Swiss Confederation (originated at the close of the 13th century), and the English Parliament, are some examples of historic significance; and the self-governing university corporations, many of them founded and chartered by the Popes, are another interesting instance. The preference shown by medieval thinking for a 'mixed' kind of government, that is a mixture of monarchical, aristocratic, and democratic elements, found its correspondence in broad fields of political reality. The Thomist school made a most illuminating distinction between 'royal' and 'politic' governance, *dominium regale* and *dominium politicum*. Regal power was absolute, unrestricted; politic power was a constitutional, responsible form of self-government. England, on the basis of this theory, at the end of the Middle Ages had become a mixed government, a *dominium regale et politicum*. "It is no yoke," proudly said Sir John Fortescue, jurist and councillor to kings, viewing the English constitution in the second half of the 15th century, "it is not a yoke, it is liberty to rule a people in this politic manner, and it means, furthermore, the highest security, not merely to the people but to the king as well."

With absolutism then, the 'politic', or democratic element in government was being suppressed, or reduced to an assent-nodding apparatus. Power, that is, the royal will, had again become its own supreme law, its own sovereign interpreter—as in the original meaning of the sentence "The king can do no wrong." Sovereignty, in the language of 16th and 17th century absolutism, meant just that sort of 'supremacy' (of which term it was the gallicized transcription), than which there is no higher authority. Law, thus, was simply the will of those in power, with no constitutional limitations drawn up against it. True, the early doctrine of absolutism did not touch the law of God, the implications of sovereignty did not extend to things supra-human. But soon enough it was discovered that the law of God calls for an authority to interpret it, and why should not this be the Civil Power, after all? Even France with her Gallican Articles came within elbow's length of that, and England, turned Protestant, went as far as the discretion of either king or parliament would care, or permit, to go. It was a further corollary of the doctrine of sovereignty, too, and a consequence of a national consciousness now wide awake, that the Catholic Church, in her head and in her ecumenic rule, came to be looked on as a 'Foreign Power', and in this diplomatic expedient is mirrored the beginning process of secularization of state power. The formal dualism, which often is an antagonism, of 'Church and state' dates from those days. The alternative to this duality was the fusion, in non-Catholic countries, of the spiritual into the secular power in the case of the national church Establishments.

A partial historical justification of absolutism lies in its midwifery services to the modern national state. It was practically a universal phenomenon in the first centuries of the modern era. But although it had its Catholic apologists, such as the great French Bishop Bossuet, it cannot be construed as representing the genuine Catholic tradition and political doctrine, or as reflecting the specific teaching of the Church. It is a fact, however, that in Catholic countries, France in particular, the hierarchy under the absolute monarchy occupied a highly privileged position, more privileged than Rome could wish, and than served the true interests of the Crown and the country. Thus, when the absolutist Régime was more and more assaulted, its critics often unscrupulously identified the Church with a detested political system, and some of them did not shrink from meditating a common ruin for both. A revolution is like an earthquake; its victims are the sinners and the just indiscriminately. And the practical conclusion from this is laid down in the admonition of the Gospel: Unless you repent, you will all perish in the same manner (St. Luke, XIII, 3).

Modern democracy, as a major political scheme, came into existence on the plea that the voice of the nations must be heard in all questions relating to their own welfare and very destiny. Democracy was the political instrument designed to rescue liberty from the hands of despotic absolutism which, it was argued, was unworthy of (if ever it possessed) the confidence, and moral support, of the peoples. Happily, democracy was not an altogether novel experiment, and democratic institutions did not have to be created from nothing, or simply from theoretical speculation. The medieval parliamentary and constitutional traditions only waited to be revived and more fully developed,—and Protestant England became the principal depository and augmenter of what may be called in truth a Catholic inheritance. For the purposes of this sketch, it suffices to point out that the two chief ingredients of democracy, namely, (1) a rule of law in conformity with the public weal, and (2) a recognition of the inalienable rights of each human being, have been bequeathed to modern times by medieval Christianity. In reasserting these fundamental notions in its struggle with absolute rule, modern democracy has but provided the legal basis and technical means, and given to the whole edifice its necessary constitutional form.

Two dates, two events in the more recent history of modern democracy have the force of symbols. They almost coincide, the years and events being the drafting, in 1787, of the Constitution of the United States, and the outbreak, in 1789, of the French Revolution. Though contemporaneous, they actually represent two different types of democracy. It is as though the ways parted,— ways that ever since have been open before the nations of the world. Entirely apart from technicalities, and the textual interpretation of documents, I simply wish to point to the difference in spirit in these two types of democracy, one of which I shall call the American type, and the other one, the French, or more accurately, the Rousseauist or totalitarian, type. And at this particular juncture, my readers are invited to bear in mind the fact that our present Western world is threatened in its very existence by a new aggressive totalitarianism that pretends to be, and in a sense is entitled to consider itself, a democracy of historical lineage.

Well then, the 'American' type (characteristic today of Western democracy at large) is constitutional in a full and comprehensive sense of the term, defining, limiting, and controlling, once for all, the exercise of state power. The cardinal point is not in what way this is done (e.g., by the separaton of the three powers, legislative, executive, and judicial), but that such a fundamental provision acting as the pivot of the whole public system has been made. State power, even if understood as the rule of the majority and construed as the 'common will', is a limited power; even a majority cannot do as it pleases, it has no title whatever to touch, and modify arbitrarily, the fundamental relationship between citizen and state. Sovereignty is not moral omnipotence (physical omnipotence being a physical impossibility, moral omnipotence being physically, but not morally, possible). To put it somewhat differently, sovereignty is, above all, the ever repeated though tacit act of cognizance of a metaphysical relationship between man and the state, a relationship given and determined beforehand, by the nature of things, and therefore not subject to alterations and infringements under any pretext; it is the free and unconditional resolution to order the life of the community in concordance with that fundamental law, whether it be laid down in a public document or not. Both the majority, or 'party in power', and the minority are uncompromisingly bound to this basic rule, and this is why the present majority is in a true sense, as it were vicariously, the representative of the whole, and acknowledged in this representative function by the minority or opposition, while the latter never will be simply silenced, and is recognized as the potential majority of tomorrow. Democracy of the 'American' type in its practical working is a sort of fair play on a grand scale.

The Rousseauist type of democracy is the exact opposite of this. It is distinguished from the autocracy of former absolutism merely in this: that sovereignty, as understood by Rousseau resides, not in the person of a hereditary king, but in the nation, and is represented by the majority, which in everything it does and wills assumes the qualification of the 'General Will'. This *volonté générale*, or will of the majority, carries everything before it, it has no compass to guide it but itself, it has an irresistible and absolute power over members of the political society, it cannot possibly go astray; whatever it does and decrees is necessarily and by definition right. The majority, or common will, imposes a religion of its own, a 'civil religion' in accordance with this conception of political society. This civil religion can never be the Catholic religion. The very idea of a legitimate opposition is, of course, proscribed; the opponents of the General Will are suffocated, morally if not physically, and forced into conformity with the sovereign will of the majority—"forced to be free"! The criterion of the Rousseauist program is the word 'sovereignty', taken in a strictly absolute sense, in its most logical, and most absurd meaning. Sovereignty, with Rousseau, is the absolute and uncontrolled power of the greater number. This, then, is Totalitarianism pure and simple—in a democratic form!

Even the French Revolution did not carry into full effect this horrible scheme. To do that, it took Bolshevism. The Bolshevist political system is modeled entirely upon Rousseau, and it boasts of being the true form of democracy. And this is full truth, if (as we have seen with Rousseau) sovereignty is taken to be its own supreme law. Right, in the Christian and Western tradition, is taken to be right independently of any political constellation. But you may in the name of your sovereign power declare right to be wrong, and exactly this is what happens in following the path laid out by Rousseau. This is no longer an advanced stage of 'secularism', as the American type of democracy is secularized. This is the disowning of the Western tradition;—it is apostasy, with all its moral implications. It considers as non-extant, and void of meaning, the notion of an eternal law, and it defiles and distorts man, by raising him above his stature when he is on the side of power, and crushing and annihilating him when he is powerless. The essence of Totalitarianism is the exaltation of naked power; and here, moreover, it displays the technical apparatus, and bears the ensign, of democracy.

It is a matter for serious consideration to us that Totalitarian democracy, as we see it today in Russian Bolshevism, should have its roots in Western soil too. The parting of the ways in modern Western history is marked by the sign of apostasy. Do away with Christianity, and democracy will inevitably revert into Totalitarianism. The system of checks and balances, and the devices to inhibit the undercurrents of despotic power present in every political system will work only as long as they are handled by statesmen and supported by a people who are conscious of what they are doing and why they are doing it. How are we to make sure that freedom will be kept inviolate? Democracy in the modern age has been designed for the restoration and preservation of freedom, but it inevitably becomes destructive of its own end when it turns totalitarian. Within the precincts of the Church human liberty has been fostered and developed more fully and comprehensively than it ever was or could have been realized in antiquity. Democracy today holds the guardianship of this liberty, while the Church, and Christianity at large, will continue to be its unceasing inspiration and its innermost source of life.

V

The Doctrinal Issue Between the
Church and Democracy

by Yves R. Simon

There is in our time a common disposition to dodge the doctrinal issues which, ever since the French Revolution, have been causing tension between the Church and democracy. Even in countries where democratic parties are traditionally dedicated to secularism, the aggressive action of common enemies has urgently suggested, for two decades or so, that some sort of alliance should replace the old conflicts. Many people would like to think that the time has come to ignore divergences that are "merely" doctrinal: enough problems will be left anyway. They argue that with all the difficulties confronting us, the doctrinal ones should be set aside as having no urgent character and perhaps no importance whatever.

Such an approach implies pragmatic postulations that bar the understanding of any issue in which Catholic doctrine is involved. In Catholicism the maintenance of the true principles in dogma and morals is always the most urgent of all tasks. Believers and unbelievers as well must recognize that the prudent management of historical situations never can supersede or render unnecessary the statement of principles and the clear definition of irreducible antinomies. In the long run lucidity is more beneficial to all than confusion. Let it be said that the need for cooperation between the Church and democracy makes it more necessary than ever that troublesome problems of doctrine be examined with entire frankness.

Between the Church and the modern state the doctrinal issues of major significance are three: (1) the general relation of the state to religion (will Church and state be united in some way, or entirely separated?); (2) freedom of belief and expression; (3) the origin and ultimate meaning of temporal power. With regard to the first two points the positions generally held by democratic thinkers are not connected with democracy in *specific* fashion. The doctrine of the religious neutrality of the state and that of unqualified freedom of expression can be asserted and put in practice by a monarchical or an aristocratic polity as well as by a democracy. They are, in essence, liberal rather than democratic. In fact, their first and most effective promoters were oligarchically-inclined bourgeois. But the problem of the origin and meaning of temporal power concerns the specific essence of democracy. The thing which is discussed (most of the time, in extreme confusion) under such headings as "origin of power," "government by consent of the governed," and "sovereignty of the people versus divine right," pertains directly to the differentia of democratic government. The literature on this subject is huge. It is often perverted by the deliberate purpose of vindicating historical appetites in terms of eternal truth. Its level is generally very low. The really valuable documents are few and not commonly read.

The main purpose of this paper is to set forth, in comparative fashion, the Catholic teaching on civil authority and a certain interpretation of democracy which, both on the side of its upholders and on the side of the Church, has many times been described as unacceptable to Catholic conscience. Whether this interpretation expresses the essence of democracy or a perversion of it is a question that nobody has a right to beg.

Less than one year after the first meeting of the Estates General, less than six months after the Declaration of the Rights of Man and of the Citizen, the Church expressed her disapproval of the theory of political authority to which the French Revolution seemed to be dedicated. At the secret Consistory of March 29, 1790, Pius VI spoke with anguish of things that were being done by the Constituent Assembly; he deplored attacks against religion and broken pledges; he traced these events to erroneous doctrines among which he mentioned the theory that none is bound by any laws except those to which he gave his consent.[1] Similar expressions were used in a num-

---

[1] *Sanctissimi Domini nostri Pii divina Providentiae Papae VI allocutio habita in consistorio secreto die XXIX Martii MDCCXC, De aerumnis regni Galliarum,* in Augustin Theiner, *Documents inédits relatifs aux Affaires Religieuses de la France, 1790 a 1800, extraits des archives secrètes du Vatican* (Paris, Firmin Didot, 1857), Vol. I, p. 2. "Per decreta, quae a generalibus nationis comitiis prodierunt, ipsa impetitur perturbaturque religio; hujus apostolicae sedis usurpantur jura; solemnia pacta, et conventa violantur. Et quemadmodum hujusmodi

ber of Church documents, the most important of which are the Encyclicals of Leo XIII, *Diuturnum* (June 29, 1881) and *Immortale
Dei* (Nov. 1, 1885), and the Letter of Pius X on the *Sillon* (Aug. 25,
1910). On the basis of these documents many hold that the Church
has proclaimed the incompatibility of her notion of authority with
the very essence of democracy. They, therefore, regard Christian
democracy and a reconciliation or alliance between the Church and
the forces of democracy as implying a doctrinal situation of dubious
character.

Among the groups which interpreted Christian democracy in
terms of doctrinal compromise, the first place belongs to free thinkers. Their mood, according to the circumstances, was either belli-
cose, inasmuch as they resented and distrusted what they considered
crafty diplomacy, or pacific, inasmuch as they imagined that the
Church was giving up a part of her doctrine for the sake of tran-
quillity. Not long ago, the same interpretation was commonly held
by traditionalists; for these, the religious and Catholic notion of
society was inseparable from traditional forms of government and
Leo XIII was a betrayer of eternal verities. Finally, the view that
Christian democracy requires some sort of doctrinal adjustment,
compromise or evolution has been popular among the Christian
democrats themselves. At the time of the great modernistic crisis
early in this century, Christian and democratically inclined circles
showed steady interest in the evolutionary theory of dogma which
constituted the core of modernism. A number of years after the
acute phase of the crisis was over—say, in the 1920's—it was often
possible to observe, among Christian democrats, a certain uneasiness and an unhappy restlessness when questions of basic attitudes
toward dogma were discussed; many of these men felt that unless a
minimum of dogmatic evolution was tolerated they might have to
give up their political ideal. The origin and the meaning of temporal authority were among the burning topics.

It is important to notice that the whole argument started in
connection with the French Revolution; throughout the nineteenth

---

mala ex falsis emanarunt doctrinis, per infectos venenatosque libros, qui in manus
omnium diffundebantur, ita quo imposterum etiam latius, securiusque evulgari,
imprimique possent ea opinionum contagia, inter prima comitiorum decreta illud
exstitit, quo libertas asseritur cogitandi etiam de religione prout cuilibet libeat,
suaque cogitata impune proferendi; nec quemque aliis obstringi legibus statuitur,
quam quibus ipse consentiat."

century it remained a French affair; the statements of Leo XIII as well as those of Pius VI and Pius X were aimed at theories erected by French thinkers into a universal pattern of democratic thought and accepted as the genuine formula of democracy all over the Latin world.

The problem that these theories claim to solve can be stated as follows. So far as common observation goes, civil societies are divided into two groups of persons, the governed, who are the great majority, and the small minority of the governing personnel. This division is not absolutely necessary, for some civil societies have no distinct governing personnel and practice government by majority vote. Although direct democracy constitutes a political type of particular importance, the more frequent case of a society governed by distinct persons should be considered first. Any such society contains a paradox which habit causes to remain unnoticed under ordinary circumstances, but is intensely felt in periods of crisis: *the multitude of the governed do obey the few that govern.* Disobedience is not rare in civil relations, but the striking thing is that it retains the character of an exception and of a disorderly happening, while obedience takes place with such regularity that broad and enduring things, like cities, states, empires and civilizations are comprised among its effects. How should this immense fact of civil obedience be accounted for? Schools of political science are not short of cynics who would answer that every act of civil obedience is traceable to constraint or to fear or to the calculations of interest. But the cynic is just as poor an observer as the idealist. Phases of extreme disintegration show that when constraint and fear, either alone or helped only by calculation, command obedience, they soon become powerless and obedience is no longer obtained with any kind of regularity. Constraint, fear and calculation can do no more than supplement the effects of ethical persuasion. They deal successfully with unruly characters so long as most citizens habitually consider that they ought to obey the orders of persons publicly described as their superiors. In short, everything takes place as if the multitudes of the governed felt morally obliged to obey the persons in government. All happens as if persons in government had the power and the right to *bind the conscience* of the governed. But how can a man bind the conscience of another man? Here lies the great paradox. To suppress it, many primitive and traditional societies mythologically attribute to governing persons a superhuman essence. The social thinkers of modern times claim to resolve the same paradox, in more up-to-date fashion, by a theory of their own, often called, with dubious propriety, the theory of popular sovereignty or the theory of democracy.

True, this theory explains the problem away; in it, obedience is interpreted as an appearance and an illusion. Let the last effects of the traditional myths concerning the dignity of the ruling person be dissipated: men in government are reduced to the capacity of agents, managers, secretaries, instruments that are traversed by power but have no power of their own. They take orders, yet, in spite of appearances, are not entitled to give any order. Apart from the violent state of affairs which constitutes the tyrannical society, all their actions are relative to aims assigned by the governed; the ways of their action are chosen by the governed. They are leaders by order of the led. *Their leadership involves no authority.* Even though the governing person is allowed to utter sentences grammatically indistinguishable from commands, the governed acknowledge no duty of obedience. Rather, the government, like hired and paid servants, takes the orders of the governed and leads them where they want to go. To call this the theory of democracy is philosophically absurd, since democracy, as a form of government, cannot have any necessary connection with a theory which explains away the essence of government. To call it "the theory of popular sovereignty" is exceedingly ambiguous, since the same expression is commonly used to designate doctrines which preserve integrally the notions of government and obedience.

As already mentioned, this theory is historically connected with the French Revolution and has been particularly prevalent where French influence has been strong. No wonder that its proper name is found in the work of a French liberal. Paul-Louis Courier (1773-1825) was a humanist, a fine Greek scholar, a skillful writer of light prose, a Voltairean, a rebel, an uncompromising adversary of Church and state (though not an anarchist), an unflinching and vainglorious defender of the little man against men of wealth and men of authority. For him the government, in a normal state of affairs, is like a cab-driver who leads his patrons where they want to go and by ways of their own choice.[2] The expression

---

, [2] Paul-Louis Courier, *Lettres au rédacteur du Censeur*, Lettre X, 10 mars 1820, *Oeuvres* (Paris: Firmin Didot, 1845), pp. 62-63. The writer describes in humorous fashion the evils that conservatives expect of a system in which the

needed to designate in unmistakable fashion the political theory with which we are concerned is now available: let it be called the *cab-driver theory.* The important thing is to convey unambiguously the notion of a leadership devoid of authority: this is done by bringing the cab-driver into the picture. He is a leader, he is expected to be an effective one, but his leadership is merely instrumental and amounts merely to the fulfillment of decisions which are not, in any sense, his own. There is no question of attributing to a cab-driver the power, right and duty to bind the conscience of his patrons. This theory can also be called *the theory of government as mere instrument of the governed* or, by abbreviation, *the instrumental theory of government.*

In the philosophy of Rousseau the cab-driver theory is marked by a richness and a subtlety which strongly contrast with the simplicity of its more popular expressions. Rousseau's major concern is to remove any system which would imply the moral submission of a man's will to the reason and will of another man. In upbringing, natural necessity replaces authority and obedience. The perfect tutor would merely provide the child with the opportunity of being taught—without being too badly hurt—by the inflexible energies of nature. In politics, the way out of relationships involving authority is the theory of the general will. Like a force of nature, the general will is impersonal and incorruptible; on the other hand, it is mysteriously identified with the will of each, so that by obeying the general will, man simply obeys himself. The essence of obedience is eliminated. Authority, as power of binding the conscience of man, has disappeared. Is real liberty adequately guaranteed by the theory of the general will? This can be doubted. The transcendent character of the general will, its superhuman infallibility, the very peculiar way in which it combines the privileges of natural necessity and those of human initiative arouse the suspicion that govern-

---

press would enjoy actual freedom: "If this abuse [i.e., the freedom of the press] should endure, every undertaking of the court would be controlled beforehand, examined, judged, criticized, estimated. The public would consider all business as their own; everything would arouse their contemptible interest; they would check the records of the treasurer, supervise the police, and scoff at the diplomatic service. In one word the nation would manage the government after the fashion of a cab-driver whom we hire and who is supposed to lead us, not where he wants, nor how he wants, but where we intend to go and by the way that we find convenient. This is a thing horrible to imagine, contrary to the divine right and the capitularies."

ment, no longer protected by its traditional vindication, has been given a new and more effective guaranty of overwhelming power. "Tyranny, claiming divine right, had become odious; he [Rousseau] re-organized it and makes it respectable, by making it proceed from the people, so he says."[3]

The system of scientific government initiated by Saint-Simon was indifferent or hostile to most aspects of liberalism, and it soon came to have little use for liberty. Yet it is easy to recognize in early Saint-Simonism an unexpected outgrowth of current liberalism. In a colorful passage Saint-Simon proposed to demonstrate that the scientific management of society procures both efficient leadership and freedom from authority. People who pursue happiness without being clear and positive about what it consists in deliver themselves, inevitably, to the judgment and the whims of the governing persons. "Imagine a large caravan saying to its leaders: *Take us where we shall be best.* From then on the leaders are everything, the caravan is nothing . . ." Unlimited confidence

---

[3] P.-J. Proudhon, *General Idea of the Revolution in the Nineteenth Century,* tr. by J. B. Robinson (London: Freedom Press, 1923) p. 118. Benjamin Constant remarked in *Principes de politique* (Paris, 1815), pp. 18-21: ". . . There is a part of human existence which necessarily remains individual and independent. . . . Sovereignty is limited and relative by essence. Where individual independence and existence begin, the jurisdiction of this sovereignty comes to an end.

"Rousseau failed to recognize this truth and, an effect of his error, his social contract, so often cited in favor of freedom, has become the most dreadful accomplice of all kinds of despotism. The contract between society and its members is defined by him in such a way as to mean that each individual surrenders the whole of his self, with all his rights and without any reservation, to the community. In order that we should not worry about the consequences of such an unqualified surrender of all parts of our existence to an abstract entity, he tells us that the sovereign, that is, the social body, can harm neither the totality of its members nor any one of them. . . . But, as soon as the sovereign must use his force,—in other words, as soon as authority must be organized in practical fashion, the sovereign delegates the authority that he cannot exercise by himself, and all these attributes disappear. Since the action exercised in the name of all is necessarily—whether you like it or not—in the hands of one or in those of a few, it is not true that by delivering one's self to all one does not deliver one's self to anybody; on the contrary one delivers one's self to those who act in the name of all. . . . Rousseau himself was frightened by these consequences; filled with terror at the sight of the immense power that he had created, he did not know in whose hands this monstrous power should be placed, and, against the danger, inseparable from such a sovereignty, he found no other protection than a trick which renders its exercise impossible. He declared that sovereignty could neither be alienated, nor delegated, nor represented. This is another way of saying that it cannot be exercised; the principle which he had just proclaimed was actually annihilated."

and passive obedience necessarily prevail. "Suppose, on the contrary, that the caravan says to its leaders: *You know the way to Mecca, lead us there.* In this new state of affairs, leaders are no longer chiefs, they are merely guides, their functions, though very important, are merely subordinate; the principal action springs from the caravan.[4] Each traveller retains his right to make, whenever he thinks fit, critical remarks on the road which is being followed and to suggest, according to his lights, the changes that he believes indicated. Since the discussion never can be concerned with anything else than a very positive and very decidable question (*are we wandering away from, or coming closer to Mecca?*), the caravan—provided it is somewhat enlightened—no longer obeys the will of its guides; its members obey their *own convictions* which result from the demonstrations that were proposed to them."[5]

Here, the cab-driver theory achieves the elimination of authority in a system of salvation through scientific enlightenment. Elsewhere, in closer relation to Rousseau, the same elimination is effected by the same theory in the more openly romantic context of a belief in the quasi-divinity of the people, as for example, the following statement made by a Paris club in 1848: "The people is the sovereign; the government is its work and its property; public functionaries are its employees. The people can, whenever it pleases, change its government and revoke its delegates. . . . Every institution which does not presuppose that the people is good and the governors corruptible is basically wrong."[6]

1. As to the sources from which the cab-driver theory derives its influence, there is in the first place the universally human desire to escape the humiliations and other hardships that obedience involves. The duty to obey another person often seems to conflict with the normal urge toward autonomy; obedience, then, seems to presuppose the mendacious attribution, to the person in command, of a dignity that no man can have, or the loss, on the part of the subject, of a dignity that all non-criminals possess by natural right.

---

[4] Notice the philosophical precision of this expression, "the principal action." If the principal action springs from the caravan, the causality exercised by the leaders is merely instrumental. This is the core of the issue.

[5] H. Saint-Simon, *L'Organisateur,* in *Oeuvres de Saint-Simon et d'Enfantin* (Paris, 1865-78), Vol. 20, pp. 195-196.

[6] Quoted by J. Belin-Milleron in "L'idée de peuple en 1848 et la psychologie collective du raisonnement," *Revue socialiste,* Vol. 45 (Paris, March 1951), 337-338.

Radical opposition to the concept of authority may lead to anarchy. But outright anarchism does not suit the taste of every rebel: such a doctrine clashes badly with our habits, puts a heavy strain on our imagination, renders history unintelligible and drives its upholders into isolation. The cab-driver theory is a handy substitute offered to whoever indulges in an anarchistic disposition but refuses to face the paradoxes and the frightening features of outright anarchy. It is, according to the felicitous expression of Maritain, a theory of masked anarchy. Thanks to this theory, a rebellious petty bourgeois can lead a respectable life, untroubled by any sense of tragedy and out of the range of police action.

2. Moreover, the cab-driver theory has the advantage of accounting clearly, easily, and cheaply for a number of democratic practices. Indirect or representative democracy is understood to take the place of direct government by the people's assembly when circumstances make the latter impossible. We would not elect legislative bodies, presidents and governors if our community were, like a New England town, so small and so closely integrated that the whole citizenry could act both as a legislative body and as an executive committee. True, even direct democracy uses a distinct personnel in the administration of public affairs. But the secretaries, managers and hog-reeves that the popular assembly uses are known to all for what they are: instruments of the people, with no right except that of carrying out the decisions of the people. When circumstances make direct democracy impossible, appearances change, but should it not be said that the essence of political relations remains the same? The men who make up the government are elected on the basis of their ideas and of their records; the principles at work in their election seem to imply that they are given orders by their electors and that they are not expected to do anything else than to carry out these orders. In democracy, positions obtained through election are temporary; the person who solicits re-election submits to a verdict whose meaning seems to be best expressed by the supposition of a purely instrumental role. Re-election, or failure to obtain re-election, are naturally interpreted as evidence of satisfaction or dissatisfaction on the part of those who hold real authority. The governing person who seeks re-election very much resembles a hired servant who tries to convince the employer that his service has been satisfactory. Thus, the cab-driver theory sums up the basic facts of democratic practice, in

direct democracy and in representative democracy as well. The theory also derives apparent support from the part played by public opinion in democratic government. In a democratic polity it is considered normal that a ruling assembly, elected two years ago on the basis of a certain program, should change its policies and act at variance with its initial program because public opinion in the meantime has changed. Such practices as sending petitions to the government and bombarding a Congressman with special delivery letters and telegrams seem also to be best accounted for by the notion that we, the governed, are the real power and that the government is related to us as a cab-driver to his patrons.

3. The lure of symmetry, operating in a comprehensive picture of human relations, gives additional verisimilitude to the cab-driver theory. Between efficient cause and final cause there is necessarily a proportion; every cause is not related to a particular end, and everything is not capable of being an end for a particular agent. Following the line of least resistance, our mind is often led to construct, between the cause and the end, symmetrical relations that the principle of proportion does not imply. An illustration may be provided in the association of the master and slave, assuming, further, that this association is interpreted, not as sheer violence, but as a normal state of affairs. This is a system primarily defined by a relation of finality: the end of the master and slave association lies not in the slave but in the master. If slaves are many, the picture is that of a governed multitude teleologically subordinated to a governing person. This is a dominion of servitude in the sense of Aristotle and St. Thomas.[7] Here finality lies where power resides, i.e., in the ruler. The person called master is both the one who exercises power and the one for the sake of whom power is exercised. Clearly, a *civil* government is not and cannot be a dominion of servitude. Even if it is granted that relations of servitude once had a normal part to play in the household, it is certain that they do not have, and never have had, any part to play in civil society. After having considered a household of the ancient type, that is, one equipped with slaves, let us direct our attention to the state, which is a community of free men. Here the temptation is great to safeguard symmetry by assuming that there is, in the latter case as well as in the former, unqualified co-incidence of power

-----

[7] *Politics,* 3.6.1278b33; *Summa Theologica,* I.96.4.

and final causality. According to the precise expression of St. Thomas, there is dominion over free men when power is exercised not for the sake of the governing person but for the common good and for the sake of the governed. Should it be said that real power belongs, in civil government as well as in servitude, to those for the sake of whom government is exercised? When government is exercised for the sake of a master, the governed are servants and authority resides entirely in the master. When government is exercised for the sake of the governed should it not be said, correspondingly, that authority belongs to the governed and that the governing personnel are merely hired servants?

In the history of many nations this lure of pleasurable symmetry was strengthened by an accident of the first magnitude. The association of civil power with master-slave relations is a common occurrence in the early phases of political entities. The king, who is supposed to rule for the sake of the common good and in no sense for the sake of his private welfare, emerges confusedly and, for a long time, uncertainly, from the landlord, that is, from the chief executive of a business enterprise using the methods of slavery or serfdom. When the citizenry become aware of the qualitative distance that separates the dominion of freedom from the dominion of servitude, when they come to realize vividly the character of civil government as dominion over free men, they soon demand that all remnants of servitude be eliminated from civil organization. Relations of servitude, situations in which the labors of a man are institutionally directed not toward his own good or toward the common good, but toward the private good of the one who rules him, may, for a long time, enjoy a great amount of tolerance, provided that they do not affect the civil government. The owner of the land will be allowed to remain the beneficiary of much unpaid labor. But the thing which will no longer be tolerated is that the king should treat the kingdom as a private estate. Many phases of the French Revolution embody a burning vision of civil society as a community of the free. Philosophers had known, for many centuries, that the state is a dominion over free men and cannot take over the character of a dominion of servitude without undergoing the most radical kind of corruption. However, these basic truths had been veiled, in a number of cases, by abusive usages and popular myths. In the earliest phase of the French Revolution the veils were suddenly lifted. A whole nation declared to the world that the state is a community of free men and cannot retain any feature reminiscent of the master and servant relationship. There was a great temptation to extend the contrast beyond the limits of its genuine significance. In an atmosphere saturated with hope and fear it seemed that the Revolution would be more complete if what was said of the final cause was also said of the efficient cause. Thus, the proposition that the purpose of government is the welfare of the governed was supplemented with the proposition that the government is the will of the governed. Pius VI was right. In the French Revolution (and in the numerous movements which followed its pattern) the principle that political government is a dominion over free men constantly trespasses the boundaries of its proper meaning and develops into the theory that government belongs to the governed as such. The revolutionary people needed continual reassurance against the danger of a confusion between civil government and dominion of servitude. Nothing could quiet their worries, short of the dogma that the governed are subjected to no authority and obey only their own will. The nightmare of a political organization directed toward the private welfare of the governing persons could be dissipated only by placing in the governed the efficient cause as well as the end of government action. Unless the citizens were declared free from genuine government and bound only by their own consent, people were not ready to believe that the government would consistently behave as dominion over free men.

Hilaire Belloc wrote: "It is impossible for the theologian, or even for the practical ecclesiastical teacher to put his finger upon a political doctrine essential to the Revolution, and to say: This doctrine is opposed to Catholic dogma or to Catholic morals. Conversely, it is impossible for the Republican to put his finger upon a matter of ecclesiastical discipline or religious dogma and to say: This Catholic point is at issue with my political theory of the State."[8] Some uncertainty and some arbitrariness inevitably attach to the expression 'essential to' in relation to things which are not, in any proper sense, essences, such as an historical event like the French Revolution. In reference to such historical aggregates, *essential* can hardly mean anything else than both important and constant. If 'essential' is so defined, Belloc's statement is false. There

---

[8] *The French Revolution* (New York: Henry Holt and Co.), p. 223.

is at least one doctrine, describable as essential to the French Revolution, which is opposed to Catholic morals: it is the cab-driver theory of government. There is at least one "Catholic point" which is at issue with the political theory of the French Revolution: it is the very definite teaching of the Church on the meaning of political authority.

For the understanding of Christian democracy it is important to remark that religious souls may be exposed in peculiar fashion to the lure of symmetry between the end and the cause of government. Christians learned from Christ himself that among them rulers should be the most humble of all and consider themselves the servants of their brethren. The Vicar of Christ is called the Servant of the servants of God. In the contrast described by Christ himself between the pagan notion of authority and the new one, the problem, again, is one of the final causality. Governing positions are commonly sought for the advantages that they bring to their holders, above all, for the satisfaction of pride and of the lust for power; Christ states that it should not be so among his followers: "You know that the rulers of the Gentiles lord it over them, and their great men exercise authority over them. Not so is it among you. On the contrary, whoever wishes to become great among you shall be your servant; and whoever wishes to be first among you shall be your slave; even as the Son of Man has not come to be served but to serve, and to give his life as a ransom for many."[9] Symmetry, in this evangelical context, may produce the same kind of confusion as in the altogether temporal context of a society becoming aware of its being, by right, a community of free men. If the character of final cause is transferred, according to the Gospel, from those who govern to those who are governed, should not efficient causality be transferred correspondingly? If the governing person is required to become a mere servant of the governed, is he not required, correspondingly, to become a mere instrument of their will? The governing person would be the servant of his brethren in two senses: (1) in that he repudiates his own interests and his own lust and endeavors to be nothing else than a thing *useful* to his brethren; (2) in that he strips himself of his proper will and takes orders from his brethren. Everything looks more harmonious and the wish of Christ seems to be more com-

---

[9] Matthew, XX, 25.

pletely fulfilled if the person in authority humbles himself twice: first, by considering himself as a means rather than as an end, then by renouncing his own will and becoming a mere instrument of the governed. The cab-driver theory, in spite of its conspicuous connection with free-thought, crept into Christian democracy at the beginning of this century. One of the main parts of the letter of Pius X on the *Sillon* is directed against the progress of a purely instrumental theory of government in circles that were intensely religious, Christian and Catholic.[10]

In order to understand in what sense the opposition of the Church to the cab-driver theory of government concerns democracy we shall consider the meaning of authority in a community which governs itself by majority vote, without any distinct governing personnel. Direct democracy extended to all government functions is an exceptional occurrence, but it is the archetype of democratic government and, in a way, of all government. Rebellious democrats see in it an ideal as well as an archetype, for it seems to achieve the elimination of authority. A people which does without a distinct governing personnel seems to have much in common with the system of the cab-driver. Whether the resemblance is essential or accidental can be decided by considering what it means to abide by the law in a direct democracy. Take the case of a citizen who, having belonged to the majority for some time, no longer does. As long as his views were supported by most of his fellow-citizens he could boast of obeying no laws and no decrees except those that he had made for himself. Until the change of majority occurred, nothing, apparently, prevented him from feeling that, through the operation of democracy, he was bound only by his own power of decision. Whatever distinct personnel is employed by the people's assembly has but the character of an instrument. Men who were no more

---

10 Pius X, *Letter on the "Sillon,"* Aug. 25, 1910. "Le Sillon place primordialement l'autorité publique dans le peuple de qui elle dérive ensuite aux gouvernants, de telle facon cependant qu'elle continue à résider en lui. Or, Léon XIII a formellement condamné cette doctrine dans son encyclique *Diuturnum* "Du principat politique" . . . Sans doute le Sillon fait descendre de Dieu cette autorité qu'il place d'abord dans le peuple, mais de telle sorte qu'elle remonte d'en bas pour aller en haut. . . . Mais outre qu'il est anormal que la délégation monte, puisqu'il est de sa nature de descendre, Léon XIII a réfuté d'avance cette tentative de conciliation de la doctrine catholique avec l'erreur du philosophisme. . . . Du reste, si le peuple demeure le détenteur du pouvoir, que devient l'autorité? une ombre, un mythe. Il n'y a plus de loi proprement dite; il n'y a plus d'obéissance."

4156/

than instruments of the people have always led him where he wanted to be led. But then his views are defeated by the majority. He may go into outright rebellion and challenge the coercive power of the community. He may also prefer the hardships of detested laws to those of open rebellion; in this case his conduct will conform to the new regulations, but his inner disposition will remain one of refusal. In either case he is a rebel. Merely external compliance, elicited by fear and calculation without any sense of obligation, is not obedience. By the same token we understand that rebellion is nothing new in his civic career. He never was a law-abiding citizen. He always has been a rebel. His rebellious disposition did not become manifest earlier because of the sheer accident of his being in the majority. In contrast, the law abiding citizen of a direct democracy does not think that his attitudes toward promulgated laws are affected in any way by his own vote. The important thing is that the law was passed by the competent authority, viz., the majority of the people; the fact that he has voted for or against it appears to him altogether incidental. When he was in the majority, he obeyed the law not because he had voted for it but because it was the law. It is natural for him to obey in spite of his own choice, for his obedience has always been genuine. This implies that it never was conditioned by his own choice. We thus come to understand that the principle of authority is as certainly realized in a direct democracy as it is in any lawful form of government.

Those functions of authority which would have no *raison d'etre* in a society free from deficiencies may be called *substitutional*. If authority had only substitutional functions to exercise, it would still be a factor of decisive importance in civil society as well as in the family. But ecclesiastical documents go far beyond the deficiency theory of government, so popular in the golden age of liberalism: emphasis is placed on the naturalness of the need for civil government. "Man's natural instinct moves him to live in civil society, for he cannot, if dwelling apart, provide himself with the necessary requirements of life, nor procure the means of developing his mental and moral faculties. Hence it is divinely ordained that he should lead his life—be it family, social or civil—with his fellow-men, amongst whom alone his several wants can be adequately supplied. But as no society can hold together unless some one be over all, directing all to strive earnestly for the common good; every civilized

101

community must have a ruling authority, and this authority, no less than society itself, has its source in nature, and has, consequently, God for its author. For God alone is the true and supreme Lord of the World" (Leo XIII, *Immortale Dei*).

I have tried elsewhere[11] to analyze those functions of authority which transcend all needs born of ill-will, ignorance or immaturity. Let it be said, in rough outline, that a society may and may not involve the pursuit of a common good through common action. A craftsman and a money-lender make up a mere *partnership* whose bond is the inter-dependence of private interests; there is no question of either of them ruling over the other; contract is the normally sufficient form of such a society; if authority is needed, it is merely on accidental grounds, namely, inasmuch as one of the partners fails to discharge his contractual obligations. In contrast with mere partnership, a *community* is a society whose *raison d'etre* lies in a good of such nature as to demand common desire and common action. The Church supports the theory that civil society is a community and that its purpose is to procure a common good characterized by completeness and supremacy in temporal life. Now, wherever there is common action there arises a problem concerning unity of action. This follows from the laws of the one and the many. Unity of action cannot be taken for granted when the agent is a multitude; it has to be caused, and if it is to be steady it requires a steady cause. In the multitude made up of rational agents, unity of action implies unity of judgment about what ought to be done, and unity of judgment can be procured only in two ways, namely, by way of unanimity and by way of authority. Experience shows that unanimity, in practical matters, is a casual and precarious thing. But it is of great relevance to transcend the data of common experience and to consider the meaning of unanimity in a society free from deficiencies.[12] If we all pursue the same common good in a disposition of perfect good will and perfect enlightenment, we shall be unanimous with regard to ways and means of common action whenever ways and means leading to the common good are uniquely determined. If circumstances are such that we

---

[11] *Philosophy of Democratic Government* (Chicago: University of Chicago Press, 1951).

[12] A community consisting only of virtuous and enlightened persons is not sheer fiction; such communities exist, but they are very small; their size never equals that of the smallest state or city.

have really no choice, if the common good admits of no more than one course of action, whoever loves the common good and knows about the circumstances adheres to this course of action. In an ideally perfect community unanimous adherence to the rule of common action would be steadily obtained when and only when there is but one means to the common good. But why should we have no choice? In most cases the common good can be attained in various ways. In most cases several means lead to the common good. It should even be said that if all particulars and modalities are taken into consideration the means to the common good is never uniquely determined. Yet the common good requires that the unity of common action be steadily procured. There is not, in the nature of things, any reason why we should drive on the right side of the road rather than on the left as they do in Great Britain; the common good, security, speed, and order in highway traffic, can be attained either by driving on the right or by driving on the left. If, prior to any settlement of the issue, some drivers prefer the right and some the left, no one should be blamed for ill-will or unsound judgment. Yet it is necessary that all should drive on the same side. In such a case and in any case involving a plurality of means unanimity cannot be a steady cause of united action. If we are all well-intentioned and enlightened we shall unanimously proclaim that one and the same rule of action ought to be followed by all, regardless of private preference. Thereby the principle of authority is posited as a necessary and natural factor of human salvation. The necessity of this principle proceeds chiefly, not from deficiencies in men and in social organizations, but from the nature of man and from the wholly-good nature of community relations.

The requirements of common action make it easy to see that the principle of authority transcends the division of government into government with and government without a distinct governing personnel. When the question is to procure the steady unity of common action, all that is essential is that all should follow,—again, regardless of private preference—the one practical judgment elicited by the power of the community (*ordinare autem aliquid in bonum commune est vel totius multitudinis, vel alicujus gerentis vicem totius multitudinis, Sum. theol.* I-II, 90.3); whether this power resides in the majority or in one person or in the majority of a definite minority is a particular issue which concerns the ways and modes of authority, not the principle of authority itself.

103

The problem of united action evidences with particular clarity the naturalness of authority in every society which is not a mere partnership. However, procuring the unity of common action in ways and means toward the common good is not the most essential function of authority. Every problem of means presupposes the settlement of problems relative to the end. The volition and the intention of the common good are necessarily anterior to any issue concerning the ways and means to the common good. We would not consider methods of unifying our common action if we had not, previously, willed and intended an object of common action. We are thus led to ask whether the virtue and the enlightenment of all suffice to procure the volition and intention of the common good. Some forms of idealistic anarchism thrive on the assumption that, if all members of a community are free from sin and ignorance, the common good is unflinchingly intended by all.

It is true that moral virtue necessarily implies a relation to the common good; virtuous persons, as a proper effect of their virtue, love the common good and are eager to sacrifice their private interest whenever the common good demands such sacrifice. But disaster follows upon failure to see the difference between the common good formally understood and the common good understood in a material sense. Virtue procures the subordination of the private welfare to the common good considered as common good and *independently from that in which* it consists. I would not, for instance, act virtuously in the pursuit of economic success if I did not steadily subordinate this private purpose to the welfare of the Republic and were not ready to give up my financial ambitions at any time, in case they happen to conflict with the common welfare. In an emergency, the needs of the nation may be such as to make private prosperity impossible or unlikely to law-abiding citizens. But who is going to determine, will, and intend the thing in which the common good consists, the content or matter of the common good, in other words, the common good materially understood? Who is going to fix the amount of taxes that I shall pay? Referring to a text of St. Thomas which should be singled out as the most profound thing ever written on the foundation of authority (*Sum. Theol.* I-II, 19.10), let us ask whether every honest person is bound to strive for the punishment of every criminal, regardless of kinship or friendship. St. Thomas wants the son of the criminal, or his wife, to oppose the death of the criminal, even though the common good demands capital punishment. These particular persons are in charge of a particular good; desiring the things that the common good demands, desiring the common good materially understood is none of their business: it is the business of the community.

Obstinately, we imagine that the common good would be more completely served and dedication to it more complete if every person willed and intended not only the common good formally understood but also the content or matter of the common good, the things in which it consists. It is hard to remove the feeling that a volition relative to the forms of the common good but not to its matter constitutes only one half of a genuine dedication and that virtue would be more complete, and society better off in all respects, if every person, in each of his actions, intended both the form and the matter of the common good. Yet it is easy to recognize here a well-known error in the metaphysical treatment of the one and the many. Since the one is an absolute perfection of being we feel that unity is absolutely desirable, and this feeling is sound in itself; it becomes misleading, however, if it is not supplemented by the realization that the ways and modes of unity are proportional to the ways and modes of being. When a thing is a multitude, forcing upon it the kind of unity that would suit an individual is a highly destructive enterprise. Such is the meaning of the famous page where Aristotle, criticizing in Plato such features of forcible unity as community of goods and wives, says that if unity is held to be the greatest good, the state should give way to the family and the family to the individual. "So we ought not to attain this greatest unity even if we could, for it would be the destruction of the state."[13] Proudhon, who was not a student of Aristotle, discusses in similar terms the communism of Cabet. "M. Cabet creates everywhere immobility; he outlaws spontaneity and fancy. The art of the milliner as well as those of the jeweller and the interior-decorator are anticommunitarian. M. Cabet, like Mentor, prescribes invariability in dress, uniformity in furniture, simultaneity of exercises, community of meals, etc. Whereupon we no longer understand why there should be in Icaria,[14] more than one man, more than one couple. Why not only good old Icar, or M. Cabet and his

---

[13] *Pol.* 2.2.1261a 15ff.
[14] The utopia of Cabet (1788-1856) is expounded in a novel entitled *A Journey to Icaria* (1840).

wife? What is the use of all these people? What is the use of this never-ending repetition of puppets, all carved and dressed in like fashion?"[15] Unnecessary uniformity is forcibly imposed unity; it is not the kind of unity that the nature of a multitude admits of and demands; unity so misconceived is no longer a perfection of being. Discrepancy between the pattern of unity and the pattern of being means sheer privation. Now, of all the kinds of forcible unity that the spirit of utopia may construct, the most disorderly and redoubtable consists precisely in the volition and intention, by private persons, of the common good materially understood. That we should all dress alike, eat the same mass-produced food, live in homes of similar design and entertain ourselves with the same motion pictures would be bad enough; yet such unnatural uniformity would affect only the more superficial part of human and social life. If the intention of the common good materially considered were demanded of each particular person, if the very matter of the common good should become an object and a form for the love and the action of each, death-like uniformity would reach the heart of men. My father would no longer be more of a father to me than any other gentleman of the same age group, my brothers would become indistinguishable from other men of my own age group, my children would disappear, together with all other children, into an undifferentiated pool; none would be more of a friend to me than the stranger who passes by, no piece of land would have a particular claim on my labor and I should not be more dedicated to my function than to any other function. Society would lose, all at once, all the goods that attach to the uniqueness of filial love, brotherly love, paternal love, selective friendship, dedication to one's homestead and to one's task. Particularity would disappear; the forms of the parts would be swallowed into that of the whole, whose very substance would thereby suffer destruction. Clearly, the common good demands that confusion be removed from human communities. The law of love extends to all men, but all would be worse off if no one were loved with preference by anyone. The land will be fruitful if each dedicates his labor to the fertility of his own piece of land and tasks will be well fulfilled if each considers his the most important of all. True, in relation to me, the task that

---

[15] *Système des contradictions économiques* (Paris; Riviere, 1923), Vol. 2, p. 300.

is mine has unique significance from the standpoint of the common good itself. Commenting on the above cited article of St. Thomas, John of St. Thomas says that if God wanted my father to die tomorrow and if I should know about his will by special revelation, God would still want me to fight for my father's survival. The welfare of my father is my own responsibility: this is how things are divinely ordered. The common good of the universe may require that my father should die tomorrow: this is none of my business. Materially considered, the common good of the universe is the business of God alone, and likewise, the common good of a human community is the business of the community. We thus come to understand that beyond the requirements of united action toward the common good, the first and most essential function of government or authority is the volition and intention of the common good materially considered. Without authority, the matter of the common good would not be willed and striven for, or would have to be willed and striven for by particular persons. In the first case, community is purely and simply annihilated, in the second case it disappears into confusion. In the relation between authority and autonomy the aspect of complementariness ultimately outweighs the aspect of opposition. So far as its most essential function is concerned, authority has a root in the excellence of autonomy. The volition and intention of the common good would not require a power of direction if such volition and intention were procured by the virtue of particular persons; but, again, if the matter of the common good became the object and form of particular wills, particularity would actually be abolished; neither persons nor minor groups would be allowed to remain themselves, to retain any life of their own, to exist and grow according to their own forms and laws. Should anarchy endeavor to preserve the meaning of community life and the primacy of the common good, it would have to become totalitarian: a paradox which may throw light on certain aspects of political history in modern times.

Against the background of a general theory of authority, discussions about the origin of civil power become clearer, simpler, more independent of accidental circumstances and passions. Obedience is no longer a paradox. Men are really bound in conscience to obey other men, although no man can bind the conscience of his neighbor. God alone can bind man's conscience, and he can bind a man to obey another man. In order to know with entire certainty that men are actually bound by God to obey other men in civil relations, we merely need to understand that the existence and the perfect operation of the civil community are things demanded by nature. A natural requirement is a divine intention.[16] If we know that man's nature requires civil community and civil authority, we also know that civil authority derives its power from God. This implies, first, that civil authority cannot be explained away, as in the cab-driver theory, and second, that no man and no group of men can claim the right to give, by an act of will, a power that belongs to God alone. On the basis of these propositions, should it be said that civil powers govern by natural right, by divine right, or by a right both natural and divine? In the language of St. Robert Bellarmine, a right which is natural is also divine, and this language is not absurd, since, again, a nature is a divine intention;[17] but much confusion will be avoided if the expression 'divine right' is used only in reference to dispositions possessing some sort of supernatural character.[18] So far as civil authority is concerned, this expression has an historic meaning which would never have been lost sight of, if it were not for the amateurishness which generally characterizes the discussions of such issues.

Briefly: the question that the so-called divine right theory claims to answer does not concern the ultimate origin of civil power but the way in which power comes to reside in a distinct governing personnel. The theory of 'government by divine right' in its more common form, holds that power is directly handed by God to the ruler, even though men designate the ruling person. In the system of Filmer,[19] designation itself is effected without the cooperation of men; God appointed Adam first ruler and the God given powers of Adam went down to kings according to the laws of hereditary transmission. Referring to Cajetan's analysis,[20] let it·be said that

---

[16] St. Thomas, *Commentary on Aristotle's Physics,* 2 les. 14 "Nature is nothing else than an idea of a certain art—viz., of the divine art—, given to things in such a way as to be immanent in them (paraphrase needed to translate the powerful "indita rebus") and by which things are moved toward a determinate end."

[17] Bellarmine, *Controversiarum de membris Ecclesiae.* Lib. 3, "de laicis sive saecularibus," Ch. 6. *Opera* (Paris: Vivès, 1870), III, pp. 10-12.

[18] See St. Thomas, *Sum. Theol.* II-II.10.10.

[19] Robert Filmer, *Patriarcha,* published in 1680.

[20] Thomas de Vio Cardinalis Caietanus, Scripta Theologica, Vol. I: *De comparatione auctoritatis papae et concilii cum apologia eiusdem tractatus,* Vin-

the problem under consideration involves (a) the person of the ruler, say, James, (b) his power, say, royal authority, (c) the conjunction of person and power. Filmer holds that man does not cause the conjunction of power and person, and much less power itself. The more moderate interpretation of the divine right theory is free from historical extravagance: power is held not to be caused by men in any sense whatsoever, but the conjunction of power and person is ascribed to human causes. This theory, fittingly called the *designation* theory inasmuch as it restricts the role of men to the designation of the ruling person, suffices to give the temporal ruler a strong position in his dealings with the Pope. Owing to hereditary transmission, which in most cases places the act of designation in the remote past, the king may even feel that the divine origin of power is more obvious in his case than in the case of the Pope (with the exception of St. Peter). No wonder that the designation theory first obtained currency in an historical context marked by nationalism, absolutism and protestantism.[21] The fact that it was taken over, in the nineteenth century, by some Catholic theologians, in spite of a firmly established theological tradition, should be described as an accident in the campaign led by Catholic thought, under emergency circumstances, against the theory of government as mere instrument of the governed.

Much evil was done by the ambiguous expression 'sovereignty of the people.' In countless books of history, political philosophy, political science, constitutional law, etc., the theory of the sovereignty of the people is described as the soul of modern democracy and its opposition to religious tradition is strongly emphasized. Then a brief paragraph or a footnote recalls that St. Thomas, Bellarmine, and Suarez also supported the theory of the 'sovereignty of the people.' The reader is left to his bewilderment. St. Thomas, Bellarmine and Suarez are no supporters of the cab-driver theory.

---

centius M. Iacobus Poffet editionem curavit (Rome: Apud Institutum "Angelicum," 1936), No. 283.

[21] See Emile Chénon, *Le rôle social de l'Eglise* (Paris: Bloud et Gay, 1924), pp. 102 ff. Bossuet has often been described as a theorist of the "divine right" of kings. In fact, he proves anxious to retain traditional views concerning the consent of the governed; see *Politique tirèe des propres paroles de l'Ecriture Sainte,* II, a. 1,2. At the same time he vindicates the theory that the king does not have to render accounts to any man, but to God alone; see *Ve Avertissement aux protestants, Oeuvres complètes* (Paris: Lefevre et Didot, 1836), VI, 222. Whether he achieves consistency remains to be seen.

It is shockingly absurd to designate any doctrine of theirs by an expression which commonly conveys the purpose of eliminating obedience and authority.

The essence of authority and that of obedience are entirely preserved in a community which governs itself without any governing personnel: this was easily established, above, by an inquiry into the relation of a citizen to the majority in a direct democracy. Such a form of government is seldom possible. That it is not a particularly good form of government is, to say the least, tenable. Yet, government exercised directly by the civil community is a *distinguished* form of government inasmuch as an essential phase of all civil government finds in it a typical realization. Suarez's expression "natural democracy"[22] is certainly foreign to the vocabulary of St. Thomas, but there is no doubt that for St. Thomas as well as for Suarez civil authority resides primarily in the civil community, not in any distinct person.[23] Petty rebels who lack the sort of fortitude needed for a profession of outright anarchism and cherish the system of masked anarchy described above can draw no comfort from what St. Thomas, Cajetan, Bellarmine and Suarez have to say on this subject. The duty to obey laws to which I have not assented, and the duty to obey men who, contingently, lead me where I do not like to go, are not called into question. At all events, men remain bound in conscience to obey other men and God alone can bind man's conscience. The controversial issue is whether the God-given power to claim obedience for the sake of the civil common good resides primarily in the civil community as a whole. The four theologians just referred to hold that it does. They hold, accordingly, that the designation of rulers—whenever there is need for a distinct governing personnel—is accompanied by a *transmission* of power. The duty of civil obedience is not explained away and the power to bind the conscience of men is not taken away from God.[24]

---

[22] Suarez, *Defensio fidei catholicae et apostolicae adversus anglicanae sectae errores,* Lib. III: "De summi pontificis supra temporales reges excellentia, et potestate," Cap. 2: "Utrum principatus politicus immediate a Deo sit, seu ex divina institutione," *Opera, XXI* (Venetiis, 1749), pp. 114 ff.

[23] See in particular *Sum. Theol.,* 1-11. 97.3, ad 3.

[24] Leo XIII, *Diuturnum illud, On Civil Government,* June 29, 1881, tr. presented by Joseph Husslein, S.J., in *Social Wellsprings* (Milwaukee: Bruce, 1940), p. 50: "Indeed, very many men of more recent times, walking in the footsteps of those who in a former age assumed to themselves the name of philosophers, say that all power comes from the people; so that those who exercise it in the State do so not as their own, but as delegated to them by the people,

Designation and transmission admit of a great variety of forms, the clearest of which—though not necessarily the most certain—is election by universal suffrage. When, in a democratic polity, the people vote, their act of choice does not create the duty to obey civil authority, (this duty already existed, and was not created by man), but the power which comes from God and primarily belongs to the community is transmitted—more or less completely—to persons designated by the choice of the people.[25] Even though the acts of designation and transmission may have taken place in the remote past

---

and that, by this rule, it can be revoked by the will of the very people by whom it was delegated. But from these Catholics dissent, who affirm that the right to rule is from God, as from a natural and necessary principle."

[25] Immediately following the text just quoted: "It is of importance, however, to remark in this place that those who may be placed over the State may in certain cases be chosen by the will and decision of the multitude, without opposition to or impugning of the Catholic doctrine. And by this choice, in truth, the ruler is designated, but the rights of ruling are not thereby conferred. Nor is the authority delegated to him, but the person by whom it is to be exercised is determined upon." It has been said that Leo XIII and Pius X rejected the transmission theory, in spite of a well established theological tradition, and gave the sanction of their authority to the theory of mere designation. Among the texts which may seem to substantiate such interpretation, this quotation from *Diuturnum* is probably the most impressive. Now, we find in it (1) a thorough repudiation of the cab-driver theory, (2) a vindication of election by the people as a method of designation, (3) a new repudiation of the cab-driver theory, obviously motivated by the fear that designation by popular vote should seem to imply that the people has not the power to bind the conscience of men (*Quo sane delectu designatur princeps, non conferuntur iura principatus . . .*)or that the rulers are mere instruments of the ruled (*neque mandatur imperium, sed statuitur a quo sit gerendum*). There is, indeed, a resemblance between the instrumental theory of government and the transmission theory. Without some sort of resemblance, these theories would never have been identified, as they so often were, under the confusing expression 'sovereignty of the people'. No wonder, then, that a criticism of the former may have seemed to be aimed at the latter. The theory of government as mere instrument of the governed is what the Church opposes. Whether the role of the people is only one of designation or whether the designation of political rulers involves a transmission of authority is a question that Leo XIII and Pius X, apparently, have not treated. On this, see E. Chenon, *op. cit.* and Heinrich Rommen, *The State in Catholic Thought* (St. Louis, B. Herder, 1945). Pius XII seems to favor the traditional transmission theory in these words: "La fondazione della Chiesa come societa si e effettuata, contrariamente all'origine dello stato, non dal basso all'alto, ma dall alto al basso" (address for the inauguration of the new legal year of the Tribunal of the Rota, Oct. 2, 1945, reported in *Osservatore Romano*, Oct. 3, 1945; quoted by J. Maritain, *Man and the State* (Chicago: The University of Chicago Press,, 1951), p. 185). These words of Pius XII would seem to conflict with some statements of Pius X in the *Letter on the Sillon* (see above) if we did not know that Pius X speaks of the cab-driver theory and Pius XII of something altogether different.

and under obscure circumstances, there remains a world of difference between the conditions proper to spiritual authority and those of temporal authority. The king is vicar of the people, the Pope is vicar of Christ and is not, in any sense whatsoever, vicar of the Church. The power of the Pope is caused by God and is not in any sense caused by men; the power of the King is caused by men inasmuch as there is transmission of power by the community to a distinct person. If the King misbehaves gravely, he can be deposed by the people as by a power greater than his. But there is not in this world any power superior to that of the Pope.[26]

This theory has often been described as a "democratic" interpretation of the origin of power. Yet its supporters never thought that it was connected with democracy in any specific fashion. It holds for kingdoms as well as for democratic polities. In fact the examples and case-histories borne in mind by the theologians who worked it out were supplied principally by medieval and Renaissance monarchies. If this theory can be called democratic with any kind of propriety, it is only insofar as there is something democratic about every organization that is *civil* and *political* in the full sense of these words. On the other hand democracy impresses upon the transmission of power a distinctive mark, inasmuch as it never allows it to be complete. Every democracy remains, in some important respects, a direct democracy. Constitutions may and may not provide that certain issues will be decided by popular vote. More important than such constitutional methods as the plebiscite is the unwritten law of democracy, which gives great power to the opinions and desires of the people as expressed by newspapers, petitions, street demonstrations, polls, ets. In the United States of America there are actually three political assemblies; one of them never meets formally but never adjourns: it is the people of the United States.

A wise polity is always, in some measure, a mixed polity, and there is no reason to question the normality and the wisdom of constitutional practices which combine the principle of government by representatives and that of direct democracy. However, this state of affairs is greatly susceptible to the accident of *ungenuine transmission*.

Let it be recalled once more that the principle of authority con-

---

[26] This brief exposition is principally derived from Cajetan, *op. cit.*

tains no requirement that cannot be fully satisfied in direct government by majority vote. In almost all cases, however, the common good demands that there be some transmission of power to a distinct personnel. Either method agrees with the universal requirements of community life, and choice between the two—an extremely important issue indeed—is entirely conditioned by the circumstances. However, the joint use of both methods may favor confusion with regard to power transmitted and power retained. People may think and behave as if power actually transmitted were still in their hands. Then, the governing persons are treated, in spite of the constitution, as mere instruments of the governed. The fundamental act of transmission becomes illusory, deceitful, fraudulent, treacherous. Authority is no longer firmly established either in the people —because of constitutional transmission—or in the governing personnel, since the implications of constitutional transmission are no longer recognized. According to the Constitution of the United States, the duty of making laws, confirming the nomination of high ranking public servants, etc., belongs to the Congress. Under other circumstances, the inhabitants of North America might have formed small communities governing themselves by majority vote. But they did bring forth a great nation whose government requires the transmission of power. When a pressure group undertakes to destroy the conscience of Congressmen through promise, threat, and bombardment by telegrams, telephone calls and special delivery letters, transmission of power becomes ungenuine, the Constitution is violated and the principle of authority ignored. Congress is treated as a merely instrumental leader whose duty it is to take the orders of the led. Such corruption of democracy into the masked anarchy of the cab-driver system takes place at the uncertain point where the increased intensity of a process and its more audacious style bring about a change in its ethical and political nature. Again, it is normal that elements of direct democracy should be preserved, even if they were not mentioned by the constitutional law, in a system of government by distinct personnel. It is normal that the whole people should be like a permanent assembly, entitled to voice opinions and wishes. And there is nothing abnormal about letting our Congressman know that if the Congress follows a certain course of action it can not only rely upon our loyalty but also expect us to go far beyond the measure of strict obligation. Anarchy begins when there is an attempt to force a policy upon the govern-

113

ment. Such an attempt implies that the assembly of the people possesses a power of decision incompatible with the act of transmission. Except in cases explicitly defined by the constitutional law, the people cannot retain, in a system of indirect government, more than a power of consultation. Accordingly, letters to Congressmen ought to be few, in order that the maddening effects of repetition be avoided, and they ought to be phrased in terms of respectful wishes, since those who send them have a right to be heard, a duty to obey, and no right to give orders.

In most concrete situations no clear line can be traced between the normal operation of democracy and practices directly opposed to the very essence of authority. At this point, some will despise a theory which ultimately seems to bring forth a picture of confusion. Such attitude is a perfect demonstration of unfamiliarity with the mystery of human realities. Let us call *recognition* the act by which we know that a certain essence, already defined and present in our mind, is actually embodied in particular experience data. Recognition can be assured at comparatively low cost in the area of technique and in related areas, but when it depends intrinsically upon virtue its cost is just as high as that of virtue. The really good citizen does not complain about the failure of the philosophers to supply him with handy criteria: the inclinations and repugnances of his virtue enable him to distinguish from each other, with great accuracy, the liberties of civic life and the conspiracies of disobedience. But virtue is rare, and the case would be hopeless if it were not that the lasting embodiment of an idea in a group may give this idea a great deal of historic weight in spite of the weakness of men. Correspondingly, everything can be expected to go wrong if the groups in which an idea is historically embodied loses sight of its own mission. When the faithful make concessions to the spirit of rebellion, the world is tempted to forget what the Church does for democracy by fighting indefatigably democracy's most familiar enemy. Other forms of government contain other threats: democracy is particularly exposed to the evil of masked anarchy.

VI

The Church and Human Rights

by *Heinrich Rommen*

I

The perpetual process—Man *vs* the State—has entered what would appear to be its last phase: the internationalization of the Rights of Man, their incorporation into the body of positive international law at a time when the international community itself is, however haltingly, feeling its way to a more solidly and homogeneously constituted form than was either the anarchism of the sovereign states or the order of the League of Nations. The Universal Declaration of Human Rights adopted by the General Assembly of the United Nations on December 10, 1948, represents the last phase of the maturing relationship of Man *vs* the State. What had been claims of natural law in the eighteenth century and as such had been made the declaratory positive law of the modern state in the Bill of Rights, declarations of fundamental rights, and similar instruments is now on the way to becoming binding international law over and above the municipal laws, penetrating even into the hitherto closed domain of municipal law.

But this "internationalization" is not the only new feature. For the Declaration adds to the traditional rights the so-called social, economic and cultural rights such as the right to social security, to a just wage, to equal access to education, etc. Such rights were mentioned in some constitutions made after the First World War and are found specifically elaborated in the new constitutions established after the Second World War, for example, in France and Italy. Nevertheless, the Declaration contains the most extensive list of such rights and, in internationalizing them, exceeds in importance the national constitutional Bills of Rights. These social-economic Rights imply claims of the person to positive action on the side of the State according to the idea of Social Justice; they do not mean, as do the traditional Bills of Rights, to limit the "intervention" of the State or to forbid such "intervention" altogether. But it would be wrong to oppose these two classes of human rights as contradictory to each other. They are actually meant to be complementary to each other insofar as the social-economic rights try to secure for the working classes that human security and dignity which the traditional rights *de facto* secured for the propertied classes. Implicitly the traditional rights had also the character of social-economic rights.

The traditional Bill of Rights directed against absolutism establishes rights "against" the State, that is, against arbitrary, unreasonable, state-intervention into a sacred sphere of personal, "private" individual and group life; they stake out prohibitive rules against state intervention in the substantive rights of Life, Liberty, Property; and they secure those procedural rights which guarantee that criminal justice and the administrative actions of the state shall follow strictly formalized procedures which place the burden of proof on the state (which is itself under the law).

In other words, the benefit of the doubt is given to Liberty rather than to the state considered as benevolent guardian. The basis of such a "watchman-state" is, of course, the idea that the citizens, enlightened by their reason and their self-interest, organize themselves in the form of the civil society with full autonomy. The free society of free individuals is the positive value. The state *qua* government, as executor of the laws, is a regrettable necessity. It has to do no more than lend the individuals legal forms for their economic and social intercourse, to adjudicate their legal disputes, and to afford protection to their persons, contracts, property, health; and to enforce moral minima of public conduct, for individuals motivated by their reasonable, enlightened self-interest organize themselves by contracts on the basis of freedom of persons, property, and contract into an ever elastic and ever changing pattern of socioeconomic relations. The principle of perfect competition in the markets of economic goods, of intellectual, political and religious ideas is the automatic regulator compelling the individual interests, without conscious intent, to serve the common interest. Thus would be produced an automatic distribution of rewards and penalties, a social harmony without the benevolent supervision and direction of the state by the enlightened despot, that immediate predecessor of

116

the watchman-state with its centrally planned mercantilist policy, its privileged estates as against the non-privileged third estate and the rightless peasants and dependent artisans.

Furthermore, political rights—those democratic rights par excellence, such as the right to vote and to be elected to public office and the abolition of the privileged estates in favor of the *citoyens* (who now form the self-governing sovereign people)—were also meant in the nineteenth century to ensure the protection of the individual from the "arbitrary," "unreasonable" intervention of the state. The nineteenth century still had the optimism of Adam Smith, the moral philosopher who wanted a system of civil freedom and economic wealth which he thought were inescapably linked together by the laws of nature. The nineteenth century pleas for general liberty and its accusations against the "state," that is, against the *ancien régime,* were optimistically grounded in the idea that if the natural laws are made the laws of the state, a social harmony continuously preserving itself by reason of the fundamental liberties and the equality of opportunity would arise.

While this theory is logical on the theoretical level, in the concrete historical world the contradictions of the Manchester-system, as it began to be called, became more and more obvious. The old legal estates with their gradations of privilege were superseded, but no society of the free and equal arose. Instead, there came into being a class-society organized around the labor-market with essentially antagonistic interests. Society divided itself into the class of owners of the means of production, and the class of propertyless proletarians, whose basis of existence was limited to short-time labor-contracts made in a highly competitive, hazardous, and wildly fluctuating labor-market in which they had no influence. At the same time the progress of industrial technology made capital less mobile and less able to change employment. Thus it became "sunk" capital and developed technological mass-production with monopolistic tendencies as a consequence. This led, then, for instance in the United States, to the paradox that the state had, in the antitrust laws, to intervene in the supposedly self-regulating society to protect it against its own tendencies. Thus the liberties claimed and realized by business men could not be realized either by the worker or by the small independent artisan; nor, later, by the independent farmer. The workers were forced, after discovering their disadvantageous situation, to utilize their political rights and to set in motion a labor movement which aimed at fuller realization of those personal rights unrealizable under the libertarian principles of the Social Harmony doctrine. But the realization of their rights forced the worker-movement to go beyond the claims for equality of bargaining power by unions, that is, organizations of self-help (often declared in the nineteenth century as inimical to a competitive society in that they implied undue restraints on free trade). The workers received the support of liberals—that new group in our industrialized society who saw that legislation protecting the rights of labor must be as strong as that protecting industry. Bargaining power was equally as important to secure the position of labor as were tariffs and free incorporation of enterprises to secure the position of the business man. The basic structure of competitive society was to be changed to assure the sort of well-rounded socialist order in which there would be an egalitarian distribution of the national income; or it was to be changed, without socialism, to conform to Christian ideas. Christian social principles stood for an economic policy responsible to the principle of distributive justice. By the development of social law in factory and labor-market, Christian social thinkers envisaged the preservation of those liberties which Adam Smith's society could not realize for all. Social law of this sort would evolve a vocational group-order of society in which the rights of individuals were protected by the rights of the self-governing functional groups to which they belonged. They would thus actively participate in the formation of their own destinies. These criticisms of nineteenth century society by various "under-privileged" groups and by the liberals led, by the end of the First World War, to an increasing acceptance of social and economic rights.

Such rights are considered to be derived from the old rights by interpretation. The first of these new concepts, haltingly and modestly set up, was that of the workers' right to organize into unions and bargain collectively. In addition, it came to be acknowledged that workers might make use of their political rights as citizens to organize labor parties and to work by parliamentary methods for social reform. Rather than to abstain from politics, workers were to participate in promoting the piece-by-piece growth of social legislation. They were also to appoint their representatives to the councils of administrative agencies which the administrative state establishes. This participation in policy-making councils was to be considered labor's collective right to co-determine the socio-economic policy of the admittedly interventionist state—admittedly interventionist because of its controls on money and credit, tariffs and investment, a policy very different from that of the old watchman-state, with its ascetic abstentions from a world that, it was supposed, could run by itself.

These slowly developed social and economic rights are fundamentally different from the rights and liberties of the original Declaration of the Rights of Man. Those were rights against the state, historically against the state of princely absolutism with its privileged classes and its rightless subjects, with its union—nay, even identification—of Church and State, with its general paternalism in education, and in its mercantilist "planned economy." The newly rising social and economic rights of the propertyless working-classes and the small family-farmers establish a positive social and economic participation in the administrative state. They seek to allow those who under the *laissez-faire* pattern were helpless, to play a cooperative role in regulating the economic system. The right and duty to work, acknowledged in so many post-World War II constitutions and in Article 23 of the Universal Declaration of Human Rights, means something very different from the "freedom" of the worker to enter the labor-market and accept any wage-offer, even one which gives him only a slight differential above starvation level. The famous "Iron Law of Wages" has given place to a state-initiated policy of full employment, to a guarantee of the right to work and of the right to social security, to unemployment insurance. Such a guarantee would be too costly in a system which permitted chronic or cyclic unemployment. If the right to just and favorable remuneration and to a family-wage is declared as a human right, then the old free labor-market pattern cannot survive; and a just general economic policy by the state becomes necessary so that certain minima of justice in wages are regularly guaranteed. A whole series of social and economic policies may stem from such beginnings: from the radical policy of total planning to the "steered" economy of a Keynesian full-employment economy, or to the Social Market-policy of the Adenauer government in Germany propagated by neo-liberals such as Wilhelm Röpke.

These great changes in the societal order have raised the question, heatedly discussed by Hayek and Röpke on the one hand, and

119

Finer and Woolton on the other, as to whether the fundamental personal liberties of the individual against the state will be able to survive in the face of the radical policy changes required if men are to be guaranteed their social and economic rights. Article 23 of the Universal Declaration, for example, says that everyone has the right to work, to free choice of employment, and to protection against unemployment. It is quite clear that conflicts may easily arise in the realization of these rights; and the question as to which of the rights in a conflict with the others actually cannot be realized without coercion is not easily answered. A man uses, let us say, his free choice to work at a certain skilled job which is rendered superfluous by technological progress. He then acquires the right to protection against unemployment, but on the condition that he accept work in another trade and location. He has, in such a case, suffered a *de facto* loss of free choice of employment. This means, however, scarcely a restriction, and even less a loss, of liberty supposedly possessed in earlier times by the worker. Actually, he was then controlled by the inescapable and for him uncontrollable and unpredictable law of supply and demand for general or qualified labor-power; his free choices were nothing else than a function of the competitive "standards" and migration policies of capital, policies of individual corporations which will now necessarily have to be influenced by the economic policy of the state.

Another characteristic of the twentieth century Bill of Rights, incorporating these new economic and social developments, is that they consider not only the rights of man as an individual vs. the state, but also his rights as a social being, as a member of a group; as a member of a trade union, as a parent, as a child with the right to education and social protection. Some of these newly declared, not simply newly created, rights were already known as derivations from the venerable old formulas of the Declarations of Rights, of the fundamental rights of modern constitutionalism, inherited from the theory of the natural rights. Such is for instance the right of the parents to determine the education of their children, the duty of the State to provide for universal, even free access to its educational institutions, from compulsory elementary education up to the university. Such were the rights of members of religious, racial, and national minorities as written into the minority-treaties, after the First World War, in Poland, Czechoslovakia, and other nations; and incorporated in many constitutions promulgated at that time.

They have been proclaimed—unofficially—by a commission of the Interparliamentary Union as the substance of the "Declaration of Rights and Duties of Minorities." In particular, such rights of minorities, recognized *de lege lata* in treaties and demanded *de lege ferenda* by the previously mentioned Declaration, included the protection of life and liberty with no discrimination against religious allegiance or forms of public and private worship; the equal protection of the laws, and equality of civil liberties and political rights; the right to the use of one's mother language in private and public life; and the right of groups to found and sustain charitable, religious, and educational institutions of their own.

It is significant that these rights were not only to be secured democratically in the municipal law of these countries, but were guaranteed also by international law, though the procedures for their enforcement certainly were not particularly effective. The minorities themselves (though they might acquire the status as "corporations of public law" in municipal law) were not recognized as subjects of international law nor was an individual member of such minorities so recognized. A member of the League might bring a violation of the minority treaties before the Council of the League of Nations as an international dispute or appeal to the Permanent Court of International Justice for a judicial settlement.

A further step towards an international Bill of Rights was the Declaration of International Rights adopted by the Institute of International Law at its meeting in October, 1929. It declared that it is the duty of states to give every person the equal protection of the law, the right to Life, Liberty, and Property without discrimination as to nationality, sex, race, language, or religion. It declared specifically the right of the individual to religious freedom and to private and public worship, the right to the free use of the language of his choice, especially in schools, and to the citizen's freedom from any deprivation by the state, directly or indirectly, of his civil liberties and political rights. Article 5 states that equality before the law must be so absolute as to exclude any direct or indirect discrimination. The same Institute adopted in 1947 a similar Declaration on the Fundamental Rights of Man as the Basis of Restoration of International Law; for an effective order of the law among the States is considered inseparable from the respect of the human person in the internal order of the State, and progress in international law is understood to be intimately bound to the respect for those inherent rights of the human person which the State must serve.

II

The rise of the totalitarian state has given the idea of fundamental human rights a powerful validation. Yet unfortunately, the novelty of totalitarian ruthlessness and totalitarian expansionist techniques has put the idealism of our human-rights concepts under a most difficult strain. Nevertheless, the future belongs to it; not least because the Church Universal is on its side. The nineteenth century liberal may scoff at the idea of being backed by the Christian tradition; but the principles of human rights not only stem historically and logically from the venerable idea of the *jura naturalia* developed since the Middle Ages, but Christian religious and ethical concepts have constituted the very inner quickening of the internal history of those human principles. The human rights we now recognize were derived as the logical juridical consequences of Christian ideas. Indeed the history of the great institutions of constitutional law, and of all parts of the law, are themselves parts and effects of the history of ideas, of culture, of developing intellectual and moral "climates." Ideas which have grown up with Christianity—and that means historically, the Catholic Church—are the origin of our human rights. Greek and Roman antiquity was not, to be sure, wholly devoid of notions of personal rights. On the basis of natural law some Greek sophists, the critics of Greek society like Hippias and Alkidamos, conceived the idea of the natural rights of all men. Yet these were sporadic cases. They cannot overbear the general attitude of injustice with which Plato and Aristotle distinguished the Greeks as called to freedom under the laws of the Polis and the rightless barbarians as fit only to be slaves of the Greeks. Furthermore, not even the Greek citizen, free under the laws, supposed himself to be endowed with inalienable, personal, human rights. However "free" the Greek citizens were, as our classical scholars tell us, and the Roman citizens under the Republic, they were free by virtue of the positive laws of their city-states. They were not aware of individual human rights, of rights of man, inalienable in character as against the positive laws. They had not the idea of a sphere of the intimate person, and of the family, staked out by the rights of man; of every man, citizen and alien, Roman and foreigner secure from any arbitrary intervention by the state. Arbitrary is here determined by these rights themselves, not by a mere procedural formality or pure legality. What "rights" there were, were political rights of the citizen established by positive law, not *jura naturalia* which would be the critical norm for the positive law. The *Crito* of Plato is here pertinent. Socrates was condemned to death unjustly, as he and his disciples very well knew and openly affirmed. *Crito* offered Socrates assistance to escape. Socrates refused. The laws of Athens were good and just, he said, even those that were the basis of his condemnation to death. That the jury used these laws wrongly did not free Socrates from obedience to the laws. The idea that the unjustly applied law itself may be wrong, and that it must be critically measured as to intrinsic right or wrong with "the idea of the law" was not mentioned. Nor did Socrates conceive of himself as a citizen possessing the right to criticize the law's justice or to speak in his own defense against an unjust law. Such criticism and such self-defense, constituting the essence of freedom and of legal reform and of progress and of a "personal natural right" against unjust laws, were beyond the comprehension of Socrates. So were the problems of law and person, authority and conscience. The Polis and its laws remained the "omnipotent pedagogue," and the appeal from its laws to the "higher law" in defense of personal rights, in defense of human rights, equal for Greeks and Barbarians, was only sporadically admitted.

Neither did Stoicism, that last and perhaps most significant philosophy of antiquity, co-eval with the idea of the *Civitas Maxima* of the Roman Empire, come to a conception of fundamental and equal human rights, in spite of its universalism and its doubts about the institution of slavery. Though the Stoics formed the *word-vessels,* in which, later, the Church fathers could mould their Christian ideas, what Bergson has to say about them remains true: That not one of the great Stoics thought about tearing down the bars which separated the free citizen from the slaves, the Roman citizen from the barbarian. Christianity had to come in order that the idea of universal fraternity, which implies equal rights and the inviolability of the person, could be realized, however slowly.[1]

For two reasons Christianity must be considered the fertile soil of the idea of the rights of the human person. First Christianity

---

[1] *Les deux sources de la morale et de la religion,* p. 72.

is intrinsically universal; it is ordained for mankind, the community of nations, not to a particular state only; it is above nation-states, national cultures and civilizations. And its purpose is not "secular" or transitory, but perpetual, to be performed within all historical climates whether they be favorable, indifferent, or unfavorable. Its purpose is the salvation of individual souls, however much they be immersed in their specific cultural pattern and "historicity." Within, yet apart from, the Greek Polis and the national and imperial state religions of the Roman Empire, the Christian community grew, its beliefs invalidating (as St. Paul made clear) the old, deep distinctions between Greek and barbarian, freeman and slave. And so, since it could not win salvation for its adherents, the State as Polis and as Imperium lost its religious life-center and became restricted to the control of merely temporal affairs. Still more significant is the assumption of the Christian that he must serve his divinely revealed truth, a truth which gives to the Church a priority over the state and over man-made, pagan forms of state-religion. The *Libertas Christiana* was established to affirm the right in conscience of the Christian to turn the citizen's allegiance away from compulsory state worship and toward a God who had revealed not only Himself but the form which worship of Him must take.

The Church of the Martyrs is in a particular sense the Church of the Witnesses. There was, of course, no subjectivism and sectarian individualism in the Church, which is itself the Holy People, the Mystical Body of Christ, the *Communio Sanctorum*, with sacramental law and hierarchical order. The *Libertas Christiana* could not be conceived as against this divine Law and the hierarchical constitution of the Church. The juridical objectivism of this institution divinely "founded," is irreconcilable with subjectivist sectarianism. Against any claims of the divinity of Emperor, Polis or Empire, that is of the temporal state, the Christian demanded his Liberty, the Church her *Libertas*.

It is an outstanding characteristic of the Roman Church that, in contradistinction to the Eastern Church's lack of resistance against Caesaropapism, it led an interminable fight for the *Libertas Ecclesiae*. The names of such Popes as Gelasius, Gregory the Great, Gregory VII, Innocent III, stand for this steady struggle for the *Libertas Ecclesiae* from the deadly embrace of the political power which at that time did not hate the liturgical life and the spiritual character of the Church, but tried to use it for its own

124

purposes, at times sincerely believing in the Church's divine mission and under other circumstances, such as the presumptions of Frederick II, using it merely to secure itself.

Libertas Ecclesiae has had two significant meanings in history. First, it has always implied a community, the Church, not to be identified with any transitory political "life-form"—neither with feudalism nor with the Carolingian ideal, the *Civitas Dei*. *Libertas Ecclesiae* meant that, whatever its positive legal guarantees might be, the Church understood itself to have its own divine mission to fulfill—a mission that set it apart as different from and ultimately independent of, the world and the world's historical structures, civil and cultural. Man was thus made a citizen of two worlds: one spiritual and the other natural and secular, distinct, though not wholly separate from each other. There stood the Church, to which a man gave devotion, spreading the gospel, inspiring men and women, providing a regimen of sacramental life and moral rectitude, influencing peasant and knight, noble and serf, burgher and tradesman, to transcend their "natural" lives and so save their souls. *Libertas Ecclesiae* meant that the Church could thus work upon a succession of civilizations and cultures, teaching, forming, educating, inspiring, but always maintaining as its *Libertas* an ultimate aloofness, a *diastasis,* so that her own substance and life, her constitution and law, could not be drawn wholly into any civilization (such as feudalism) to perish with it when it should come to an end.

And so the second meaning of *Libertas Ecclesiae* came to be freedom of the spirit for the religious man against secular Powers and Dominations. The act of Faith and the life which it initiates must be free from secular oppression. Man is not wholly immersed in his biological-national or even cultural forms of life; man transcends with his person, with his conscience, all such historical, accidental conditions of existence. Such ideas were inconceivable to the ancients, to whom politico-cultural existence and "religion" were one, though there may be prefigurations of these ideas in sophist and Stoic philosophy.

It might be pointed out here that the pagan Roman Empire came to realize with a premonitory clarity that with the Church, the *Ecclesia,* and its demand for *Libertas,* whether of herself as *Corpus* or of her members as individual citizens, an "incompatible" element had entered the pagan world. Rome, as is evidenced by her Pantheon, was tolerant and indifferent to the national religions of the people it subjected to its political rule. But it reacted almost instinctively against that small *secta Christianorum* and persecuted this "Church of the Martyrs" with the full might of its police apparatus. Even the philosopher emperor, Marcus Aurelius, participated in this persecution. It was a unique fact that none of the many "sects," oriental or occidental, were made to suffer as was the *secta Christianorum,* though it never ceased to pray for the secular ruler and preach civil loyalty to the temporal laws. This had been taught by St. Paul and St. Peter, by Clement I, and by Justin, the martyr, in his famous Apologia for the Christians. The reason for the persecution was that Christianity put intrinsic limits to the powers of the Realm: not only the limits of the natural law as it was already known but also those of the divine law of the Founder of its Church. The latter took precedence in any conflict with the "temporal" law. The great struggle between the spiritual law of the Church and the temporal law of the secular State began. And it should be made clear that the *Libertas Ecclesiae* included the religious liberty of the Christian against the secular authority— not, of course, as the Reformation redefined the phrase: as religious liberty in the sense of freedom from the authority of the Church. The Christian conscience must be free to live according to the revealed law, just as the Church must be free and untrammeled to follow its divine mission.

Constantine in his famous Edict of Toleration of Milan (311 A.D.) wanted to make the Church and her moral authority a political prop for his imperial rule, and her bishops and dioceses administrative props for the political structures of the decaying Realm. Thus arose the great danger of Caesaropapism: that the Church might become part and parcel of the Realm as a political structure. In that event, the bishops and the Pope would assume the functions of political administrators and morale builders of the Empire, and mass-conversions would make the Empire nominally Christian, but in reality still temporal and secular.

We see, thus, how the painful and often disappointing struggle for the *Libertas Ecclesiae* within the Western and Eastern parts of the Empire began. The final issue of the struggle in the West might be called successful; but in the East, where it ended with the submission of the Orthodox Church to the Byzantine emperors, the result was failure.

126

From the beginning, in the West, the Latin Church was essentially successful in its struggle for the *Libertas Ecclesiae*. However, the waves of the migrating Germanic tribes early flowed over the ruins of the Western Realm, and upon this tide arose the civilization of the Middle Ages. And then the struggle for the *Libertas Ecclesiae* began again in earnest.

The natural piety of the Germanic tribes together with their conversion to Christianity produced the idea of the Holy Roman Empire. Charlemagne meditated upon the *Civitas Dei* of St. Augustine and, misinterpreting it, made it the great design for his and his successors' political plans. To the time of Ludwig the Bavarian in the fourteenth century, this idea of the Holy Empire, the *Sacrum Imperium,* was the formative dream of the German Emperors. It harbored immense dangers for the *Libertas Ecclesiae*. Among the threats with which it was pregnant were the character of the Germanic law and the natural piety with which the Germanic tribes were willing to accept the Emperor as the Vicar of God on earth, and the feudalistic concept of the majesty of the Emperor.

During those dangerous centuries there were, nonetheless, some significant victories for true Christian liberty. Great Christian champions appeared in the persons of Gregory VII, Alexander III, and Innocent III. There was Gratian's treatise on canon law. Scholasticism arose. New religious orders arose. The Franciscans especially aided in the struggle. And as the cities grew, the striving for the *Libertas Populi* also grew apace. So, likewise, did the *Libertas Ecclesiae* find its supporters.

We must not be confused by the fact that this struggle for the *Libertas Ecclesiae* was conducted in the terms of the medieval civilization and in its frame of reference. When the disputants of those times spoke of *Potestas,* they did not mean a Machiavellian power for power's sake, amoral and meaningless. *Potestas* meant liberty to the disputants. *Libertates* and *Potestates* as legal terms are often interchangeable. In the letters of a Gregory VII, the *Potestas Ecclesiae* as opposed to the *Potestas Imperii* is treated substantially as the *Libertas Ecclesiae,* as the concept that the Church as a spiritual society with its canon law, its sacerdotal offices, and its jurisdictional autonomy, must be freed from the interference of the "sacred" majesty of the Emperor. Thus *Potestas* was conceived of as serving the *Libertas Ecclesiae,* not as a power to be used for its own sake.

That in this struggle the legal forms of the feudal order which was so dangerous to the *Libertas Ecclesiae* were used as weapons by the Popes to protect this *Libertas,* is again quite understandable, though it led to tragic consequences: a widespread secularization of the Church which necessitated the not always successful reform movements of which the last, in the sixteenth century, led to the final dissolution both of the unity of the Church and of the unity of the *Sacrum Imperium.* Gregory VII, Innocent III and Alexander VI (in his famous Motu Proprio *"Inter cetera"* 1493) used the feudal legal forms to dispute the claims of the Emperor, based on a sacralised feudal law, because the propagandists of the Emperor were not less theocratical than those of the Popes, and all were influenced more or less by a misinterpretation of the Augustinian *De Civitate Dei.*

Scholasticism, from Peter Abelard on to St. Thomas Aquinas and John of Paris, distinguishing sharply, as it did, between nature and grace, philosophy and theology, faith and reason, criticized at least implicitly the Augustinian devaluation of nature, reason and philosophy and arrived at a different elaboration of the *Libertas Ecclesiae* from that of the theocratical partisans of the Pope. In the thinking of the Scholastics, the political order, the *civitas,* belongs to Nature. So does political authority, which derives its competency from the people whose temporal common good it serves. Political authority is autonomous in its ordering of the temporal common good; it is legitimized and limited by the natural law and by the revealed divine law, but not, *prima facie,* by the canon law. Scholasticism insisted upon the distinct natural and temporal character of political life as opposed to the supernatural and spiritual character of the Church. It was on philosophical grounds, rather than upon the basis of the positive public law of the Empire, that the Scholastics considered that the duties and rights of subjects and of political authority are independent of the supernatural order of Grace. The later Wycliffian doctrine that the prince who lives in mortal sin cannot demand the allegiance of his subjects was explicitly opposed by the Scholastics' view.[2] St. Thomas states that neither simple misbelief nor even the apostasy of the ruler *eo ipso* destroys the duty of political loyalty due to such a ruler by his Christian subjects. But it is, he says, possible that the apostate

---

[2] *Summa Theologica,* II,II, quaest. 12 a. 2.

ruler may by declaratory judgment of ecclesiastical authority be pronounced deposed as a punishment for his apostasy. Thus only according to the positive public law of his times is such a declaratory judgment recognized; for it was the Church which blessed the covenant of Prince and People in the sacral act of crowning and taking the respective oaths; thus it was considered the competency of the Church to declare the breach of covenant if and when the Prince apostasized.

The temporal common good was considered a genuinely independent, though natural, value. It is natural, John of Paris says, that nations, since they are different in character and in way of life, should have their own states and different constitutions, because what suits one people may not suit another. Consequently, there is little room for a universal monarchy with the Emperor as Lord of the World, as Head of Christendom. Still less would there be room for a sacral monarchical ruler, quasi-divinely instituted by such rites of consecrating and crowning an Emperor as those upon which Eichmann reports so interestingly.[3]

The Scholastics were equally indifferent, philosophically, both to the Papocaesarism of the Curialists who would have made the Pope the overlord of Church and World and to the Caesaropapism of the Legists who would have wished the sacred Emperor to be the overlord of the World and Church. Though they made obeisance to the general political ideas of their time and to the positive public law of their feudal world, and might have appeared, at times, to be partisans of the claims of the Pope or of the Emperor, philosophically they distinguished sharply between the Church universal as a spiritual society and the pluralism of temporal secular states.

The introduction and assimilation of Aristotle's *Politics* into the medieval world of political ideas was certainly, though by no means intended to be, a revolutionary act, because it deprived the temporal ruler, whether Emperor or King, who did not recognize a political superior, of the particular sacral character which was claimed by and for him since Charlemagne. The Scholastics thus brought back the principle that the *Libertas Ecclesiae* is best guaranteed by the restriction of political authority to its proper field, the temporal common good. Such consideration of the common good might or might not include the idea of religious homogeneity.

---

[3] *Die Kaiser-Krönung im Abendland,* I, p. 23 ff.

Thus we see that the Church was not considered the source of the State, nor its superior. The Church was considered to be ordained to the realization of a value much higher than that of the State, but it does not follow that the Sate is subordinate in causality to the Church. It is simply that the Church enjoys a higher dignity.[4]

III

It would not be too far fetched if we were to say that the struggle for the *Libertas Ecclesiae,* which practically often meant the many *libertates, immunitates,* and *privilegia* of ecclesiastical office holders, courts, and the canon law they administered, worked also in favor of the many tendencies of cities and vocational groups which, before 1000 A.D., granted liberties, immunities and privileges for cities and their inhabitants, for the guilds and their members, and for the rural yeomen-farmers, from the typical burdens of feudal law and feudal lords. The Magna Carta of 1215, which King John was compelled to grant, is the most famous, but by no means a singular, example of such charters of liberties, immunities and privileges. It was significant mostly for the simple fact that, by reason of particular circumstances, it endured the many political upheavals which occurred between 1215 and 1789, while other similar charters were buried by political changes such as monarchical absolutism and wars of religion.

The many charters of "liberties, rights and franchises," of "immunities and privileges," which we encounter in the history of the Middle Ages, more and more frequently, from the tenth century on, originate almost always as the result of the demands of burghers or members of merchant and trade guilds to be freed from the bonds of feudalism. If one studies the slow development and enlargement of such liberties and immunities, one can see how each additional liberty frees man further from the many bonds of feudalism, until the self-government and the *Libertas populi* of the medieval city (and not seldom, also, of the yeoman in rural districts) is accomplished.

The legal device by which such liberties were acquired sometimes took the form of perpetual privileges granted by the feudal lord or the overlord to immigrants, as with the newly founded

---

[4] John of Paris, "Treatise on the Royal and the Papal Power," Goldast, II, p. 134.

towns and villages in East Germany; sometimes the granting of such freedoms was the price paid by a feudal prince for financial or military help by burghers of an already existing town; and sometimes these expansions of freedom came as the result of a peace-treaty after a successful rising of the citizenry against the lord, as was the case in the famous *Conjuratio Magna pro Libertate* in Cologne against the Lord-Archbishop (1112 A.D.). By reason of their origin such liberties might appear as only corporate liberties of the city and not as subjective liberties and rights of the individual citizens. But the sources, on the contrary, tell us that though these liberties were acquired through the mediation of the city, they nevertheless were *jura singulorum* and as such recognized, when the cities became sovereign, as valid also against the city-government. We find also that many charters speak of "all free citizens, wealthy and poor," or "without consideration of rank and avocation."

Among the types of liberty thus gained in the Middle Ages, we find freedom from feudal services and taxes; freedom of movement (important for merchantmen and trades-journeymen); freedom to acquire, hold, and dispose of movable and immovable property; freedom from unreasonable and oppressive taxation; and the right (*jus*) to be tried by the city-court and by one's own peers, even though the accuser may be the feudal lord or his successor. Furthermore, no one might be deprived of life, or property, or suffer damage to his body except by formal trial before a lawfully constituted court; that is, there was to be no punishment *sine legali judicio,* a standing formula since Otto III's privilege to the citizens of Cremma (996 A.D.). Freedom from arrest without proven cause and right to bail had already been recognized in the eleventh and twelfth centuries, though that freedom harks back to the eighth Council of Toledo (683 A.D.). The famous Golden Bull of Hungary (1222 A.D.), by no means a copy of or derived from the Magna Carta, also contains a clause against arbitrary arrest and is in many respects as elaborate as is the Magna Carta. The freedom from search is also recognized in many parts of the Continent before 1215 A.D. The equality of all men—Jews and heretics as well as Christians—before the Law was fully recognized in the famous German Law-text, the *Sachsenspiegel,* and by the equally famous Superior Court of Magdeburg, the decisions of which had the rank of ruling cases. (It would, of course, be wrong to forget

131

the political disabilities of Jews or Saracens in the Middle Ages.)

Not only serfdom, so typical of the socio-economic feudal system, but even slavery, was still customary in the Middle Ages. The latter came into being mostly as punishment, or as a consequence of men's being taken prisoners of war. These survivals of injustice are evident from the discussion of the theologians, who rather uncritically, yet with an uncomfortable conscience, seem to accept the Aristotelian doctrine of "natural" slavery, though they make it less provocative by explaining it as being not *in prima intentione naturae* but being caused by original sin and thus belonging to the *jus gentium,* that rather opaque body of law somewhere between natural and positive or civil law. Yet the *Sachsenspiegel* declared simply "that slavery and also serfdom have their origins in unrighteousness. They have been introduced by force. What earlier times regarded as unlawful custom wants now to be held for law" (II, 42, 6). Such ideas about the institution of serfdom and slavery were more widespread than conservative theologians allow us to assume. Witnessing to this are the many peasant-risings and their legal claims, which after the Flemish rising (1323) become more and more vocal. Against the increasing demands made of the feudal lords the "old liberties and rights" are stressed. But not only these. The natural and the divine law is more and more quoted.

The "Reformation of Emperor Sigismund," a widely read pamphlet written by a cleric in 1480 A.D., affirms that servitude is against the Divine and the Natural law, and that it is an unbearable crime for a Christian to say to another Christian, "Thou art mine." To fight against servitude is a divine work. The propaganda of the *"Bundschuh,"* the secret society of the rebellious peasants, also declares serfdom to be intrinsically wrong since all men are created free by God. And the third Article of the famous Twelve Articles of the Peasants (1525), at the start of the Great Peasant War, condemns serfdom as un-Christian, since "we are all, rich and poor, redeemed by Christ's precious blood; and, therefore, according to Holy Writ, 'We are free and will be free'."

We come to the conclusion that all through the Middle Ages, not only in towns and cities, but also in whole territories, a struggle for securing the rights of life, liberty, and property were going on. This struggle was not one of whole nations, for the nation-state had not yet developed. It was a struggle of smaller communities, of the members of certain strata in a hierarchical society. The Magna

Carta was only one among many charters claiming rights against governmental authority, and its particular dignity rests more on the fact that it was never wholly submerged by princely absolutism than on the fact of its uniqueness. Furthermore, the struggle for securing such "positive" rights, liberties, and immunities was not initiated by a powerful radical ideology as was the case in the eighteenth century. It was more a pragmatic and concrete struggle for the specific rights of groups, of guilds, of settlers, of members of the nobility, of cities and towns and of the yeomanry against the feudal order.

However, we should not assume that motives of a spiritual and philosophical character were absent in this struggle. On the contrary, Christianity certainly contained such motives. However much the individual might be immersed in his group and conditioned by his station in that stable and "hierarchical" society of the Middle Ages, he transcended all these circumscriptions by his particular dignity as a Christian called to a higher citizenship in the true city of God, in the Church considered as the "Holy people," and in the Heaven beyond. The Middle Ages were the era of never-ceasing social criticism of all institutions which stood in the way of the realization of this dignity. Feudal institutions slowly yielded to the critical attacks Christianity made upon them. Still more important, the Church itself survived a life-and-death struggle against its own feudalization. Finally, the medieval social order and its institutions as the effect of the Church's influence, proved to be incapable of enduring. They had to be—and were slowly—transformed or abolished as a consequence of Christian ideas. Before God there is no discrimination of worldly rank and family status. The asceticisms of the friars constituted a constant criticism, not only of the old religious orders, but of all of feudal society. The friars' preaching, while no summons to revolutionary action, chipped steadily away at the ideological foundations of feudal society, at the superior-blood *mystique,* at the hereditary pride of belonging to the leading families, at the identity of status and wealth, at the *splendor familiae,* at the contempt for the lowly born serfs. The friars praised "poverty," and they glorified the poor as the particular "children of God." It is very difficult for us today to understand the tremendous effect of the sermons of the friars, those wandering preachers, with their blistering attacks upon the society in which they lived. In a society of lavish "conspicuous consumption," of the wealth of the few and the poverty and servile status of the many, suddenly the "poor of and in Christ" appeared, recruiting especially from the ranks of the upper strata of medieval society. It is no wonder that these great spiritual movements—some of them regrettably turning into heretical sectarianism like that of Waldo's followers— became the parents of more democratic and individualistic trends in philosophy and politics. Poverty meant freedom not only from wealth but from the society that made feudal status and wealth the basis of inequality and serfdom. John of Salisbury and Bernard of Clairvaux had already praised the "poor"! John also had fought for the *Libertas conscientiae* under God against its violation by the political power of the Emperor who demanded obedience as the *Vicarius Dei* on earth. Bernard had praised the spiritual man who is truly free, because he is, like a Stoic, indifferent to the "World," and he found in the "poor" Pope the true vicar of Christ, the crucified.

Thus it was not strange that the first effort to give the charters of liberties a philosophical understructure was made by the friars, especially by William of Ockham. The latter developed a well-constructed theory of "natural rights." They are to be considered powers or faculties based on the Natural Law as an objective rule. They empower or authorize a person to act, to own a thing, or to dispose of it. Such a right is a liberty as distinguished from a *licentia*. The latter is merely a permission to do something granted by a revocable *gratia* of a superior and is distinguished from a right by the fact that only the latter can be enforced by action before courts. Such a natural right is a subjective, individual, or collective liberty based on those objective rules of Natural Law which lay upon all the obligation to respect this right.

Ockham distinguished between natural and positive man-made rights. To the former belong especially liberty and property. Liberty is the right to independence, initiative, and self-determination, flowing from the rational nature of man. It follows that slavery and all forms of servitude must be products of man-made laws and cannot be based upon Natural Law. Natural liberty can only be lost by voluntary action, i.e., by contractually giving it up to another person; or a person can be deprived of it judicially *ex justa causa et culpa* and for no other reason. Likewise Ockham contended that the right to private property is a natural right. Under a slight but significant change of the previous scholastic doctrine,

134

which ascribed property as an institution either to the *jus gentium* (following the Roman Law) or to mere human law, Ockham said that under the conditions of fallen human nature private property becomes not only a useful, convenient institution, but a strictly necessary one. It is thus of divine ordination as a dictate of right reason. The concrete positive law regulating the use, the forms, the acquisition and the disposal of property are of course of mere human law. Yet anterior to these human laws of property is the natural right to property given by God and nature. Nobody consequently may be deprived of this right without his consent (*volenti non fit injuria*) or without just and reasonable cause in formal procedures. Ockham thus gave the positive *jura et libertates,* mostly "granted" or acquired by agreement and thus somewhat weak, a sound foundation in Natural Law. They are not to be delivered to the whims of discretionary authority, but they are to be understood as true rights, of which the holders cannot be deprived without just cause established before courts or by the vote of assemblies. A mere contention of a discretionary authority was not sufficient to deprive a person of these rights since he was protected by the right to vindicate them in courts of law.

We must not make the mistake of imputing modern ideas to medieval writers even though, like John of Salisbury, they use a term like "freedom of conscience" or, like Gregory VII (in his letter to the people of Venice) a term like *"Libertas populi."* We can make no simple identification of liberty, in the modern sense, with medieval man's longing for liberties. What medieval man wanted was the securing of his economic and civic activities within the hierarchical society of those times. He had no notion of overthrowing that society for any egalitarian liberty or liberal democracy such as we conceive of in modern times. He wanted to secure his concrete liberties. He had no idea of himself as a solitary self-centered individual, nor as an agent in the building and reforming of society and the State. He had scarcely any conception of himself as an individual capable of self-determination and self-fulfillment in all the fields of human endeavor—cultural, political, social, and economic. The liberties which he conceived of were to exist only within the basic framework of a "sacral" society—concrete freedoms from restrictions upon economic and civic activities.

IV

In the light of this discussion we may better understand that most troublesome institution of the Middle Ages—the Inquisition, which seems in so stark a contradiction to modern liberty of religion and of conscience. Let me say at once that I will not defend the Inquisition. The greatest majority of Catholic theologians agree about the dark side of this historical, non-essential, institution of the ecclesiastic society. It would be easy to collect condemnations of this institution by famous theologians; and I am sure that, so far as theology is concerned, it will be adjudged a regrettable affair of the past. But, while the Inquisition certainly is indefensible, it is not inexplicable.

The Inquisition was, as the name suggests, a judicial inquiry about religious dissent, about the propagation of heretical sectarian doctrines. Religious dissenters, heretics, were from time to time persecuted after the Church became the Church of the Realm, because religious heterodoxy was all too easily construed to be political disloyalty or as an attack on the religious political substance, on the way of life of a society in which religion and politics, canon and civil law, the Emperor's and the Pope's office, were so intertwined *de facto* that the violations of the laws of the one were all too easily considered also violations of the laws of the other. Canonical excommunication often drew after it such civil law consequences as dissolution of the bonds of political allegiance, and political crimes such as tyranny, or civil crimes such as murder and rape, were often followed in turn by canonical punishment.

The unity of that politico-religious society, under the impossible ideal of realizing the *Civitas Dei,* was almost totalitarian in character. In spite of the clear distinction between the competencies and powers of the distinct societies, Church and Empire, and between the *Libertas Ecclesiae* and of the sacerdotal office and the Canon Law, the unity—if not the identity—of both societies in Christendom with the preeminence of either Emperor or Pope was much more effective than the fine distinctions of the schoolmen or the longing of Saints for the spiritual Church. To belong by baptism to the Church was all too easily considered the basis of political homogeneity and loyalty. To be a Christian was the condition of political rights.

This strong feeling of unity, religious and political, which was by no means foreign even to that strange "un-Christian" Emperor Frederick II, led easily to the civil intolerance and persecution of non-conformists which is associated with the Inquisition. If even the sincere ruler is perchance convinced that religious heterodoxy is necessarily also political disloyalty, or that religious unanimity or conformity is the *prima facie* basis of political unity and of civic loyalty, then religious heterodoxy becomes all too easily proof of political disloyalty and revolutionary conspiracy. This was the case in the Middle Ages, as it was the case in Elizabethan England, and in Calvin's Geneva. Only when the Church and State are understood to be independent societies, their laws different in competencies and object, with the duties of citizen and the right of secular authorities based on natural law not on supernatural authority, only then is it possible to distinguish and to keep apart the two societies, their laws, authorities, and allegiances.

Practically this was not done in the Middle Ages. Consequently, Jews and Mohammedans could not acquire civil rights, though they might be—and mostly were—protected in their rights to life, to certain granted liberties, and to property. They could not be compelled to have their children baptized. Their religious services were to be tolerated. On the other hand, heretics, i.e., validly baptized persons who in spite of several formal summonses to give up their heterodox opinions stubbornly persevered in them, presented a presumably homogeneous society with a dangerous problem.

The approach of the theologians and churchmen was to a degree rather legalistic. The Christian promised at baptism to remain faithful to the Faith. Ergo, he was held to keep it and if he became heretical, he had broken his promise; he consequently ought by spiritual and secular law to be compelled to honor his promise and desist from heresy. Furthermore, because of the unity of civil and religious society, he who violated the faith by public or external heresy was also held to have committed a crime in temporal law, because heresy was by all medieval theologians considered as a disturbance of the public order of Christianity. Consequently, heresy was first an affair for the spiritual courts; and after being established there, became an affair of the temporal courts by reason of the public law of Christendom. But infidels and Jews were to be tolerated.

Such was the way of thinking from the first Christian Emperors all through the Middle Ages, up to the victory of civil tolerance.

137

And this thought was common to Lutherans, Calvinists, and the New England divines as well as to Catholics. Rightly or wrongly, in those universally Christian societies, the question as to whether a man shocked by ecclesiastical abuses, could in sincere conscience fall into "heresy" (and thus be subjectively not guilty of heresy) was never seriously discussed. Such involved psychological questions were scarcely aired in such a non-individualist society. It should be remarked also that in medieval society a critique of religious abuses could usually be made within the Church, issuing even in reform movements, without being considered heretical. The similarity and the difference between St. Francis and Waldo are striking in this respect.

If punishment of heretics in the canonical sense by secular punishments (which rarely included capital punishment) had been carried on for centuries, what made the Inquisition so abominable to modern man and so to be regretted by modern theologians?

I think it must be said that the peculiar horror of the Inquisition was a matter of two things.

First, there was the introduction and ecclesiastical sanction of torture as a means of getting evidence not only from suspects but even from mere material witnesses. Torture (*quaestio*) had become a means of getting criminal evidence in the old Roman Empire predominantly for capital crimes and high treason (as with the Christian martyrs). Ulpian was full of misgivings about this *res fragibilis* and St. Augustine complained bitterly about the misery caused by it to innocent people.[5] The non-Romanized Germanic tribes did not use torture. But this was more because they did not yet know public criminal prosecution, leaving the prosecution of crimes to the violated person or his family. Oaths and ordeals were the customary means of evidence.

When the public peace in the eleventh and twelfth centuries was disturbed so wantonly by the robber-barons and the feuding lords, the public authorities had to take over public prosecution of crimes. Thus a new mode of procuring evidence became necessary —the official search for it, or "inquisition" (inquirere), regardless of the request of the violated person or his kin. Hence arose the questioning of witnesses to get evidence against the arrested suspect, to get a confession, the queen of all evidence. To get a con-

---

[5] *De Civitate Dei*, XIX, c. 6.

fession, torture began to be used and looked upon as necessary for criminal justice.

By the beginning of the thirteenth century, torture had thus reappeared. The *Sachsenspiegel* (1220) ignores torture, but some thirty years later the *Schwabenspiegel,* influenced by Roman law and by Curialism in its political theory, recommends it, as do some other Germanic laws, not similarly influenced. The Roman Inquisition was an institution that slowly developed, in the form of special regional courts with a supreme tribunal in Rome, for the detection of the many, rather secret, heretical movements sprouting everywhere at the end of the twelfth century. Its tribunals superseded the ordinary episcopal courts which had, up to then, rather inefficiently and often very arbitrarily tried to stamp out heresy. The real black mark against the Inquisition was the order by Pope Innocent IV in the Bull, *Ad Exstirpenda* (1252), to apply torture as a means of getting evidence from suspects, not only for self-incrimination, but also for denunciation of fellow-heretics. This order was directed to all courts, secular and spiritual, not only to the tribunals of the Inquisition; it thus gave torture a kind of supreme sanction. The Bull cautioned against excessive use of torture. A confession could be accepted only after, not during the torture, and outside the torture-chambers. It was to be "free and spontaneous" and without the infliction of "force or fear." That sounds like bloody irony and can only be condemned as hypocritical. Even if we give the inquisitors every benefit of the doubt and assume that they followed to the letter the rules that torture should only be applied as a means of last resort, we may be sadly certain that, between the fervor of the heretic and the fanatical passion of the defenders of the faith, the laws were not seldom flaunted.

Secondly, the Inquisition employed the shocking device of having the death penalty pronounced and executed by the temporal authority. But what if the temporal power was not itself convinced of the victim's guilt, or wanted to be more merciful, or tried to save a heretic for political reasons? In that case, the temporal authorities themselves could be declared *"Fautores heresis"* and would become subject to prosecution by the Inquisition. This was indeed a vicious circle.

That it seemed such to the people of the Middle Ages is doubtful. The heretic was considered an actively subversive agent. At least he was so considered by the ruling classes, who at that time often composed the higher clergy and the higher political authorities. They were thus connected by common family and political interests. Not a few heresies, all those, for instance, which contained Manichean tendencies or those which argued that by mortal sin dominion was lost or those which denied the sacredness and the goodness of oaths—in a society that was based on a pyramid of oaths and allegiances—were *de facto,* within the moral and ideological framework of that practically universal and single society, Christendom, subversive of that historical stage of human development. In that sacral society, in which the Faith was the very foundation of religious and social homogeneity, heresy could be considered with some reason not only as a danger to the Faith, but as a political and social danger as well. Repressive action will in similar cases always be taken even by political authority.

What the forms of repression in any society will be is not a theoretical question, but depends on the general moral temper, the intellectual climate, the humanist tendencies of a given civilization. Two hundred years ago we had cruel penal justice even for a mere youth of fourteen years of age. One hundred years ago we still had legal slavery in this Christian country, in spite of the idealism of the founding fathers and great liberal Bills of Rights in state and federal constitutions. Thirty years ago those of us with awakened consciences smarted under the Sacco-Vanzetti case. Today our consciences are disturbed by the fanaticism of anti-communists who appear ready to play havoc with our liberties. On the other hand, one has only to study the penal part of the Canon Law, up to the presently valid code, and the Concordats with even predominantly Catholic countries, in order to know that the modern Bill of Rights and the inviolability of the sincere conscience must be jealously respected by a Catholic civilization, if ever the dream of a wholly Catholic world is to be realized.

V

Everywhere under absolute monarchy, even those rights and liberties which were generally respected in the Middle Ages were often submerged by the *Raison d'Etat.* Religious toleration was first accepted by so-called Catholic States in Poland and in Switzerland after a victory of the Catholic party. The Edict of Nantes was made long before Protestant states showed any signs of tolerance;

its breach was condemned by Catholics with the same feeling of shame as Protestant liberals might feel about the persecution of Catholics in Elizabethan or Puritan England. The cause of such persecution, of course, was the assumption that only religious conformity to the Church of the Prince who had become definitely the spiritual authority in Protestant states and who claimed at least the control of the jurisdictional, the external, organizational life of the Catholic Church within his nation or territory, could guarantee unquestioning political loyalty and filial submission to the Father-Prince. Religious dissent, recognizing especially the Pope's jurisdictional primacy *in spiritualibus* was considered as incompatible with this kind of political loyalty. Hence the era of State-Churchdom.

But such an identification, based essentially on a mockery of the Divine Right, was in contradiction not only to the Scholastic political theory, but came into increasing conflict with the "Spirit" of the times. The Enlightenment, with its Deism, its criticism of revealed religion (of whatever Christian denomination), and with its nurturing of non-conformity, did much to destroy the idea of a state Church. When Canisius in 1550 recommended that the Inquisition, spiritual in character, be introduced in Germany to fight against the spread of Protestantism (a spiritual counter-attack similar to what Luther had recommended against the *Schwarmgeister*), Ignatius of Loyola advised firmly against it. But "Divine Right" Kings had no qualms. They were willing to see religion made political, and the Church debased to an instrument of thought control, at least so far as its organizational relationship to the Crown was concerned.

Thus the dubious unity of Church and State was attacked from two flanks: from the idea of the *Libertas Ecclesiae* and from the individualist rationalism of the philosophers who wanted to destroy both Absolutism and its ideological prop, the Church. The *ecrasez l'infame* of Voltaire meant the destruction of both. Furthermore, the ruling classes of the Ancien Régime apostasized in great numbers and went over to unbelief. Everyone wanted Freedom—the rising entrepreneurial class from the planned economy of princely mercantilism; the philosopher, from a rather inefficient censorship of literature and sciences; the freethinker, from what he considered an enforced religio-political ideology; and the rationalist, from the servitude of Reason to a State-religion. "Man is born free, but everywhere he is in chains."

141

The "Christian Monarchy" itself was already "secularized"; it had lost its concrete legitimacy in the intellectual world of the ruling classes in the eighteenth century, however much the simple faithful, the farmers and artisans, still lived secure in their traditional faith.

Thus became explainable the enthusiasm of the Great Revolution, the Declaration of the Rights of Man and of the Citizen, and the falsification of freedom of religion into persecution of the Church and of religious belief. And thus also it becomes understandable that Catholic writers and churchmen should not have greeted the Revolution with complete trust, however much not a few of them were ready to accept the *Novus ordo saeclorum* in its initial liberating epoch.

In the Anglo-Saxon countries the Revolution was not a violent break with the past and a radical (if shaky) new construction, but a slow evolution, and the traditional forms were slowly (as by a kind of osmosis) transformed. The free non-conformist groups had done their part to save the intellectuals as well as the masses from a hasty Erastian identification of State and Church. Thus, in those countries, it was not only anti-religious Rationalism that pleaded for freedom, but the Christian consciences of non-conformists; there an amicable separation of Church and State could be accepted by practically all as a rule of political prudence.

It was different in Continental Europe. There the Restoration and political romanticism followed as a violent reaction against the terror and against the revolutionary promulgation of the civil religion in 1792 which secularized Gallicanism. And the romantic political writers of that period (and many churchmen who misread the signs of their time) thought that by such a reestablishment, a bygone historical form of political and social life could be simply continued, and that the positive gains of the Revolution (what was genuinely humane and Christian in the new order) could be simply suppressed. They did so in an unforgivable misinterpretation of the conservative character of the Church, of its *Libertas,* of its ability and duty to adapt its external forms of pastoral service, its teaching, and its missionary work to social changes, in that they, at least implicitly, contended that the new secular, not necessarily "secularized," state with its Bill of Rights, its civil tolerance, its democratic constitution was intrinsically anti-Catholic.

In addition they were guilty of a methodological error. They pleaded that the new Democracy with its equal protection of the law, with its political and legal equality of all citizens, with its personal and political rights of the individual, was born tainted with the quasi-original sin of godless Revolution. They asserted, consequently, that its characteristic institutions could only be interpreted and applied in the spirit of a rationalist and often violently anti-Christian ideology. The Church in France insisted on interpreting the new democratic institutions as intrinsically unacceptable, as if contaminated with injustice from their very origin.

But this was a great error. Delivery from State-Churchdom, from Absolutism, from a Regime which was already "secularized" and morally corrupt, and a turning to greater freedom was a historical and moral necessity. Furthermore, political institutions such as the Bill of Rights, representative government, and political equality in their positive constitutional form are not absolutes. They are not metaphysical or theological truths. They must be judged according to their concrete service to that common good to be realized in and by an historical society. They are practical maxims restricting government, organizing it, legitimizing it.

Thus tolerance is a practical maxim, not a metaphysical absolute truth. It might at one period in history be based on a great respect for the individual conscience, even though that conscience might lead the individual to errors not found in the ages of faith. It might be based, at another time, on a judgment of prudence that tolerance is more favorable for the common good than is enforced conformity. It might be based, falsely, on theological indifferentism, that is the thesis that there is no true religion, that objective truth is a fiction; the State, then, would assume a neutrality that must eventually lead to a new quasi-religion, a Rousseauist *religion civile*. This neutrality can easily show the same disregard for the religious convictions of Christians as was shown in times of intolerance. But only this one kind of tolerance—that based on indifferentism—leads to evil consequences. The other bases of tolerance (since they represent non-trespass on the individual conscience) are unassailably right. In other words tolerance is a practical prudential maxim which takes into account the inviolability of consciences, the common good, and the interests of religion and public morality. Even the most tolerant or free state cannot afford absolute tolerance even toward "private" religion. For such absolute total tolerance would issue in anarchy just as surely as absolute intolerance issues in tyrannical totalitarianism.

Furthermore, the criticism by theologians and Popes of the wrong philosophy out of which decent political institutions historically sprang should not have led to the rejection of the positive institutions themselves.

The Belgian Charter of 1830 contained all the usual liberties, of religion, of conscience, of speech, of press, of assembly. The Cardinal Archbishop of Malines wrote to the National Congress which was deliberating upon the new constitution: "We do not want any privileges. Perfect liberty with all the consequences—that is what we want." Another Catholic publicist wrote: "The Liberty of all has become the condition of the Liberty of us Catholics." Another succinctly states: "To demand freedom of opinion does not mean to assert that all opinions are equally good. . . . Wherever a society has ceased to be unanimous in its religion, a positive religion ceases to be a social law and the State, the necessary expression of all the needs of that society, must restrict itself to protect the civil security of all citizens without discrimination." Gregory XVI, certainly a conservative, author of *"Mirari vos arbitramur,"* when informed by Cardinal Sterkx about the proposed Charter, declared that he had no feeling of uneasiness (*inquietude*) whatever about it. And the great Catholic leader, Deschamps, stated in 1856 that no pontifical utterance existed regarding any incompatibility of the Charter with Catholic doctrine and that there was not the slightest papal reservation about taking an unqualified oath to the Charter.[6] Similar views may be found among theologians and representative authors in Germany, France, Switzerland, the Netherlands and, of course, in England and the United States.

A certain diffidence against such utterances stems from a feeling that they might be only the products of clerical opportunism. Those who are thus suspicious will recall Montalembert's famous plea for the "Free Church in the Free State," which was later adopted by Cavour in his fight against the papal temporal sovereignty. Doubters will also remember our modern American principle of the absolute separation of Church and State. But it would be only common sense to say that the situation in a predominantly Catholic country

---

[6] Georges Goyau, *Catholicisme et Politique* (Paris, 1923), pp. 112 ff.

is a special case. If a people is universally Catholic, then it is quite clear that that fact will find reflection in its political life and in its laws, since the common good of such a people will contain religious elements. To demand under such conditions absolute separation of State and Church and a-religious public schools would be simply ridiculous.

In our days Spain is often cited as an example of Catholic opportunism in regard to the Bill of Rights. Yet religious freedom is guaranteed to all Spaniards with the qualification that religious dissidents from the State-religion shall have only the right to private worship, in simple prayerhouses. In the *Civiltà Catolica* Father Cavalli (in agreement with the great majority of the Spanish bishops) criticized this "legal" tolerance granted to the small Protestant groups (perhaps one thousandth of the population, half of them alien residents), saying that they deserved only a practical tolerance (*tolleranza di fatto*). But that is by no means an official opinion of ecclesiastical authority, as has been pointed out repeatedly by recognized theologians.[7] Also in contradiction to Cavalli's ideas is the weighty opinion of the late Archbishop McNicholas of Cincinnati that "if tomorrow the Catholics constituted a majority in our country, they would not seek a union of Church and State. They would then as now uphold the Constitution and all its amendments, recognizing the moral obligation imposed on all Catholics to observe and defend the Constitution and its amendments."[8] In this respect there are numerous testimonies of similar bearing from members of the hierarchy in many countries. The only State where a different attitude partly prevails is Spain. But Spanish practice is not to be identified either with Catholic doctrine or with universal Catholic practice.

St. Thomas defended the natural right of the parents to determine the education of their children, and asserted that to baptize the children of Jews or Saracens against the will of their parents represented a grave violation of this natural right. This right was positively recognized in the order to the civil governor of Rome by the latter's temporal ruler, Pope Benedict XIV in 1747, concerning

---

[7] *Vie Intellectuelle,* October, 1948, 294 ff.; Father Pribilla's essay on "Tolerance" in *Stimmen der Żeit,* April, 1949; Franz Thyssen in *De Situatie van de Protestanten in Spanje,* Utrecht, 1951; John Courtney Murray in *Theological Studies.*

[8] Wilfrid Parsons, *The First Freedom,* p. 83.

baptism of Jewish children. Children of Protestant parents cannot, therefore, be compelled by the State against the will of the parents to attend Catholic public schools.

A great confusion comes into this question of precedence of religion by a common misuse of the term "heretic." A heretic, as was said above, is a baptized and therefore lawful and *bona fide* member of the Church. The heretic makes, as the Greek word implies, a choice; he chooses on his own authority, in contradiction to ecclesiastical authority and tradition, certain parts of the whole body of doctrine, denying others or distorting and misinterpreting established parts of the doctrine. (The apostate repudiates the whole of the faith.) It is essential to the definition of a heretic that he formerly held the doctrine of the Church and that, then, he should have made a personal choice, substituting his private opinion on a doctrine of faith for that of the Church. It is essential, further, that he should stubbornly persist in his "private" choice despite being formally and thoroughly informed of the error of his opinions. Consequently, there is at least an implied supposition that he continues to hold to his wrong opinion in spite of better knowledge. It is essential also that the heretical opinion be externally manifested; otherwise it is a violation of the moral law of Faith known only to God. The external heresy is, therefore, punishable *in foro externo* because in this sense heresy is a violation of the social order and the established faith and doctrine of the Church in subordinating this doctrine and faith to one's own "private" faith and doctrine. What punishment is inflicted for the offense of heresy in canon law, for instance automatic excommunication or the latter after a formal trial or administrative procedure, or what civic consequences, if any, the sentence of ecclesiastical tribunal or administrative authority will have, are to a great degree a matter of changing positive law, both canon and secular. Pius XII in addressing the Roman Rota, the Supreme Court of Canon Law, stated that the offense of heresy cannot leave the Church indifferent. "Without doubt," said the Pope, "the tribunal charged with the defense of the Faith has in the course of centuries taken forms and methods not required by the nature of the things but nevertheless explainable in the light of particular circumstances. . . . If it may seem to the modern mind that the repression of delicts damaging to the Faith has, in past centuries, gone beyond just limitations, modern society shows generally in this respect insensibility and excessive indifference." The Pope then cited Lactantius (fourth century): "There is no need for violence and injustice, because religion cannot be imposed by force . . . therefore, nobody is kept with us against his will." He concludes: "If the Church after having gained certitude about the fact of heresy and apostasy punishes those guilty, for instance, by excommunicating them from the Church, then the Church remains strictly within the domain of its competencies, within its domestic jurisdiction, as it were" (*Allocution* of October 6, 1946). Let that stand by itself.

Now all citizens who are born Protestants, Old Catholics, etc., are by definition not heretics. The German language calls them more appropriately *"Andersgläubige."* The official liturgical and diplomatic language of the Church uses the term "dissident brethren" for individuals and Protestant "Congregations," "dissident oriental Churches," "dissident Churches."[9] They never subjectively and externally belonged to the Church, though their baptism might be valid; they have never had full knowledge of the full Faith and did not make a "choice." They are objectively "in error" though subjectively they are of sincere conscience. Any attempt to violate their conscience even by indirect political pressure would be objectively wrong. "A society in which the only means to make a career would be to be a Catholic would be a society in which the right of sincerity is menaced."[10] Furthermore, a Protestant as long as he sincerely believes in the divine truth of his religion is, according to Catholic doctrine, not even permitted deliberately to doubt it. This right of sincere conscience in matters which do not directly concern the secular public order, or, to use a more appropriate term, the temporal common good, has to be respected by State and Society. The "persecution" of heretics in the Middle Ages by the secular branch was a consequence of a practical identification of Church-"State"-Society, just as the persecution of Catholics in some American colonies was based on the identification of Society with a particular Christian sect. With the victory of the doctrine of two perfect societies, Church and State, (each sovereign and independent in its own field and thus separate, though cooperating for the same people who are members of both) it is quite clear that the personal rights of all, especially the

---

[9] M. F. Congar, O.P., *Divided Christendom,* 1939, Appendix IV.
[10] J. Leclerrg, *Vie Intellectuelle* (February, 1949), 109.

freedom of conscience, have to be protected against unjust and unconstitutional intervention. For the essentially secular State had, in matters of religion, no original competency after the Church was instituted by God. Even in a "Catholic" state the government has no right to violate the consciences of the religious minorities as long as their external acts do not disturb the public order.

It would be well, if all exaggerated claims of absolute rights of religion, speech, and press were dropped. Not even the most liberal democracy recognizes an absolute right of subversive conspiratorial groups to freedom of speech, press, and assembly. To change the constitution only the use of constitutional means is permissible. An absolute freedom of religion, of speech, of the press is recognized in no liberal democracy; but these rights, meaningful only in politically organized society, are always restricted by the values which are the substance of the constitution and the essential parts of the common good. Jefferson, in his rationalist optimism about the victory of truth and reason in free discussion with error and unreason, is only right as long as Robert's rules of parliamentary procedure are observed and as long as spurious fanaticism and passions do not drown the sincerity of open reason.

Much misunderstanding, and the fear that the Church and Catholics do not sincerely and without surreptitious mental reservation recognize the freedom of religion, of conscience, of speech and of the press stem, I think, from a lack of judicious information, for which indubitably not a few Catholic writers may be involuntarily responsible. Especially in the great struggle of the nineteenth century over the ideas of 1789, the conservative anti-revolutionary writers have contributed much to this misinformation, for they appeared to be, as they certainly wished, the standard-bearers of the official Catholic doctrine. Yet partisan as they were, propagandists more than scholars, they often were not only far off the mark but they lacked especially the judicious circumspection, the sensitivity for the fine nuances, the prudent comparison and evaluation of apparently superficially discordant doctrinal utterances which only a mind trained in scholastic distinctions can harmoniously unite into a balanced body of doctrine. On the other hand non-Catholics are full of old tales, remembrances of bygone times, of prejudices confirmed by the careless conservatives mentioned above.

In fine, let me state expressly that the French Declaration of the Rights of Man in 1789 voted by the bishops and by the clergy of

France and the modern Bills of Rights from that of 1688 to those of the new constitutions enacted in many countries after the Second World War contain no phrase, no word that expressly and necessarily implies a formal negation of Catholic doctrines. These documents hold that the freedom of religion from state intervention, that is, civic freedom of religion, not based on theological indifferentism, is best protected by political freedom; that freedom of the press is good in itself; that freedom of speech and of discussion is essential to the growth of individual persons as well as to the furtherance of the common good which, today, is not entrusted to the hands of a divine right monarch (always a suspect figure to serious Catholic theologians) but to the peoples who have grown mature. As to freedom of speech, let me recall the instruction of Pope Paul III on the rules of debate for the Council of Trent: that each member should have the right to full freedom of speech in all matters before the Council and that nobody should be silenced even if he uttered a manifest heresy, as long as he promised to submit to the final decisions of the Council.[11] Consequently the Church also accepts fully the human rights as declared in the Universal Declaration of December, 1948. No religious community has suffered more than the Church in the totalitarian states, because the latter better recognizes the Church's defense of human rights than do its detractors in the democracies.

VI

About the Church's attitude to the so-called socio-economic rights only a few words have to be said. These rights are, for the most part, the direct and indirect consequences of the basic organizational pattern of that particular historical socio-economic order which is called Capitalism, free enterprise system, free market economy, etc. Its rise from the pre-capitalist order was, as has been said above, simultaneous with democracy and a strongly individualistic conception of natural rights. In apparent contradiction to the democratic ideology and to the economically relevant personal rights was the situation of modern workers, that is, the earlier artisans and guildsmen, the earlier (before the liberation of the peasantry) serf or agricultural servant and the small craft-shop-owner, dispossessed by the rise of the factory system. They all appeared

---

[11] Theiner: Introductio XIX.

now with the legal mark of the free seller of labor-power as a quasi-commodity in the economic system. As was said above, they only theoretically were profiting from the new rights; actually their condition was that they only rarely could use these rights. Quite significantly they called themselves "Wage-slaves."

Thus the specific social problems of Capitalism arose. And society was much more conscious of them, because the tremendously increasing productivity of the socio-economic system offered a good chance to rid society of the phenomenon of mass-poverty in spite of the Ricardian-Malthusian pessimism which considered it as institutionally conditioned. Furthermore, the very ideological basis of democracy, of *weltzugewandte* piety, and the highly increased appreciation of personality opposed the blatant misery of the industrial masses caused by their ruthless exploitation. The Church was from the beginning somewhat suspicious and uncertain of this new order. It was inspired, *de facto,* though not by any intrinsic necessity, by a whole mixture of ideas and motives of which at least some, such as the threatening materialism of an acquisitive mind, the extreme individualism, and the attempt to substitute for the moral law the economic law, were unacceptable to the ethics of the Church. Furthermore, if we consider the high social mobility, the horrible industrial slums, the dissolution of the family, and the hardening of human relations in factory and slum, the destruction of the old order to which the pastoral methods of the Church had adapted themselves caused almost insuperable difficulties for pastoral work. Additional causes were the dissolution of traditional forms of social life, of manners and customs which, with their religious foundation, had earlier been strength and comfort in trials, the *"Vermassung"* and the wildness of leisure time pleasures, the impossibility of meeting mass-misery by the usual means of charity and of reaching pastorally the tempted souls in tremendously enlarged parishes. Faced with these almost insurmountable difficulties, some Catholics (a minority), politically alienated from democracy and romantically glorifying the medieval social and political order, out of protest against capitalism remained in an ineffective negative position. Others, troubled in their consciences and eager to help immediately, and not particularly concerned about ideologies, embarked on programs of social action. Their main argument was the mutual interdependence of morality and a decent living-standard: the old maxim of St. Thomas that without a minimum of

150

earthly goods, determined by the particular socio-economic civilization, the practice of the virtues would require ethical heroism which cannot be demanded generally nor for any length of time. After some discussion, which the history of Catholic social thought extensively reports, a general agreement was reached for furthering the self-help organizations of the workers (unions, co-operatives) and for imperiously demanding, on the basis of distributive justice, social legislation to suppress obvious social injustices, to prepare a more just social order, and above all to foster the self-help organization of the workers. All efforts and plans for overcoming the violent class-conflicts issuing *de facto* in the class-struggles so typical of the capitalist class-society should be encouraged. For example, practical cooperation of employers and employees for the particular common good of their industry and vocation within the framework of the national and even of the international common good should be developed.

The famous Social Encyclicals, "Rerum Novarum" of Leo XIII (1891) and "Quadragesimo Anno" of Pius XI, are not so much documents that originate and give initiative to these efforts; rather, they sanction or approve the efforts already successfully made, they encourage and they warn of extreme demands and wrong ways and means. Thus, they can only be appreciated against the background of the history of Catholic social action originating in the free initiative of laymen, workers, intellectuals and industrial entrepreneurs, and of priests and bishops motivated mainly by moral and pastoral reasons.

Catholic social thought and action, based firmly on theology and on natural law approved by the supreme authority, and reliably directed by it, has thus recognized for many decades that all social action aims at the restoration and preservation of the human personality and dignity of the worker as man, as a Christian, and as citizen, in the factory, in the political community, in "society." While equally rejecting Marxism and the concept of the absolute rights of private property, Catholic social thought stresses the private and the social character of property, and demands the "redemption of the proletariat by a wide distribution of industrial property and the introduction of institutions which fulfill for the individual, but especially for the family, the main property-function, namely: secure liberty and social security. It is the duty of the State, by legislative intervention and by an active economic policy, so to arrange the social order that the demands of social and distributive justice in our society may be realized under full realization of the rights of the workers and of other classes such as the family-farmer, the small businessman and the independent craftsman. The right to associate freely in trade unions, the right to a just wage which will include the right to a family-wage and a decent living-standard, and finally, the right to strike, if that is the only means to realize these rights, were all recognized long before actual legislation acknowledged them. Similarly the state, in the interest of the common good, is strictly obliged to realize social justice. All have a right to participate in the common good on the basis, first, of their dignity as men and citizens, and then according to their own contribution to it in their various vocations and professions. If a whole class or group by reason of the malfunctioning of the (free) social order of the market society does not participate according to its functional contribution in the common good, then the state has by corrective legislation the duty to make the social order work justly. The state should not violate the principle of subsidiarity, but should put at the disposal of the injured groups such social institutions as credit unions, which they may administer themselves.

Catholic social thought early recognized the right to social security in its various aspects. Much of the modern social security legislation in many countries has been developed, if not always under the initiative of Catholic social reformers, always at least with their fervent support. There is not a single human right enumerated in Articles 22 to 28 of the Universal Declaration which Catholic social reformers, when it was in their power, had not already put in legal form many decades ago, in national laws and constitutions. Proof of that is that the modern constitutions which contain more elaborated catalogs of social and economic rights, the Weimar constitution of 1919, the French and the Italian constitutions of 1946 and 1948, the Bonn Constitution of 1949 of Western Germany, have all been established under the decisive influence of the Christian democratic parties, "the democratic parties of Christian inspiration," whose political programs are profoundly influenced by the traditional ideals of Catholic social thought. What is especially meritorious in these programs is a zealous defense of free social action of social groups, wherever they satisfactorily can realize justice, as against a so-called social progress ideology which wants to charge the administrative State with all these tasks, making it a bureaucratic care-for-everything State (*Versorgungstaat*). Characteristic, furthermore, is its recognition of the rights of groups (the family, the religious community, the universities and the free schools, of the municipalities), in other words, of a kind of social federalism somewhat akin to Jeffersonian ideas and hostile equally to *laissez-faire* individualism and to those Marxist ideas of socialist uniformity and mass-collectivism which prepare for the ascendancy of the totalitarian state.

In the struggle for an effective bill of human rights honest men everywhere will find—and will be glad to do so—a mighty ally in the Church. Catholics will find in this struggle their inspiration in the Faith; honest men, in the social doctrine of the Church which being based also on the Natural Law common to all men, can give by its long and tried experience and practically proven prudence, powerful support to the "recognition of the inherent dignity of all members of the human family (as) the foundation of freedom, justice and peace in the World" (Preamble of the Universal Declaration).

VII

The New Situation of Continental Protestantism After World War II

by Karl Thieme

Non-Catholic Christians of the Occident have two names by which they characterize themselves: they have used the name 'Protestants' ever since their representatives at the Diet of Spires (1529) protested against the majority's resolution to defer any further change in religion to the decision of a general council. Thus, 'Protestants' are revolutionists against the Roman Vicar of Christ, and 'Protestantism' is in itself a negation. As 'Evangelicals,' however, they indicate what they would insist is the basis of their creed, God's Word in the New Testament.

In the beginning also this word 'Evangelical' had an aggressive sense: the pure evangel, as Luther understood it, was contrasted with an alleged corruption of the Gospel by the human additions of Roman tradition. But beginning with the Pietist movement in the seventeenth century, apart from the polemical sense of the word 'Evangelical,' there arose in Europe an irenic understanding of it. Today it may be said that among those who try to be really Evangelical Christians there is an ever increasing number who question whether Luther's 'pure' Evangel is really the unshortened fullness of the Gospel. This question implies another: Is it really possible to understand the Word of God without listening to the Catholic tradition as its exegesis?

It is remarkable that these questions are now asked precisely in those countries—Luther's Germany and Calvin's France—in which the ecclesiastical schism of the sixteenth century arose; that in the same countries also the mutual Christian brotherhood—feeling of Evangelicals and Catholics, notwithstanding a continuing doctrinal separation, is most accentuated and at work. For instance it is no mere formality that there was an Evangelical address to the first postwar 'Catholic Days' (1948) at Mainz, (1949) at Bochum, (1950) at Passau, and a Catholic one to the 'Evangelical Church Days' (1949) at Hannover, (1950) at Essen, and (1951) at Berlin.

There are two principal reasons for this new development. We may appreciate the first if we ask where, in Europe, the old type of Protestantism is still strongest. The answer, of course, is, in Sweden with its Lutheranism and in Switzerland with its Calvinism, that is, in the two countries where there was no common suffering of all believers in the revealed God (Jews, Catholics and Protestants), no persecution of them by the enemies of God and men. It was common suffering in this persecution and mutual help in the face of it that brought closer the separated Christian brethren in Germany, France, Holland and elsewhere. After the War the displacement of millions of Catholics and Protestants from the eastern lands had a similar effect, although this movement also occasioned much friction. A second reason, more important in matters of principle, is this: the study of Holy Scripture and of the literature of the apostolic and patristic age produced a new understanding of the institutional and charismatic, the static and the dynamic foundations of Christian life, i.e. of the Church and her ministry, hierarchic and prophetic. In discussing these points no attempt will be made to treat each group and country individually. The emphasis will be upon the political, sociological and theological aspects of ecclesiastical developments in the German fatherland of Protestantism, and this will be followed by some observations about the other Protestant communities of the European continent and about the 'Oecumene'.

The great change of the last decades is the weakening of belief in human reason, in science and in progress, along with the all but complete disappearance of the religious liberalism nourished by this belief. Only radical Marxism still asserts the absolutely scientific truth of its system, thereby discrediting science the more. The mass of bourgeois and even a great number of the intelligentsia no longer require scientific proof of religion or *Weltanschauung*. Now they examine its capacity to satisfy the psychological or social needs of mankind or seek its validity in the life and moral behavior of its believers. This change presents new opportunities and new dangers to religion. Scientific apologetics have lost the interest they commanded fifty years ago. The bitter controversy with rationalism has dwindled away and the battle cry of 'progress' makes little impression. But along with the superficial views of 'objective truth' the more profound concept of it is fading, and men readily think that any comforting belief may be right. Yesterday their faith may have been the Nazi program, succeeded by occult teaching and later perhaps by a psychological system, and tomorrow it may embrace another political savior. That is the situation in all of Europe, with, of course, some differences between more sceptical nations such as the Italians, French, Swiss, Netherlanders and Scandinavians, and those more inclined to faith even in the midst of their disillusion, such as the Germans, the Spaniards and the English as well. To the anxious observer such is the spiritual world in which the great drama of modern Protestant Christianity develops.

The constitutions and movements of the continental Protestant churches vary considerably. Relatively the most conservative is the Swedish Lutheran Church (7 millions) and its 'bishops' and the Archbishop of Upsala, bound by the legislation of the state; the most progressive is the 'Hervormed' Calvinist Church of the Netherlands (more than 3 millions) with a new synodal constitution which defines the task of Christ's Church as first, the continuation of the Lord's discourse with the people of Israel, secondly the preaching of the gospel to the heathen and, third and last, ministering to the people of the Netherlands.

The largest number of Protestants within one territory are the Germans. In the Evangelical Church in Germany (*Evangelische Kirche in Deutschland, EKiD*) twenty-seven regional churches, each with its special character, are united. Including the separated Bremen Church their adherents number 39,800,000. At Eisenach, below the Wartburg, where Luther translated the Bible, EKiD on July 13, 1948, adopted a constitution (*Grundordnung*), which provides for a federalist organization, midway between a federation of churches analogous to the United Nations and such a federal state as the United States. Like a federal state EKiD has a plurality of governing organisms:

1. Up to 80% of the "Synode," corresponding to a House of Representatives, is elected by the (directly elected) member church synods;
2. In the Conference of the Churches, corresponding to a senate,

every member-church has one delegate, (*not elected by the people*) but nominated by the government of this member-church;
3. The 'Council of the EKiD,' corresponding to a cabinet, is composed of members chosen by the "Synode" and the Conference of the Churches together.

The President of this Council, and thus of EKiD as a whole, is Bishop Otto Dibelius of Berlin, author of *The Century of the Church* (1930). Dibelius, minister at the Potsdam Garrison Church when Hindenburg and Hitler celebrated there the beginning of the Third Reich (March 21, 1933), was later on a vigorous opponent of Nazi terrorism. The Vice-President is Bishop Hans Lilje, Hannover, former Secretary of the Christian Students Union and well-known writer on religious subjects. Chief of EKiD's foreign relations ministry ('*Kirchliches Aussenamt*') is Martin Niemoeller, former submarine captain, critic of Hitler and concentration camp prisoner, and now President of the Hessian church at Wiesbaden. Since the dismissal of the "catholicizing" Propst, Hans Asmussen, Kirchenrat Heinz Brunotte, Hannover, a friend of Lilje, has been the chief of its chancellery. Analogous to a federal state in all these things, the EKiD nevertheless corresponds to a federation of states by reason of a further element of the constitution. Whenever there is presented to the Synode a church law involving 'confessional' difficulties for a group of her constituent confessions, (Lutherans, Calvinists, or *evangelisch-unierte*, United Evangelicals, that is, members of churches where Lutherans and Calvinists have been united since 1817), a special provision goes into operation. The constituent groups are divided into the three 'conventions' (Konvente) and each one of them has a right of veto. This arrangement was necessary because the Lutherans otherwise would be able to decide every issue. In the EKiD there are thirteen Lutheran regional churches (over 20,000,000 people), twelve United churches (over 19,000,000 people), and two Reformed (Calvinist) churches (400,000).

Prior to the establishment of EKiD the Lutherans had formed their own organization, the United Evangelical Lutheran Church of Germany (*Vereinigte Evangelische Lutheranische Kirche Deutschlands, VELKD*), mainly centered in Franconia, Bavaria (around Nuremberg) and in Hannover, but without the participation of the Lutheran churches of Wurttemberg, Oldenburg, Lübeck and Eutin. The members of VELKD, in close liaison with world Lutheranism, recognize only this Lutheran community as the church, united under one Bishop, Meiser of Munich, in one common faith expressed in the *Augustana* (the Protestant confession before the Augsburg Diet of 1530), and in one liturgy, the *Hymn Book of the Evangelical Church*. In their view EKiD is merely an organization for common Protestant church policy and, consequently, without doctrinal authority. In the Lutheran ranks, the 'right wing' of German Protestantism, one may find a man such as Hermann Sasse, former editor of the Evangelical Church Year Book, an opponent of Hitler and Erlangen professor of theology. Sasse quit the Bavarian Lutheran Church because it was not Lutheran enough. He then joined the more "orthodox" little group of *Alt Lutheraner,* connected with the Missouri Synod.

The revolutionary tendencies of the 'left wing' of German Protestantism are political rather than doctrinal. Its core is the Brethren Councils (Bruderräte), united in a *Reichsbruderrat* with Martin Niemoeller as President and Pfarrer Mochalsky of Darmstadt as Secretary. These Brethren Councils had their origin in 1933-34 when Hitler's German Christians drove out the old church governments of northern and central Germany. Under Reichsbishop Müller new bishops of doubtful character were imposed on the churches. In the face of this campaign pastors and laymen formed these voluntary Brethren Councils. These, assuming emergency functions of church government for the non-German, or better, anti-Müller, Christians, examined and installed pastors. They retained these functions until new legitimate church authorities were set up after Hitler's defeat.

The churches of Bavaria, Wurttemburg, Baden, Hannover and Westphalia remained 'intact,' that is, they did not suffer from the imposition of German Christian leaders. In these areas the Brethren Councils did not take over the government of the Church. Instead, they sought to be the conscience of the Church. This involved the criticism of compromising arrangements made between their bishops and Hitler or his Gauleiters. Since the meeting at Eisenach, these *Bruderräte* aspire to an analogous function, which they call the prophetic watchman's ministry of the Church. This means a constant prayerful vigilance to the end that EKiD really becomes a confessing Church—"not a Church, asleep in its security. *Ecclesia semper reformanda est.*"[1]

The gulf between the typical Lutherans and the leaders of the Brethren Councils is not at all a matter of fundamentalist and liberal tendencies. The religious liberalism of men like Harnack is all but dead in Germany. So is its counterpart—apologetic conservatism. German Protestant ministers no longer risk their appointments, as Traub did forty years ago, by discussing such a question as whether Christ was really born of a Virgin. In public almost no one denies it. Today their discussions center around whether it is more important jointly to confess the Augsburg Confession or jointly to confess whatever appears to be the true Christian answer to actual public questions. These might include a confession against German remilitarization or against a form of anti-semitism and in favor of Christians protecting Jewish cemeteries.

This, of course, involves two meanings of confessions: one involves strict adhesion to the complex of traditional articles of Christian faith; the other is the act of professing whatever appears to be the divine order for the here and now and of rejecting contemporary temptations, for example, the totalitarian state, militarism and lack of social responsibility.

Those who insist upon the importance of unequivocal confession of the traditional Christian faith, especially the Lutherans, are primarily concerned to clarify the objective truth of revelation held in common. Like the Catholics they see no possibility of eucharistic communion with Calvinists who deny Christ's corporal presence under the tangible species of bread and wine. On the other hand, they tend to a certain Lutheran quietism, as their opponents say. This involves an assurance of salvation without works, a trust in vested rights and goods, spiritual as well as material.

It is precisely this attitude that is a red tag to the confessing churchmen, many of them Calvinists—or Crypto-Calvinists as strict Lutherans would say. These confessing churchmen emphasize present rather than past decisions. In 1934 they believed that it was more important to issue the Theological Declaration of Barmen in defense of the Church's autonomy, attacked by the German Christians, than to repeat the Augsburg Confession, which no one had attacked at that time. Point 5 of this Declaration was the most

---

[1] Promulgation of the Brethren Council, Oct. 16, 1948, in *Herder Korrespondenz*, III, p. 233.

anti-hitlerian. This damned as heresy the opinion that the state should provide the exclusive and total organization of human life, and that as a consequence the state thus fulfills the mission of the Church.[2] As an evidence of the Brethren Council's influence on the constitution of EKiD, its preamble refers to the Barmen Declaration after the Apostles', Nicene and Athanasian creeds and various confessions of the sixteenth century.[3]

These confessing churchmen fear that the strict confessionalists will be content with the mechanical repetition of the old confessions and fail to resist Satan in his current masquerade. The confessionalists, on the other hand, fear that the confessing churchmen may eventually forget and even sacrifice the heritage of tradition. This is not exclusively a matter of eucharistic doctrine, the principle point of Lutheran-Calvinist controversy. The fear extends to other points and, indeed, the fear has, to some extent, been justified. While Lutherans emphasize the claim that they and the Calvinists are members of great international communities of genuinely common faith, they also insist that the members of the churches of the Prussian Union of 1817 have no really common confessional basis with anyone else on this earth. The Lutherans have proposed that this group should divide into its constituent elements, the small flock of Calvinists and the overwhelming majority of Lutherans, who would then assume together with those of VELKD the absolute domination of EKiD.

This Lutheran appeal failed. Indeed on February 20, 1951, Bishop Meiser, "with sorrow, even confounded," as he wrote, had to protest against the formal reconstitution of the Evangelical Church of the Old Prussian Union. This is a federal church with six member churches under Bishop Dibelius. The members are Rhineland, Westphalia, Berlin-Brandenburg, North Saxony, Pomerania and Silesia—the churchmen of East Prussia having been wiped out. The reconstitution of this Union was the fruit of a long internal and external struggle. Externally the small but vigorous Reformed Church of North West Germany under President Middendorf fought, partly by formal non-cooperation with EKiD, against the expulsion of the Reformed elements from ecclesiastical community with the Lutherans. The dissolution of the Union would

---

[2] *Herder Korrespondenz*, II, pp. 266 ff.
[3] *Herder Korrespondenz*, II, pp. 263 ff., 342, 397 f., 514 ff.

have given the Lutherans an overwhelming supremacy in EKiD. Internally, the preservation of the Union was made possible by the Lutheran-born "Brethren Council" adherents who held mutual communion services even with those Calvinist brethren who do not believe in Christ's corporeal presence. Their argument in this matter is that doctrinal differences should demarcate only theological schools and not the churches. The new prospects of common ground in understanding the gospel seem more important to them than the ancient doctrinal conflict. In their own opinion they have not fallen into the doctrinal indifferentism from which the Union arose in 1817. In the restoration of the Union in 1950 they profess to anticipate a genuine church of the future. Dr. Heinemann, the president of the EKiD's Synod, and former cabinet minister under Adenauer, has argued that the Lutherans themselves, for example, Althaus, Stauffer and Jeremias disagree on fundamental questions without forming separate churches.

The Lutheran answer to this argues that the nonconfessionalism of Karl Barth has actually begun to undermine the sacrament of baptism. In a basic attack on "theologians of Niemoeller's type," Asmussen reproached them for placing man's temporal welfare ahead of eternal salvation, for preaching a new millenarianism. That this charge has some basis may be seen in Niemoeller's proposal to base his preaching of the gospel on the fact that modern men no longer ask for a merciful God but for a merciful neighbor.

Here the confessional controversy of German Protestantism (and of French as well) reaches political ground. As a rule the confessionalists are conservatives in politics, in commitments to the military defense of western civilization and in economics. On the last subject the confessionalists would be divided: one group approaches the neo-liberalism of Röpke and Hayek, without publicly supporting the anti-collectivist slogans of those spokesmen; the other group calls loudly for social reform, as, for example, Emil Brunner has done in *Gerechtigkeit* (Justice), the manifesto of moderate social reform for continental European Protestantism. The "confessors" on the other hand seriously sympathize with Marxian Socialism (politically, not philosophically) and are sharply opposed to any church propaganda for a capitalistic crusade against Soviet Russia. Heinemann and Niemoeller argue for Germany's unarmed neutralization between East and West. These men, and Catholics of similar views, for example the famous poet and opponent of Hitler,

Reinhold Schneider, are not "fellow travellers." A distinction must be made between a very small group around the well-known Swiss theologian Karl Barth, whose influence is far greater on foreign than on Swiss churches, and the rank and file of Brethren-Council Christians on the other.

Even Barth is no crypto-communist. Asmussen has reproached him for explicitly defending the total state.[4] This is going too far. At any rate Barth has several times denied that he ever did so. But he did praise Stalin as "a remarkable thinker," a man whose "high human stature" ("Format") cannot be confused with mere charlatans like Hitler, Goering, etc. He has said that for the Christian solution of economic problems the choice is limited to socialist reforms. Among these the Christian must choose the most efficient judged on the basis of the greatest social justice. This means that the solution need not imply even an assurance that man will not have to act against his conscience.

The practical consequence of this attitude in matters of Church policy may be seen in the fact that Karl Barth's authority induced the Hungarian Calvinists to conform with the Hungarian Communist government. The Hungarian Calvinists broke the common Christian front in defense of confessional schools against the state's usurpation. They reproached Cardinal Mindszenty for making a "political," not a religious, fight. Their Bishop, Bereczky, who was elected as a result of Barth's direct influence, opposed the Toronto declaration about Korea (1950). Thus in August 1951 he appeared at the World Churches Assembly only as an observer and not as a member.

Barth himself at Herborn (March, 1951) demanded for Germany "the bold course of unarmed neutrality." But even there, amidst seventy of his friends and followers, no full agreement was reached. Relatively few progressive German Protestants share Barth's naive views about Stalin and about Bolshevism as the national "temple-building of the awakened Slav race," with "radical Marxism" as the temple's frontispiece.[5] It is not Soviet sympathy, but an entirely understandable antipathy to anything suggesting Hitler's "Swastika Crusade" against the East, that gathers support among German Protestants (and others) for Niemoeller's and

---

[4] *Ibid.*, IV, p. 85.
[5] *Dogmatik,* III, 3, 126.

Heinemann's unequivocal and Schumacher's equivocal fight against remilitarization. Even those who have freed themselves of wishful thinking and reluctantly recognize the necessity of military preparations fear the consequences of a restoration of militarism. The bases for their fear are very real in a country where hundreds of thousands of former professional soldiers await their new day. Its advent may involve a new fascism, a totalitarianism of the right as the only weapon against Bolshevism, the totalitarianism of the left. The Germans have been told in the course of "reeducation" by the allies that they should have resisted Hitler in the early days, before it was too late. Thus, they distrust all propaganda for an ideological union against the East, even when it is presented in the name of world brotherhood. In addition, there is a confessional distrust of America's indifferentist humanitarianism, similar to the distrust Father J. LaFarge expressed in *America* (January 27, 1951).

The political decisions of German Protestants about defense are complicated by questions about Germany's national destiny. Before the Anschluss with Austria, the Protestants with their two-thirds majority dominated the Reich and had a disproportionate percentage of the leading positions in politics, cultural activities (especially the universities) and economics. Today in the west German Federal Republic they are about one-half of the population and feel that they have been supplanted by the Catholics who have a superior political organization dating from Catholic minority days. Thus, as Niemoeller has frankly said, even considerations of confessional politics urge the German Protestants to refrain from any action which might finally divide Germany into western and eastern satellite states. When Niemoeller was asked for his opinion about a western German state, he indicated his opposition, for he believed that it would mean a Russian eastern German state as well. The German Catholic bishops did not see matters in that light. This difference of approach caused Niemoeller (1949) to describe the Western state as "conceived in the Vatican and born in Washington." Further, Niemoeller, disregarding the difference between western-free and eastern-manipulated elections, has said that Adenauer's legitimacy was as insubstantial as that of Eastern Germany's chancellor, Grotewohl.

Niemoeller, of course, failed to consider that the Protestant bishops in the so-called "intact churches" of southern Germany replied affirmatively to the question of the Allied Governments:

Shall we form a German state out of the Laender which we occupy? The reply, then, was not made on a confessional basis but according to one's generation, generations more expressive of character than of years. Niemoeller and his Brethren-Council friends are typically young and dynamic men, ready to risk all in order to gain still more. The bishops of the "intact churches" in communities which have not experienced revolution are as a rule older men and of a more static character. As they see it, their ministry is to keep the community in its traditional ways, to examine and judge suggested changes and not to jeopardize the church. Until 1933 men such as these held the higher church positions in Protestant Germany and almost everywhere in the world. In northern and central Germany they were then excluded from office. The ensuing struggle with Hitler's German Christians was conducted not by the old church leaders but by the dynamic non-legalistic type which formed the emergency church government, the brethren councils. After 1945 these men were gradually supplanted by the old leaders. "The old administrative experts won the victory over the theologians," said Asmussen. His old friend and recent opponent, Niemoeller, was almost the only one of the "young" confessors to hold an outstanding position in EKiD.

This is no mere triumph of a managerial ruse over harmless idealists. The prophetical aspirations of the latter are so high that they make impossible the normal functioning of a large organization, especially when it is ceaselessly disturbed by the quarrels of uncompromising theologians.

The basic aspects of this conflict are revealed in the Conference Report, *Evangelische Selbstprüfung,* which expresses the views of the most outstanding German supporters of Barth. In the well-known monthly, *Die Wandlung,* some radical Protestant critics of the church electoral laws go even farther than the Barthians. These radicals criticized the fact that the active, that is, practising church members favored the church electoral laws. The latter provision retains some element of hierarchical order, for it approaches the belief that the church should be governed according to its objective traditions and not according to the subjective will of its members. The criticism advanced by the Barthians runs as follows: "These laws produce two classes within the church: passive members and active ones. The passive members have the right to pay contributions, the active ones to spend them. . . . Thus is created the standardized church-Christian, the orthodox Pietist, who is the sole and dominant force in EKiD today, both in the ranks of clergy and laity, in church government and in parishes, who conscientiously maintain this exclusivism."

This criticism from the left ("The Church is too hierarchical") is answered by Asmussen's criticism from the right: "The structure of ministration is as sick as it was before 1933" because ministration was exclusively considered as the task of preaching instead of the gift of salvation. "Prophet to the right, prophet to the left, the secular between them," as Goethe put it. The poor church counsellor has a difficult task in steering his ship through the wild waves of our time.

Behind the sociological conflict of static and dynamic types, old and young, jurist and theologian, Asmussen's remark reveals the more profound ecclesiastical contradiction between the hierarchic and prophetic conceptions of the church's ministry and the two types of ecclesiastical structure corresponding to them.

The head of the French Reformed Church of Basle, Jean-Louis Leuba, an editor of the French quarterly, *Verbum Caro,* does not view this contradiction as a necessary one. In his book *Institution and Event* (Paris, 1950)—hierarchical institution and prophetical event—he attempted to show the difference between and the unity of the two modes of Divine operation as expressed in the New Testament. God acts through St. Peter and the Apostles as through an "institution which He established for all time, whereas He acts through St. Paul and later men of the spirit as through 'events' which His Spirit has frequently roused up in the Church's history." Leuba's argument proceeds to emphasize that the twelve Apostles recognized Paul's ministry as not derived from theirs (Galatians, 2, 9. they "gave to me . . . the right hand of fellowship" instead of "laying their hands upon him," as was done in the case of Stephen and all the other members of the hierarchic ministry). Paul, himself, recognized the Twelve's apostolate, for, as he wrote, without their consent I "had run in vain," Gal. 2, 2. Thus, on the basis of the New Testament Leuba believes that the two modes of Divine operation are united. But to distinguish his position from the Catholic one he has to assert that subordination "in potestate suprema et regimine," as defined by Innocent X, is a Romanist error, the complete subordination of St. Paul to St. Peter, the very reverse of the usual error of Protestantism, which recognizes only the Pauline charismatic or prophetic ministry.

Those who hold this error, and they are the overwhelming majority of continental Protestants, are not at all obliged to acknowledge hierarchical institution. For them every visible organism of the church is and remains, as for Luther himself, a "secular thing," designed to secure the undisturbed prophetical preaching of the pure Gospel. In their preaching, too, they prefer a "profane" language, wherever this will not be too shocking for a tradition-bound flock.

Here they often encounter opposition, not only from older people but from the young who look more for liturgical elevation and priestly consolation of their hearts than for the prophetical admonition of their intellects. Organized in the small but energetic Berneuchen Movement, so called because many years ago its members met in the former monastery at Berneuchen, Brandenburg, this last tendency has had its greatest influence in the liturgy and church music. This revival of ancient choral singing is possibly the most important religious development in continental Protestantism. It is the popular form of a Christian revival, which in its theological expression is not accessible to the masses and in its expression in sermons is frequently more forbidding than attractive. By singing the old sharp and vigorous community songs of the sixteenth and seventeenth centuries in place of the sentimental and egocentric melodies and texts of the succeeding centuries, the Protestant young people acquire a new sense of the church *"kirchliches Selbstbewusstsein."* The significance of this has not been sufficiently appreciated, though it increases as every new generation learns these songs.

The importance of this choral singing was revealed at the Evangelical Church Days, especially that in Ber'in in 1951, when hundreds of thousands, singing together, expressed their faith and hope in God (and their protest against Bolshevik terror). Along with knowledge of the Bible, and psychologically even more important, choral singing is Evangelical Christianity's best weapon for her adherents in this century of the concentration camp. These two are the points on which even the self-critical Protestant feels superior to the Catholic, whose youth movement has so far been unable to introduce its fine *'Kirchenlied'* or a similar hymn book into all the German dioceses.

The same multiple schism, manifest in EKiD, is to be observed in the Amsterdam Oecumene. The early stages of this movement towards the federation of the churches, in the days of the leadership of the Swedish Archbishop Soederblom and the Stockholm Conference (1925), were considered to be pro-Catholic in tendency. Later, notably under General-Secretary Visser t'Hooft (Netherlands), the influence of radical Protestantism increased. As a result of this development, even Karl Barth, a most vigorous opponent of its initial direction, returned from the Amsterdam Conference (1948), as, to use his own words, a "converted oecumenic man." Possibly it would be more exact to say that he was the man who all but converted the oecumene to his conception of the church as a purely profane "Community of Christians, renouncing all hierarchical claims derived from the Incarnation and renouncing the authority delegated by Christ to the Apostles."

Thus, there has been a confluence of the anti-papal feelings of the majority of American Protestants and British non-conformists and of the rooted distrust of any Catholicizing tendency among the great majority of continental evangelicals, especially in Switzerland, the Netherlands and Germany. Nor, I fear, is the dominance of this tendency likely to be short-lived. It is no mere accident that the evangelicals are represented on the World-Churches-Council by Niemoeller. The latter, very likely because in his concentration-camp period he came very close to the Catholic Church, is now the most strenuous enemy of whatever appears to him as "political Catholicism." After the common Christian resistance to the Nazi occupation, the persistence of the old form of Huguenotism in France, as of the Waldensians in Italy, is not matter for surprise. It is more astonishing that a similar spirit appears even in the Netherlands. In 1950 the Netherlands Reformed General Synod issued a Pastoral Letter concerning its relations with the Catholic Church. Instead of revealing evidence of friendly discussion between Catholic and Reformed theologians, the Letter largely repeated the old slogans of "political anti-Catholicism" along with some, at best, questionable affirmations of serious theological controversy. To this letter, professors of the Catholic University of Nymwegen wrote a reply (Utrecht, 1950), which even many ordinary Calvinists recognized to be superior to the attack.

Alongside this overwhelming left wing of Continental Evangelical Christianity, there is the center composed of German and Scandinavian Lutherans. In their outlook they are torn between their attachment to traditional Catholic remnants in their doctrine and the no-less traditional sentiment of anti-Catholic protest. In this division of feelings they are, of course, true to Luther. The right-wing of the oecumene consists of Anglicans, small high-Church groups and the Orthodox. These with their sacramental and hier-archical conception of the church's ministry have no concentrated body of adherents on the Continent west of the iron curtain. The large majority of the members of any of the Continental Evangelical Churches or free churches approve the decisively Protestant tendency of Barth and Niemoeller in matters of church policy, even where there are disagreements about the latter's political opinions.

But there is also a significant minority seriously concerned with the improvement of inter-confessional relations. Where this concern takes a primarily political form, as in Germany, these people join or favor the great Christian political party of Western Germany (the Christian Democratic Union), consisting of Catholics and Prot-estants. Although the voting strength of the CDU is largely drawn from the Catholics, there is complete religious equality in the party. Where their concern is a moral one, they join the "Societies for the cooperation of Christians and Jews" (analogous to the American Councils). Through these organizations they attempt to uproot anti-Semitic, anti-Catholic and anti-Protestant prejudice and to pre-vent a re-appearance of the hatreds sowed by Hitler. Where they are particularly eager for religious peace or, even, eventual reunion of the separated brethren in Christ, they often join the "Una Sancta Movement," which calls for a "creative peace between the Christian Confessional Communities." Apart from this popular movement, there have been serious conversations, approved by EKiD's authori-ties and the Holy See. In these meetings responsible Protestant and Catholic theologians frankly discussed the serious differences con-cerning faith and order, which separate the Evangelical and Catho-lic communities. Possibly there has not been such serious and re-sponsible discussions since the seventeenth century correspondence of Leibniz and Bossuet.

The impulse to these exchanges and meetings came from the persecution which they shared. But the fruitfulness of this new con-frontation is also derived from the reconsideration of their respective traditions. The memory of their common suffering will fade in time; new grievances and reawakened mistrust may erode the sense of community and the impetus for common action. On the other hand, the steadily progressing study of religious fundamentals in both camps has produced a recognition of the fact that their separation is not so easily legitimized as the preceding generation believed.

There are some Protestants (and even more Catholics) who believe that the reunion of Protestants and Catholics will be decisively assisted by a new and better understanding of Luther. This apparently was the hope of the late Protestant scholar, Dr. K. A. Meissinger, who founded in Munich an Institute for Reformation Research. He was happy to write a preface to a book entitled *Agreement on Luther*, by the Catholic Balling, which popularized the findings of the Catholic historians, Lortz and Herte, who, in criticizing traditional Catholic views of Luther as oversimplified and partisan, have done an important revisionist work. Similarly, Meissinger dealt with "Luther oekumenisch," first published in the Catholic *Hochland* and later in a collected volume, *For Conversation Between the Confessions* (Munich, 1940). This literature has had but a weak echo among the rank and file of Protestants. Even the well-informed (but rather Liberal) Protestant church-historian, H. Hermelink (Tübingen) rejects this new Catholic approach to Luther. "Lortz," he said, "was too favorably treated by Evangelical criticism."[6] As long as Catholics regard Luther as a heretic and not as a prophet, Hermelink finds their viewpoint unacceptable, even when they recognize the genius of Luther and see at least, in part, the foundations of his grievances in the abuses of the late medieval Church.

In the long run the discussion about Luther returns to a discussion of Holy Scripture. Hermelink has also perceived this and has quoted the Catholic, Bishop Besson: "Our fathers divided over the Bible and under the Bible we shall unite again." This position is greatly reenforced by reading the leading scholars of the New Testament and Early Church History. For more than thirty years the Biblical doctrine of the Church has irresistibly revealed itself to serious investigation as fundamentally Catholic. As early as 1929, in a famous little book *Die kirche* (republished in Theological Tracts, Munich, 1950) Erik Peterson, Protestant Professor at Bonn, con-

---

[6] *Katholizismus und Protestantismus im Gerpräch um die Una Sancta* (Stuttgart, 1949), p. 45.

verted to Catholicism in 1930, stated that the detailed findings of his colleagues, Holl, Kattenbusch, Loofs, and even Lietzmann, converged on a recognition of the legitimacy of the Roman Church.

This development has been accentuated by the studies of such men as Oscar Cullmann (Basle) on the early Christian Credo and service, Markus Barth on the apostles as eye-witnesses (Zurich, 1946), Heinrich Schlier on the uninterrupted line of tradition from the last Pauline to the first Clementine Epistle, and last but not least, J.-L. Leuba, whose work has already been mentioned.

Not only the ecclesiological but also the soteriological content of the New Testament is seen by some Lutheran theologians in a sense different from that of Luther; Max Lackmann (1949) in an exegesis of St. James' Epistle explicitly criticized Luther's "faith alone" and won some agreement. Even the Lutheran Bishop, W. Stählin (Oldenburg) formally rejected the Lutheran "alone," that is, "by faith alone," "the Holy Scriptures alone."[7]

The reader who restricted himself to those books would have the impression that there was a general theological return of the Evangelical Christians to Catholic positions. This would be very wide of the mark. Most of those authors are isolated scholars or vigorously resisted outsiders, including Bishop Stählin in his own church, for the majority of Lutheran pastors are more or less his open adversaries. When, for example, a Protestant pastor recognized the authority of St. Peter, as R. Baumann did in *Das Petrus Bekenntnis und Schlüssel*, he lost his office and had to undergo trial in accord with the new doctrinal and disciplinary constitution, which his Church, the Lutheran Church of Wurtemberg, had adopted.

Alongside this neo-conservative trend in New Testament exegesis there is a kind of liberal revival. Its spokesman is Rudolf Bultmann, who seeks to free the Gospel from its alleged mythological elements, and has assigned to himself the task of demythologizing it (*Entmythologisierung*). He does this in agreement with the rationalist scheme of proclaiming all facts which present difficulties for human belief as mythological fictions. This trend differs from earlier liberalism in one important respect. Earlier liberalism used the Gospel to inculcate a belief in progress and morality. Bultmann reduces the gospel to an existentialism of decision, a vague appeal to live in the

---

[7] *Allein: Das Recht und die Gefahren einer polemischen Formel* (Stuttgart, 1950).

unceasing consciousness of God's eternal presence and our responsibility to Him.

With the dynamic character of this Biblical theology the Barthians find kinship. This appears in a discussion of the Hessian Synod, which refused to censure Bultmann. It may also be seen in Hermann Diem's brochure on the principles of hermeneutics.[8] Here he strikingly and pertinently parallels Luther's eucharistic teaching with Luther's interpretation of Scripture. Diem opposes this to the Catholic position, which believes that it has God's Word in the Bible even *ante et extra usum,* as it also believes in Christ's presence under the species of bread and wine even *before and apart from the reception* of Communion.

The Lutheran Bishop Haug (Wurttemberg) is no Lutheran in this Barthian sense. In 1951 he issued, to the pastors of his church, a pastoral letter, which reproached Bultmann for emptying Christ's career of the historical character of His life, death and resurrection, and for abandoning belief in Christ's enduring presence in the Church. At the EKiD synod at Hamburg (April 1951) Bishop Dibelius repeated much the same criticisms.

Here we find the Protestant Bishops claiming a doctrinal authority, which was mainly exercised by the Theological faculties from the days of Luther until 1933, when the Marburg Faculty opposed the exclusion of "non-Aryans" from the Church's ministry by the German Christians and the Erlangen Faculty approved the exclusion. This same authority was wielded in 1950, when the Lutheran Bishops attacked the papal proclamation of the doctrine of the Assumption. This attack was first read by the head of VELKD, Bishop Meiser, in a service at Kulmbach (Nov. 5, 1950). The Evangelicals were almost unanimous in their protest, but the protests ranged from the sharply aggressive and exaggerated views, which asserted that the Blessed Virgin had been defined as "co-redemptrix," for example, in the Austrian Bishop May's proclamation, to the genuine brotherly concern expressed by Max Thurian.[9]

On the whole, the intensity of theological criticism and religious concern among German and French Protestants was in sharp contrast to the indifference of Swiss Protestants. The majority of the latter issued a statement to the effect that such a characterisic

---

[8] *Grundfragen der biblischen Hermeneutik* (Munich, 1950), pp. 5 ff.
[9] "Le dogme de l'Assomption" in Leuba's *Verbum Caro,* No. 17 (1951).

Catholic definition in no way affected them. This concern proves, far more than books or articles can, that the largest part of continental Evangelical Christians no longer live in a world wholly apart from the Catholics and that in the last decades something has happened to draw the separated brethren together.

Something has happened. What will happen in the future? The dispassionate observer will not overlook the fact that only a small minority of those, who as children have been baptized in a Continental Protestant Church, and who do not formally leave it, may really be called Evangelical Christians. Some have become such during Hitler's persecution or in the course of Stalin's persecution east of the iron curtain. Catholic and Evangelical religious life is more fervent in the hungry east than in the well-fed west, as all participants in the Berlin-Church Day (1951) agreed. But among the majority of western Protestants the religious revival of the war years and the first post-war years did not last long.

The "free-churches," drawing support from North America, seem to have some success among the broad masses. Apart from them, there still exist the old freethinkers, Marxian materialists, and biological racialists. Among the somewhat better educated there prevail Gnostic and occult tendencies, which advance today as they did in the late days of the Roman Empire until a follower of these movements, Julian the Apostate, mounted the imperial throne.

Perhaps an analogous development will come from the successes of the late Dr. Steiner's Anthroposophy (a 'heretical' branch of Mrs. Besant's theosophical movement), or from Professor Jung's psychological school (Zurich) with its esoteric quasi-religion, which every summer fascinates the participants in the Eranos Congress at Lake Maggiore. If a new persecution should come from such a quarter or from Bolshevism, then Evangelical Christians and Catholics will face the direct challenge to understand each other and the Jews, who, like themselves, have been persecuted by Apostate brethren and unconverted heathens. Christians and Jews are believers in the same God of Moses and the Prophets, Isaac, Jacob and Abraham, and, according to Romans, XI, 26, the Jews will be believers in Christ before the end of history.

To promote such mutual understanding there are three approaches, which are happily not neglected by an elite of Continental Protestantism. These are incessant prayer, personal contacts and intense Bible study with the object of expounding the veritable word of God and not of reading into it one's own prejudices. If Catholics, Protestants and Jews in increasing numbers follow these approaches, then the recent changes in Continental Protestantism will not be merely partial and ephemeral. Instead they will work the beginning of the fulfillment of Christ's prophecy: "There shall be one fold and one shepherd" (John, X, 26).

VIII

The Present State and the Problems of the Missions of the Catholic Church

by G. Naidenoff, S.J.

Every period has its own particular way of evaluating events and conditions. A hundred years ago the missionary renaissance was magnified with an overflowing lyricism. Here for example is a sample of the prose of 1840, an expression of triumph: "The Church has only to glance at the vast regions of the Orient. Immediately avenues open up; ships knife the seas; these rapid messengers (the missionaries) fly on the wings of the winds; the air echoes the name of Jesus. Thirty kingdoms and islands without number are conquered for the Faith. . . . The most deep-rooted prejudices, the most cruel superstitions, all fall and vanish at the very name of the God of the Gospels."

Fifty years later, when Europe was asserting its superiority and its hegemony over the world, the heroism of the missionaries still burned but their pen was dipped in another ink: "Everything in China is pagan," one of them writes, "not only souls, but the blood, the atmosphere and the soil; the demon seems to have given men a double original sin. . . . What a sad, sad people! They do not have the Gospel and when they do, it will still be a sad people; they will always lack the exquisite gifts which God has given the peoples of Europe . . ."

I have quoted these two examples, not in order to underrate our predecessors, but rather to warn our contemporaries against other excesses which might prevent them from having a true, realistic and profound idea of the missionary work of the Church.

Men in our times like to measure everything with exactness; they think that statistics are the most eloquent expression of facts. They wish to use the procedures of mathematical investigation as much as possible in the religious field. It was no doubt in answer to this demand for precision that the recent encyclical *"Evangelii Praecones"* gave its spiritual summary in figures: "In 1926 there were 400 missions, at present there are 600; then there were not 15,000,000 in these regions, today there are nearly 28,000,000. In this same year, 1926, the foreign and native priests were 14,800 in number, today there are more than 26,800."

These figures are true as such but they immediately become false if we fail to determine our bearings, which alone give them a complete meaning. If we do not, we risk provoking fifty years hence the same smiles and as much indignation as the inflated imaginations of the romantics or the feeling of superiority of the Europe of yesterday now cause us.

World Population and Catholic Population

The principal contemporary religious event is the prodigious increase of the world's population and the relative stagnation of the Christian population. It has been said that the essential thing, at the present time, is not the clash of incompatible ideologies but the fact that each year 25,000,000 more people are born than die. We can agree with this, if it is specified that this increase is not uniform over the globe and that the difference of birth rates—which vary greatly according to countries—is provoking, without emigration, a decisive upheaval in the density of human population.

The population increased by 200,000,000 between 1937 and 1948, but this tidal wave does not affect all countries equally; far from it. In fact, the 200,000,000 increase breaks down as follows:

6,000,000 only for Western Europe
28,000,000 for the Soviet world
30,000,000 for Africa—especially Arabs and assimilated groups
43,000,000 for the American hemisphere
87,000,000 for Asia

It is, therefore, true to say that the most important events of our time are not the rise of the Russian red star, nor of the American white stars, but the fact that, according to the latest statistics of the United Nations, Asia will soon have, in spite of the good birth rate of the two Americas, two-thirds of the world's populatin.

In Asia it is no longer a matter of amorphous and easily-handled masses, but of men as well organized and alert as those of the West, whose tutelage they have shaken off while retaining western techniques. The same will soon be true of Africa. The techniques of the West belong to the whole world at the very moment when the world no longer belongs to the West.

Now this rise of peoples is not favorable to Christianity, for it particularly favors the non-Christian masses. In thirty years the Catholics have increased in theory by 100,000,000 while the non-Catholics have increased in fact by 400,000,000. In fact, as of 1950, taking the maximum figures for baptized Catholics, there are:

> 226,000,000 in Europe
> 178,000,000 in the Americas
> 24,000,000 in Asia
> 17,000,000 in Africa
>   2,500,000 in Australia-Oceania

It is hardly an exaggeration to say that the western hemisphere (the Americas and Europe) is Christian, and that the oriental hemisphere (Asia, Africa) is not Christian. This means that the population reservoirs are in inverse proportion to the reservoirs of Christianity.

There is another aspect of the world religious situation which too easily escapes the attention, especially that of the Americans. In the United States, where religious faith increases year by year among the Catholics as well as among the Protestants, people do not perhaps realize that the most formidable missionary force at present is atheism.

Atheism—the First Missionary Force of the World

It is customary, in giving missionary statistics, to count in round numbers, 400,000,000 Catholics, 400,000,000 Orthodox Christians and Protestants and the enormous mass of 1,600,000,000 non-Christians. But people forget to point out that there is growing in this Christian and pagan humanity a huge army of men and women who maintain with heads high that religion is out of date and that God does not exist.

Atheism threatens all religions. Confucianism, professed by the whole of China, by many Indo-Chinese and Koreans, has completely disappeared as a religion and has not been replaced by anything else than practical irreligion, made worse by the militant atheism imported by Communism. Madam Sophia Zen says in cynical, and for us, profoundly sad terms: "The missionaries should at last understand that the present generation of China is corrupted and intolerant; neither the fire of Hell, nor proselytism will succeed in turning young people away from the atheism which they have accepted. Better still, the elders of this generation are not alarmed by the atheistic tendencies of their youngers for they themselves are for the most part atheistic. In truth Russian culture will perhaps be surprised that its areligious character, considered as somewhat diabolical by Western civilization, is accepted with good grace and with serenity by the very ancient Chinese civilization because its cultural foundation is equally atheistic, or at least agnostic."

Japanese Shintoism, in spite of its revival, is no doubt destined to join Confucianism in the museum of religions if we can believe Baron Satsuma: "I do not consider Shintoism a religion. . . . The Japanese people are almost completely indifferent to religion."

Buddhism, a deep rooted, active religion with a missionary zeal in certain countries like Ceylon, Burma, a part of Vietnam and Japan, is dying in the souls of a host of intellectuals, and especially among youth. The latter, desirous of efficiency and terrestrial achievements, are rejecting Buddhism, a religion which preaches the death of desire. In a study made shortly before the war at the Imperial University of Tokyo the students were asked: "What is your religion?" Of the 4,900 asked, six replied that they were disciples of Confucius, eight were Shintoists, sixty Christians, 300 Buddhists, 1,500 atheists and 3,000 without any religion. In 1949 a similar study made at Kyoto gave an identical result; among the students only 14% admitted the existence of God.

Africa, in turn, has perhaps been more touched by religious indifference than by Christian evangelization or Moslem proselytism. Dr. Aujoulat writes: "Young Africans have passed, without transition, from fetishism to atheism, sometimes after a short period as Christians." Even more numerous are those who, after contact with European life, have adopted a new and tyrannical cult, the cult of money. They have become materialists in fact, and without knowing it. Their rapid multiplication constitutes nonetheless one of the most visible and disturbing elements of the evolution of Africa. In France the words of a Communist political leader are often quoted: "We are very grateful for the missionaries. They teach the Africans to read. We teach them to think."

Atheism today is the normal state, religion the exception. Atheism is more redoubtable since Communism is its ardent propagandist and even transforms it into a religion. Here is what a high Russian official in Switzerland has written: "Stalin is neither a saint nor a cynic. He is a fervent apostle who does not hesitate to use any weapon he thinks effective. . . . Every weakness in the fulfillment of the program of power is a sin without remission. . . . The Party is the Church; furthermore, it is a reserved chapel. The irrational, emotional and religious element unquestionably plays a role. There are suicides not only in case one is excluded from the Party, but for a simple accusation, even because one has not been admitted. . . . The Party, with its hierarchy, is its clergy. The role of Stalin is both vast and limited, like that of the pope in the Church. . . . The Regime is adored, loved and hated in an inextricable whirlpool of admiration, rancour, veneration and disgust. It is a god, a father, best friend, a demon. . . . Millions of men, dozens of peoples, feel and know that it is the flesh of their flesh."

Thus, thanks to the Communist Church, atheism, so universally widespread, finds its moral and mystical justification, and transforms itself into a sort of conquering and irresistible religion, like the religion of Buddha of old, which, incidentally, under the shock of Communism, is going back to its atheistic origins. The "Young Buddhists" movement of Shanghai, a missionary writes, rejoices over the advent of the "New Democracy," for it will lead them back to their most ancient and most authentic tradition, remind them that God does not exist and cannot exist, and that Buddhism is not, properly speaking, a religion.

Is it not with a tremendous melancholy that we hear this concert of voices proclaiming the irreparable anaesthesia of the religious sense of humanity? The axiom of old Plutarch has long been repeated: "It is easier to build a city in the air than to build it without gods." Let us look about us in the universe. Man has built a kingdom on earth; he seeks no other and does not admit that the perspective of a problematical after-life troubles his plans. We cannot deny that the most active and most universal missionary force at the present time is a negative and destructive force, if we accept the French philosopher Maritain's definition of a believer as one "whose life is so constituted that if God disappeared his life would no longer have any meaning." It is not an exaggeration to say that nearly a billion individuals have no anxiety nor religious sentiment.

178

The Solidarity of the Believers

The common peril of atheism has had as its counterpart a bringing together of believers who, in their affirmation of a hereafter, feel a solidarity before those for whom the earth is enough. It is especially among Christians that this need of coming together is most noticeable. For four centuries the struggle between Catholics and Protestants has been bitter, and has resulted even in massacres and martyrdom. The wars of religion were cruel and produced an almost unbridgeable gulf. But today a Catholic priest and a Protestant pastor can walk together in the countrysides of southern France and say: "These fields have been sprinkled with the blood of our ancestors shed for their faith." They can speak so, for, henceforth, they see rather what brings them together than what separates them.

Among the Protestants, ecumenical assemblies and efforts of fusion have multiplied. Events have helped them especially in the missions. The Protestant Churches in Japan have become unified like those of southern India. The Bangkok conference of 1949, which grouped the native delegates of all the Protestant churches of the Far East, strongly insisted on the absolute necessity of the union of Christians.

Among Catholics Unity Week has become a universal fact. More and more numerous are those who, in agreement with the hierarchy and subject to its directives, are impatient to hasten the hour that God alone knows when all Christians will assemble on the mysterious roads opened by grace.

If among Christians the nostalgia for unity has causes more profound than the present crisis, other believers wish especially to form a common front against a common enemy. This feeling is especially strong among the Moslems. The editor of the review *As Salam* has written: "At the present time, all religions which proclaim the sovereignty of God have understood the danger which threatens humanity. Islam and Catholicism, after loyally fighting each other for centuries, are studying the possibilities of a common Crusade against the all invading paganism, immorality and reversal of human values."

This basis of understanding is fragile, like the reason which has provoked it. It does not exclude painful reverses; upsurges of fanaticism, secret persecutions, and attempts at modernization in the secret hope of remaining master of the terrain. Moslems consider that in the present breakdown, they are contributing a formula for the future to which all could rally. Surprises are not excluded; thus in mid-1950 the leader of 80,000,000 untouchable outcasts of India decided to embrace Buddhism after having studied and rejected other religions.

It is comforting to note in the turbulent history of religions this widespread desire for cooperation, mutual aid and understanding.

Shortly before the bamboo curtain fell on China, the Archbishop of Nanking, Yu Pin, founded the society of five religions in order to neutralize the effects of materialism. We have seen American prelates like Archbishop John O'Hara, then Bishop of Buffalo, exhorting Buddhist monks in their monasteries in Japan, while these declared themselves ready "to fight on the side of the Catholics in the battle for the defense of Japanese spiritual interests." While at Bethlehem on Christmas, 1949, the Archbishop de Provenchere of Aix, France, received the following telegram from the best known sheik of Algeria: "Are united in thought and prayer with you at Bethlehem, Christmas night, anniversary birth of Mouloud Sidna Aissa (Jesus) for union of Christian and Moslem believers for world peace and justice. . . . " It is understandable that after such words a chief of the Moroccan Istiqlal could say to the author of the present article: "We should found an International of the spiritual-minded." An Algerian has written him that he was "proud to fight at his side on another level for the triumph of the eternal truths."

This regrouping of believers has contributed a great deal to the purifying of polytheistic religions. No doubt, new superstitions, even new religions have come into being, like the Caodaism of Vietnam which has succeeded in grouping more than a million faithful, like certain pseudo-Christian sects of black Africa, but one wonders to what extent idolatry in the classical meaning of the word still exists today. When fetishism still survives, its holders, when they attain a certain level of culture, try to prove that it is a matter of intermediate beings comparable to the saints and angels. This road to monotheism prepares the ways for the God of Christian revelation.

However, this can also provoke a certain spiritual saturation of soul which turns it away from a more profound search. This is observable in minds as eminent as those of Gandhi and Tagore; it is noticeable in a host of people who prefer a religion in their own image to revealed dogma.

The Church Overcomes Nationalism

The division in each country between believers and atheists not only has as its counterpart a bringing together of different religious confessions; it has contributed in the missions to the nationalization of religions considered up to now as foreign importations. Political leaders notably have experienced, as in the time of Constantine, all the spiritual aid they could expect from the social and moral dynamism of the Christian faith.

It would be then a profound error—and too many Europeans are still inclined to make it—to see in the unfurling of nationalism throughout the world a serious obstacle to evangelization. The events of the last ten years have practically nullified the work undertaken by Europe in the last fifty years. As a result of world changes and the weakening of Europe after 1940, Asiatic countries have rediscovered or affirmed their independence while Africa, especially Moslem Africa, is rapidly following the same road. Confederations, or unions of states replacing empires, certainly maintain numerous unequal juridical bonds, but sovereignty is scattered more and more each day. Since 1926 a number of nations have acquired complete international rights:

Iraq—1932	Indian Union—1947
Saudi Arabia—1927-1932	Pakistan—1947
Egypt—1936	Yemen—1947
Syria—1941-1946	Viet Nam—1945-1948
Lebanon—1941	Burma—1948
Korea—1945	Ceylon—1948
Jordan—1946	Israel—1948
Philippines—1946	Indonesia—1949
	Libya—1951

This independence, gained or conquered for the most part by the shedding of blood, did not spare that of the missionaries. But by a happy consequence almost all the new countries have realized that "the missionaries of the Gospel exhort all men to fraternal relations which raise them above the rivalries of national frontiers." Numerous official acts and diplomatic relations established between the Holy See and non-Christian countries,—India, Indonesia, Lebanon, China, Egypt, Liberia, Pakistan—are striking examples.

In the feverish and irritable Moslem countries one notes with astonishment that, in spite of an overheated fanaticism always ready to explode in irrational acts, Christians are not mistreated and are even invited to participate in the general movement. In Egypt, ecclesiastical dignitaries, both orthodox and Catholic, have appeared in public with the Moslem religious leaders.

In countries where evangelization is not hindered, as in India or Japan, nationalism has simply accelerated the constitution of a native clergy and hierarchy, to the great advantage of the universal Church. In the Christian countries we are inclined, as a result of a still unresolved past, to distinguish between mission lands, that is lands to be Christianized, and our own lands, which give men and money, and provide the missionary spirit. This attitude is legitimate, but time is making it increasingly antiquated. In a very few years, the geographical notion of mission territories and mission-sending countries will be effaced. The establishment of a hierarchy reduces more and more the number of regions which ask abroad not only for fraternal aid and subsidies, but even for spiritual direction and leadership.

In his radio broadcast of Christmas 1945, His Holiness Pius XII declared: "Once the life of the Church, in its visible aspects, spent its strength preferably in the countries of old Europe, whence it spread, like a majestic river, to what we might call the periphery of the world; today it appears on the contrary like an exchange of life and energy between all the members of the mystical body of Christ on earth. Many countries on other continents have, for a long time, gone beyond the missionary stage of their ecclesiastical organization. They are governed by their own hierarchy and give to the whole Church spiritual and material goods, whereas before they were only receiving them."

This is what we ultimately owe to nationalism. Now such a change, such an exchange, is of extreme urgency, if one thinks of the shortage of missionaries and even their decline in numbers, in spite of appearances.

Available Missionaries

There are two ways of conceiving the missionary clergy. First, one can note with satisfaction its substantial increase in the last twenty-five years and note that the number of priests in the missions is proportionate to that of the faithful. Hence, the latter can receive a sufficient and regular spiritual food. It is held, in fact, that one priest per 1000 faithful indicates real religious health.

But one can estimate the number of priests in proportion, not to the number of faithful, but to the general non-Catholic population. We should indeed envisage the situation in this way if we are speaking of missions. Otherwise, we are only speaking of a Christian islet in a pagan sea. In Viet Nam, for example, the clergy is flourishing: villages are scattered and isolated among the rice fields. One finds, without transition, a completely Christian village with its Church and its curé next to a completely pagan village where neither a European nor a native priest has ever penetrated. The Communists exploit the situation with real skill. They let the Christian village quietly stagnate in its ancestral ways while they work to improve the organization of the pagan village. In a short time the standard of life of the pagan village will be so superior to that of the Christian village that the latter will be definitely annihilated: any further missionary work will no longer be possible either within it or without. And yet, there persists a tendency to note in the statistics the satisfactory number of Viet Nam clergy—which is true certainly if one considers the clergy as parish priests, but false if one considers it as a missionary clergy.

We should raise here, in passing, the question whether the missionary work in itself belongs to the clergy or the laity. Without going into a long discussion of the question, let me say that I support the thesis of Father Seumois, O.M.I., of Ottawa University, who asserts, with excellent arguments, that the task of the priest is to be the pastor of the faithful while that of the laity is to be the missionary. It is the laity's job to bring the future flock to the pastor.

However that may be, the present structure of the missions requires of the clergy the twofold task of being pastor and missionary, often a contradictory position and one which requires of them an effort beyond their capacities.

Now let us visualize the question in a more general way as that of the clergy in the world. Here, according to my estimation, is the relative situation of the Catholics and the clergy: for 32,592,000 practicing Catholics, North America (the United States and Canada) had 53,135 secular and regular priests in 1950, an impressive figure in proportion to the faithful. But if we maintain the concept of the missionary priest, that is to say, the relation not to the Catholics alone, but to the total population, the situation is much less encouraging.

Latin America in 1950 had the ridiculous figure of 24,500 priests for 154,000,000 presumed Catholics. Europe had the uncertain figure of 215,000 priests for a number of Catholics at present impossible to determine. Africa had 9,400 priests at the beginning of 1950 for the number, certainly high, of 17,000,000 faithful. Australia had 2,470 priests, Asia 12,590 and Oceania 3,600. This gives a total of 320,695 priests, unequally divided as we shall see even in the heart of Christianity.

In Holland and England there is one priest for 400 faithful, in Canada one for 500, in Belgium one for 600, in France one for 900 baptized Catholics. I have just used the term "baptized Catholics" for France, and not the word "faithful." The distinction, which may not be immediately obvious to an American Catholic, is very clear to a European. In France there are 52,000 priests. This number makes it the most numerous national clergy in the world. There is a population of 35,000,000 baptized, of which about 15,000,000 have recourse from time to time to the clergy, and of which about 4,000,000 are practicing Catholics, to which number we must add 1,000,000 children who attend Catholic schools. We can, in any case, consider that France has a sufficient clergy and is not a missionary country in the usual sense of the word: she does not need a foreign clergy to renew herself. What she does need is a new distribution of the clergy, too numerous in certain dioceses, too few in others, and a different social distribution, for too many priests have been drawn from the traditional milieu attached to the past, usually referred to as bourgeois, while the masses, looking toward the future and social liberation, have been asking Marxism to lead them and to "save" them.

The situation is analogous in Italy. In Spain the clergy, still suffering from the terrible persecution of 1936-1938, which put to death 7,300 priests, has leaned too much on official elites while the people suffer in silence and wait.

So far we have only stressed the problems of distribution in speaking of the clergy. Now we must point out the lack of priests. In Poland there is one priest for 2,000 Catholics. This figure is reduced to one for 6,000 throughout South America and to one for 8,000 in the Philippines.

But what are these last figures in comparison with those in mission countries? In them, no doubt, there is always at least one priest for 1,000 Catholics, but also one priest (missionary) for 100,000 inhabitants. Or to put it another way: in Europe one cannot cross thirteen square kilometers without finding a priest, two religious and at least a church tower; in Oceania they are spread over 280 kilometers, in Africa over 500, in Asia over 2,130. Between thirteen square kilometers and 2,130 there is a tremendous difference.

But this is not the most serious difficulty. We have been justifiably encouraged in the last twenty-five years because the missionary clergy has considerably increased, from 14,800 to 26,800. But in order to evaluate this figure accurately, we must note, besides the corresponding increase of the population, that this increase marks less an improvement in the number of foreign missionaries than a happy flourishing of the native clergy. In 1925 there were 10,000 foreign priests; today they number 15,000. There were then only 4000 native priests; now there are 12,000.

The following is even more symptomatic. In 1935, of 50,500 missionary religious, 18,000 were natives and 32,500 were foreign. Today, in a total of 61,000 there are 38,000 native and only 24,000 foreign. Thus, the religious who go to the missions have decreased in 15 years by about 8,500. If we compare the 24,000 valiant missionaries to the 600,000 religious who work in Christian lands the disproportion becomes scandalous. This means that in spite of the pleas of the Sovereign pontiffs many have not yet understood the urgency of the missionary needs. Numerous active congregations and numerous contemplative convents have not yet placed in the first rank of their preoccupations, concern for the diffusion of the kingdom of God beyond the narrow frontiers of their diocese or country.

These observations place in true proportion the small contingent of native clergy, the fragile plant which must, whatever the cost, become the vigorous tree with the shortest possible delay in order that, in the words of Pius XII, "the Church, having planted deep roots, can without the help of foreign missionaries, prosper and grow." This growth has already begun, for example, in Indo China, where the Church has nearly 2,000 native priests for a Catholic population of 1,600,000. Likewise, the small Christian community in Japan, which had only 38 priests and 29 major seminarians in 1920 for 78,000 faithful, now has, in 1951, for a population of 142,000 faithful 195 priests and 180 major seminarians. These figures are promising for Japan, since in thirty years the number of Catholic priests has quadrupled, while the number of seminarians has quintupled for a Catholic population that has doubled. In India the 3,000 native priests supported by 1,300 major seminarians can hope to take charge in the near future of their 5,000,000 Catholics.

Africa, although evangelized much more recently, shows an even more rapid increase in the number of priests. In 1939 there were 7,608,000 Catholics, 388 native priests, and 844 major seminarians for the whole of Africa; in 1950 there were 1,100 priests and 1,250 seminarians for 19,962,844 Catholics.

While insisting on the dramatic shortage of clergy in proportion to the total population, we must rejoice at the rapid progress which shows the wonderful vitality of the native churches in this fulfillment of papal instructions. But this progress towards religious autonomy is taking place in countries which are prey to ideological disturbances, the destroyers of ancient traditions. We must, therefore, have a clergy spiritually disciplined, of unquestionable orthodoxy and unflinching devotion to the Roman Pontiff. The native clergy has the heavy task of taking over the Christian heritage which became successively incarnate in the Greek, Latin and western world, and which today must assume a form in harmony with national aspirations without betraying the message of Christ. On the spiritual plane, especially, they should remember that, in the beautiful comparison of St. Paul, they carry "a treasure in perishable earthenware." They need the support of the universal prayer of Christians of all races, in order to carry out the instructions Pius XII gave them of being "the burning lamp which reflects the splendor of all the virtues on the Christian people."

We have already stressed above, in regard to nationalism, the establishment of the hierarchy in the mission countries. Let us recall simply these words of the encyclical *Evangelii Praecones:* "Twenty-five years ago all pastors at the heads of missions were foreigners. Since that time, 88 of these missions have been entrusted to the native clergy; in numerous places the establishment of an ecclesiastical hierarchy normally constituted, with bishops chosen from among the inhabitants of the place, brings out more clearly how much the religion of Christ is of itself Catholic and how little it can be considered foreign in any place on the globe."

The constitution of the hierarchy, the progressive development of a native clergy, the dramatic shortage of missionaries, the favorable evolution of nationalism on the Christian level, the solidarity which contemporary conditions have fostered in believers, the missionary powers of militant atheism and the fundamental modifications caused throughout the universe by the uneven increase of population—these are, in general terms, it seems to me, the most important points.

Now we must take up the particular situations by turning first to the most striking one in the Church today, the development of the Church in America and the Anglo-Saxon world.

America and the Anglo-Saxon World

In general, it is with astonishment and a touch of scepticism that Europeans observe the intense vitality of the Catholic Church in the United States. The appearance and evidence are, at first, not easily believed, all the more so because, for example, the American nation includes millions of non-believers as well as twenty-eight million Catholics. By reason of the novelty and boldness of their approach to the modern world, their astonishing capacity for adaptation, and their religious practice, faithful and without intellectual complications, these Catholics are a source of comfort for the Universal Church. The Church in the United States receives some 120,000 converts each year. Its clergy numbers 43,000, and its religious 150,000. To these figures may be added the growing number of universities, hospitals, and, especially, the abandonment of spiritual isolationism. It is common knowledge that the Americans have been most generous in contributions, but it should be added that their missionaries have increased from 2,000 in 1940 to 4,400 in 1952.

Until recently people tended to confuse Catholics with Latins, that is, with people related to the Romans by language and civilization. To give one example, among many: the saints of the nineteenth and early twentieth century, canonized by the Church, are, with the exception of a German and an Austrian, all of Italian (29), French (19), or Spanish (5) origin. The center and the heart of Christendom was Europe, both by reason of its mass of Catholics and the intensity of its thoughts and spiritual life, for both its initiatives and the authority were Christian.

That is no longer so today. The simple play of numbers brings to the fore in the Church, a people, who, unlike the Latin world, look on the future less as a formidable enigma than as a conquest calling for the most youthful optimism.

When I speak of the Anglo-Saxon world, I mean a Catholic world which has emerged in a Protestant environment, in contrast with the Graeco-Oriental world and the Latin world. While the churches of France, Spain and Italy have retained an absolute continuity with a past of over a thousand years, the Anglo-Saxon churches underwent the Protestant interlude and were, for a more or less long period, detached from the Catholic Church. During the last century they were considered as missionary lands. They are characterized by a neo-Catholicism whose common characteristics justify the regrouping of the countries we have found in the *Catholic Directory* published in London in 1951. This English annual lumps together, when counting the Catholics of Great Britain, the almost 25,000,000 Catholics who form part of the Commonwealth and Ireland with the 43,000,000 Catholics under American influence (this includes the Philippines). This procedure is not arbitrary, for all the Catholics thus included are aware of common aspirations in spite of divergencies and differences, and have a common idea of the world and the great religious problems.

Scarcely a century ago the Dutch Catholics were outlawed. To-day they form 40% of the population. Their religious life is intense and profound, their family life pure and prolific. Protestants accuse the Dutch Catholics of pursuing demographic politics in order to become the majority in the country: "Children, children, children" seems to be their motto. In fact, it is a matter of moral health in homes where birth control slogans are rejected. Almost all the little children go to Catholic schools. The school and the family are the two pillars of Dutch Catholicism.

In England, where unfortunately the birthrate is low, the Catholics are winning the battle for children too, and, in spite of the plague of mixed marriages between Protestants and Catholics, they have every reason to be optimistic.

In Canada, despite a sharply different origin in French Catholicism, there is the same common stream, which brings the Americans and Anglo-Saxons together. This it is which influences their manner of being Catholic. A Canadian Jesuit defined it in these words: "We love life." Therein is to be found the source of their inexhaustible optimism and hope.

188

A significant development in the Catholicism of the United States is the increasing vocations to the religious and clerical life. In 1922, for a Catholic population of 18,000,000, there were 22,500 priests and in 1948 the numbers of the clergy reached 42,300, while the Catholic population had increased by one-third.

The most extraordinary phenomenon of the United States is the remarkable increase in the number of vocations for the contemplative life. The attraction of the Trappist life, which requires the most severe cloister and the radical elimination of comfort, is a noteworthy example. After fifty years of failure in trying to plant the monastic life in the United States, there has suddenly developed a rush. In 1943 there were only three Trappist foundations in America; there were four in 1944, five in 1947, seven in 1949, and nine in 1951. The American Trappists have the largest number of novices in the world, nearly 300. Similarly, at the time of the foundation in 1949 of the first Trappist convent for 50 Trappist nuns, there were 500 applications for admission. At Christmas 1950 the candidates numbered 800. This prodigious return to a 700-year-old past has only one purpose: "To be alone with God."

The laity, after a long period of passivity, are in turn assuming their responsibilities and are introducing Catholic principles in the social life among the millions of unbelieving citizens. They know how to use every modern means, including the cinema and the radio. In the domain of the speculative intelligence, so dear to certain Europeans, notably to the French, the American Catholics, even if they had this special turn of mind, could not allow themselves the dangerous liberty of an unlimited reflection. Since almost all of them come from immigrant origins, and for long years were entirely preoccupied with earning their daily bread, they have to assert in their ethics and their simple and rigid principles a compact solidarity in the face of a Protestant world which until recent years was hostile, and which still remains the master of finance, politics and the state.

On the strictly missionary level the American and Anglo-Saxons have taken the lead. On the Tercentenary of the Jesuit martyrs of North America Pius XII said: "This is the hour of America. The missions await the answer." Indeed, we may say in conclusion, that we must all one day go through an Anglo-Saxon-American phase of Catholicism just as we have all been, through our ancestors, spiritually Semites, Greeks, Latins, and Occidentals.

South American Anxieties

The situation of Latin America is quite otherwise. While the 27,000,000 Catholics of the United States are confronted with 70,000,000 non-religious citizens and nearly 50,000,000 Protestants; while the 5,000,000 Canadian Catholics live amidst 7,000,000 non-Catholics, Latin America rests quietly with the idea that she is completely Catholic. Yet she is undergoing nonetheless a very serious religious disintegration. The most dramatic of the dangers comes from the deplorable shortage of clergy. In this vast area from Mexico to Argentina and Chile, there are less than 25,000 priests for 154,000,000 souls. If we take as a basis for measurement one priest for 1000 souls, which is the average for the Christian countries of Europe and is necessary for the needs of the flock, Latin America needs 100,000 more priests and 200,000 more religious. Souls are literally dying from spiritual hunger, and it is understandable that Protestant propaganda, carried on very intensively today, finds hearts ready to be nourished by it. The shortage of Catholic clergy permits the unfurling of two antagonistic forces on the country: first, an ardent Protestantism, active and full of spiritual overtones, and secondly, Communism which, relying on social evils, rivals in speed the disciples of Jesus Christ.

A Mexican Jesuit said with some humor that it would not be difficult to describe his country by citing phrases each of which would belie the preceding one. This seems to be true for all the countries of Latin America, where the religious and social contrasts are such that one should be surprised at nothing. People continue to believe that persecution rages in Mexico, and are surprised that on a first Friday of the month one can count 5,000 communions in a parish of 15,000 souls in Mexico. Their surprise increases when they learn that on the coast religious practice is almost nil. In Colombia one could name a number of places which never see a priest and never receive the help of religion; at the same time the French Little Sisters of the Poor have pointed out that the country which gives them the most vocations throughout the whole world is Colombia. The Sisters of St. Vincent de Paul and others are practically of the same opinion.

Like several other governments of Latin America, Brazil is officially Catholic. But of the 51,000,000 inhabitants not 20,000,000 of them practice their religion; in certain dioceses ten times as large as Belgium there is only one priest for 6500 souls.

Worse still are the conditions in countries that lack such contrasts. Here people live in general indifference and debility, in spite of a small Christian and priestly elite who see very clearly and very sorrowfully the terrible situation.

In Peru, for example, the whole population is officially Catholic. Yet if we consider the small number of priests, the poor formation of the laity, and the great distances, we can be absolutely sure that a very large part of the population is totally unable to attend church or to receive the sacraments, and, in a large measure, unable to know its own religion. For a country of 7,500,000 inhabitants, as large as a sixth of the United States, with a terrain as varied as that of Utah, there are only 1500 priests.

It is easy to multiply examples. In Chile 50% of the marriages are not blessed by the Church. In one parish of 9,000 inhabitants, 60 people made their Easter duty. In another of 22,000 inhabitants, 450 made their Easter duty. In a third of 40,000 souls, 800 women and 250 men attend mass. In Chile 4,000,000 out of 5,000,000 are deprived of all serious religious influence.

While the population of Latin America, which is very prolific, has a future full of promise, the Catholic Church risks suffering there an irreparable disaster, even if vocations to the priesthood increase and the laity emerges from its lethargy. The native clergy do not suffice. Foreign missionaries are necessary. Already the excess of Spanish and American vocations are going there. This has been a regular feature of Church history, and if we recall that the local Churches of every country have all originally, and at certain difficult moments of their history, needed help, we should perhaps not call such help foreign.

It is precisely towards such a situation that Europeans fear they may be moving, after having been themselves the apostles of the universe and the founders of modern missions in Africa and Asia.

Africa

Africa has been called the great hope of the Church today. This is, however, an exaggeration. Apostolic work there is meeting with varying success and varying obstacles.

At the two ends of the continent the large number of Christians have planted a flourishing Church of the Western type; that is to say, alongside of unquestionable examples of religious life there arise occasions of scandal and often clashes unfavorable for the spread of the Faith.

Islam is making serious headway in Africa. About half of the 170,000,000 Africans are Moslems. If we visualize Africa as a trapezoid having at its southeastern base a triangle one can say, in a general way, that the trapezoid is Moslem and the triangle fetichist. Regions only slightly Islamized form the trapezoid-triangle axis. Of the 80,000,000 Moslems only three million are outside of the trapezoid. They can also be divided into two parts: one-half Arab or assimilated, the other Islamized negroes. The 35,000,000 negroes can, in turn, be divided into two groups, a half (14,000,000) being in British Nigeria. In general, the negro Moslems, who retain their pre-Islam customs, are less refractory than the Arabs subject to Christian influence. Certain converts even say that Islam was for them the road to Christianity.

The Moslems of North Africa, who for nearly fourteen centuries have replaced the flourishing Christian areas, are impervious to the Gospel, but they are impressed by contemplatives like Father de Foucauld. They admire this interior and mystical life which they know that they cannot find in their own religion.

Until recently the Africans asserted that they were unshakeably spiritual-minded. Indeed, Africa is still one of the corners of the world where men are most inclined to discern the life of the soul behind the rigidity of matter. But it is certain that materialism is spreading. A certain number of the missionaries are showing signs of discouragement, for they have the impression that the ground gained on one point is lost on another.

This pessimistic outlook is compensated for by the marvelous success in the Belgian Congo, Uganda, Urundi, Nigeria and in the whole of British East Africa. In these regions, "the Holy Spirit breathes like a tornado." Let it suffice to say, for example, that in Uganda in 1948 there were 941,000 Catholics, and that in 1950 there were over a million. Likewise in Tanganyika there were 664,000 in 1948 and 710,000 in 1949. In Kenya there were 287,000 in 1948, and 323,000 in 1949. In the Belgian Congo there were 500,000 in 1927; there are 3,500,000 today.

One may wonder whether these encouraging figures compensate for the losses in human substance which Africa has suffered. It is subject at present to a declining birthrate which makes its future questionable. The usual causes, alcoholism, venereal diseases, polygamy, and the break with traditional tribal life do not suffice to explain it. Doctors know how many unhappy African families come to them because of their grief at having no children. This sterility should be the subject of careful studies which could, by a large scale contemporary example, discover the causes of this still mysterious fact of the rise and decline of races. Certain peoples at a given moment of their history lose the desire, and then the possibility, of surviving. It is not a question of individuals taken one by one, but of a whole race whose spiritual, moral, psychological and psychic equilibrium has been broken. Taken individually, the men and women want to have children, but they cannot. They are sterile in spite of themselves. It is the whole race which is struck. Human groups have been effaced from history like the branch of a tree which grows to a certain point, stops, withers and dies. We must face the implications of this really troubling fact for our too materialistic minds: moral factors can influence biology to the point of determining its laws.

Shall we see a growing Christendom appear in a declining African world? Or—since it is a question of moral factors—can the presence of Christianity overcome the germs of death? At present we do not know the answer.

The Anguish of Western Europe

An analogous question may be raised concerning the ancient Christianity of Europe, which lives in dread of the prospect of being crushed under the Soviet wheels. But instead of inspiring courage this anguish annihilates the will, partly infected by a mysterious lassitude, which may be the temporary consequence of recent shocks or a sign of biological exhaustion. The most significant thing is that this new temper differs from the usual post-war attitude. It does not mean a frenzied search for pleasure after the restrictions and horrors of war, but rather among the young it is a need and a demand for a morose and cynical enjoyment and among older people a need for an unquiet repose. This is the present temper which makes souls unconcerned about divine affairs, while at the same time obsession with the collectivity attracts the most energetic and determined towards a sort of social atheism, which they regard as the necessary condition of vigor and balance in action.

Political conditions in Western Europe are favorable. Almost all nations are in the hands of men who are Christian and sometimes even profoundly Christian. Spain is governed by a leader who proudly proclaims himself Catholic. In Portugal Salazar has attempted to realize a Christian order in a markedly personal way. Ireland officially professes Catholicism, and its constitution begins with an invocation to the Holy Trinity. Italy has entrusted its destiny to outstanding militant Catholics whose piety is of an exceptional type. In Belgium the victories of the Catholic party are simply the official consecration of the decisive influence of a team of believers. Holland is applying Christian principles and recently had a professed Catholic as its prime minister, for centuries an inconceivable development. In Western Germany the destinies of the fragile state of Western Germany are in Catholic hands. Everyone knows that the sovereign of Luxembourg leads the country according to the norms of the Gospel. In the French government many ministers like Pinay, Pleven, Bidault, the two Schumanns, Letourneau, Aujoulat, etc., are profoundly Catholic men, several of whom inspire their action by prayer and daily communion. In short, nearly all of Western Europe is governed by Catholics.

In Western Europe everyone can practice his Faith openly. Anticlericalism is dead. As a Catholic priest always wearing the characteristic soutane, I have travelled, over the last 10 years, between 60,000 to 70,000 miles in every direction without ever having heard anyone in France mock or insult me. All I have met is sometimes a great indifference, sometimes a scowl or an unfriendly glance; that is all.

But this is perhaps the worst. While in mission lands souls die of spiritual thirst and hunger, in the West, where one has only to offer a hand, the masses seem to have no appetite for God. We are not going to count the number of fallen away Christians in Western Germany or in certain regions of Belgium, nor meditate upon the astonishing success of the Communist party in Italy, nor repeat the picture given by Father Godin in *France Pays de Mission*. Everyone knows that the percentage of practicing Catholics is small compared to the total population. We have given some figures above for France. Soundings made in rural areas and in the towns agree, so that we can accept these figures without trying to explain them away by saying, "It has always been like that."

Quality and depth compensate indeed for quantity, but one should have no illusions. It is not good to rely on the elite alone in a mass civilization. For the mass of human beings one needs massive means. Today the radio, press, and cinema are the best preachers of materialism. As long as they have not been baptized there is no hope for a Christian society, even with outstanding elites and a radiant holiness. But this supposes an organization of Catholic Action conscious of the real forces which move the country and possessed of an exact sense of proportion, for there is a proportion between the leaven and the flour which should be respected. A discipline must be maintained at whatever price when one is a minority. A disciplined and active minority can do anything on condition it realize that it is a minority.

The elite and the holiness have a twofold meaning: they are either the flowering of a balanced and faithful Christian society or they are the heroic survivals of a world destined to disappear. Hence it is possible that God, in spite of this elite and this holiness, is tired of Europe and that the Christian message is being carried elsewhere.

It must be recognized that it is impossible to classify and characterize the Church in each nation, although some of them, for example, Portugal, Belgium, Italy or Germany, have an important place in the Christian development of the world. Fatima, in Portugal, exercises a powerful attraction and plays an extraordinary role not only in the spiritual renewal of Portugal but of all the Catholic world. The missionary vitality of Belgium has justly taken form in a doctrine of apostolate to the infidels, and this doctrine would have made its impress, even apart from the striking personality of the famous Father Labbe. Spain, Germany and Italy are separately treated in this volume.

French Catholics, among whom the dechristianization has been strongest and the demoralization of the masses most widespread, are obliged to have more virtue and, especially, a constant and fruitful spiritual anxiety; in the field of theological reflection, in the search for methods, sometimes they appear like a gigantic workshop, sometimes like an experimental station or a laboratory, for is this not what we must call the many tentative efforts of Catholic action and community life? In this work of innovating and pioneering there is a dangerous illusion: that of believing that because they have made contact with the enemy, they are making progress. Because they have been the most dechristianized they think they know the best ways of re-Christianization. They know their efforts are applauded by those whom they consider the most farsighted in other nations without seeing that they annoy, irritate and scandalize the great mass of believers who find, in the traditional forms, a sufficient haven of shelter for their average virtue, and a safe port from which they can optimistically attempt the open sea of the modern world.

The Martyrs

While Christians of the West, with varying success, live through the experience of a religious liberty, which is only dampened by the zeal of certain governments, fifty million Catholics find themselves condemned to the suffocation of their religious life. On them the Iron Curtain has fallen rigidly and implacably.

In the Baltic countries, the persecution, begun with the first Soviet occupation in 1940, was resumed after the German defeat and has continued without restraint. In Latvia the Soviets have allowed the bishop of Riga and in Lithuania the bishop of Paneverys to continue. The bishop of Liepaja is in the West, that of Kaisedorys has been officially deported, and of four others nothing is known. The faithful of Lithuania have suffered atrociously. Informed Vatican circles estimate that 500,000 Catholics have been deported.

Albania has not been less ferocious towards the Catholics. As in the Baltic states, one bishop (of Pulati) has been maintained as proof of the regime's religious liberalism, but the regime has imprisoned the bishop of Durazzo for twenty years and has shot the other two bishops of the country. Of 110 diocesan priests the latest official governmental figure accounts for only forty-two. What became of the others?

While the sensational trials of Cardinal Mindszenty and Archbishop Stepinac have received international attention, they have also masked the more important fact of the enormous number of victims. A Vatican computation estimates that in Eastern and Baltic Europe more than 10,000 priests and religious have been killed, deported or exiled. Titoist Jugoslavia has slain, imprisoned or deported more than 2,000 Catholic priests. Outside the spotlight of publicity the lower clergy, religious, and laity have been subjected to "administrative" imprisonment, exile or execution on such pretexts as that they are "enemies of the people" or that they obey "foreign authorities." Their devotion to Rome is an inexpiable crime under a regime which recognizes no international authority except itself.

The situation in Rumania casts a sinister light on this aspect of Communism. There, the Catholic Church of the Byzantine rite (1,563,000 people) was abolished by decree on December 1, 1948. Its five bishops were arrested, and two of them are dead. The fate of the 1,800 diocesan clergy has varied, according to their willingness to submit to the Patriarchate of Moscow. The same conditions prevail among the Uniates of sub-Carpathian Russia (3,000,000 people), who have been forcibly joined to the Orthodox Church. The refractory Uniate clergy has been killed (5,000 priests) or sent to Siberia.

The Church of the Latin rite in Rumania was spared for a time but later four of its six bishoprics were suppressed. The bishops of the two other sees, having refused to accept the Church Statute imposed by the Government, were arrested (June 26 and 27, 1949). One month later, fifteen religious orders were dissolved and their monasteries confiscated. As the result of a series of trials, the representative of the Holy See was expelled, and many priests and laymen received various punishments, usually forced labor. Then on March 15, 1951, a Directional Council, twenty-seven members, of whom fourteen were priests, received from the government the task of founding a national Catholic Church. This action was followed by other religious trials in which all the accused pleaded guilty, and admitted, in the words of some of the accused, "to having been driven by the representatives of the Vatican in Rumania to the course which led to the present catastrophe."

The Czecho-Slovakian government has been most successful in maneuvering to achieve a Church organically tied to the structure of the totalitarian state, a Church with each of its members personally committed to the regime's doctrines. After the usual attacks on the Vatican as a foreign power, enemy of Czech democracy, accomplice and tool of the United States, there occurred five public trials designed to eliminate the strongest members of the clergy by vilifying them. Each of these trials involved an attempt to break down the will of the accused by means of introducing moral confusion in the victim's conscience through skillful psychological pressure.

Finally, as in Rumania, the religious houses were liquidated;

between April and October 3,000 religious were deported.

In the storm Archbishop Beran appeared as the living symbol of Catholic integrity. Seven other bishops have been arrested, five are under house arrest for refusing an oath, analogous to that of the Civil Constitution of the Clergy during the French Revolution. Five others have taken the oath. Rome has made no pronouncement.

The confusion of souls is probably greater in Hungary, where there are signs of a growing movement of apostasy.

Only in Poland and East Germany are there all the symptoms of a vigorous spiritual resistance. But terrible anguish presses upon the future. Men and women frequent the sacraments more than ever before. But the youth are monopolized by the new regimes and are pressed to forget the past and to live by the precepts of Marxism.

In sum, there are behind the iron curtain sixty-six dioceses deprived of bishops. Of the latter, thirty are in prison or doing forced labor, six are under house arrest, and fourteen have been killed or have died in prison.

To this European martyrology must be added that of China. It was in 1947 that the great storm erupted from the north. In April, 1948, the twenty-one invaded dioceses counted 336 expulsions, 127 imprisonments and 122 dead among the clergy. When the persecution continued after the complete Communist victory, it was soon evident that the persecution was not the result of mere disorders. The hope for compromise was belied during 1950 when the new regime unequivocally set to work to implant the Marxist ideology.

At the beginning of May 1952, there were twenty-two bishops in prison, at least 300 priests, brothers and sisters. Simultaneously, of 3,046 foreign priests in China (in 1948), there remained no more than 1,080; of 400 brothers only fifty-two and of 2,036 sisters only 600. The native Chinese clergy is closely watched and subjected to constant pressure to accept a schismatic national Church. The three million Chinese Catholics, after a brief hesitation, is resolutely committed to the stand defined by the courageous Abbe Tong, "My whole soul to God and the Holy See and my body to my country."

The Orthodox Church

This painful striking of a balance would be unjust and false, if the revival of the Orthodox Church were not mentioned. After having been atrociously persecuted, after having been, at any rate in the minds of the Soviet leaders, annihilated, the Orthodox Church is no longer a shrivelled old woman, praying alone in the smoke of candles. Now it is a youth struggling on the European battlefield. The Orthodox Church, with scrupulous fidelity, has resumed the liturgical splendors which characterized its past.

In spite of widespread accounts in the West, however, there is no Orthodox Church of the Catacombs. This title should be reserved for those who perished under persecution during the early years of the Soviet regime, for those who prayed and worshipped in secret. But the Orthodox Church now enjoys freedom of worship.

The Orthodox Church today includes one patriarch (Moscow), three metropolitans, twenty-six archbishops, and forty-nine bishops. Of the seventy-nine episcopal sees, forty-eight have been established since 1944. According to the estimates of the Russian religious authorities, more than 200,000 persons use the facilities of the fifty-five churches of Moscow.

But, alas, if the Faith is reborn, in the Soviet Union, it is that of the Patriarch Alexis, the gatherer—around the "Holy See" of Moscow—of the Orthodox of the whole world. It is not a Catholic faith. On the whole, the people's democracies are impenetrably closed to Catholicism. Not a single Catholic priest has openly entered the immensity of Russia as a missionary priest in more than thirty years. Not a single foreign missionary can enter Communist China.

It is well to recall that other countries are setting up the same barricades. There is not a Catholic missionary priest in Saudi Arabia, Baluchistan, Afghanistan or Tibet. Between Rome and nearly a billion of mankind there is a complete separation.

Burdens of Asia

Asia has been intentionally left for the conclusion because there the most radical upheavals are taking place. Tomorrow she will weigh most heavily on the destinies of the universe. Today she is, of all the continents, not only the least Christianized, but the one in which Christianization progresses most slowly. Up to the last World War conversions in Asia and Africa were going at the same rate. Since then the situation has changed sharply. Asia was being converted more rapidly yesterday than today, while in Africa the situation is reversed. But while the negro population of Africa is hardly increasing, the population of Asia is increasing so fast that the pagans are increasing faster than the Christians. Conversions do not suffice to make up the difference in favor of Christianity.

The stagnation, and in some places, the decline of the number of Christians in Asia, are extremely disconcerting. It seems that Asia has been too busy with the problems of the present life and of temporal reorganization to have that leisure and sufficient freedom of soul which alone opens the way to the eternal questions.

For nearly a century Asia has been wavering between its age-old structures and the ideal of life imported from the West. The die has been cast. Asia has chosen the West. All the nations of the Far East show an exasperated determination to have complete political autonomy. But they are just as determined to assimilate the techniques of the West, and even to surpass it in efficiency.

Communism has seized upon all the rancors and all the aspirations of Asia. It is spreading even in regions as Catholic as the Philippines. Since the Chinese Republic finds itself bound to Russia the empire of Genghis Khan has been reconstituted. Communism, like a scourge of God, requires all peoples, willy nilly, to turn over a new leaf, to drop the civilization of their ancestors for the enigmatic civilization of tomorrow, which is bought today at the price of a fierce barbarism. Let us suppose optimistically that the red wave, like a heavy rain on granite, leaves Asia intact. It is no less true that the transformations will be inevitable because they are desired by everybody.

In the making of this new world, the Christians are a small group. If we skip the Philippines, which are a special case, we find 12,000,000 Catholics among 1,300,000,000 people. The Protestants are a little less numerous than the Catholics.

In India a recent magnificent council asserted, before the eyes of all, the vitality of a Church long rooted and alone remaining firm in a country which, according to Nehru, "does not know where it is going." No doubt, too, the Protestant congress at Bangkok, which brought together delegations from diverse countries of Asia, has given promising signs.

The increase of Catholics and Protestants in Japan still remains very small. At least this time, it seems that no persecution can stamp out the Christendom founded four centuries ago by Francis Xavier and renewed under our eyes by the fervent aid of all peoples and all congregations. But in any case nothing can console us for the loss of China.

In China, indeed, the crisis of vocations is serious and the falling away of a certain number of Catholics points to a stagnation and even a decline which antedates communism. Father Damboriena, a missionary and historian of the missions in China, writes: "We believe that the figures do not reflect the real situation. They count only the new converts which swell the flock every year, but forget to lop off the number—perhaps even larger—who fell away during the war as a result of destruction, disintegration of families, lack of missionaries, emigration, etc. . . . Missionaries are unanimous in recognizing it." These words were written in 1938. What should be said now, with the complete withdrawal of foreign missionaries simply a question of time? The Chinese Catholic Church, with its 3,000,000 faithful drowned in the largest population of the globe, is the Church most in need of our prayers in order that she may, after being buried like a seed in the earth, grow up and flourish more vigorously in the spring-time God will one day send.

No matter where one looks in Asia, except in the Philippines, the churches there are weak and fragile. There is everywhere, even in the Philippines, the poisonous attraction of Communism.

Yet there is a ray of hope. In the West Communism appears to be like a degraded Christianity, a diabolical ersatz of the message of Christ. In the Far East it could become—but this is God's secret—the agent of Him for whom, without knowing it, all the Attilas and all the conquerors have marched. Without offering any too long-term hypotheses about the future, we should note that all the Christendoms of the Far East have been recruited, in a large part, among the little people, the poor villagers, the proletariat. The missionaries, in fact, were criticized for not having evangelized the elite. Today this situation may have certain advantages. Most of the Christians of the Far East have no capital, social prestige or political position to save. They have only their Christian Faith to strengthen them against Marxism. It will not be difficult for them to bear the burden during the revolutionary torment and to rise up intact tomorrow. Mixed with the mass of their fellow citizens, they need not fear, like many of their brothers in Europe, being accused of a "bourgeois Christianity," of a "class" Christianity. They can even be, as a result of the violent social upheavals of communism, dispersed among the pagans with whom many, seeking refuge in their Catholic villages or parishes, have not, up to now, associated. Thus, with the paralysis of scattered, or closely watched priests, there can arise in Communist Asia, quite spontaneously and without being officially supported, an authentic apostolate of the laity such as the primitive persecuted Church knew during the first three centuries. This is our great hope: that the little Christian people become the leaven in the immense meal, and prepare the day when those who will then be directing the destinies of the country will understand, like Constantine, that the future belongs to Christ.

It is not impossible either, that after the period of reconstitution, the Orthodox Church may become strongly missionary, and the more readily as the public authorities see in it an excellent product for export. In November, 1950, an event seemingly trivial but of great significance took place in Moscow. In that month the Patriarch Alexis, assisted by two metropolitans, an archbishop and two bishops, consecrated for the first time a Chinese priest bishop of the Orthodox Church. The new bishop has his see at Tientsin, a large port south of Peking. This missionary action is certainly painful for us but it may, by taking the Orthodox Churches beyond their national frontiers, lead them, by a counter-shock, perhaps even to Rome, as Protestant missions have led Protestants to ecumenism. Lenin said that the road from Moscow to Paris passed through Peking. It is not forbidden, from a Catholic point of view, to hope for a distant tomorrow, and one in conformity with human history, when Christianity, after passing through its Mediterranean and Atlantic phases, will end one day on the shores of the Pacific in the Christian reconciliation which can alone spare the West a disastrous night.

All this emphasizes the increasing importance which the shores of this immense ocean are going to have in the life of the Church of tomorrow. The Pacific era has opened for the world; it should open also for the Church. Although Christianity is solidly planted in the American hemisphere it has only weak positions in Asia. We should all strengthen them with all our force.

Each of us wants to know how he can personally modify the general situation of the world and contribute to solving the missionary problems. The first condition, it seems to me, is to see them as a whole, to measure exactly the facts and the elements involved in the light of the words of Marshal Smuts: "Every problem which is not seen in world terms is a badly stated problem and therefore insoluble."

In a general way, Catholics do not have over-all perspectives and when missions are involved, more appeal is made to their hearts and pocketbooks than to their intelligences. Now whoever does not understand why he gives and does not know what he is to love will one day refuse to give and refuse to love. Hence it has seemed to me indispensable not to separate the missionary Church from the old Christendoms, and to try to have an idea of God's plan for the world. God's plans are as inscrutable as He Himself but, at the same time, as knowable as He Himself. We must recognize His mysterious plan, whose perspectives and measures escape us, and, at the same time, the close solidarity between the body and soul of human societies. There is no growth nor decline of the Church; there is the majestic unfolding of history under the eyes and direction of God.

I can conclude in no better way than by quoting the beautiful words of Nguyen Van Ai, president of the Catholic Action of Viet Nam: "We are most keenly aware of the pressing need of feeling the palpitating life of the Church, persecuted here, glorious there, but, it must be admitted, too parceled out, scattered and multiple to have achieved the veritable characteristic of the Church: unique, universal, that is to say Catholic."

"We must come together if only to have a less vague idea of the meaning of the universality of the Church. This concern for the universal life of the Church must constitute more than a luxury for a few Catholics; it must win the heart of each of us. For the most serious problems of the present world are not those of a few but the problems of all of us.

"Would it not be desirable for the different Catholics of Europe, Africa and Asia to meet more frequently in order to understand each other and to become steeped in the real concerns of the Church? May we one day come up to the problems which concern man in general and our Catholic life in particular according to the true dimensions of the present world.

"May we feel more pressingly the need of feeling more united in Christ, better adapted to the new conditions of the world in order to be able to bear . . . witness of the Church, that is to say, witness of unity and love."

IX

Catholicism and the German Public

by Otto B. Roegele

German Catholicism, today, is in a painful state of transition. The great political and social catastrophe which the German people experienced under Hitlerism, the Second World War and the breakdown of the Reich, placed the Catholics in a completely new situation in many respects. Only with great difficulty are they finding their way and proceeding to master this situation. An understanding of this difficulty will be made easier by recalling the historic bases from which German Catholicism must emanate today. In the past lies a time of stability, of assured Church property which did not change basically from the wars of religion of the sixteenth and seventeenth centuries until 1944-46. Moreover, the years after 1870 had brought an inner consolidation and a slow, but steady increase of the public influence of the Catholics. According to the census of (May 17) 1939, there were 69,700,000 people living in the area of the German Reich apart from Austria. Of these, 33% were Catholic, and 59.8% Protestant. The Catholics lived predominantly in the southern and western parts of Germany. The north and the east were, save for minor exceptions like the Catholic Ermland (East Prussia), purely Protestant. The seven million inhabitants of Austria, which was incorporated into the German Reich early in 1938, are almost 90% Catholic. Their influence, however, upon the whole of the German situation lasted only for such a short time and was hampered by so many difficulties that it was almost negligible.

I. Historical Fundamentals

The various confessions practically lived in closed settlement areas. This was a consequence of the territorial split up of Germany during the times of absolutism, when the Church property question received a definite solution in each territory and the principle *"cuius regio eius religio"* was established. A greater mixture of the religious groups originally existed only in a few areas (namely, the former "Free Imperial Towns," Cologne, Aachen, Lübeck, Frankfurt, Nurnberg, Ulm, Speyer, Worms, Augsburg, Strasbourg, Rothenburg o.T., Heilbronn, etc.). The increasing mobility of population which accompanied the industrialization of Germany and the growth of the great cities partly wiped out the sharp frontiers between the settlements of the confessions.

When in the years from 1830 to 1848 a new wave of freedom spread through Europe, Germany also moved with its swell. In Germany, the liberal program of limiting absolute monarchies by constitutional arrangements was mingled with a passionate desire for national union. The Catholic representatives of the parliament in the Frankfort *Paulskirche* joined together on this issue. Everywhere the Catholics hoped that the new constitutional era would bring them civil equality and greater freedom. The highly-gifted publisher Josef von Görres became the spokesman of this struggle for freedom of the Church. The *Kolner Wirren* (Struggle in Cologne) had greatly roused the Catholic people. Because of his resistance to the Prussian regulation concerning religiously mixed marriages the Archbishop of Cologne, von Droste-Vischering, was put into jail, where the Archbishop of Posen followed him. King Friedrich Wilhelm IV of Prussia had to set both bishops free again, allow them free intercourse with Rome and establish a special "Catholic division" in the Prussian ministry of religious establishments (1841). The unsuccessful end of the negotiations in the *Paulskirche,* however, and the resistance of the northern Germans against the restoration of a Reich which included Catholic Austria, buried the great hopes of the German Catholics. Nevertheless, the emancipation of the citizens had made some distinct progress in the Protestant German states.

The war of 1866 which forcibly drove Austria out of German history, finally destroyed the idea of a "dualistic solution" (including Prussia and Austria) and delivered western and southern Germany into the hands of Prussia. The Kingdom of Hannover was annexed by Prussia. Thus a bridge was built between the original Prussian territory and the newly won Rhineland. At the same time the last remains of the traditions of separate states were destroyed.

The foundation of Bismarck's Reich in 1871 naturally shifted Germany's political focal point from Catholic Vienna to Protestant Berlin. After 1871 the Catholics in the German Reich were a clear minority group. Accordingly, their political organ, the Center Party, which in effect was a Catholic one, and significantly had in Windthorst an anti-Prussian Hannoverian as its leader, became an instrument of the struggle for effective equality. The *Kulturkampf* of the seventies shed light on the situation: Bismarck was defeated and repealed his discriminatory laws. Thereafter the Catholics were stricken by an all but inextinguishable fear of not being "national enough." The *Kulturkampf* offered to German Catholicism the opportunity to prove the strength which it had amassed in the struggle against Protestant state absolutism. But the impress of the *Kulturkampf* was lasting, and the feeling that Catholicism cannot develop its powers and possibilities in a state dominated by Prussia has persisted into the present.

Thus, since 1871, the public behavior of German Catholicism has been antithetically orientated, not as in French Catholicism, against the form of government (that is against the republic, because the Catholics were royalists), but against the division of power in the state, because the Catholics were southerners or Rhinelanders and therefore against the hegemony of Prussia. That is also the reason why the tradition of federalism of western political philosophy has always been extremely lively and active in German Catholicism. Hence even today its chief political efforts are pointed towards the equal treatment of the confessions in the selection of government and administrative personnel.

This basic antithetical feeling, useful as it may have been as a driving force and for concentration upon political possibilities, led, in the field of *spiritual life* to a ghetto-like seclusion from contemporary cultural life, to atrophy and resignation, to an acceptance of inequality. In connection with this it was important that the age of the Enlightenment darkened, and even extinguished, the memory of the Christian Middle Ages, and that the fashionable German philosophy in the 19th Century was Kantian idealism with its "categorical imperative" (very useful for the Prussian state, its officials and military men). The educational ideal was the classicist humanism of Goethe and Schiller, the political rule was the totalitarian ideology of Hegel, neither of which grew, territorially or spiritually, on Catholic soil. Thus, the Catholics stood completely against the "spirit of the time."

The end of the Empire of the Kaiser (1918) did not change the predominance of Prussia over Germany, but gave to the German Catholics greater mobility. They received an equal chance in the civil service. The Center Party acquired a key position because of the particular structure of the German party system after 1918, and participated in the *responsibility of governing* far more than its quantitative strength would have suggested. Although the Center Party held only about 70 seats (out of 600) in the Reichstag, it secured the Chancellorship of the Reich in 8 of the 14 cabinets between 1918 and 1933.

Hand in hand with this increase of *political* influence went the liberation from the cultural ghetto. New forces from the groups of the youth movement (*Quickborn, Neu-Deutschland, Hochland*) emerged into vigorous activity. The thorough preparatory and educational work in the social field, which the *Volksverein für das katholische Deutschland* (centered in München-Gladbach) had achieved, bore fruit. The Catholic social conception, a living tradition in Germany since the days of Bishop Emmanuel von Ketteler of Mainz, began to distinguish itself from the Socialist, and sometimes was even successful in the fight against Socialism. Franz Hitze, professor of theology, became a successful parliamentary spokesman for Catholic social teachings and was responsible for considerable progress in social legislation. Karl Sonnenschein, former secretary general of the *Volksverein* and one of its fascinating orators, was known as the "apostle of Berlin," a prototype of the modern big city priest whose ministration to souls included every assistance to bodily needs. Anton Heinen won lasting importance as a popular educator. In the field of youth care, nursing institutions and hospitals, and homes for children, Catholic specialists and institutions were very prominent.

The political ideal of the Center Party during the Weimar Republic (1918-1933) was not, however, so clear as it had been in the period of the antithesis. Political forces were spent on the small game of party politics for offices and maintenance of the principle of parity. The representative of the Center Party, Matthias Erzberger, went so far—contrary to all south German federalist tradition—as to sponsor a financial reform which deprived the Laender of power and favored the central authority. Bismarck had not dared to do that in his boldest centralist dreams. This lack of a clear and steady program became the undoing of the Center Party when Hitler came. The representatives of the Center Party were decisively influenced by the vote of the former Reichskanzler Heinrich Brüning, for the famed "Ermachtigungsgesetz" (Enabling Law). Basically they had given in to the idea of a centralist form of government. They had no principled objections against a further concentration of power, and mistakenly saw, in Hitler's promises, an adequate guarantee against the abuse of this power.

II. *Results of the Church Struggle*

The Concordat, signed in Rome between the Holy See and the German Reich on July 20, 1933, led many Catholics to believe that the Hitler regime sought an honest understanding with the Church, especially because, in its beginnings, it bettered public morality. Many took seriously the statement that "positive Christianity" was a part of the Nazi program. Later the Concordat was systematically disregarded, although freedom of religion, restricted to Church services, was maintained. The psychological consequences of the Concordat were absolutely harmful; it hid the fundamental contrasts between Hitler's doctrine and Christianity.

Hitler's fight against Christianity found German Catholicism better prepared in that it could start off from its own successful tradition of resistance against Bismarck and his imitators. The loss of political representation—the Center Party had anticipated its prohibition by self-dissolution on July 6, 1933—and the paralysis of the Catholic organizations by thousands of restrictions, later on by outright prohibition, increasingly forced a return to the original form of church life, the parish.

Forceful expulsion from the field of political and social activity by the totalitarian state led the Catholics to the rediscovery of the parish and, for the first time, to a *full* use of its missionary possibilities. Unfortunately, after the period of persecution it has often been forgotten how dearly this advantage had been bought; many still refuse to emerge from the parish position to which they had been driven back. They will not reoccupy the territory, once lost, but now accessible to them. Today, this legacy of persecution appears most prominently in youth work.

The period of persecution had another, very important result:

the comprehensive improvement of the relations between the two great Christian confessions.

For the first time since 1871 German Catholicism in the "Third Reich" confronted a Protestantism which was not allied to the state at all, but found itself in the situation of a minority group. Those forces in German Protestantism which clung to their faith and objected to National Socialist intervention in the church order, won more and more support from the people. Some *Landeskirchen* as a whole had preserved themselves untouched and had not surrendered to Hitler—for example, Wurttemberg with Landesbischof Theophil Wurm, and Bavaria with Landesbischof Meiser. A strong feeling of solidarity developed during the persecution, and bridged the centuries-old differences between the confessions. They suddenly discovered that what they had in common was more powerful than their differences. It is impossible to exaggerate the strength of this new Christian feeling which even affected and brought back to the church men who had long been separated from it.

This development explains why no Catholic party was founded after the war. Instead of the Center Party, there was a party embracing *all* Christian forces, a party which called itself the "Christian Democratic Union" (CDU), and in Bavaria the "Christian Social Union" (CSU).

Numerous meetings of leading clergymen of both confessions, such as those between the chairman of the "Council of the Evangelical Church in Germany," Dr. Dibelius, and the chairman of the "Fulda Bishops Conference," Cardinal Dr. Josef Frings, revived the hope that a lasting cooperation would also be established in charitable and social fields, between the *Caritasverband* and *Evangelisches Hilfswerk*. In many places churches had been destroyed. When the Catholics were fortunate enough to have their church, they put it at the disposal of other confessions, and *vice versa*. Today, Catholics enjoy these guest rights in 700 Protestant churches. The church authorities who, in former years, had violently objected to this joint use of churches on grounds of principle, now not only tolerated this *brotherly help,* but some even instructed their pastors to grant it.

The greatest hope of German Catholicism during the time of persecution was its youth. Before Hitler there was a flourishing organizational life, with a spirit of freshness and a careful differentiation answering the needs of natural and professional groupings

(*Jungmännerverband, Quickborn, Neu-Deutschland, Heiland, Jugendbund des Katholischen Frauenbundes*). Though National Socialism was able to destroy the external forms of these organizations and prohibit their newspaper *Junge Front* (later *Michael*), which is recognized, over all Germany, as a symbol of manly resistance, the regime did not gain the apostasy of youth from its ideals. The young people met on a parochial level and in the rooms of the parish. The prohibition of religious instruction in the schools led to voluntary religious instruction by priests in the parish, and the majority of the Catholic children went to these sessions regularly. This extra-curricular instruction was free of all state influences and restraints and could aim more directly at the substance of the faith. Besides, as the teaching activity was half-illegal, the attraction of the forbidden doubtless strengthened its educational effect. This state of affairs had the disadvantage that everything was much more dependent on the individual personality of a priest than under normal conditions. This disadvantage was outweighed by the intensity with which the religious could operate now by the direct radiation of personalities. Never before had there been so many vocations to the priesthood as in those years of persecution, although the study of theology did not mean, as in former times, exemption from military service. On the contrary, candidacy for the priesthood involved severe disadvantages in military service, often an assignment to extremely dangerous points of the fighting front and permanent political supervision.

This religious springtime of German Catholic youth did not and could not come to full realization, because the ranks of the most active and promising were cruelly decimated during the war. Out of about 20,000 members of a Bund of Catholic high school (Gymnasium) boys almost 50% were killed during the years 1939-1945. There are high school classes which do not count a single survivor. Nonetheless, the *spirit* of the Catholic youth has, to an astonishing degree, become the common and undisputed property of German Catholicism. As a consequence of the forced withdrawal to the redoubt of the parish, the style of the youth movement became a style element even in liturgical life and influenced the *whole* realm of ceremonies in the church. In Germany the youth movement before the First World War and between the two Wars had the *élan vital* which promoted the great spiritual reforms within the church (eucharistic and liturgical movements, the Lay Apostolate, the rediscovery of Holy Scriptures as an inspiration for the Christian life), and gradually won their acceptance by all the people in the church. The liturgical movement had a special importance because it gave a sense of genuine reform to believers, in an epoch of crumbling forms, and created a real community in an era of collectivism and of Hitler's "racial community." The ideas and views of the youth movement, which broke with the historicist tendencies of the nineteenth century and emphasized a stark simplicity, the proper use of materials, and "modern" art currents, today decisively influence the building of churches and church art. It has had a revolutionary effect on edifying literature—the use of the Schott Mass book was successfully promoted by the youth movement—and on the prayers printed for devotional exercises. The German Catholic Days inescapably appear to be demonstrations inspired by young men.

III. *Territorial Changes*

In 1932, the area of the German Reich contained 25 dioceses. As a result of the Potsdam decisions of the Allied powers the following have been lost to Poland and Russia: the diocese of Ermland (*Frauenburg*), the "praelatura nullius" Schneidemuhl, almost the whole of the Archdiocese of Breslau, the part of the bishopric of Berlin east of the Oder, and a part of the bishopric of Meissen.

The partition of the rest of Germany into zones of occupation rendered impossible for several years the free movement of persons, goods and money between the zones. No fewer than 10 dioceses were cut by zone frontiers. After the foundation of the Federal Republic of Germany in May 1949, these difficulties almost completely disappeared in western and southern Germany, but they were heightened for those dioceses which are cut by the frontier between the Federal Republic and the Soviet zone, the Iron Curtain: Wurzburg, Fulda, Paderborn, and Osnabrück. In this area almost insuperable difficulties impede the movement of the clergy. Communication between the pastors and their superiors is grievously hampered. Not only are there two political systems of irreconcilable contrast, but there are also two currencies, two postal systems, etc. For an inhabitant of the Federal Republic it is technically easier to get permission for a trip to France or Argentina than to the Soviet zone of Germany.

IV. *Material Damage*

The destruction wrought by the aerial war in Germany has enormously influenced church life. In the diocese of Aachen 85% of all church buildings were destroyed; in the diocese of Münster only 200 out of 573 churches remained undamaged; in the diocese of Trier only 124 out of 834 parishes suffered no damage to buildings or real estate; in the Archdiocese of Cologne only 211 out of 954 churches were undamaged, and in the city of Cologne itself, which once had 104 churches, among them some a thousand years old, there was only one left undamaged.

It will take many decades for the parishes to recover the material resources which they had before the war. General poverty and the necessity of building factories and dwelling houses first, make the situation even more difficult.

In spite of all this, many churches and buildings belonging to the Church in Western Germany have been rebuilt during the six years since the end of the War. The willingness of the Catholic population to sacrifice has been admirable, and the state authorities and the occupation powers have lent a hand by granting money and credits. For example, 200,000 marks were given from the McCloy Fund for the reconstruction of the famous St. Geron Church in Cologne.

In the Soviet zone some construction has been carried out. Here, however, the situation is different because of the reception of displaced persons. After Silesia and the Ermland came under Polish administration, no closed settlement of Catholic areas existed. Here the problem was not the reconstruction of destroyed churches or the construction of new ones, but primarily the establishment of new parishes and emergency churches in an area which hitherto had contained very few Catholics.

The financial situation of the Catholic Church in the Federal Republic is excellent in spite of the high expenditures. The State levies from every Catholic a church tax which is about 7 to 10% of the wage or income tax. Since the state taxation after the war reached an almost confiscatory height, the revenues of the Church have increased considerably. (The scale of the wage tax for a married couple without children is: from 750 DM—176.50 DM; from 1200 DM—414 DM; from 2000 DM—918 DM.)

V. *The Lack of Priests*

The lack of priests is of fundamental importance for the present state of German Catholicism. The reasons for this shortage are the quantitative weakness caused by the war and postwar years 1924-25, the losses in the concentration camps, the numerous casualties among priests and theology students during the war at the front and at home and in the prisoner-of-war camps, and the complete lack of whole classes of high school boys as a result of the criminal use of fifteen to seventeen-year-old boys as soldiers in the last phase of the War.

The Archbishop of Cologne had been able to ordain only thirty-five priests per year during 1939-1946 while the average in former years had been eighty. The diocese of Münster cannot normally fill 500 pastoral positions. The losses in Münster may be broken down as follows: thirty priests were in concentration camps, and nine of them died; forty priests fell at the front, eighty are missing, and ten are still prisoners of war in Russia; of the 271 students of theology 267 had to join the army, of whom seventy were killed, while thirty are still missing.

Even worse are the losses of the east German dioceses. Ermland had 393 priests in 1944; when the Russians marched in a third of them were killed or died of starvation or disease; another third were detained by the Polish authorities or deported; only 136 clergymen are now available to minister to the souls of their countrymen.

That is why the lack of priests is extremely great in the *Diaspora*. The situation has been aggravated by the fact that the Germans expelled from the east are mostly Catholic, and have been transplanted into areas which were formerly solidly Protestant and have no well established Catholic Church organization.

VI. *The New Diaspora*

On April 1, 1948 there were the following categories of homeless people in the four occupation zones of Germany:

Evacuees caused by bombing	2,000,000
Displaced persons	800,000
Driven from the east	11,071,000
Fugitives from the Soviet Zone to Western Germany	817,500

In the meantime many of the evacuees have returned to reconstructed houses in the big cities. The number of displaced persons has been reduced by repatriation and emigration. On the other hand, the continued flow of fugitives from the satellite states has kept the figure high. The fugitives from the Soviet zone grow daily. Today, it is still likely that there are 15 million homeless people in Germany.

The expulsion of the Germans living east of the Oder, a measure resolved upon at Potsdam, cost the lives of 3 to 4 million Germans. Out of the 11 million who escaped from the eastern German frontier, almost exactly half are Catholic. When these people were distributed over the rest of Germany where state authority and economic production were then completely disrupted, it was not possible to arrange the distribution according to religious membership. More than three-quarters of the expelled Catholics were ushered into purely Protestant areas. Suddenly, dioceses, where till then only a few Catholics had lived, were swelled in numbers by people who had nothing, neither work nor home, and had gone through the most horrifying mental experiences. For example, the Bishopric of Meissen had 225,000 Catholics in 1939 and 185 priests. By March 31, 1947, 516,000 Catholics had emigrated there, but there were only sixty-three priests available.

It is the historic merit of the *Bonifatius Verein* that it mobilized all the forces of German Catholicism in order to give effective personal and material help to the huge new diaspora that had appeared over night.

German Protestantism confronted the same situation. Just as there are no longer any purely Protestant areas, so there are no longer any purely Catholic ones. In 1910, 2,300 villages in Bavaria were still solidly Catholic, while in 1947 there were only nine. The figures for purely Protestant villages are 244 in 1910, and none in 1949. In 1947 Munich, commonly considered to be a metropolis of Catholic Germany, had 51.14 mixed marriages for every 100 purely Catholic marriages. In Luther's town, Wittenberg, once solidly Protestant, the Catholics today form 18% of the population. The population of Schleswig-Holstein increased 100% during one year, from 1.39 to 2.51 million people. Every fifth Catholic in Germany is an expelled person.

VII. *The Confessions and the Division of Germany*

The statement of Pastor Martin Niemoeller that the Federal Republic of Germany was "conceived in the Vatican and born in Washington" sheds light on the controversy over the effect of the division of Germany on the Christian confessions.

Before 1938 there lived in the area of the German Reich about 70 million inhabitants, 33% of whom were Catholics and 60% Protestants. In the Soviet zone there are about 17.5 million people, 3 million of whom are Catholic. These figures reveal the magnitude of the Catholic Diaspora. The Federal Republic has 47.6 million inhabitants, of whom 50.7% are Protestant and 45.2% Catholic.

Protestantism in the Federal Republic has no clear quantitative majority. The political center of the new state does not lie in Protestant northern Germany, but in the predominantly Catholic Rhineland. The importance of the south German *Laender* has grown. The *Land*, Prussia, formerly the power center of the Imperial Reich and the Republic, has been divided into newly created *Laender*, at least two of which (Niedersachsen and Nordrhein-Westfalen) have a population with anti-Prussian tendencies. The former free Hanseatic cities, Bremen and Hamburg, have become independent city states again; their interests were consistently opposed to the Prussian military state of yesterday.

No wonder that the eye of a man like the former submarine commander Niemoeller, seeking for power positions, looks to the Soviet zone. A fusion of the two areas would, of course, restore the old proportion of 2:1 between Protestants and Catholics.

It is false and unjust to attribute the dividing of Germany or its continued division to the sectarian selfishness of the Catholics. The real history of this tragedy is only too well known. Apart from that, the German Catholics cannot overlook the fact that the present arrangement is injurious to their own co-religionists in the Soviet zone. The oppression of Christianity in the Soviet zone is in its effects harder on the 2 million Catholic displaced persons than on the almost exclusively Protestant natives, who are professionally and socially established and need the help of the anti-christian state for their daily living less urgently than the displaced persons do for their own rehabilitation.

The Christian Democratic Union (CDU) is at present the strongest party in the Federal Republic. It bears the chief burden

215

of responsibility in the Federal government and in the majority of the *Laender*. Within the CDU the Catholic element prevails. This results in part from the fact that the Catholics have always had a political grouping and were able to put their voters and leaders at the disposal of the CDU, while Protestants were not able to do so. Besides, Catholicism in Germany has—thanks to its tradition—a more direct relation to political life in a parliamentary democracy than Protestantism. The consequent greater political dynamism and discipline benefit the CDU today. The other parties with Christian elements in their programs have only a local importance: the German Party has its home in Niedersachsen, Bremen and Hamburg and is tied to the Guelph tradition of the Kingdom of Hannover which had been forcibly annexed by Prussia in 1866; the party is faithfully Protestant. The Bayern Party (Bavarian Party) exists only in Bavaria; it is strongly Royalist, xenophobe and anti-Prussian and has liberal and Catholic wings. Its chief support comes from the farmers, the clergy, and government officials. The new Center Party in Westphalia and the Rhineland is practically, not in theory, purely Catholic-clerical; it stands close to the socialists in social and economic policies, and its vaccillating foreign policy is not free from tendencies towards neutralism.

Unfortunately, in the course of the six years since the end of the War the good relations between the confessions have not been everywhere untroubled. These difficulties have not arisen because of the statements from Rome requiring caution in any co-operation involving matters of truth and of worship. The differences arise in the political field.

The Protestants believe that in the CDU, and in all those governments established or partly established by it, the Catholics enjoy an excessive predominance. They point to the almost equal proportion of the confession in the whole population of the Federal Republic. The Catholics, for their part, emphasize the fact that the political support of the CDU has come far more from Catholics than from Protestants, and that the minorities of the Protestant voters have received particular consideration in that Protestant candidates, rather than Catholics, have usually been put up in confessionally-mixed electoral areas. Out of the 139 CDU representatives in the Bundestag, about forty are Protestants; it is generally estimated, however, that the Protestant share of the 7 million CDU votes is far less than one-third. Nevertheless, the CDU has cast its vote for a Protestant *Bundespräsident* and a Protestant *Bundestagspräsident,* and the confessional statistics concerning the composition of the Federal authorities, issued from time to time by the Federal government mostly as a defense against reproaches, show that the proportion of Protestant officials, especially in higher ranks, is larger than the Protestant proportion of the population.

Nevertheless, the mere fact of such a controversy proves the deterioration of the relations between the confessions as a result of the struggle for political power.

This, however, has not reached the point of serious attempts to destroy the politically acting community of the confessions. Every thinking man can grasp the fact that the Christians would lose their political advantage if they gave up the comprehensive party of the CDU. The old Center Party, its name burdened in more than one respect, does not even have much attraction for Catholic circles, and it is more than uncertain whether Protestantism could succeed in forming its own political organization if the CDU should ever cease to exist.

VIII. *Political Questions*

The German Catholics had no reason to mourn over the state which perished with the unconditional surrender in the Spring of 1945. Hitler had never left any doubts about his intentions to destroy the Catholic Church in Germany as soon as the War was over and the Catholic soldiers were no longer needed.

Thus, in spite of the immense loss of lives, the destruction and the lack of all necessities of life, a sense of liberation swept through the lands of the German Catholics when the Allies put an end to the National-Socialist regime. In various places, clergymen took the initiative, after all state and community authorities had disappeared, and surrendered their towns to the approaching troops in order to save them from final destruction. The Abbess of the venerable Benedictine Convent of St. Walberg at Eichstätt led her nuns out to meet a group of American tanks in order to assure them, in the name of the inhabitants of the town, that nobody had other than peaceful intentions. This Abbess may stand as one example among many.

Even the unfortunate experiences of the early period of the occupation could not discourage the forces in German Catholicism which were ready for honest reconstruction. It was bitter for them, in the beginning, to see how one-sidedly the occupation forces preferred Communist and extreme Socialist elements when authority had to be delegated to Germans. One example may serve as an illustration: the "Catholic" licensee of the first German newspaper to be licensed in the U.S. zone, the *Frankfurter Rundschau,* was the Communist Wilhelm Karl Gerst. Along with a second Communist as representative of the Party, he was made publisher and owner of that paper. His work for Catholicism, as long as the occupation forces permitted his activity, chiefly consisted of smear articles against German bishops and of Communist propaganda.

A juster division of power was established only after the first democratic elections for the *Laender* parliaments. These elections, held in the U.S. zone on June 30, 1946, resulted in 2.6 million votes for the CDU, 1.8 million for the Socialists, and about 400,000 for both the Communists and the LPD. After that it was no longer possible to conceal the preference of the people.

When the *Laender* constitution had to be prepared, all those great political questions arose which have always been eagerly studied by the Catholic intellectuals. The lesson drawn from the times of the Bismarckian Reich, the centralistic Republic, and the totalitarian Hitler regime, all clearly called for a federal organization of the new Germany. The historical situation corresponded to this concept because the Allies demanded that autonomous *Laender* should first be created before a union on a broader base could be thought of.

While many German forces refrained from co-operating in this construction of a new state form, for they could envisage a national structure only on centralizing lines, the Catholics went zealously to work. The Catholic politicians, especially in southern Germany (Bayern, Oberschwaben, Baden) and in the Rhineland, saw the long-awaited possibility of achieving their ideal of a federal Germany organized on the basis of cultural regions.

This was the reason why the Catholic influence on the shape of things was rather considerable in the beginning. This influence first conflicted with the socialist ideas of a great central state which would provide no intermediary of any importance between the highest authority and the communities, and, later on, also with the centralizing leanings of the "Free Democrats." But circumstances were favorable and a federal organization was achieved. Recently, there has been a strengthening of the forces which aim to destroy the federal constitution because they regard it as irrational and too expensive. Unfortunately, the political education of the Catholics has not kept pace with developments. As a result, the mass of the voters face these problems without any understanding, although the parliamentary leaders are often exceedingly well-informed. In view of this lack of proportion it must be expected that in the near future centralizing tendencies will get the upper hand and, in the long run, effect some changes in the constitutional structure.

The chief problem of the new state, however, is the reserve with which the population regards its origin and growth. In this respect the Catholics are no exception. There are numerous reasons for this attitude. After all, the Germans have received their new state at the hands of the Allies. A century of political continuity was interrupted and in many respects the new creation could not and would not be tied to the old. The new capital was located in Bonn, a town which had never played a role in German history. The lack of tradition of the newly created state could not have been emphasized more clearly.

It should be added that the left-wing forces did all in their power to convince the German public that the new regime was merely the product of a "conspiracy of socially reactionary and clerical circles." The civic conscience of the Germans, undermined by the nationalist inflation of the Third Reich and stunned by defeat and by the occupation regime, is still completely off balance. The moral authority of the new state is low among the people. Criticism of the government, the Parliament, and the authorities is common—regardless of the party to which the critics may belong.

It is, undoubtedly, a serious limitation of German Catholicism that it has been unable to form a clear and conscious civic attitude among its members. Nor are there any promising efforts under way to make up for it. Social-political and cultural-political questions dominate Catholic discussions, while fundamental questions of state policy receive little consideration. This is all the more tragic because the historic opportunity of German Catholicism today is in the field of state policy, especially as all other groups, the socialists included, are irremediably and in principle incapable of presenting a clear and comprehensive political conception of the state.

IX. *Questions of Foreign Policy*

The Catholics are reproached not only for failing to take the initiative in restoring the national unity of Germany, but they are also accused of making their foreign policy subservient to the Vatican. They are blamed for subordinating the needs of the German people to the interests of the "triangle Rome-Paris-Bonn."

It is certainly true that the great majority of German Catholics are determined to do all in their power to achieve a united Europe. It is also true that they consider this end, and the securing of the freedom and independence of this Europe as more urgent than the fusion of the Soviet zone and the Federal Republic. They have reached this position not because of an anti-Protestant bias or an unconscious fear of the numerical superiority of the Protestants in the east, but because of their conviction that their German countrymen in the Soviet zone will be served by the elective strength of the west.

Another point is that German Protestantism, with its Prussian, Hohenzollern, *kleindeutsch* tradition, largely thought and thinks nationalistically. Only with difficulty can it accept the idea of giving up a part of the national sovereignty in favor of a European federation, while this idea corresponds to the universalist occidental world view of the Catholics. This development is quite apart from the fact that there is also a kind of Latin groundswell for Europe, a view which, of course, is not necessarily Christian or Catholic. This view prevails almost exclusively in the south and west of Germany, and these are Catholic areas.

But these contradictions should not be exaggerated. Today, the Protestant politicians of the CDU are pledged to work unstintingly and without reservation for the union of Europe. In the course of the Adenauer administration this foreign policy has become the true unification formula of the CDU. This end has enabled the Adenauer cabinet time and again to hold together and focus conflicting forces in economic, social and domestic politics generally.

German Catholicism, however, is not free of tendencies which oppose a firm alignment with the west. Some have sought a neutralist utopia. For example, the Chairwoman of the Center Party, Helene Wessel, and Inge Scholl, the survivor of the Scholl sisters of the University of Munich who were executed by Hitler, have expressed such sentiments. Others are prepared to deal with the Russians to secure a kind of "provisional government" for all of Germany. There are many shades of opinion between these views and the firm pro-western view. In general, it may be said that among the Catholics an inclination towards socialism accompanies willingness for an agreement with the east, and that, even here, the philosophical rejection of Bolshevism is joined with a criticism of the capitalistic west.

This is particularly apparent in Catholic discussion about German participation in the western defense system. The position of the poet, Reinhold Schneider, who is widely known for his opposition to Hitler, may be cited as typical of many German Catholics. Schneider, who certainly does not favor Bolshevism and does not lack the courage to oppose terrorist threats, is against German participation in Western defense. His refusal involves an opposition, based on pacifist principles, to modern war, even a war to resist an unjust attack. The importance of the principle must be emphasized, even though his hope for a peaceful settlement with the east is supported by his impractical view that the Russian people can be diverted from Bolshevism by the convincing example of true Christian life. Others oppose German association in Western defense because they believe that Germany would be the battlefield and, consequently, would be doomed to utter destruction. Very few suggest that their refusal to serve in the cause of freedom springs from resentment that the Germans have been blamed for fighting in behalf of tyranny.

Catholic analysis of the relations of Germany to the East and West is especially complicated by such difficult problems as the incorporation of Berlin and of the Soviet zone into the German state. Even to many Catholics the recovery of German national unity seems more important than the preservation of the civil liberty of the West German state. As the inclusion of the Soviet zone would mean a socialist majority in parliament, nationalist and Marxist opinions converge on this issue.

Among the German Catholics, socialism, anti-capitalism and neutralism have romantic and even utopian features. Such views are held particularly by the younger generation and the intellectuals. These have had no adequate political training. Moreover, the spiritual isolation of the German people during the Hitler regime and the years after it had a destructive influence on the older generation.

X. *Social Questions*

Immediately after 1945 there was no time for the consideration of theoretical questions of social and economic policy. Practical

221

help for the millions of needy was an overwhelming imperative. In meeting the varying demands of this work *Caritas,* with its 121,000 professional workers and 700,000 volunteer workers, achieved wonders. In 1945-46 the *Caritas* organization of the Archdiocese of Munich, alone, distributed 6,731,787 kilograms of food. In that region 11,000 people were fed daily from the kitchens of *Caritas.* During this period the Archdiocese of Munich raised 5,400,000 marks. These efforts of the Catholics were, of course, inadequate for dealing even with the direst need. Generous assistance received from abroad made a deep impression on the German people. Thus, by the autumn of 1947, the Vatican had sent 6,000 tons of food, the National Catholic Welfare Conference provided 5,000 tons of clothing and food, and 780,000 Care-packages were distributed through the agency of *Caritas* to German beneficiaries.

To the measure that the Germans participated in the handling of public affairs, they perceived the great economic and social-political problems and sought an answer. The failure to create a main study center, such as the earlier People's Association for Catholic Germany, for the consideration of these questions was unfortunate. As a result, the social efforts of German Catholicism were based on different methods and moved in different directions. At first, the search for a reconciliation between socialism and Catholicism was a dominant concern, but practical politics, especially the consequences of the economic liberalization achieved by the CDU Minister, Ludwig Erhard, established a preference for what is called a "social market economy." This view is opposed to planning theories, and in favoring the free play of the market also supports the use of strong social-political controls.

In this program, then, there are two elements of diverse origin. The whole social-political controversy in German Catholicism centers around the weight which each element shall carry in any particular case.

Since 1945 the principal conflict has been over the establishment of workers' co-determination in industrial establishments and handicraft work. The Catholic Day at Bochum—an assemblage of 600,000 Catholic laity—had supported co-determination. On this matter employers and employees were united. Only after the trade unions had vehemently taken up the Bochum program and were achieving political effectiveness did opposition develop among some Catholics. There were serious disputes in CDU and the Catholic organizations, which even now do not exercise a weighty influence on the course of political affairs. After lengthy deliberation parliament passed a law, which established co-determination in the coal and iron industries and almost completely satisfied the demands of the trade unions.

This example indicates that the failure to reestablish Christian trade unions (alongside the Socialists, Communists and others) also had its unfortunate side. By its very nature, the Catholic Workers Movement, which has more than 200,000 well-organized members, can influence politically only its trade-union members; it can not operate as an independent force. When it vigorously opposed exaggerated demands for co-determination and the extension of co-determination from works' councils to the central offices of the trade unions, it failed to secure a hearing. The existence of a well-led, unified trade unionism was vital for political and economic peace in the first years of Germany's post-war reconstruction. But it can not be readily said that the failure to establish Christian trade unions and the establishment of a workers movement on a purely religious level have in sum proved to be inexpedient. The pastoral possibilities among the proletariat have, thereby, developed more than they have lost.

In the center of the social political struggles of German Catholicism are the problems of the housing shortage and of the economic and spiritual needs of large families.

Some Church authorities have given the fine example of offering Church-owned property for settlements. There are in almost all dioceses co-operative organizations which have offered to the homeless and to young families neighborly help and loans for housing. The "new home" undertaking, for which Father Magnani provided a plan with the simplicity of genius and the great drive of a forceful priestly personality, has been successful and widely imitated.

Even more important, because more effective, has been the effort of the CDU to secure state money for the constructing of homes. In the first years of the Federal Republic's existence, its money has made possible the building of more than 300,000 dwelling places.

Efforts to establish family allowances, such as exist in a number of states, are under way. These funds would be designed to supplement the salary inadequacies of those with large families.

At the commencement of the new state's existence, those who had lost all their possessions during the bombing or land warfare strongly demanded an "equalization of damage." In principle this demand called for the confiscation of all the remaining national resources, which would then be redistributed in proportion to the amount of property held by each person at the beginning of the war. There was much concern with this problem even among the Catholics. Practical difficulties make it impossible to consider an all-embracing solution. Moreover, in the meantime, many successful efforts have been made to rebuild a new life in a new dwelling place.

For those, unable because of old age or unfortunate circumstances to find employment, the initiative of the CDU has provided "Direct Help." This token share of a damage equalization payment assures at least a subsistence minimum. The Socialists, where they have dominated the *Laender* governments, have done as little in this as in home construction. Nevertheless, with astounding humility, they have described the accomplishments of the CDU as inadequate.

XI. *Cultural-Political Questions*

The disunity in social-political views is in contrast to the impressive accord on cultural-political matters.

In drafting the *Laender* constitutions the Catholic authorities sought to secure a constitutional settlement of the school question. They hoped for an arrangement which would respect the right of the parents to determine the character of the school, and thus permit the establishment of denominational religious schools, wherever the parents desired them. Because of the different political majorities in the various *Laender,* this hope was realized in only a few instances (Bavaria, South Wurttemberg, Rhineland-Pfalz). In the preliminary work on the fundamental law of the Federal Republic it seemed doubtful that a decision would be taken in favor of this parental right, for the school question was in the sphere of the *Laender's* competence. When it was decided to introduce, as a minimum, a general declaratory clause, there was no majority to support it. As a result, the Catholics had to be satisfied with securing the provision of Church supervised religious instruction in all schools. The question of parental right and of denominational schools were left to the *Laender.*

All German universities and high schools are either state or municipal institutions. There are no Catholic high schools. But in some universities Catholic influence is not inconsiderable. Many universities have Catholic theological faculties. In all university cities there are special student chaplains. The outlook of the majority of professors, however, is not definitely Christian.

Unfortunately the Catholics had no influence on the reformulation of marriage law, for this was arranged by the Allied Control Commission. This law preserved many National-Socialist provisions, which ran counter to the Catholic position. Thus, paragraph 48 of the new marriage law included a provision that a marriage could be broken even against the will of the guiltless party.

The whole cultural-political program of German Catholicism in its contemporary form expresses statist assumptions, which have developed in Germany since the days of Absolutism. There are, as yet, only some strivings for a new program, which would be based on the Catholic conception of the autonomy of the cultural realm in view of the substantial weaknesses that appear in the cultural program of any state, even when controlled by Christians with the best of intentions.

Where this still uncommon mistrust of statist authority does appear, it takes two forms. First, there is in the political realm mistrust of simply trying to reshape the contemporary (in particular, Prussian) authoritarian state according to the proper concept of Christian views. This is paralleled, especially among the younger generation, by cultural-political views which decisively favor a greater independence of public cultural authorities and a freeing of the Church and education from political connections. Many vaguely look on the "free school" of the French as an ideal, although they have to recognize that the economic and, especially, the spiritual bases for such an arrangement in Germany are simply not present at the moment.

XII. *Condition of the Press and Reviews*

The press policy of the occupation powers considerably changed the character of the German press. At first, party journals were not permitted. Instead, the first journals were jointly put in the hands of trusted representatives of the four permitted parties. Later, when party papers were tolerated, the CDU journals, corresponding to the denominationally mixed character of the party, were not simply Catholic organs, as had earlier been the case with the organs of the Center Party. The only exclusively Catholic daily, which was licensed in 1948, had little significance apart from its own region.[1]

The Church press (diocesan and parish papers) went through an unexpected growth after 1945. Today, these papers have more than 6 million subscribers. The diocesan papers have 2 million, the Catholic Sunday journals have 300,000, and the illustrated papers 315,000. The rest of the total is made up by organization journals (1,900,000) and the journals of religious orders and missions (1,000,000).

The monthly reviews have experienced a similar increase. To the venerable *Stimmen der Zeit* and the widely respected literary review, *Hochland,* there has been added the *Frankfurter Hefte,* which serves as the spokesman for the leftist tendencies of German Catholicism. The *Neue Ordnung* is devoted to social-political and Church affairs. The review, *Wort und Wahrheit,* which is published in Vienna but has German editors and authors, is growing in significance and maintains a brilliant literary style. It is concerned with the renewal of life within the Church and with the preservation of the healthy elements in politics, considered from a European point of view.

The broadcasting system of the Federal Republic has responded to the explicit ecclesiastical request for the transmission of Sunday and occasional feast-day services. Some stations offer five minutes of prayer every morning. On the other hand, there is practically no Catholic influence on the rest of the radio programs. The whole complex of the Northwest German Radio System, which reaches the most populous areas of Germany, is dominated by socialist elements, as a result of British occupation policy. The situation is not much different elsewhere.

The Catholics lack professional technical experts, who could by their professional competence effect a change in this condition. The interest of the hierarchy has unfortunately been restricted to the rather limited concern with the broadcast of religious services. They have failed to appreciate the possibilities which the main programs offer.

Catholic influence in the field of film production is even smaller. But efforts are being made to enable the Catholic population to be critical of each film on aesthetic and moral grounds and to develop

---

[1] The *Rheinischer Merkur,* edited by the author of this article, is a weekly which is primarily a political journal but also deals with economic and cultural matters. It has won a respected place in German journalism. Editors' note.

their own judgment. To this end the work of the "Church Film Service" is important. It publishes a periodical, which is placed on Church bulletin boards and is mainly distributed by Catholic youth organizations. The participation of Church representatives in the so-called "Self-Control of German Films" is of little value, because the representatives of the film industry control a majority of votes and, therefore, can block any unfavorable verdicts.

XIII. *Future Outlook*

From the foregoing it appears that barely calculable factors, internal and external, determine the course of German Catholicism. In his widely noticed pastoral letter, "Growth or Decline of the Church," the French Cardinal Suhard asked whether the difficulties of contemporary Catholicism should be considered as symptoms of decline or as growing-pains. The very same question must be asked with reference to Germany.

A comparison with the situation in France reveals that the development towards laicism, towards the secularization of public life and towards the religious indifferentism of the masses is still not so far advanced there as in France. In Germany Faust's rule still holds: "One-third of the baptized practices its religion regularly, another third, considering itself Catholic, practices irregularly, and the remaining third has no direct relation with the Church at all."

The Church is still a power in public life. In many places it preserves the remains of the thousand years of feudal brilliance and has, also, gained in the last one and one-half centuries a new moral prestige, which is recognized even by people far removed from the Church.

German Catholicism, however, was not reduced to the challenging extremities experienced by the French. National-Socialism was diabolically motivated in not carrying through the separation of the Church from the State. Hitler even collected the Church taxes and paid the bishops, priests and Church officials. The bureaucratic elements of German Catholicism survived the persecution without major injury. They are no more receptive to the modern world than they were twenty or fifty years ago. They show no inclination to adjust themselves or to come to terms with the modern world. The active missionary life expresses itself in the field of pastoral care. Recently many young men have been appointed to the Ger-

227

man episcopate. For this to be effective, it will also be necessary to replace the fossil element in Church bureaucracy.

On the whole, German Catholicism lacks that urgency and power of initiative which the awareness of the Existentialist crisis and the return to religious sources instilled in French Catholicism. German Catholicism is free of the turmoil of a consciousness of crisis. It still feels too secure in its traditions and in the assured possession of property, damaged but not destroyed.

The phenomenon of the loss of the working classes was eventually recognized, and the pastoral and organizational measures for winning them back have been in operation for some time. There is little public awareness of the fact that after the First World War the religious spirit of the country people was threatened and that after 1939 the center of the religious danger shifted to the country, especially after the influx of eleven million expellees. Pastoral care in the countryside appears to be dominated by old ways of doing things. In the twentieth century the Church is in danger of losing the country, as the industrial proletariat was lost in the nineteenth century. For this reason it is perhaps not only a misfortune, but also a blessing, that the urbanization of the rural areas continues, for with the cinema the city also brings a missionary impulse and the work of the lay apostolate to the countryside.

The political future of German Catholicism is dependent on its success in providing the Christian parties with competent Catholic leaders on every level. The Christian parties, and especially the CDU, have, of course, most of the voters. But they lack the professional politicians needed to make the Party a politically functioning machine. It must be the task of the Church organizations to work extensively in the realm outside of politics, where the principal political decisions occur. The objective of this labor should be to rouse the interest of all Catholics in politics and to assure their technical equipment so that this interest will be effective.

Education in political methods is almost completely lacking. But there is useful work done among the youth organizations in teaching them group techniques, the methods of leading discussions and presiding at meetings. The job of political education will not be easy, for the Catholics share the general German tendency to look for decisions from authority. They, too, are deficient in initiative, and place obedience before resolution and discipline before civil courage. Even the slow progress of the Lay movements has

228

been caused primarily by their own irresolution rather than by the occasional objections of the Hierarchy.

On the credit side of the balance sheet there are the high moral quality and the outstanding scholarly education of the German clergy. Regard for the Church increased during the persecution. In the conflict with the Bolshevist system of the east the Catholic Church has daily revealed a new vitality and steadfastness in the face of terror. This particularly impresses the German people, for whom the "iron curtain" is open and who have experienced the terror. Between the wars the religious zeal of the young exercised an increasing influence in local communities and public life as well.

There is still dominant today a pastoral attitude concerned exclusively with caring for the Catholics. In the long run this would certainly impair the missionary movement. The determined search of French Catholicism for a strategy of reconquest appears only among some individuals in Germany. There, the facade of religious life has prevented the recognition that Germany, like France, should be considered and dealt with as a missionary country. But in Germany, also, where the facade is collapsing, a willingness to recognize the facts is growing, and the heroic spirit needed to regain the masses is present in many individuals.

Germany is ripe for a second Boniface, embracing, purifying and setting all in order.

X

Contemporary French Catholicism *

by Adrien Dansette

I. *From the Revolution to World War I: the Two Frances*

To explain what Catholicism is in contemporary France would require a whole volume. It would be easy to sketch an external picture, to explain its organization, to outline the visible activity of its secular and regular clergy, to describe the hierarchy of the former and to enumerate the various orders of the latter, to explain the role of the laity by describing the network of institutions included in Catholic Action, and to accumulate statistics. But when the reader had absorbed this mass of information he would know hardly anything because the essential part, the soul or spirit of French Catholicism, would escape him. Rather than to give simply an external picture we have decided to use another method. We shall dwell less on space and more on time, that is, instead of describing a situation we shall try to bring to life an evolution. No doubt we shall not cover exactly what might be expected of us. We believe, however, that our effort will not have been in vain if we explain its origins, at least in the recent past, and its transformation, if we show the realities of French Catholicism and their complex relationships and describe its richness and its diversity. In brief, we shall try to satisfy the reader's curiosity and to awaken in him the desire to study the subject further.

It is always difficult to understand the religious situation of one's own country because religious questions touch us so profoundly and because the facts about them often go back to the obscurity of a very distant past. It is hard to circumscribe them and to disen-

---

* Translated by James A. Corbett.

230

tangle them from so many others with which they are intimately mingled.

It is even more difficult to understand the religious situation of another country, especially when the traditions of that country have, as in the case of France, a very special character.

Under the Old Regime Catholicism was the religion of the State and of the French. The French monarchy was called the Most Christian Monarchy. The King was the representative of God; he had been consecrated with holy oils. The great acts of life were religious acts. Attacks on the Faith, blasphemies, and sacrileges were punished by the courts. There was no place for disbelief.

One should not conclude from this that France was an idyllic country from the religious point of view. There have always been what are called "the two Frances." This does not mean that there has been no French unity; there are few countries where unity is more complete and where local particularisms present less danger. It simply means that from the religious point of view we should recognize in French history two traditions whose origins go very far back and which have not ceased to perpetuate themselves and, sometimes, even to come in conflict with each other.

There is the Roman tradition of the Church, heir of the Roman Empire, and hierarchized on the model of the imperial administration. It is the tradition of royal power united to the religious power, the authoritarian tradition which under diverse forms flourished at the end of the Middle Ages, and again in the seventeenth century. Louis XIV was the political incarnation and Bossuet the religious incarnation of this tradition.

There is also the Gallic tradition stemming from nature and reason which, confronting the authoritarian and ascetic ideal of Catholicism, proclaims the right to joy and the claims of reason. It is the tradition of the medieval fabliaux, of Rabelais, Molière and the encyclopedists of the eighteenth century.

These two traditions vie with each other down the centuries of history; Catholic France and the France of the Revolution, the France of the *Syllabus* and the France of the Rights of Man, the France of the Right and the France of the Left, the France of authority and the France of liberty, the France of conservatism and the France of reforms.

After the authoritarian reign of Louis XIV, which came to an end in 1715, there was a strong reaction dominated especially by

Voltaire. The *philosophes* taught liberty, ridiculed religion, and undermined the foundations of Catholicism. But, rather curiously, as they lived in a society where the Church was intimately linked to the State, they could not conceive of another arrangement. Although they remained unbelievers they proclaimed the necessity of religion for the people. This point of view explains what happened during the Revolution. The Church of France, known as the Gallican Church, was so closely linked to the Monarchy that the blows which fell on the Monarchy also fell on the Church. Both collapsed together. The members of the Constituent Assembly, the Assembly of 1789, were legists formed by Roman history and by the Encyclopedists. They had no idea of a Church separated from the State. They did what they saw the king do; they legislated as he had on religious affairs: "We are a national convention," one explained. The Constituent Assembly therefore gave a new organization to the Church without consulting the Pope or the episcopate. This was the Civil Constitution of the Clergy.

Confronted with this Constitution, the clergy hesitated. Most of the bishops rejected it; the lower clergy split into equal parts; the Pope condemned it. France had in fact two Churches: one which refused and one which accepted the Civil Constitution of the Clergy. The latter was called the Constitutional Church. This was the official Church which adopted the doctrines of the government and became republican with it.

The Catholic Church, swept away with the Monarchy, and persecuted by the Revolution, remained monarchist and became counter-revolutionary. The course of events led Catholicism to ally itself with monarchist, conservative and reactionary forces. This fact gives the key to the future. Under new forms the two Frances perpetuate themselves.

The France of the Left triumphed momentarily with the Revolution. Like most revolutions, the great Revolution evolved toward extremism. It not only persecuted the Catholic Church, but it soon persecuted the Constitutional Church and replaced it with religions which had nothing in common with Christianity. There were, in order, the cult of Reason, the cult of the Supreme Being, the Theophilanthropic cult and the Decadarian cult—a word derived from *decadi,* the day of rest every tenth day, which replaced Sunday, because that day was too closely linked with Catholic worship.

During the Consulate order returned under the strong hand of

Bonaparte whose policy was one of national reconciliation. He wanted to fuse the two Frances, the France of Catholicism and the France of the Revolution. While retaining the reforms of the Revolution he decided to restore the Catholic altars. The Concordat, negotiated with Pope Pius VII in 1801, decided the relations of the State and the Church until 1905.

By the terms of the Concordat, Catholicism was recognized by the French State no longer as the religion of the State as it was under the Old Regime, but as "the religion of the majority of Frenchmen." The bishops named the pastors and their assistants. The government named the bishops; the Pope conferred their spiritual powers. The government paid the salaries of the bishops and the priests.

The Concordat was in short a transaction between the two Frances. The persecution stopped and worship was restored. The Church was recognized as having a special position as regards the State; its clergy was paid. But this was not a unique place that the Church enjoyed, for Jewish and Protestant worship was granted similar rights. Hence, the State was no longer Christian and the Church had to accept freedom of conscience. Nor, as under the Old Regime, was it a body having its own life, its own assemblies and its own independent sources of income.

As a result the Church of France had a completely different attitude towards the Holy See. Under the Old Regime the Church had been Gallican, that is, while recognizing that the Pope had a special authority, this authority was limited by that of the bishops meeting in their assemblies. But the Church lost confidence in a State that had ceased to be Catholic. During the nineteenth century it gradually turned toward the Holy See. Ultramontanism succeeded Gallicanism. Whereas the Gallican Church had been known for its independence of the Holy See, now, the Church of France finally became subject to it without reservation. The proclamation of the dogma of papal infallibility in 1870 was a decisive date in this regard.

If, under the regime of the Concordat, the State was no longer Catholic, this did not necessarily mean that it would not act as a Catholic state. Its attitude towards the Church varied with the fluctuations of politics. When the First Empire fell, royalty was restored and for fifteen years there was a clerical upsurge which tended, to some extent, to give the Church a situation comparable to the one it enjoyed before the Revolution. In 1830 this clerical regime was overthrown and the Church suffered an anticlerical reaction under the Voltairian monarchy of Louis Philippe. In 1848 another revolution replaced the monarchy of Louis Philippe with the Second Republic which was not hostile to the Church because the new government opposed the preceding regime. The Second Empire followed the Second Republic. It was a clerical regime which considered the Church as a force for order capable of propping up the civil power. At the beginning of the National Assembly which, after the war of 1870, replaced the Second Empire and continued, in its broad lines, its religious policy, there was in the country a strong and progressive republican upsurge which triumphed partially as early as 1876 and completely in 1879.

The republicans were then the complete masters of power. Who were these republicans? While the Church, except for a few months in 1848, remained constantly a force of the Right bound up in part with the monarchists, the republicans were leftists. They followed the cult of the great Revolution, and were animated by an optimistic conception of man. They divinized science and believed in indefinite progress. Catholicism appeared to them as a power of darkness, in full decadence and destined to disappear rapidly. Thus, as soon as they were in power, their principal concern was to accelerate the fall of this force of the past which still stood before them. Their attack occurred in two waves and centered on three points: the Congregations, teaching and the Concordat.

The first wave developed between 1879-1889. Its first victims were the Congregations. Hostility to them was very old and was very strong. It went back to the decadence which struck the monastic orders during the eighteenth century, to the fact that as great landowners they were the target of popular hatreds, and finally to the action of the Jesuits who had been supporters of papal policy, the merchants of Ultramontanism who had been expelled from France in 1764 before being suppressed by Clement XIV in 1773. The Concordat of 1801 did not mention the Congregations. They were extremely prudent in reestablishing themselves at first, then multiplied and flourished after 1840. As most of them had no legal status the government dissolved them in 1880. The measure was applied, however, only partially. It should be noted, moreover, that the expelled Congregations reconstituted themselves during the next fifteen or twenty years.

234

The action of the republicans in the field of education was even more important. Their principal reform, accomplished by Jules Ferry, aimed at primary education. At the time it was in the hands of or under the influence of the Church. The Republican government, however, created a free primary school system which was obligatory and laic and without religious instruction.

After a period of appeasement a second wave of anticlericalism was unleashed from 1899 on by the Dreyfus affair. The accusation of treason made against the Jewish officer divided France into two camps, the two traditional camps. The Dreyfusards, who defended the innocence of Dreyfus, triumphed. These were men of the Left who had fought for the triumph of the principles of liberty and justice. As the Church was, as a whole, on the other side, on that of the anti-Dreyfusards who supported authority and order and did not wish the condemnation of Dreyfus to be questioned, she suffered the consequences of defeat.

This second wave of anti-clericalism, which was much more violent than the first, raged until World War I broke out in 1914, but in a most violent form up to 1906. There was no persecution in the strict sense of the word, though Catholics became second class citizens. Although they were not harmed personally or denied their liberty, they were, however, excluded not only from power but denied favors by the government especially in the public administration.

The Congregations had to suffer again. Two religious orders were compromised in the Dreyfus affair: the Assumptionists because of their publications and their committees before the elections of 1898, and the Jesuits because of the influence they were supposed to have exercised on the staff officers who tried to quash the affair. There is no denying that a large number of army and navy officers belonged to the bourgeoisie which sent its children to Jesuit colleges or other Catholic colleges. The Assumptionists were scattered and a law was voted in 1901 which required the Congregations to be authorized by the Government. Because the Assumptionists were denied this authorization, a large number of them were forced into exile in order to be able to live according to their rule. Furthermore, a law of 1904 forbade those belonging to Congregations (not only as groups but individually) to teach.

The most important step taken against the Church was the repeal of the Concordat—a logical measure in view of the circumstances. The government was composed of positivists, atheists, Free-Masons,—all adversaries of the Church. French Free-Masonry is rigorously antireligious, whereas by the terms of the Concordat, the state continued to recognize the special position of the Church and even to subsidize her, to name the bishops and to pay the salaries of the clergy. This situation could not last.

The abrogation of the Concordat was an old article in the republican program. Ever since the Second Empire, the republicans had been demanding that France should desist from maintaining a lie, from recognizing cults, and should abandon the Catholic Church to the slow death which awaited her. Yet the republicans had hesitated to break the Concordat because they had seen in it an instrument which permitted moderating the hostility of the Church and of preventing the bishops from organizing the struggle against the Republic. But before the Church was given her liberty the religious were expelled, and the Church's influence on education was reduced as much as possible.

The abrogation of the Concordat took place in two steps. First in 1904, the government of the Republic broke diplomatic relations with the Holy See as a result of divers conflicts, particularly over the nomination of bishops which the government wished to name without any prior understanding. Then it attacked the Concordat itself. The Catholics were very hostile to the break for many reasons. The first was doctrinal, for the Church approves the union of the two powers, the spiritual and the temporal, and condemns separation in principle; the second was historical, for separation had been achieved only momentarily during the Revolution under conditions which left painful memories. Finally, there was the practical consideration that the suppression of a budget of 35,000,000 francs paid by the state raised difficult problems. How would the Church provide for the support of the clergy, the maintenance of church buildings, and the work of her organizations?

The Law of Separation of the Churches and the State was voted in December 1905. It stated that the Republic neither recognized nor supported financially any cult. The state would no longer name the bishops and suppressed the budgetary provisions for the cults. The Church henceforth depended solely on the Holy See and could organize herself as she pleased. The Law provided for associations of laymen to conserve the ownership of the Church's property.

The Law established the new position of the Church without

consulting the Church in the person of the Supreme Pontiff (although this Law constituted an abrogation of the Concordat concluded with the Holy See). Since Pope Pius X considered that the association of laymen, as provided for by the Law, did not assure respect for episcopal authority, he condemned the Law of Separation.

As a result the Church did not establish any associations, and in conformity with the Law, its possessions were assigned by the State to benevolent organizations. The Church lost, therefore, not only the money which the state had provided, but even her own possessions.

If the Church was obliged, in order to exercise her juridical rights, to adopt the forms provided for by the French Law for moral persons, she won, thanks to the separation, the freedom to control her own internal organization. Henceforth, it would be the Pope and not the French government who named the bishops. Would bishops, free as regards the State, become the masters of the Church under the control of the papacy?

For this there would have to be not only bishops, but an episcopate, which could unite in episcopal assemblies forbidden by the Concordat. In fact, during the thirteen months which followed the vote on the Law of Separation, the bishops met three times in plenary assemblies in order to determine the position they should take as regards the Law. The bishops, who had been in large part named by Leo XIII, the Pope of conciliation, favored accepting the Law with certain reservations. This displeased Pius X whose policy, as we have seen, followed an intransigent course. That is why he refused to authorize further assemblies. There was therefore properly speaking, following the Separation as before it, no French episcopate but a smattering of bishops who lacked the means of establishing a common policy and even of mutually exchanging ideas.

This situation tended to change in time. On the morrow of World War I the return of Alsace and Lorraine to France raised problems which the cardinals and archbishops studied together. Thus was begun the Assembly of cardinals and archbishops which met yearly at first, then twice a year and which maintains a permanent secretariat between sessions. Finally, in April 1951, a plenary assembly of the episcopate met for the first time since January 1907 in order to define a common policy on the school problem and to study new methods of pastoral action.

Intransigent Catholicism and Liberal Catholicism

This brief summary of the relations between Church and State from the end of the Old Regime to World War I may give the impression that the conflict between the Church and the society born of the Revolution ranged on one side all the republicans, who were also the adversaries of Catholicism, and on the other all the Catholics, who were also adversaries of the Republic. That would be a simplification, for the reality is much more complex. We have distinguished two great traditions, a tradition of the authoritarian and religious right and a tradition of the irreligious and liberal left. But it is likewise true that there was within the Church herself during the nineteenth century, alongside the dominant tradition, another tradition, a liberal tradition which tried to reconcile the Church with this society by disengaging her from alliances with the forces of the Counter-Revolution. While the intransigent Catholics have a pessimistic conception of man and unceasingly recalled his need to be subject to an authority, the liberal Catholics, although they believe in original sin, also have faith in liberty and do not deny a certain sympathy for revolutionary optimism.

Liberal Catholicism made three great attempts during the nineteenth century to bring about a reconciliation with modern society. The first, on the morrow of the Revolution of 1830, with Lamennais, Lacordaire and Montalembert, was condemned by Gregory XVI in 1832 for doctrinal errors; the second in 1848 and 1849, with Lacordaire and Ozanam, was stillborn as a result of the movement of intransigeance provoked by the temporary triumph of the Roman Revolution which drove Pius IX from the Papal States. Taken up by Montalembert during the Second Empire, it was stopped again by the encyclical *Quanta cura* and the *Syllabus* of 1864. The third developed between 1890 and 1898 and this time under irreproachable doctrinal conditions, for it was instigated by Leo XIII himself, who counseled French Catholics to accept the government of the Republic. This was called the policy of *Ralliement*. But this third attempt failed in large part because of the Dreyfus affair which, by exciting old passions to the highest degree, prevented any understanding between the two Frances.

Social Catholicism and Christian Democracy

While the Catholics, in spite of the efforts of a minority of them and the support given by Leo XIII at the end of the nineteenth century, were attacking the political foundations of modern society, the social foundations of this very society began to crack. Of the three Orders of the Old Regime, only the first two, the clergy and the nobility, had been suppressed; the third, the Third Estate, that is the bourgeoisie, had triumphed and had made modern society a bourgeois society. Now, the economic transformation of the nineteenth century assured the development and awareness of a fourth estate, the working class. Yet the industrial revolution imposed wretched conditions upon the growing working class; the proletariat was born. The Church, as a whole, did not seem to be moved by the social problem, and the socialists criticized the Church for her complacency towards the wealthy bourgeoisie, a complacency similar to that she had displayed in the political order towards reactionary governments like those of the Restoration and the Second Empire.

Yet, from the very beginning, there were Catholics—they were later called social Catholics and their doctrine Social Catholicism— who sought a remedy for this special form of misery, this material and moral misery which is the misery of the proletariat. As early as 1822, there was a Catholic workers association and Lamennais, followed by others, raised the problems created by the existence of the proletariat.

Social Catholicism was born in two different milieux: in the legitimist aristocracy, and in the lower bourgeoisie and intellectual middle bourgeoisie. Thus, there developed two Catholic social traditions, which held certain convictions in common; that human dignity must be defended; that the moral and material improvement of the lot of the proletariat were interdependent; and finally that the institution of the family was of fundamental importance.

But these two traditions evolved separately. The first gave rise to a conservative social Catholicism inspired by the memories of the Christian Middle Ages. It dreamed of a society in which the upper classes of society would play a paternalistic role. The second worked for a Christian democracy anxious to promote the welfare of the working class in a spirit of equality.

The tradition of conservative Catholicism had the Marquis de La Tour du Pin as its theorist and the Count Albert de Mun as its moving spirit. It gave rise to the movement of workers' Circles which, after enjoying a certain success following the war of 1870, soon went into decline because its paternalistic spirit could not win the workers, and because, in a more general way, it was in profound disagreement with the general evolution of French society.

It was under the form, or at least the influence, of Christian democracy that Social Catholicism finally won out in the heart of French Catholicism. But it suffered many vicissitudes and setbacks: the failure of Ozanam in 1849, the failure of the movement of democratic priests (born of the encyclical *Rerum Novarum*) at the end of the century, and the failure of the *Sillon* of Marc Sangnier which was condemned by Pius X in 1910.

The *Sillon* deserves a brief parenthesis. Marc Sangnier gave to the young people whom he grouped together in the last years of the century the mission of living Catholicism, of being penetrated with the thought of Christ, and of making it penetrate each one of us. Their duty was to live it individually and to live it collectively as well, first within the *Sillon* movement, "a great friendship which one shared if one had the common soul," in which differences of class, customs, dress, and language disappeared, in which a new elite would develop with elements furnished by all classes; and to live it outside the *Sillon,* for the interior life of its members required of them a democratic zeal, since democracy was for Marc Sangnier "the social organization which tends to require the maximum of the conscience and the responsibility of each one."

The *Sillon* was a movement for popular education and owes its originality to its leader, Marc Sangnier, an exceptional inspirer of souls and an orator with a moving lyricism. He formed an elite of young Catholics of outstanding moral value and gave them a new style of thought and action. His fraternal and apostolic conception of Catholicism led him to leave the field of popular education in order to extend his activity to the social and political spheres. As his movement was, on the one hand confessional, while, on the other, his political program was ardently republican and democratic, it was inevitable that he should eventually come into conflict with the religious authorities. They could not permit, from the point of view of discipline, that he veer towards politics and withdraw from episcopal authority the Catholics, priests and faithful, whom he had organized with the approval of the ecclesiastical hierarchy for a uniquely religious purpose. Neither could they tolerate, from the doctrinal point of view, that he appear, if not explicitly, at least by the general conduct of his movement, to maintain that Christianity implies democracy. In short, Marc Sangnier committed to the advantage of the Republic and of democracy the same error made during the whole nineteenth century by the majority of French Catholics to the advantage of monarchy.

The importance of *Sillon,* in spite of the condemnation which suddenly destroyed it, lay in the shock it gave to an admirable minority of young Catholics. It was an experience that deeply marked their entire lives and consequently the evolution of French Catholicism.

The two currents, of conservative social Catholicism and of Christian democracy, joined in the *Semaines Sociales,* a sort of travelling university, which meets for a week once a year in a large city and which from 1904 on elaborated the doctrine of social Catholicism. Yet we should note that in 1914 social Catholicism exercised only an insignificant influence on legislation and on the working class.

The Crisis of Modernism

Catholicism was in conflict with the world not only on the political and social levels, but also on the intellectual level. This conflict took on all its fullness and meaning at the time of the crisis of modernism.

From 1860 on the French elites were as a whole guided by a few great key ideas: a religious admiration for the great Revolution, a proud conception of man, and also an unlimited confidence in the infinite possibilities of reason and of science. They were influenced by the criticism of Kant and the personalism of Renouvier who claimed that conscience alone should determine the moral law, by the evolution of Spencer and Darwin who excluded all intervention of the supernatural, by the positivism of Comte who rejected the earlier theological and metaphysical ages. Comte put aside the search for causes and admitted only the facts of experience, while Taine and Renan exemplified this positivism in its naturalistic aspect before it was popularized by Zola. Taine wrote that science should henceforth attack the soul and Renan thought that he had proved that Jesus was not a divine being. A great scholar, Marcellin Berthelot, asserted in imperious words: "The world today is without mystery . . . the notion of miracles . . . has vanished like an empty mirage."

The historical foundations of religion appeared to have been undermined by the discoveries of the newly created auxiliary sciences of history, philosophy, archaeology, and palaeography which questioned the contents of the Scripture, revealed the borrowings of which the Old Testament was composed and the personal tendencies of their authors, discussed the origins, the composition and the dates of the Gospels, the meaning and the object of the message of Christ, and the foundation of the Church. Historical criticism made heavy attacks on ecclesiastical history. It revealed the play of external influences on the elaboration of dogmas, and shed light on the relations of Christianity to earlier religious systems. It seemed that the supernatural was both excluded by philosophy and written off by history.

Now the Church, on emerging from the revolutionary torment, devoted herself entirely to the work of ecclesiastical reconstruction which turned her away from the field of scholarship. She had prepared priests capable of refuting Voltaire but not Renan, as those of the eighteenth century were capable of refuting Calvin or Jansen but not Voltaire. As Eugene-Melchior de Vogue wrote: "theological protest continued to follow the triumphant principles (of 1789); but it followed them in a stagecoach when it had the railroad at hand."

It was inevitable that the Catholic elite should one day become aware of its intellectual backwardness. This occurred with the creation of Catholic Institutes, an application of the Law of 1875 on the freedom of graduate teaching, the last success scored by the Catholics before the conquest of power by the anticlerical republicans. It was from this new awareness that modernism was born; it arose at the confluence of rational criticism and the renaissance of clerical studies.

Modernism may be taken to include all the efforts undertaken by men who, beginning as believers, reformers of the Church because her defenders, tried to correlate the Catholic religion with the intellectual and moral needs of their times. We should emphasize, in order to avoid all misunderstanding, that the Holy See gave to the word modernism a more restricted meaning by condemning, in 1907, under this name a body of erroneous doctrines which tended to modify the doctrinal basis of the Catholic religion on the pretext of adapting it to modern needs. On the historical level from which we are considering the matter, modernism thus conceived is only one aspect of the vast intellectual fermentation which the Catholic world of the time knew.

French modernism was primarily biblical and philosophical. From the biblical point of view it had, sometimes, the merit of freeing the Old Testament from literal interpretations which had become unacceptable, and sometimes, as with Loisy, instead of answering the exigencies of criticism, it finally surrendered Holy Scriptures by pieces to the scientific criticism of the period which the future showed was not always well-founded. From the philosophical point of view French modernism, with Blondel, LeRoy, and Father Laberthonniere, observed the insufficiency of scholasticism as it was taught in the religious world of the time and tried to present to the modern soul a Catholicism which was not repugnant to it. It sought to complete its rational dialectic by the inductive method in order to throw a bridge between Catholicism and rationalist philosophy. Some of these attempts were not approved by the Roman authorities.

In spite of regrettable errors, modernism expressed the new vitality of the Catholic intellectuals, who finally became capable of meeting the problems which the rationalists alone pretended to be able to solve.

Modernist errors provoked at Rome and in the Church in France a necessary reaction, but one which in turn ended in excesses. In fact this reaction unfortunately overshot its mark. Certain Catholics improved on the papal strictures. They boasted of professing an "integral" Catholicism and called themselves "integral Catholics." This won for them and their ideas the names of integralists and integralism. Integralism proposed to defend Catholic truth against the attacks of modernists. But this definition misses the essence of integralism. Integralism is not a specifically new thing. It brought to the intellectual problems which modernism tried to answer tendencies of mind which had already displayed themselves in other domains, particularly in politics. The integralists were the successors of the intransigent Catholics who fought the liberal Catholics during the nineteenth century. They developed the same principles, but with an increased vigor which assured their achievement of an important position in intellectual life. Profoundly penetrated with the idea of original sin, they placed no confidence in man. They considered faith under its objective aspect and distrusted its subjective manifestations. They constantly referred to traditional facts and did not consider them susceptible of new de-

243

velopments. Characterized by an exclusive cult of Thomism, they made frequent appeals to the ecclesiastical hierarchy in order to draw attention to those of its members and the faithful who appeared to deviate from this philosophy.

This attitude was not without danger for the Church, because it involved the risk of inhibiting all intellectual effort, identifying doctrine with a routine conformism and making Catholics a group secluded from the modern world and little desirous of understanding it.

II. *The Morrow of World War I*

Religious Pacification

World War I had a profound influence on the position of French Catholics. After the victory the clergy was accepted in the national community. It had done its duty at the front. Priests of the older generation had served as stretcher-bearers and attendants of the sick and wounded; younger priests had served as chaplains or simple soldiers. The veterans preserved feelings of comradeship, fraternity and respect which prevented the revival of the prewar religious struggles.

On the other hand, while religious questions dominated politics before 1914, after 1919, with the application of the Treaty of Versailles and the problem of reparations, international questions held first place in the minds of men. Domestic politics, financial and economic problems took on an increasing importance.

Hence, the anticlerical republicans suddenly found themselves on the defensive, a point which they expressed in the myth of the "untouchable laws." By this they understood the settlement by which the Third Republic had organized the lay state and the lay school. The republicans well knew that these laws, like any others, could be modified. By calling them untouchable they asserted that these laws constituted the foundations of the regime and that they would not allow them to become an issue.

In fact certain of these laws were amended or were not enforced. The Law of 1901 on the Congregations is a case in point. It was morally impossible to tell the members of the Congregations who had returned to France to fight that they had to go back into exile if they wished to live according to their vows of religion. Although the Law was not abrogated until 1942 it was no longer applied and the religious who so desired returned freely to France and resumed their community life.

Moreover, it had become clear during the war that the absence of French representation at the Vatican had not been in the national interest of France; consequently relations between France and the Holy See were resumed in 1921. The Chamber of Deputies approved this step by a large majority, and the Senate, confronted with a *fait accompli,* agreed.

Finally, Paris negotiated with Rome concerning the juridical status of the Church of France. As a result of the condemnation by Pius X of the Associations, the Church no longer had, as we have seen, the legal means of ownership. As jurisprudence, since the Law of 1905, had constantly favored the ecclesiastical hierarchy in the few cases of associations which had come before the courts, the Holy See in 1924 accepted in a slightly modified form the Associations set up by the Law of 1905, under the name of diocesan associations, so that the Church recovered the legal right to her own property.

But the Chamber of 1918, composed of war veterans, gave way in 1924 to a Chamber of radicals whose first government decided to suppress the embassy at the Vatican, to enforce the law concerning the Congregations, and to introduce lay legislation in Alsace and Lorraine. Alsace and Lorraine had returned to the national community in 1918 with the legislation which governed them in 1870, that is, in particular, with the legislation provided by the Concordat. The government had solemnly promised the maintenance of their local liberties. The government of 1924 pretended that the peoples of Alsace-Lorraine were favorable to the introduction of lay legislation. In reality these proposals raised a storm of protest in Alsace and Lorraine and the government recognized that its persistence would produce a grave crisis.

In the rest of France the unanimity of the Catholics against the application of the Law of 1901 on the Congregations was also manifested. An imposing association was formed, the National Catholic Federation, which organized a vast campaign of lectures. The government, impressed by the extent and the vigor of the movement of protest, dared not apply the law.

Finally, although the Chamber voted the suppression of the Embassy at the Vatican, when the Chamber fell in April 1925, the new government hastened to declare that it was abandoning all projects hostile to the Church including the suppression of relations with the Holy See. The elections of 1924 were the last with an anti-clerical character reminiscent of the prewar days. The rapid fall of the government which tried to revive anticlericalism shows that these struggles belonged to days gone by.

The Political and Social Evolution of Catholicism

Although its evolution did not follow a single path and involved many contrasts, French Catholicism, during the ten years which followed the first World War, worked, as a whole, through varying vicissitudes, to the pacification of the relations between the Church and the State, and, in a more general way, to a conciliation between Catholicism and the world.

Benedict XV and Pius XI again took up the policy of Leo XIII, that is, the policy of rallying the Church to the Republic. This time it had a lasting success. The effort encountered the ill-will of the episcopate, in large measure because Pius X's policy towards the French government had been intransigent. We shall see how Pius XI finally overcame, at the time of the *Action Française* affair, the passive opposition of the episcopate. He transformed it gradually by naming, to vacant sees, especially after 1926, during the nunciature of Maglione, men who had not ben subject to a conservative formation and who were social minded.

The development of social Catholicism was characterized by three important events during this period: the foundation in 1919 of the Confederation of Christian Workers which the Holy See supported (and which has not yet attained 150,000 members), the creation of the first specialized movement of Catholic Action, and the appearance of a political party inspired by Catholic social ideas.

As early as 1885 Albert de Mun had tried to create a Catholic party with a Catholic social program, but had failed. The royalists had replied that a Catholic party already existed—theirs. The Popular Liberal Action Party, founded by the Catholics of the *Ralliement* in 1901, to which de Mun himself belonged, had been influenced to a certain extent by social Catholicism. But it was only in 1924 with the creation of the Popular Democratic Party that the social Catholics possessed a party, one of whose objects was to incorporate Catholic social principles into legislation. In truth, the constitution of the Popular Democratic Party was for the democrats of Christian inspiration and for the social Catholics only partially successful. They did not do their best and did not succeed under the Third Republic. Many social Catholics remained attached to other political groups and its political representation in the Chamber remained very weak. Not until the upheaval of World War II, which broke the traditional framework of French politics, was there formed a large party inspired by social Catholicism.

Many Catholics, however, remained attached to the conservative parties which they had supported during the nineteenth century. The old monarchist party which grouped behind it about half of the French electors after the war of 1870, saw its members gradually fall away as the Republic continued to exist and to appear as a stable government. In 1918 the monarchists maintained with difficulty only a few strongholds in the West and South of France. But a new party put new life into royalism; the *Action Française* which, if it was not an electoral power, exercised a profound influence on the Catholic world.

The nationalistic doctrine of its leader, Charles Maurras, had many origins, but its religious thought had two essential sources: paganism and postivism. Maurras admired the Hellenic world and the Roman emperors for having subjected to their discipline "the Jewish visions and the Christian supernatural," and the Church for having "truncated, reworked and transformed" in the missal, the "turbulent Oriental writings." Following Auguste Comte, at the time of the Dreyfus affair, the time when the *Action Française* was born, he divided the French into "the proponents of order and anarchists"; the Catholics and pagans, positivists and atheists were considered to be the proponents of order, the Deists, Jews and Protestants were counted as anarchists. The latter, according to Maurras, dreamed of the rights of the individual and of an ideal France governed according to republican, liberal and lay principles. But for Maurras it was not the individual who counted but society, the real France and all that made it strong. Now, observation, which permits disengaging the laws of political science like those of physics and of chemistry, teaches that the prosperity of French society depended upon the return to the political form and religious tradition which had fostered France in the past. This religious tradition was Catholicism, not the liberal Catholicism of Lamennais and Lacordaire, but an intransigent Catholicism, faithful to its dogmas and its discipline which experience had proved to be conformity with the national interest. He wanted the Catholics, atheists and positivists to work for the restoration of this Catholicism.

It was on these foundations that after the establishment of the paper, *Action Française* in 1908, a union of this new political movement, the Catholic integralists, and conservatives, was formed.

The reasons *Action Française* and the integralists acted as they did were not the same. The integralists worked for the triumph of religious truth, the *Action Française* for the defense of a certain concept of French order. But they had the same enemies: the Republic, democracy, liberalism, modernism. The *Action Française,* considering the total restoration of the theoretical rights of the Church to be useful for the national health, agreed on the political level.

On the other hand, the *Action Française* found followers among the bourgeoisie because it based the social superiority which they pretended to have on political science. It found these followers especially among the Catholic bourgeoisie and also among the mass of the Catholic faithful, whose political opinions were determined by religious convictions, because this Catholic bourgeoisie and the Church's membership were pleased to see in the *Action Française* a party which fought vigorously against "the persecuting Republic" and categorically affirmed the most absolute Catholic positions.

This religious following did not realize that the external Catholicism to which the *Action Française* was linked was a sort of dechristianized Catholicism. *Action Française,* by deducing its principles from the lessons of empiricism, refused to recognize in fact that the political order can not be separated from the moral order. The resulting nationalism ignored the religious and moral principles which every Christian nation ought to accept. It did not scruple to use any means at its disposition in order to attain its ends.

We should not be surprised then that the Holy See was led to consider the *Action Française* as a political school whose conceptions derived from a naturalistic view of man, of society, of religion and the state.

A few of Maurras' books had been referred to the Holy Office even before World War I and put on the Index by a decree of Jan. 26, 1914, but Pius X decided to suspend the promulgation of this condemnation because he thought that Maurras, although a doctrinaire deserving of condemnation, helped the Church in the fight which he was leading against modernism and the *Sillon*.

Twelve years later, in 1926, after an investigation made by a Belgian journal, Cardinal Mercier became concerned about the pernicious influence exercised by the *Action Française* on the Catholic youth of Belgium. Then Pius XI, after a personal study of the question, gave a strong warning to the *Action Française* through Cardinal Andrieu, archbishop of Bordeaux, and finally, because of the resistance of Maurras, solemnly condemned it.

The *Action Française* openly revolted and pretended that the condemnation was motivated by political considerations. Charles Maurras' refusal to submit stemmed from many causes, but the counsel of the theologians of the *Action Française*, who urged him to resist, revealed one of the principal aspects of the affair: it was an episode in the fight led by the Catholic integralists against Pius XI, whom they considered a liberal. Catholics can hardly pretend to be more Catholic than the Pope, and can only lose in such a struggle. They lost it precisely through the defeat of the *Action Française*, a defeat which also, after many long years, involved the disappearance of integralism.

Although the laity of the *Action Française* generally resisted, the clergy, with more or less good will, were obliged to submit. The clergy were, incidentally, the object of a rigorous purge which weeded out those priests suspected of being favorable to the *Action Française* from all positions where they might exercise influence. After 1928, the young Catholics, for the most part, escaped recruitment by the *Action Française*. A movement which no longer recruits from the bottom is a movement in decline. We shall soon see that the Catholic youth took an entirely different orientation. Let us note for the moment that the *Action Française* affair involved the abandonment of a monarchical regime by the Catholics. Pius XI did not condemn the *Action Française* for political reasons, but, in fact, his condemnation had that political result. Hence the success of the *Ralliement* of the Catholics to the Republic in which the Holy See had only partially and temporarily succeeded under Pius X. Catholicism was disengaged from its long alliance with parties opposed to the regime, from its traditional identification with one of the two Frances, the one which had been constantly defeated by the other during the nineteenth century.

The Intellectual Evolution of Catholicism

The intellectual evolution of French Catholicism during the first ten postwar years also led to a reconciliation of the Church with the age.

From the Catholic point of view it was still dominated by the quarrel over modernism. Father Sertillanges professed an assimilating modernism. Though Jacques Maritain remained faithful to his intransigent Thomism, this did not prevent him from becoming the philosopher of Christian democracy. Edouard Le Roy undertook an enormous project of disciplining and synthesizing intuitive thought. The exegetical work of Father de Grandmaison was dominated by the desire to meet both the modernist and integralist dangers.

But viewpoints changed as the rationalist doctrines which gave birth to the modernist movement decayed. The nineteenth century was proud of its rationalist and scientific work which had temporarily given Catholic intellectuals a sense of insufficiency and had given such a painful character to the modernist movement. Now the weakness of this movement began to appear. Against scientism there occurred a general reaction dominated by the intuitive thought of Bergson. Science gave up trying to embrace everything in its successive deductions and no one any longer looked to it for a total explanation of being. It was recognized that each particular science rested on uncertain concepts; indeterminism even dominated in mathematics and physics. Thus the barricade which seemed to be such an obstacle to Catholic thought collapsed.

III. *From the End of the Third Republic to the Present*

Religious Policies—Vichy Regime and Fourth Republic

If we turn now to the second half of the interwar period which began about the thirties, we shall see that the Catholic world entered upon a profound transformation.

Without any doubt this transformation appeared least in Church-State relations, although these relations were definitively and peacefully maintained. After the failure of the anti-clerical reaction of 1924, there was no serious quarrel between the Church and state.

Gradually republican statesmen desisted from demonstrations of hostility to the Church, and it is even quite striking to note that while the radical upsurge of 1924 provoked a crisis in the religious policy of appeasement, the much more leftist socialism of 1936 in no way disturbed this pacification. The official authorities maintained good relations at the time with the ecclesiastical authorities.

With the defeat of 1940 the Third Republic collapsed and a new regime replaced it, that of the French State, symbolized by Marshal Pétain. There can be no doubt that at the beginning this regime met the wishes of the great majority of the French. But its policy towards Germany, which gradually turned in the direction of collaboration, caused it more and more to lose the support of public opinion so that at the time of the Liberation it represented only a very small minority of the country. However that may be, the ecclesiastical authorities, in accordance with the traditional doctrine of the Church, recognized the new power which, in a general way, was based on the conservative forces of the country, and consequently on the majority of the Catholics. The alliance was in a way an historical fatality, since the new regime was born of a reaction against the Third Republic which had so long been hostile to the Church. The contrast of the two Frances did not disappear.

The official personalities of the Pétain regime took severe measures against the republican ideology and rendered homage to Christian principles. They also granted the Church more tangible satisfaction; some favored the Congregations and others the confessional school.

At the end of 1940, the law of 1904 which had prohibited Congregations from teaching was abrogated—in fact, it had not been applied since 1914. Then, in April 1942, the Law of 1901 which subjugated the Congregations to governmental authorization was modified. Religious, living in a community according to their vows without having secured official authorization, were no longer subject to prosecution. Future "legal recognition" of the Congregations seemed easily obtainable. The Congregations, satisfied with the toleration they had already enjoyed, did not use this new facility, no doubt because of the uncertainty of a regime dependent upon the outcome of the war for its future.

The aid given to Catholic teaching was more substantial. Since the abrogation of the Concordat, the Catholics found it difficult to maintain their schools and this difficulty increased as large private fortunes dwindled after the war due to the impoverishment of the country and inflation. Furthermore, they feared the public school for it was in the public school, especially in the primary schools, that the old spirit of hostility to the Church was most vigorously maintained by the teachers. During the years following World War I the Catholics campaigned for what they called proportional allocations to the schools. Their grievance was that parents who sent their children to Catholic schools paid twice for the instruction, once in taxes for the support of the public schools, and a second time for tuition in Catholic schools. The campaign lasted a long time because it challenged the principle of laicity; the lay state refused to subsidize institutions which were not laic.

The Vichy regime, by its law of November 1941, admitted the principle of financial aid to private elementary schools. The state recognized that these schools which handled one-fifth of the children, saved the state the cost of educating them; consequently the state granted an aid which was justified on the grounds that the resources of the private schools were insufficient. These subsidies, however, jeopardized the principle of laicity for the future.

At the time of the Liberation, although the Resistance was largely composed of leftists and Communists, there was no anti-clerical reaction because the head of the government, General de Gaulle, and several of his ministers were Catholics and particularly because the Catholics had also played a notable role in the struggles of the Resistance. The Catholics of the left, especially the heads and members of the Popular Democratic Party and the heads and members of the Christian labor unions were, as a rule, in the Resistance. The National Council of the Resistance was presided over by a member of the Democratic Republican Party, Georges Bidault, who later became one of the presidents of the council of the Fourth Republic.

Nevertheless, serious differences arose between the new regime and the Holy See. The government of General de Gaulle demanded that the Papal Nuncio accredited to the Vichy government be replaced. Then he asked for the retirement of a certain number of bishops who, he believed, were compromised by collaboration. Finally, after laborious negotiations, three bishops were induced to make a "voluntary resignation."

On the school question the Liberation government, after having

252

suppressed the legislation of the Vichy regime, drew up a solution based on the distinction between private school instruction for which, by reason of the principle of laicity, no financial effort could be given by the state, and education which could be entrusted to youth movements (including Catholic movements) which were to receive financial aid from the State. This proposal provoked so much dissatisfaction that it had to be dropped.

Because numerous religious had taken part in the Resistance it was impossible to undo the modifications of the Laws of 1901 and 1904 which Vichy had made. It is difficult to see, furthermore, how a government which was not anti-clerical could reestablish laws which, at the time they had been abolished by Vichy, had not been applied for more than twenty years.

Thus, if we sum up the religious policy of the Liberation government, we note with surprise that this revolutionary government, which replaced the regime of Vichy and refused to restore the Third Republic, though no decision was made on the point by an elected assembly, revealed itself on religious questions to be a rather routine government which returned to conventional prewar practices.

But the *status quo* was no longer possible. From 1945 to 1950 monetary devaluations, the progressive increases in the school budgets, the new impoverishment of the French resulting from the recent war, were such that the private elementary schools could no longer meet their burdens. It was indispensable that they receive state aid in one form or another. This thorny question, which involved the laicity of the state, once again brought the two Frances face to face. The financial embarrassment of the private schools was such as to require urgent measures. It seems that the evolution of public opinion, the difficulties encountered by the public schools in accommodating the new classes of children reaching school age, increasingly numerous because of the growth of French population, and finally the election in June 1951 of an Assembly in which a majority seemed willing to listen to the claim of private schools, justify the hope that in the coming years the state will make an effort in favor of the religious schools.

The school problem was not the only one which required legislative action. Would the youth movements also be helped? And the Congregations? The Congregations of men, though not authorized, had enjoyed the legal toleration established by the law of 1942; but this situation is juridically insufficient for the handling of their property.

The Congregations of women were governed by an old law of 1825 whose terms belonged to horse and buggy days. We should note, too, that the agreement reached between the government of the Republic and the Holy See in 1924, on the diocesan associations, gave the Church a juridical means of possession which does not apply to religious orders. Here, again, legislation was insufficient. Finally, the two provinces recovered in 1918, Alsace and Lorraine, were still subject to the regime of the Concordat. There was no serious question of applying to them the present French laws. Perhaps the best means of adjusting this abnormal situation would be to improve the laws so that they could be applied to all of France.

Legislative modifications, therefore, are desirable. Nothing is ever perfect. But it can be said that, except for the reservations made on the school problem, the Church in France has for a long time adapted herself to the laws of the Third Republic as they have been amended and applied. Today, she is happy about this regime of separation which had been voted against her will. If she has lost some material advantages, she has been able to recover in poverty, a freedom, an independence, a dignity and a spirit of the apostolate which explain her grandeur and strength today.

The Political Evolution of Catholicism

The evolution of the political attitude of Catholics is germane to this normalization of the relations of Church and State, and *vice versa*. Religious quarrels no longer disturb the forum because the Catholics, especially the clergy, do not indulge in anti-republican politics. It is, however, also true that the lay Catholics and the clergy cease to carry on anti-republican politics because those political quarrels no longer disturb the forum.

Between the two World Wars the majority of Catholics remained faithful, if not to the parties aggressively hostile to the Republic, like the *Action Française,* at least to the conservative parties. The Popular Democratic Party which drew support from only a minority of the Catholics took great care to avoid being a confessional party. For their part the clergy gradually withdrew from their traditional political associations. The Assembly of Cardinals and Archbishops of 1936 urged the clergy not to be associated with political parties and the directors and militants of Catholic Action not to be at the same time directors, representatives or propagandists of a political party.

On the morrow of the Liberation a new democratic party born of the Resistance, was founded, the Popular Republican Movement which replaced the Popular Democratic Party. Why this new party? Partly because the Popular Democratic Party had been divided by Vichy, some of its members voting full powers to Marshall Pétain, others refusing them. But it was largely due to the fact that there was a conflict between the old leaders of the Popular Democratic Party and the young founders of the Popular Republican Movement. Finally, the spirit of Resistance to the Germans, being necessarily a revolutionary spirit, gave the founders of the new party a more advanced outlook than that of the leaders of the Popular Democratic Party. The members of the Popular Democratic Party joined the Popular Republican Movement and most of the leaders of the Popular Democratic Party were gradually absorbed by the new party.

The Popular Republican Movement profited, at the time of its foundation, by the collapse of the rightist parties whose leaders, compromised by the experience of the Vichy Regime, could not run for election, or if they did, were defeated. Its deputies in the Chamber were ten times more numerous than those of the Popular Democratic Party had been. For a short time it was the largest French party. As it was seated in the center of the National Assembly, it played an important role in French politics after the war.

Many wondered whether this situation would not be transitory and whether, with the inevitable recovery of the rightist parties, the Popular Republican Movement would not decline to the level of the Popular Democratic Party. This recovery took place in the form of the *Rassemblement* of the French people, the party of General de Gaulle who, indeed, won half of the votes of the Popular Republican Movement in the elections of June 1951. But the Popular Republican Movement, with the 2,330,000 votes it retains, remains a large party. It profits from the momentum already gained, from the need for a renewal felt by a part of its rightist followers, and by the fine years in the specialized movements of Catholic Action. The fact that the Popular Republican Movement has taken root in the country is very important in the history of French Catholicism. Of course, this party is not a confessional party, but its electors are recruited in large part from Catholic circles. It is the first time that, on the political level, Catholics are not grouped in the rightist parties, but divided between the rightist parties and a party seated in the center of the parliamentary semicircle, and whose economic leanings are nearer to the managed economy of the Socialist Party than was the liberalism of the old conservative parties. The Church is thus released from the compromises with the forces of political and social conservatism which resulted in so much criticism from her adversaries.

We should mention, as we finish our consideration of the political action of Catholics, the tactics of the "outstretched hand" used by the Communist Party since the legislative elections of 1936. The General Secretary of the French Communist Party, Maurice Thorez, then proclaimed: "We offer our hand to Catholics—workers, employees, artisans, peasants—we, who are laic, because you are our brothers, and like ourselves burdened with the same worries." This tactic, at the time, made an impression on only a small number of Catholic intellectuals. Since the Liberation, collusion between the Communists and some elements of the Catholics has been favored by the memory of their joint struggle against the German oppressors. A small group of "progressive" Christians, very weak numerically, composed almost solely of intellectuals, who often adopt the same positions as the Communist Party although they remain independent of it, has developed since the Liberation. The late Cardinal Suhard admonished them on this score and silenced one priest who had become a propagandist for the movement. However, "progressive" Christians do not consider that the decree of the Holy Office of July 1, 1949 applies to them because they do not preach continual collaboration with the Communist Party.

Modern Civilization and Dechristianization

Since the separation from the State, the Church has regained an ardent spirit for the apostolate. The forms which this apostolate have taken would have astounded the Catholics of the turn of the century. For they express, as incidentally do the new orientations of the Catholic mind and spirituality, the renewal of Catholicism which began to be manifest in the thirties.

The thirties are from every point of view years which marked the end of the old world, or rather the awareness of this end. Up to that time men had not realized the full importance of World

War I. Only a few farseeing minds foresaw the drama to come. One of the most penetrating observers of the time, Paul Valéry, said: "Everything is threatened by the magnitude of the event" which "witnesses the powerlessness of the ideas men have trusted in." Drieu la Rochelle spoke of the "great questioning which is taking place." Proust revealed the multiplicity of the human mystery, Freud explored its unsuspected testimony, Romain Rolland set forth the reply of Hindu thinkers to Western anxiety, and Jean-Richard Bloch proposed the Marxist solution. . . . And suddenly an economic depression began in 1929 in the United States, an economic crisis from which the modern world emerged only during a new world conflict. It was time to realize that a new epoch was beginning.

Without always being aware of it, young elements of French Catholicism acted as if they realized that an historic period was finished, that a new universe was in the making amidst the sufferings of fantastic catastrophes, and that the mission of Catholicism was to enlighten with its message the night of this mysterious future. The old political quarrels, which had occupied the attention of Catholicism during the nineteenth and the early twentieth centuries, lost their bitterness, and became of secondary importance or disappeared. We have already seen that the period 1920-1930 saw the liquidation, in large measure, on the political and intellectual level, of the rivalry between the two Frances and provided for the religious minded, and the irreligious, an understanding which further reduced the future clash of these two Frances.

New problems emerged to replace the old political ones. In order to understand their emergence, it is necessary to consider the true religious situation of France, the answer which each Frenchman gives to the religious problem. We shall then see, that if the two Frances no longer find themselves so brutally at odds, it is because there has developed between them a third France which is neither the France of religion nor the France of irreligion, but the France of indifference, and because Catholicism, relaxing the intensity of the struggle against less aggressive adversaries, developed a spirit of apostolic fervor towards these masses of indifferent Frenchmen.

Believers, and not Catholics alone, not only in France but in all countries, have many illusions about the depth of conviction of those who are statistically classified as belonging to their religion. They count as Catholics, or Protestants, those who are born, live

257

and remain within the rites of their religion although they do not have any faith in the truth of it. In the last thirty years, very serious studies have been made in France. These make it possible to estimate, to a certain extent as regards the past and more accurately as regards the present, what was and what is no longer the faith itself, but the manifestations by which it is expressed, that is, religious practice. Briefly, they distinguish particularly the faithful, that is, those who go to Mass on Sunday and make their Easter duty, the seasonal Catholics, that is, those who are content to go to Church for the important events of their lives (baptism, first communion, marriage, and death), and finally, the dissidents, that is, those who remain away from the sacraments even on those occasions.

The dechristianization of France (and of other countries) is not, as many imagine, a recent phenomenon but goes back to the Old Regime. It is difficult to deal with religious practice during the Old Regime, for religious practice then was obligatory in principle. But even then it was not always observed especially in the large cities; for example, two-thirds of the population of Bordeaux failed to make their Easter duty. It is very striking to see how differently the French Revolution affected the several regions. It may be supposed that where the official dechristianization was accepted without resistance, the Faith was not very deep. Thus it becomes possible to draw a geographical map of religious practice which in its main lines is not very different from what is observable today. It reveals that the Faith was intact in Flanders, in most of the West, the Basque country, the Massif Central, Alsace; but there were important proportions of unbelievers in the large cities and a halo of indifference around Paris. Burgundy, the Loire valley, the plains of the Center, and a large part of the Southwest were largely dechristianized, while the rest of the country seemed to live in a state of lukewarmness which is not incompatible with regular practice. At that time, the upper classes in cities generally lost their faith especially under the influence of the philosophy of the eighteenth century, while the people as a whole were more faithful.

During the first part of the nineteenth century, the religious map underwent no fundamental changes; its features simply became sharper. Changes occurred rapidly, however, under the Third Republic. The old causes of dechristianization which had diversely acted according to regions remain; for example, the Faith defends itself with more difficulty in cities, along highways and rivers, wherever ideas are the object of intense mixing or rapid circulation and where the believing elements of the upper classes lose their authority because they emigrate or no longer exercise their traditional patronage. But then new causes appear. Jules Ferry's reform of teaching was without doubt a cause of dechristianization; the teacher, who is an important person in the village, exercised an influence opposed to that of the pastor. The other laic laws played a similar role, particularly the Law of Separation, as did the activity of an administration composed of people hostile to the Church.

Less visible, although even more important, is the influence of the techniques of the modern world. The percentage of rural population is diminishing in relation to the urban population. The countrysides themselves are becoming urbanized. The development of the means of travel and of diffusing ideas involves a greater mixing of individuals; and also a more rapid movement of merchandise. In brief, an open dynamic economy, the capitalistic economy which, multiplying exchanges for profit, creates new needs and whets the appetite for profits, has taken the place of the old stable and rural economy whose aim was limited to satisfying the essential needs of existence. Dechristianization does not result from these techniques themselves. The railroad, bicycle, automobile, the newspaper, cinema, radio and TV and, in general, the machine and its products which play the role of agents of dechristianization are no more pagan than the horse and boats which were the agents of Christianization at the end of the Roman Empire were Christian. But modern techniques overthrow the old modes of life in which the Church had a large part and create new economic and social structures to which the Church has not adapted itself.

This is particularly true of the large worker concentrations which, developing outside all Christian traditions, are almost entirely ignorant of Catholicism. To them Catholicism appears as an enemy, because it seems to be bound to capitalism. The industrial suburbs of Paris, for example, are almost completely pagan.

If there was an unquestionable dechristianization of the rural and urban population during the Third Republic, there has also been, since the middle of the nineteenth century, a progressive Christianization of the bourgeoisie. This class began to come back to the Church after the Revolution of 1848 because it saw in the Church a force for order capable of keeping the people obedient. This movement increased after the Dreyfus affair because the

Church appeared to be an institution necessary for the moral life of the country. Later, its motivation gradually became more spiritual and religious. Among the intellectual elite there were, on the eve of World War I, more and more signs of a living and active Faith. They increased and multiplied. The young Catholic students assert themselves everywhere today. In certain large schools they are the majority of the students. The Catholic students of Paris march in the spring pilgrimage to Chartres every year, inspired by the memory of Péguy. Nearly 10,000 of them go, although this pilgrimage takes place near examination time. Another characteristic sign is that before the First World War there was an intellectual snobbery which made it difficult for the young Catholic intellectual to assert his Faith; this snobbery today works rather in favor of Catholicism.

The Renewal of the Apostolic Spirit

Around 1930 a new apostolic spirit replaced the old defensive and politically active spirit. This new spirit, considering the problems of Catholicism as they were revealed by research on religious practice, devised new methods. The spirit of the apostolate assumed wholly new forms, at first in order to obtain a hearing from the Third France (of indifference) which had increased in importance, especially under the Third Republic. Later, as the sense of the disintegration of the old world became sharper, the innovations were designed to build future society in a Christian way. This transformation took place among the clergy as well as among the laity.

The separation had its repercussions on the number of vocations. There were more than 56,000 priests in 1877 and about the same number in 1901. By 1913 the number had declined to 54,000 and then fell to 47,000 in 1929 and to 42,500 in 1949, a number which seems to constitute a stable level. The large classes ordained under the Second Empire and the early Third Republic formed a backlog which for a long time halted the fall in numbers. The annual figures for the new priests, which attained 1,675 in 1875 and 1,753 in 1901, fell to 825 in 1913, then rose and became stabilized from 1930 at around 1000-1100. The regular clergy, more directly affected by the laws at the beginning of the century, showed a greater elasticity than the secular clergy, and has nearly reached its maximum in priests. In spite of this decline there is in

France one priest for every 686 Catholics. This is a high ratio which is bettered only by Switzerland, England, Canada, Belgium and the United States.

At the time of the Concordat, when the village priest, a great recruiter, noticed a pious boy, he easily obtained permission from his peasant parents for him to enter a little seminary, whence he moved to the major seminary. This recruitment produced a clergy of high spiritual value. Foreigners who come to know the French clergy are always edified today, even more than yesterday, by its exceptional moral qualities. The Separation, besides causing the Church a loss of prestige, created for the priests an economic insecurity which discouraged families from permitting their children to devote themselves to the priesthood. Hence the decline in the number of priests. But the new conditions led to the formation of a different kind of clergy. The priest of the Concordat who was treated by the State as a government official and was assured of a career with a guaranteed income, ended up by acting somewhat like an official of the spiritual order confirmed in his rights and strong in defending them. His journalists inculcated in him a rigorous conception of the rights of the Church and the conviction that the monarchy was the only regime capable of assuring respect for them. He believed it his duty to join the battle to safeguard the temporal positions of Catholicism.

The new clergy does not come from the same milieu. It is no longer almost entirely rural. A part of the missing rural vocations are replaced by urban vocations, in large part bourgeois, and also, as a result of the development of Catholic worker organizations, by vocations among the working classes. Under the influence of this change and a more peaceful political atmosphere, a new type of priest is developing. Disengaged from every temporal connection with the state and maintained by his very poverty in a spirit of the priesthood, he is led to rejuvenate his parish by the apostolic spirit or to rekindle the religious vitality of the faithful by social action outside of the old structures in which it vegetated, instead of allowing the routine of a modest living to weaken his zeal as a fisher of souls and the quarrels of the forum to excite his partisan passions.

A profound dualism has established itself in modern society. Alongside of those who remain attached to the Church, there are those who not only individually but collectively live outside the Church. The parish remains "the primordial cell of the Christian society," but the present situation imposes, besides the task of defense and preservation, that of penetration and conquest, of leading back to the Church those who no longer know her or who do not know the road. But how can we penetrate an indifferent or hostile society whose members are unaware of the Church?

Priests and laity have given a twofold answer to this question. Let us begin with that of the laity which, chronologically speaking, came first. It is the answer given by the specialized movements of Catholic Action.

Catholic Action is not only the grouping of the religious and social works of Catholicism. It has taken on with Pius XI the form of a new institution corresponding to the needs of the present time. In view of the dechristianization of the masses the relative ineffectiveness of the older organism of the parish first became apparent, as well as the difficulties, and sometimes the practical impossibility, of the individual apostolate. This change of temporal structure and the powerlessness of the priest to meet it, led to the appeal to the layman, who inescapably finds the religiously indifferent all around him. Thus, the role of the laity in the specialized structures best suited for the spiritual conquest became official and permanent. The action of the laity, the apostolate of the like by like, was henceforth organized in conjunction with the hierarchy which inspires and directs it.

The formula was first applied in Belgium among the Belgian Young Christian Workers, then it was adapted in France thanks to the Catholic Association of French Youth. This Association, founded in 1886 by Albert de Mun, has grown slowly and wisely. Although it was at first associated with the tradition of aristocratic social Catholicism, it has accepted the policy of the *Ralliement* and gradually taken on a more democratic character while retaining an essentially bourgeois leadership. Its principal formula for action was the study circle in which young people became initiated, under the direction of a chaplain, in the theses of social Catholicism. From 1927 on the Catholic Association of French Youth which, before World War I, was practically eclipsed by the more dynamic and audacious *Sillon,* but whose prudence avoided difficulties with ecclesiastical authorities, underwent a profound transformation in a few years. When it gathered in its study groups young people of every social class without distinction as to origin, it transformed itself into a federation of specialized youth movements in which each group of young people belonged to a given social milieu. Thus arose, one by one, the Young Christian Workers (J.O.C.), the Young Christian Farmers (J.A.C.), the Young Christian Sailors (J.M.C.), the Young Christian Students (J.E.C.), the Young Christian Independents (J.I.C.) for the bourgeois, and also the corresponding feminine movements, except for the Maritime Youth. Adult groups were then formed to extend and maintain the work of the youth groups.

During the years prior to World War II the clergy organized in an attempt to reach the fallen away Catholics, drawn away by modern life from the traditional framework of the parish which no longer exercised sufficient attraction on them, and also the fallen away Catholics who, no longer understanding the rites of the Church, never enter. This is an effort which is growing and taking on the most diverse forms in order to make sacred things more attractive.

In 1942 a seminary was opened at Lisieux whose object is to supply priests to the French regions where they are most urgently needed. Directed by religious and seculars animated with an admirable apostolic spirit and formed as a result of a profound knowledge of the living conditions of the people, it brings together every year an increasing number of students and priest-students who come to this vivifying atmosphere to learn these new methods. There were thirty there in 1943 and 160 in 1947, although the buildings were damaged by bombardment. By the pooling of experiences and the omission of all routine, self-directing groups are formed and associate an intense interior life with a zealous spirit for the apostolate. Elsewhere in the suburbs of Paris, a new order called the Missionary Brothers of the Countryside was organized at the same time. It has the same general orientation and has developed rapidly. It forms small communities which, in collaboration with existing parishes, take charge of the apostolate of dechristianized sectors. There is no diocese in France where there are not a few teams of priests who work to rejuvenate and coordinate apostolic action.

Although this young and admirable clergy agrees on the end, there are divergencies on the immediate methods and objectives. Some, starting with existing structures, consider the parish as the community which should embrace all those who live within its boundaries. They look to have the faithful taken up in a movement of collective piety. The liturgy is made more living by the practice of prayer out loud, by the choice of simple canticles, by a public explanation of the Mass in French, by the explanation of the sacraments on the occasion of their celebration (baptism, marriage, etc.) by the celebration of paraliturgical ceremonies on the occasion of popular feasts. It would require a special study to explain the efforts made outside the walls of the Church in order to achieve what one of these priests calls "a Christianity which pervades the streets. . . ."

Others would start from bases other than the parish, thanks to the direct preaching of the priest adapting himself to those whom he wishes to reach. This is the formula of the priest-worker whose work has been authorized by the highest ecclesiastical authorities. These priest-workers are not parish priests disguised as proletarians, but worker-priests, that is, they live the worker's life like other workers. This effort, born of the apostolate of clandestine priest-chaplains in the Forced Labor Service imposed during the German occupation, has been too recent to permit a considered judgment.

It is not possible to speak of the apostolate of the French clergy without briefly mentioning its missionary apostolate. It is at first disconcerting to realize that during the nineteenth century, while she was carrying on a long and difficult struggle in her own country, the Church of France dominated the activity of missions in the world. This situation seems to have its modern origins in the rediscovered vitality of a clergy which reformed itself very rapidly after the Restoration. It was normal for her youth to go beyond the frontiers. The missionary movement began about 1830 and, after 1860, developed very rapidly with the colonial expansion of the great powers. The missionaries followed the soldiers.

France enjoyed privileges in the Levant in virtue of the capitulations, and in China thanks to the treaty of Tien-Tsin in 1858. These privileges facilitated the activity of the French missionaries, priests of the Foreign Missions of Paris, Jesuits, Lazarists, and Franciscans, Christian Brothers and the Daughters of Charity.

It is primarily new orders who went to the other continents. The religious conquest of Africa was undertaken before the middle of the century by the Holy Ghost Fathers, then by the Fathers of the African Missions of Lyon and the White Fathers, starting in 1856 and 1866 respectively.

Oceania became in 1826 the field of action of the Picpus Fathers and in 1836 of the Marists. The Sacred Heart Fathers of Issoudun devoted themselves to the apostolate of New Guinea beginning in 1881. The Canadian missionary activities of the Oblates of Mary Immaculate began in 1841.

In the middle of the eighteen-seventies there were 6,100 missionary priests; of these, 4,500 or 75% were French. France alone played a missionary role three times more important than that of all the other nations together in the missionary expansion of Catholicism. A half century later, in 1930, the total number of missionary priests had increased to 8,398 but among them the French numbered only 3,000—less than 36%.

This decline stems from several causes. After the formation of German unity and Italian unity, German and Italian missionaries sought to be free of the tutelage of French missionaries, and, as nearly all missionary institutes depended on international recruitment, the very zeal of French missionaries led to the entrance of an increasing number of foreigners. On the other hand, the Law of 1901 on the Congregations gave a temporary impetus to French missionary activity by forcing Congregations to settle abroad; but it later slowed down greatly the recruiting of new men by preventing them from having novitiates in France.

Finally, it is in the nature of the missionary apostolate to work in order to become unnecessary. The new Christian communities born of its action, tend little by little to have their own priests. Benedict XV and Pius XI understood, moreover, that the awakening of nationalism among the colored peoples involved the risk of making the missionaries appear as agents of the white race; these pontiffs insisted upon the development of native clergies. Thus, the general development of the world diminishes the importance, at least relatively, of missionary action and consequently of French missionary activity, which, according to a classification by nations, still outstrips others.

The Intellectual Vitality of Catholicism

In the field of French Catholic thought during the last twenty years there is also observable a determination to participate in the world, to adapt the eternal to the daily, to find Christian doctrinal solutions for problems which menace everything.

We have already mentioned the distant origins of this new activity of the Catholic intelligence. Its birth seems to date from the morrow of the condemnation of the *Action Française* which caused a profound crisis of conscience. In any case, since the last world conflict it has developed extraordinarily. We can not even outline it in a few pages. Let us consider rather a few key points.

In 1932 Emmanuel Mounier founded *Esprit,* a non-confessional review which brought together all sorts of Catholics and Protestants. He wanted to study man in himself and in the community in which he was "committed." Committed is the essential word. He and his teams, with the insolence of their age, proposed to renew the world in the name of principles, and one of the essential principles was the primacy of the human person in things social and economic. The influence of *Esprit,* which is a vigorously anti-conformist and innovating influence, is considerable.

A decade or so after the *Action Française* affair, the Spanish civil war produced a new crisis for the conscience of French Catholics. The Spanish Popular Front was definitely anticlerical and antireligious. One must admit that the alliance existing under the old regime between a privileged Church, an autocracy which was very rich and very little conscious of its duties, and an army on the alert for possible *prononciamientos,* was bound to bring about such a reaction. Nevertheless, Franco posed as the avenger of religion persecuted by the Popular Front, and gave to his reconquest of Spain the air of a crusade. The Spanish Catholics are not, however, unanimous in supporting him. Among Franco's adversaries there are the Basque Catholics and the Catalonian Catholics who are partisans of provincial liberties. In France Mauriac and Maritain, *Esprit,* and *Sept,* the Dominican weekly, opposed Franco. They represented a minority, while the majority of Catholics held opposite views.

On the morrow of the Liberation it was inevitable that Catholic circles, as a result of the events they had lived through, should be the object of a remarkable ferment. New groups arose to spread their ideas in new reviews, new books and lectures. We might cite for example *Jeunesse de l'Eglise* and *Economie et Humanisme,* both of Dominican inspiration. Both—the second with less sensational intensity and more intellectual rigor—fearing lest the Church be no longer animated with a living faith if she remained too closely attached to a particular cultural tradition, ruling classes and the money powers, sought a more communitarian way of life for the believers. If, at the other extreme of the Catholic horizon, there is a small group of integralist tendencies whose organ is *La Pensée Catholique,* the great Jesuit review *Les Etudes,* while retaining the wisdom and prudence proper to an old institution, has manifested an understanding of the most generous tendencies. This serious-minded review has revealed an interest in studying philosophical problems, which appeared after the age of scholasticism, and in going back beyond this philosophy to the Biblical and patristic sources (a field in which Father Danielou is one of the eminent specialists). We shall at least mention the name of Father Teilhard de Chardin, but omit any effort to sum up his very rich and warmly debated thought. Some, observing that his thought expresses confidence in the great contemporary current of collectivization on condition of collaborating with it through and in love, believe that it constitutes a transposition on the planetary level of the immanentism which was, on the individual level, peculiar to modernism before 1914.

These comments would be incomplete if we overlooked the role of the *Semaines Sociales* and that of the French Center of Catholic Intellectuals, founded after the war. The *Semaines Sociales,* nearly a half century old, have clearly understood that the social question is not simply one concerning the relations between management and workers. Hence, at each of their annual sessions, they study contemporary social life as a whole under its most varied aspects. Before an audience of several thousand, for a week every year, the French Center of Catholic Intellectuals treats, after long preparation in study meetings, some question of major importance for Catholic thought. Its constant concern is to apply this thinking to the preoccupation of the moment.

Everywhere then we find the will to discover in Catholicism the principles which may guide and direct the building of the society which is slowly emerging amidst contemporary torments.

Catholic Literature

The literary renewal of French Catholicism is well known; hence it is less necessary to speak of it. It goes back to the years before 1914. The mysterious apprehension, sometimes the lucid conception, of a profound crisis, already discernible among some of their elders—it stands out like a vision in Léon Bloy—guided numerous convert writers toward the same faith. They were especially the fruit of a sometimes diffuse and indirect influence, that of all the spiritual or Catholic thinkers who for thirty years traced the frontiers of scientific ambitions and brought to man, with the "action" of Blondel and especially the "intuition" of Bergson, more or less direct means of attaining the mystery of Revelation.

The message of a number of these writers is specifically Catholic, that is, it involves a Catholic view of man and of society. Claudel gave a spontaneous and lyrical expression to the obscure and hesitating aspiration of many hearts toward religion. His work, consisting of pieces of unquestionable, and, perhaps, imperishable beauty exercised a great influence on young writers (Jacques Rivière was converted by him). It "can only be explained," Henri Clouard writes, "by a Catholic conception of the world not only in its construction as a whole and in the contours, but in the detail of detours, the familiarity of life and of hearts." The *Georgiques* of Jammes are Christian: he sees God in nature; the sacerdotal poetry of Le Cardonnel moves in the supernatural; Péguy never ceased singing of the Catholic mission of France. And how many novelists have, in different degrees, habits of thought and feeling which gives them a Christian view of life and of the problems it raises for men. Georges Goyau expressed, in another way, this fact of the penetration of Christianity among Catholic writers. He sees their literature dominated and inspired by the idea of the communion of saints: "it draws from it, with Huysmans and Baumann, an exegesis of suffering; with Leon Bloy, Claudel and Retté, a philosophy of life; with Péguy, the intelligence of the life of the Church."

In fact these writers do not have an identical conception of Christianity nor, especially, of its social projection. Their messages, quite different on this point, can be reduced to two of which one appeals to tradition and the other to fraternity.

Bourget, the principal herald of traditional Catholicism, was anti-democratic (*L'Etape*); he believed in the aristocratic function (*L'Emigré*), and supported a strong organization of the family (*Un Divorce*). His profound thought aimed to give the aristocratic and bourgeois elite the notion of duty necessary for the exercise of their role. René Bazin, in his constant preoccupation with a return to the earth and the faith, and Henri Bordeaux, with the worship he never fails to render the family, developed in different ways this solid doctrine. The thesis of the social utility of religion comes to life again, this time sincere and noble, under these forms. Napoleon saw in Catholicism a factor for order, Cousin an instrument of bourgeois domination; Bourget made it the unalterable cement of societies strongly conceived because he admires its marvelous knowledge of human nature as expressed in the doctrine of original sin.

The messages of Bloy and Péguy are quite different. The first Christians believed in the early return of the triumphant Christ; their successors were lulled to sleep while waiting, that is, they compromised with the world; Léon Bloy did not weaken. He announced the coming of Christ and, at first, that of the apocalyptic times which no one foresaw at the dawn of this twentieth century when, instead, others were hailing its triumphant march. He awaited with a constant impatience this epoch of justice which would offer its society, rid of its bourgeois and its wealth, to God: "One does not go to Paradise in one year or ten years, one enters it today when one is poor and crucified." No one has more violently castigated modern society, its state, its banks and . . . its Church: "Each day the infinite multitude of the disinherited cries louder and louder: You have no right to enjoy things when your brother suffers." Such is the socialism of Bloy, a socialism which has nothing in common with the economists and politicians, an evangelical socialism of Christian poverty.

This socialism is not very different from that of Péguy who, while adhering to the Catholic faith, did not deny his socialist faith. His socialism was not anti-religious; his Catholicism was not anti-socialist. Péguy rejected the bourgeois Catholicism installed in "comfortable positions" and returned to the traditions of the Christian mysteries. Why should it be that when Christianity is mentioned "in the land of St. Louis and Joan of Arc, in the city of St. Genevieve," everyone thinks that Marshal MacMahon is meant? "Why is talk of the Christian order identified with May 16th?"[1] And again: "Christianity is socially only a superior religion for the higher classes of society of the nation, a miserable sort of elegant religion for supposedly elegant people." It is a Christianity which does not want to pay "the temporal costs" of "eternal salvation."

Although he was born in 1845 Léon Bloy, little read and little

---

[1] This is an allusion to the dismissal by Marshal MacMahon on May 16, 1876 of a republican ministry although it had been maintained by the parliamentary majority chosen in recent elections.

understood in his own lifetime, may be compared with Péguy, whose influence was to fuse with his to increase that of both together, while that of Bourget and the traditional novelists weakened.

On the morrow of World War I, after the disappearance of Bloy and Péguy, Catholic writers, with rare exceptions like Claudel, continued to try to demonstrate the truth of the solutions offered by Christian ethics for the problems of individual and social life, and their apostolic preoccupation gave to their work a certain conventional character. The new Catholic literature, on the contrary, no longer envisaged the projection of religion on the person or society, but the very drama of the Christian (its development corresponding to the development of spirituality). This literature reveals the drama and describes it in its total nudity. What is man in the unity and diversity of his soul and his carnal form? What can original sin, grace, religious vocation and the communion of saints do to him? The point is to reach the human reality in its essence for, dominating all the others, the supreme problem for the Christian is that of the struggle against evil for the goal of eternal salvation.

Although an unbeliever, Estaunié, by studying religious anguish, foresaw this type of literature which two great names were to propagate, Georges Bernanos and François Mauriac. In 1925 the first, whom Mauriac considers the founder of the new Catholic novel, caused a belated, violent and glorious eruption in the world of letters with *Sous le Soleil de Satan*. Its familiar heroes are priests chosen not because of their clerical functions but because the Christian adventure is lived by them to the point of paroxysm. The heroes of Mauriac, who reached literary maturity as early as 1922, kept in their heart, this human heart "full of filth" as Pascal put it, "a vocation for the infinite" susceptible of carrying them above themselves.

Non-Catholic critics at first refused to understand the very nature of these tragedies of souls—and the heroes who live them, unusual priests and morbid faithful, have scandalized and continue to scandalize the faithful who are not all church wardens—yet these attendant circumstances do not detract from the fact that a literary revolution, inconceivable a half century earlier, has taken place.

Under different forms this same search for the depths of Catholicism, this same aspiration toward a Christian vision of man and of the world is also the essential characteristic of other writers who are not tormented by the problem of evil to the same degree. A Claudel does not try to Christianize society: he moves within an essentially Christian society. Following the example of the medieval mystery plays, Henri Ghéon's plays, conceived for "the faithful people," are a "prolongation of his prayer," an "illustration of his faith."

Catholic Spirituality

The insufficiency of the rational effort of a century, the successive catastrophes which have tragically shed light on it, the unrest which has resulted from it, the feeling of the progressive ruin of an old society, of the painful birth of a new society are also expressed by the evolution of Catholic spirituality. This is the least well-known part of the subject of our survey because the most difficult to study.

In the nineteenth century Catholics envisaged their religion primarily from the moral point of view. They sought in the Church less the indivisible realm of God than the traditional external organization which provides prescriptions for the rule of life and duties. They loved the pomp and the feasts, especially those whose human values interest everybody (like All Saints day, for example) and the practical virtues of their saints (the justice of St. Louis, the charity of St. Vincent de Paul, and, one might add, although her sanctity was proclaimed only later, the patriotism of Joan of Arc). God was certainly not absent from the thinking of Catholics, but they felt little need, or rather, the curiosity of their piety liked, instead of going directly to Him, to follow, at the risk of going astray, the roundabout ways of particular devotions: the rosary, the months of St. Joseph, of Mary, of the Sacred Heart, the souls in Purgatory, the scapular, medals. These views, not always related to theology or the liturgy, were bound up, especially among women—wasn't French Catholicism a religion for women?—with a sentimentality that was satisfied with extraordinary phenomena, or romanesque representations. The cult of the Sacred Heart, as it was generally practiced, both the revelations and the messages of Margaret Mary Alacoque, to whom it owes its diffusion, and the bad taste of those images of the Sacred Heart which made of it an object of worship distinct from the Person of Christ, is a good example.

Now diverse influences concurred to overthrow this spiritual life within two generations, starting at the end of the nineteenth century. The oldest, and perhaps the most important has been, since the opening of the Catholic Institutes, the theological renewal. The works of specialists have been popularized in elementary theological works like those of Father Plus, for example, which are read by the mass of the clergy and the elite of the Christian people and bring their attention to the essential notions of Catholicism. By turning their fervor to God they turn it away from particular devotions. A liturgical awakening has accompanied this renewed interest in theology: missals are taking the place of "prayer books to be read during the Mass." The Missal of Dom Lefevre, which has had great favor, was published in 1920.

At the same time a controversy arose as to the meaning of the mystical life. Those who considered its ways as exceptional and its expression as belonging to the marvelous followed Father Poulain whose ideas were expressed in 1901 in *Les Graces d' Oraison.* But in numerous books published between 1896 and 1932 Monsignor Saudreau envisaged the mystical life as the natural prolongation of the life of grace which all Christian souls should normally attain. In 1921 the Dominican review *La Vie Spirituelle,* which had been adding its bit for the previous two years, received the approbation of Benedict XV: the Pope "constantly draws the attention of souls to the conditions required for the progress of grace, of virtues and the gifts of the Holy Ghost whose perfect expression is found in the mystical life." The Abbé Bremond, for his part, has helped awaken aspirations to this life by revealing in his *History of Religious Sentiment in France since the Wars of Religion,* unfortunately broken off at the end of the seventeenth century, the largely ignored past of Catholic spirituality.

After World War I other influences of diverse origin contributed to favor the renewal of the spiritual life. There were, apart from the trials endured during the war itself, the frustration of the hopes of victory, the return to Catholicism, beginning before the war, of numerous intellectuals who infused in it a new virility, and fiinally, the creation of Catholic Action movements which stressed the notions of community and commitment.

What is, thereafter, more and more striking among young Catholics—and especially since the Second World War—is the spiritual sincerity, the appetite for human and divine life, the appeal to

God through grace and the earthly conditions to which it applies in their existence. Instead of the conformist, individualistic Catholicism of 1901, the Catholicism of the law, of obligations of practice and of sentiment, theirs seems both more personal and more social, a Catholicism inspired by the theological virtues and proclaimed by direct testimony. Exercises in prayer have given way to this permanent prayer which is the very life of the Christian, the exclusive search for individual salvation has given way to that of work in the marketplace for the salvation of the world. The tendency of these young people to transpose their spiritual living into a sometimes ill-considered activism has understandably prompted reservations. But it should not be forgotten that they have replaced the somewhat passive religion of their fathers, who believed that they lived in a stable and unchanging society, with a conquering religion in a society that has lost the sense of being the master of its own destiny.

How can we fail to wonder what is the significance of the posthumous destinies of Theresa of the Infant Jesus, canonized in 1925 only twenty-seven years after her death. She is the first French mystic and saint who has had popularity, a popularity which no other saint knew to such a degree and which spread with a prodigious rapidity. If one thinks of other great French saints loved for their practical virtues the fact appears quite singular, and the miracles attributed to the little Sister do not suffice to explain it. She exercised such an attraction so quickly because she answered the most recent aspirations of piety. A living incarnation of the simplifying work of thinkers who have explained the essence of theological and mystical truth, she attained God and lived with Him, without any learned analysis, without recourse to learned arguments, nor to exceptional moments of sensibility or sudden illuminations, but simply by "the little way of spiritual childhood," by the confident surrender of a soul filled with love. She offers to men of our time the highest and most accessible type of asceticism.

These are a few brief lights shed on the highways of Catholic spirituality. We have left in the background the most well-known of them, that traced by Pius X, because it deserves special consideration. The great acts of his pontificate are consecrated to communion, the frequent communion of adults (Dec. 10, 1905), of children (Sept. 15, 1906) and to the early age at which these could receive the sacrament (Aug. 8, 1910). No one contributed more than this Holy Father to lead the faithful to the most direct and most complete purity of Catholicism, and thus to prepare the spiritual conceptions of the young generations which seeks above all the truth in Christ, in his Person and in his Word. Thus Catholicism owes to this Pope more than to any other whatever new effectiveness its message possesses in the modern world. He seemed to be out of touch with the modern world, and his pontificate was simply a series of temporal failures. How the detours of history, or religious history more than of any other, because it touches what is deepest in the soul, break through the oversimplified classifications historians resort to in order to be understood! There is no true history which does not make allowance for a share of mystery.

Is it not also true of the whole history of French Catholicism which a half century ago appeared to be in its agony, and today provides the spectacle of such an ardent fervor?

XI

The Church and Catholic Activity
in Contemporary Italy*

by *Michele Frederico Sciacca*

I. *From 1848 to the End of the First World War*

The first half of the nineteenth century may be considered the period of the ideal preparation for the political rebirth of the Italian nation, the period which gave the Italian Risorgimento its intellectual and moral content. As a consequence, in this period the closest ties prevail between all cultural manifestations and political life. Even Catholicism (except in the case of Mazzini and his followers, who considered the function of the Church exhausted), was called upon to fulfill a political task, to become Italian and national, the unifying force of Italian hearts, the revivifying power of the Italian genius, both liberal and civil and, having reestablished its position in the modern world, the dynamic principle of a new era of culture. Evidently there was here a confusion of the necessary with the contingent, historical circumstances with that which is above history and therefore eternal. The chief theoretician of a "civil Catholicism" and of a Papacy at the head of a reconstituted Italian polity was the philosopher Vincenzo Gioberti (1801-1852), whose position in political theory is called "neoguelfism" and the primary text of which was the work *Primato morale e civile degli Italiani* (The Moral and Civil Primacy of the Italians), published in 1843. The Church, as the depository and the interpreter of Revelation, has always had its principal seat in Italy; therefore, Gioberti argued, Italy, among all nations, has a moral and a civil primacy. His object was to induce the Church to place herself at the head of the movement of Italian renewal and to persuade the Italians to support her in this great work of cultural rebirth. This

---

* Translated by A. Robert Caponigri.

notion was also the source of the project most characteristic of neoguelfism, that of a political confederation of the Italian states with the Papacy at its head. In a word, Gioberti sought to create in Italy a national Catholicism, in order to eliminate the antithesis between the traditional religion and the Italian renovation and to arrive at an alliance between patriotism and religion. This idea involved the conception of the Church as a manifestation of human civility or culture, having her first movement from God and her gaze fixed upon God in her perpetual dynamism. Thus the Church would become an integral element in progress, in a manner equal to divine truth, and herself subject to the process of civilization and of cultural becoming. And hence flowed, too, the necessity of a Catholic reformation, in order to transform the traditional physiognomy of Catholicism, now summoned to play its part in a vast political strategy.

The strategy (and Gioberti's idea was such, dictated more by political motives than by a sincere love of the Church and of Catholicism), was in part successful, for the Italian question became a movement of public opinion, but very soon revealed its equivocal structure. Gioberti, encouraged by the wide success of the *Primacy,* did not hesitate to attack the Jesuits openly, first in the *Prolegomeni al Primato* (1845) and later, and more violently, in the *Gesuita moderno* (1847) and in the *Apologia del Gesuita moderno* (1848), expressing with ever greater clarity and explicitness his doctrine of a progressivist Catholicism. The controversy between Gioberti and the Jesuits places in contrast "civil religion" and traditional and conservative Catholicism. The *Prolegomeni* served in part to make clear the equivocation between Catholic liberalism and integral and authentic Catholicism. It became clear how radically the liberal and progressivist Catholicism of Gioberti, envisaging the renovation of the civil and religious conscience of the Italians, by means of a close marriage between religion and culture, between the religious and the cultural magistry, was in opposition to the conception of Catholicism and of its mission which the Curia and the Jesuits entertained. A Catholicism which is an "instrument of culture" necessarily encountered resistance, and sharp resistance, from traditional orthodoxy. Evidently Gioberti and other Catholics, more concerned for Italy than for the Church, for a moment saw, or deluded themselves that they saw, in her an instrument for the realization of their political purposes. The Church lost no time in disillusioning the neoguelfs, but her reaction struck not only at this equivocation, but at modern culture *en bloc,* in this way generating the alternate equivocation of a Church inexorably hostile to all modern progress. These equivocations have been for the most part clarified and the Giobertian manner of formulating the problem, fundamentally erroneous, has long been dead without hope of renewal and without regret. Evidently, that "civil and national Catholicism" so contracted and reduced the function of the Church as to identify her with the task of resolving the problem of Italian independence, and to consider Catholicism as the instrument of a civil and national renovation. Far better is the vision of Antonio Rosmini (1798-1855), the greatest Italian thinker of the nineteenth century, who clearly posits (as do the Jesuits) the problem of "Catholic civilization," which is a thing very different from "cultural Catholicism": the Church works from within and not from without, not so much moving the heart as striking the reason or intellect with the aspect of the invisible truth and restoring life and thought, new and at the same time Catholic, to civilization and culture. This is the sense of that which Rosmini calls "the full and living instruction" of consciences.

Not all the principles of political liberalism were in opposition to the doctrinal and dogmatic complex of the Church, but, in relation to the times, the attitude of the Papacy could only with difficulty have been either different or more conciliatory. Liberal individualism, which places the liberty of the individual above all else and the meaning of life in the free and unlimited deployment of the nature of the individual (identifying liberty with the liberty of nature), which makes of individual liberty a dogma, could not and cannot be accepted by the Church, not only because it is in opposition to the Christian and Catholic conception of liberty, but also because it tends to identify liberty with the will, which is the negation of liberty. All this is apart from the serious social consequences of this concept, such as the liberal notions of property and of "economic liberalism" which are fundamentally antisocial. On the other hand, the political interests of the Papacy in its character as a sovereign state were menaced to the point where the temporal power of the Pope, together with his very freedom of action, as spiritual head of the Catholic world, was compromised. All these and other circumstances explain and justify the negative attitude of the ecclesiastical hierarchy (the Papacy and the Episcopate) concerning the liberal ideology, for this negation involved the defense of clear-cut religious, moral and social principles as well as certain religious institutions (the existence of religious orders, church property, civil recognition of religious marriages, etc.). The encyclical *Mirari vos arbitramus* of Gregory XVI (August 15, 1832) is the first explicit condemnation of liberal principles (liberty of conscience, unlimited freedom of opinion, separation of Church and State, rationalism applied to theology). Subsequently, Pius IX in a letter to the bishops of Italy (1863), condemned religious "latitudinarianism," that is, the doctrine which, for the purposes of salvation, places all religious confessions on the same plane, and, as a consequence, does not hold that adherence to Catholicism is a necessary condition of salvation. About a year later there followed the encyclical *Quanta cura* (December 8, 1864) and the famous *Syllabus,* published in the form of an appendix to the encyclical itself, in which "naturalism," "communism," and "socialism" are condemned (without, however, any allusion to their socio-economic doctrines).

In its eighty articles grouped in ten paragraphs, the *Syllabus* condemned "modern errors," that is: (1) pantheism, naturalism, absolute rationalism; (2) moderate rationalism; (3) indifferentism and latitudinarianism; (4) socialism, communism, secret societies, biblical societies, and clerico-liberal societies; (5) errors concerning the church and her rights (the subordination of the acts of ecclesiastical authority to state approval, etc.); (6) errors concerning civil society whether in itself or in its relations to the Church; (7) errors concerning ethics, whether natural or Christian; (8) errors concerning Christian marriage; (9) errors concerning the civil power of the Roman pontiffs (the idea that the temporal power is incompatible with spiritual power); (10) errors referring to contemporary liberalism.

The *Syllabus* had tremendous repercussions and excited violent and impassioned controversies. The adversaries of the Church and of the Papacy exploited it without scruple as unanswerable evidence of the impossibility of reconciliation between the Church and the needs of modern culture and of the social and political life of modern society and decried the "obscurantism" of a "retrograde" Catholicism. Thus, as a consequence of the failure of Giobertian neoguelfism, of the condemnation of liberalism and of other modern errors, and the rigid development of the political policy of the

278

Vatican into forms of conservatism, the cultural climate of the second half of the nineteenth century is quite different from that of the first half of the century. As a matter of fact, in opposition to the preceding period, integral laicism characterizes Italian life in general after 1860. The spirit of laicism, the frequently verbose and extravagant protestations of so-called "free thought," the deification of liberty, of man, of science, etc., frequently gave rise to vulgar forms of anticlericalism and of antireligion.

Naturally, in these controversies and in the conflict of opinions and of interests, political circumstances had their part. It must be noted that the internal and external political life of the new Italian Kingdom was anything but easy and simple from 1860 to 1870. Controversies and dissensions between republicans and monarchists, conservatives and revolutionaries, diversity of cultural conditions and social development between the different regions, brigandage (both political and non-political) in the South, aversion to Piedmontese centralization, the slightest participation of the great majority of people in political life, the restlessness of the lower and upper middle classes, rendered the work of government difficult and wearisome. The questions of Venezia and of Rome remained unresolved. The latter, by far the more complex, weighed upon Italian political life, disturbed consciences and had anything but happy effects even upon cultural activity. The unfortunate efforts of Ricasoli, the convention of September, which displeased everyone and solved nothing, Mentana, Porta Pia, the plebiscite, and the Law of Guarantees, indicate the phases of this episode which for many years convulsed Italian life and even the political schemes of Napoleon III. The publication of the *Syllabus* occurred in the midst of these circumstances and rendered the moderate political strategy of the Right more difficult; it brought upon the Church the aversion of lay culture and unleashed that violent anticlericalism which, without justified motives or because of the excessive importance given to certain secondary problems in preference to other principal concerns, continued its perverse course for forty years. The opposition to the Church and to the antiliberal attitude of Pius IX contributed also to the alienation of Catholics from political life and the further impoverishment of the classes which participated in it. Mazzini never desisted from his lamentations over this Italy, so different from the Italy of which he had dreamed; the young Carducci directed the arrows of his satire against it; Cardinal Antonelli, convinced that the unity would soon give way, even thought, according to the neoguelf program of Gioberti, of a republican federation. Passions were high, serenity absent. The formulation of the dogma of the infallibility of the Pope when he speaks *ex cathedra* on matters of faith and morals, a purely theological question, had serious political repercussions and appeared as a further reenforcement of the antiliberalism of Rome.

Naturally, in this new cultural and political climate, the still living representatives of the culture of the first half of the nineteenth century—Gioberti and Rosmini had both died prematurely—such as Lambruschini, Capponi, Tommaseo, even Mazzini himself, the Galluppian pacifists in the South, the Giobertians who were also numerous there, and the neo-Thomists, all found themselves cut adrift, in disharmony with their times, concerned over the evil effects which, especially on the young, the new ideas could not for long fail to exercise. If one but thinks of the climate of ardent spirituality and religion which is characteristic of the first half of the nineteenth century, prevalently Catholic, in part Jansenistic, but in both aspects, intimately felt and profoundly experienced, it is possible to explain quite easily the disastrous impression which the "new doctrines," the agitated and aroused passions, the indifferent and irreverent attitudes toward religion, must have made upon those noble spirits. The official culture, "rosminian" in the widest sense of the term, feared that this revolutionary laicism would dethrone it (as, in fact, happened) and would become the recognized governing and ruling force of the mind.

The attitude of the Catholics, at least in Italy, was one of diffidence and detachment from the liberal, lay state, which was indifferent and hostile toward religious institutions, advocated "separatism" between Church and state and was in the hands of men whose formative influences had been rationalistic and illuministic. This was the reality supporting the attitude of "absenteeism" from political life on the part of Catholics both in Italy and in other liberal states. "It was the mistaken strategy of those filled with nostalgia for the divine-right monarchies and for the theory of the solidarity of the Altar and the Throne."[1] Many Catholics, especially the higher clergy, hoped for a return to older ways, counting

---

[1] M. Bendiscioli, *Chiesa e societa' nei secoli XIX e XX* (Milano, Marzorati, 1951), p. 78.

upon the intrinsic weakness of the new Kingdom. They believed that with "non-collaboration in Parliament and in the local administrations," with "absenteeism" on an organized scale in the elections, they might reduce the representative organs to an incapacity to function in public administration, and so bring about the dominance in those organs of the extremists, who in provoking disorder would justify "reaction" and the reestablishment of the older forms of organization."[2] This absenteeism of Italian Catholics with respect to the liberal state was officially sanctioned by the *non-expedit*, that is by the declaration of the Holy See that "it was not proper" for Catholics to participate in the elections of political representatives of a state which had deprived the Pope of the Patrimony of Saint Peter and whose king and government had as a consequence been excommunicated. This is the source of the formula: "neither elected nor electors." Absenteeism did more actual damage to Catholicism itself than to any other party, to the degree that it permitted the legislation of the new Italian state to develop under laicist and antireligious influence, so that in effect masonry controlled the entire administration as well as the educational establishment, which became entirely laicized. The "Civiltà Cattolica," a review published by the Jesuit fathers, reacted most vigorously and conducted some memorable polemics. The situations were exasperated and exacerbated, while the activity of the liberal Catholics, who accepted the new state and sought to work within it to the benefit of religious institutions, achieved few tangible advantages for the Church in her difficult situation. Most grave was the perturbation of conscience among those who sought to be at the same time "good Italians" and "good Catholics," as was the disagreement between "liberal Catholics" and "clerical Catholics." Under such circumstances the liberal-constitutional state of the first half of the nineteenth century evolved into a lay state in opposition to the Church, with great damage both to Italy and to Italians. The "Roman Question," made sharper, rather than resolved by the "Law of Guarantees" (February, 1871) unacceptable to the Church, continued unresolved, and weighed upon and dominated the entire life of a state which called itself lay but which was ninety-seven percent Catholic. From that time a question imposed itself which is neither merely political nor merely Italian, but is actually proper to western

---

[2] *Ibid.*, p. 79.

and international culture: how to achieve concord between Church and culture, in such a way that the world may not have merely Catholics, on the one hand, and a modern civilization which is not Catholic on the other, but a true Catholic culture. It is a problem of uniting what has been separated, of composing a scandalous divorce and not of extending a conflict or an indifference. This problem will persist and its solution prove impossible so long as those who think in harmony with the modern world hate the faith and those who believe nurse suspicions and reservations against modern culture.

Meanwhile socialism or social democracy began to take consistent form against liberalism and political democracy. Social democracy opposed liberalism as "bourgeois" (in so far as the liberty which it defended favored in practice the interest of the industrial and commercial bourgeoisie) and championed the right of the laboring classes to vote. It placed in the foreground the economic needs of the working class or proletariat. Under the spur of socialism (which, with Marx, took the name of communism), the liberal state was constrained to extend the franchise and to make concessions on the question of political eligibility, thus permitting hitherto unrepresented classes to achieve representation in the state. With respect to the Church, and despite the generally humanitarian or religious character of the first theoreticians of socialism (that socialism which Marx called "utopian"), the socialistic ideologies presented themselves, from the beginning, as more dangerous than the liberal, and afterwards ever more negative and disturbing. "Absenteeism" increasingly appeared as a mistaken and dangerous tactic. "It became clear that such tactics did not provoke the fall of the new regime but gave a free hand to the extremists, and that these proved not only to be anticlerical but also to have socialist leanings, under the stimulus which the rapidly growing working-class movement was exercising. Therefore, under the urgency of social danger, there took place first the participation of Catholics in the administrative elections (communal and provincial), which led to the administrative control by moderates, displacing the radicals, in such important places, as Rome; thence the way led to official electoral pacts by means of which the votes of Catholics were made to converge upon the moderate candidates who committed themselves to a policy considerate of the needs of the Church. There was created as the immediate result an organization designed to achieve this result, the "Electoral Union of Italian Catholics," reestablished by the anticommunistic "Civic Committees" in 1948, which drew together the work of the Catholic congresses and issued annual reviews. These affirmed the Catholic doctrinal positions with respect to the problems of the hour."[3]

Even the attitude of the Papacy underwent those modifications suggested by the changes in the situation. In the encyclical *Quod apostolici muneris* (October 28, 1878), Leo XIII condemned the program and the method of socialism; but the same great Pope in another encyclical *Libertas, praestantissimum* (June 20, 1888), gave a greater value to liberty than the *Syllabus* had given, while the encyclical *Immortale Dei* (November 1, 1885) had three years before outlined the "Christian constitution of States" in which there was affirmed the indifference of the Church in regard to the forms of government as long as it guaranteed and preserved the fundamental needs of Christian life. It recalled that the "Church has always been in favor of civil liberty untainted by intemperance." A positive position with respect to the needs of the working class was taken by Leo XIII's famous encyclical *Rerum novarum* (May 15, 1891), which urged that there should be a more concrete concern for the workingman's condition, predicted a new order in economic life, which would render less harsh the inequalities between social classes, and delineated a new order for their relationships.

The *Rerum Novarum* signalized an important date not only for Italians but for the world. To it are to be traced the origins of the organizational experiences of Catholics in the social field, their criticism of the capitalistic system, the syndical Catholic associations for the improvement of the working class (the so-called "white syndicates"), and the substitution of the "social function" of property for the individualistic concept of "private" property held by liberalism. In this way the Church: (a) made her own the demand of the masses for a revision of the economic system; (b) condemned socialist and communistic doctrines; and, (c) rejecting the method of violence, sought solutions based on Christian principles of solidarity and fraternal love.

Of necessity, the Catholics found themselves in the thick of the political battle against liberals and socialists, but with a greater understanding of the concept of political liberty as inseparable from

---

[3] *Ibid.,* p. 86.

social liberty, in a position of the "center" which might satisfy the needs of political democracy and of social democracy in harmony with Christian principles. With the elections of 1913 the Catholics entered officially into the Parliament and thus brought to an end the formula of "neither elected nor electors." This involvement in political life has proved to be an indubitable good not only because the nation has been able to avail itself of the services of very able men and because the laicist legislation has been, bit by bit, moderated but finally because it has contributed to the relaxation and prepared the way for the solution of the "Roman Question."

After the First World War (1914-1918) the weight of the imposing cultural, social and syndical power of the Italian Catholics made itself felt in a tangible manner and led to a true revision of the laicist laws, despite the resistance of lay Masonry and of the sociocommunists. Then came Fascism, not without the collaboration of certain conservative Catholic circles, and a new situation arose.

II. *The Lateran Pacts and the Solution of the "Roman Question"*

The accusation, frequently advanced by her adversaries, that the Church had lent her support to Fascism and that it was compromised by Fascism and appropriated it, is false. Just as she did not attach herself to liberalism, even when it presented itself as a Catholic liberalism, nor to any other political party or theory, so the Church maintained her independence with respect to the Fascist dictatorship. Nor did she spare Fascism, as she had not spared Marxism, from her condemnation. This attitude of the Church is recognized even by writers who, while calling themselves Catholics, have heaped severe and frequently unjust criticisms upon her. Thus, for example, Jemolo: "It may be recognized without qualification that there was no heretical principle, no proposition against dogma, against orthodox history or against morals which was even tentatively advanced by Fascist men or journals of any authority, which was not immediately refuted by pontifical acts, by very authoritative ecclesiastical reviews or by the *Osservatore Romano* with the zeal and the precision, the theological and the juridical sense, which distinguishes men of the Church. Those who for twenty years lent an avid ear to every voice which, in opposition to Fascism, reaffirmed the Christian values, remember perfectly the condemnation of totalitarianism, with the defense of the rights of the individual and of the family, as well, of course, as those of the Church, the replies made

284

to the conception of a Catholic Church more the heir of the Roman imperial spirit than of the preaching of the prophet of Nazareth, the repudiation of the thesis concerning "living room" which renders legitimate wars of conquest; they remember all, even the condemnation of the doctrine that it is licit to equate the intention with the completed or effected crime, implied in the article in the *Osservatore Romano* which announced the sentence of death passed on the anarchist Schirru who was guilty of having had the intention of killing the 'Duce.' Whoever wants to defend the Church from the accusation of having concurred in any point of the perverted doctrines of Fascism can compile a well documented defense, which would demonstrate that at every moment the right doctrine was taught and defended."[4]

Another writer, laicist and anti-Catholic in the extreme, Calamandrei, in a speech (March 1949) to the Constituent Assembly on the insertion of the Lateran Pacts in the new Italian constitution, said: ". . . at a certain moment, during the years of greatest oppression, we were aware that the sole newspaper in which it was still possible to find some accent of liberty, of our own liberty and of the common liberty of all free men, was the *Osservatore Romano;* for we knew that anyone who bought the *Osservatore Romano* risked being bludgeoned; because a free voice was to be found in the *Acta diurna* of our friend Gonella; because when the racial persecutions were begun, the Church rose up against the persecutors and in defense of the oppressed; because when the Germans were hunting down our sons to torture them and to shoot them, these our sons, of whatever party they may have been, found refuge . . . in the canonical precincts and in the convents. . . ."[5]

The fact that the Conciliation was affected under and with the Fascist Government signifies nothing so far as the alleged "Fascism" of the Church is concerned; the Conciliation is an act which transcends the contingent circumstances of a political regime and prescinds from the fact, that is to say, from the fact that this regime may be of one cast or another, so long as it is legally constituted and recognized. For the rest, the concordats between the Church and the State are very frequent especially in the history of modern times; from the end of the first world war, the Church, though not always

---

[4] A. C. Jemolo, *Chiesa e stato in Italia negli ultimi cento anni* (Torino, Einaudi, 1948), pp. 680-681.

[5] Quoted by Jemolo, *op. cit.*, p. 703.

with equally good results, has established as many of these as possible with regimes of very different cast. Indeed, in modern times the concordat has become a necessity, in so far as, on the one hand, the state has its own national theory, informed by the concept of its own sovereignty over its own territory, and on the other, the Church has the dual character of universality and supernaturality. This theoretical contrast determines the necessity of a *modus vivendi* between the two powers, of mutual concessions for reciprocal advantage. A concordat between the Church and the Italian State was especially imperative, for the Papacy had its seat in Rome, the capital of the (then) Kingdom of Italy. With the seizure of Rome (1870) there had been opened the exceedingly serious "Roman Question," which was to continue unresolved, despite half a century of controversy. Thereafter, the Pope considered himself the "prisoner" of the King of Italy and sought to vindicate that minimal sovereignty which was necessary to his autonomy as spiritual head of the Catholic world. The problem was not simply and solely Italian, but international. A solution of this question was reached on February 11, 1929, by Pope Pius XI, for whom Cardinal Pietro Gasparri acted as Secretary of State. The Lateran Pacts comprise: (a) a Concordat; and (b) a political Treaty for the solution of the "Roman Question," with the consequent recognition of the State of Vatican City. The treaty became effective with the exchange of ratifications on June 7, 1929.

The Pacts of St. John Lateran have had historical, political, religious and juridical consequences of enormous importance not only for Italy but for the entire world. The solution of the "Roman Question" may be considered as definitive since it fulfills all the necessary conditions, being *bilateral* (the Law of Guarantees [1871], by contrast, was unilateral since it was never accepted by the Church), *Italian, territorial* and *international*, without foreign interference. "A bilateral solution, thanks to the just, natural and direct agreement between the two interested parties, the Holy See and the Italian State; an Italian solution, because there were no guarantees from any third power; a territorial solution, because, while Rome remained the recognized capital of the Italian state, the State of Vatican City was established under the sovereignty of the Supreme Pontiff. It must be added, further, that the territorial solution has been integrated with other juridical and economic guarantees, established in the treaty, and the appended Financial

Convention. To complete the Conciliation there had further been established a Concordat, intended to regulate the conditions of religion and of the Church in Italy."[6]

The bilateral solution on a territorial basis was indispensable: a *minimum* of territorial sovereignty is the condition of action for the Church. The words of Pius XI, pronounced on that same date, February 11, 1929, are as clear and as eloquent as could be wished on this point: "It has been our desire to demonstrate in a peremptory manner that no territorial cupidity motivates the Vicar of Jesus Christ, but only the consciousness of that which it is impossible not to demand; for a certain territorial sovereignty is the universally recognized and indispensable condition for every jurisdictional sovereignty; as a consequence, the necessity of that amount of territory without which that jurisdictional sovereignty cannot subsist, because it would have no place to stand. We have as a matter of fact taken that point of view which the Blessed Saint Francis took: enough of the body to keep it in unity with the soul. It is only right that we reserve to Ourselves the right to observe that the territory which We have reserved to Ourselves and which has been recognized as Ours, is, materially speaking, little enough, but at the same time it is great, the greatest in the world, from any point of view other than the material from which it may be viewed. . . . The "little" Vatican City is the spiritualization of the temporal power of the Popes and is the minimal indispensable condition of the highest Sovereignty on earth. For the Church and for the Catholic world it has been a great conquest, which signifies above all territorial independence and visible liberty for the central government of the Universal Church, protection of the family by means of the recognition of the civil effects of canonical marriage, the possibility of influencing more directly the education of youth by means of religious instruction in the schools."[7]

What were the ideas and what the motives which inspired the Lateran Pacts? In the first place, the times had changed and the problem had now reached a final form: the controversies were spent, the ideas clarified and the terms of the question precisely formulated. On the one hand, the Vatican had become convinced: (a) that an Italy without Rome as its capital was an impossibility, just

[6] A. Piola: *Dalla Concilazione alla Constituzione* (Genova, Lupa, 1950), pp. 21-22.

[7] Quoted by Piola, *op. cit.,* p. 84.

as the dissolution of Italy's political unity had now become impossible; (b) that the Roman question was no longer a problem of international interest and that there was no hope, as there had been in the time of Napoleon III, of any foreign intervention; (c) that it would be both impolitic and unpopular to restate the problem in terms of territorial extension, for to do so would give the appearance of a purely political issue dictated by attachment of the temporal power. To pose the problem in terms of the autonomy required for the spiritual teaching mission of the Church, however, would emphasize its dominantly religious aspect and would consequently attract the sympathy and the support of all Italian Catholics. On the other hand, Fascism saw in the solution of the knotty question an occasion or opportunity for claiming credit in support of its own authority, its prestige and its solidity, without mentioning the increment (and extension to new areas) of the sympathy of those Catholic currents which from the beginning had supported it. In a word, for Fascism (which in its principles was not Catholic) the solution of the question was dictated by political strategy and only in view of the advantages which the regime might draw from it; for the Vatican it was suggested, once the bilaterality and the territoriality were respected, by dominantly religious motives, in the sense that the solution promised to establish peace and to foster among Catholics a unity which in the present and, above all, in the future, would reenforce and render more effective their political and social action. If the question were not resolved at that time, it would have proved much more difficult to resolve it after the fall of Fascism, on account of the resurgence of lay Masonic factions and of Communism; and on the other hand, it would have constituted one more problem for Christian Democracy and a further source of discord between liberal and conservative Catholics (and among Catholics without exception), discord which the groups of the extreme left would not hesitate to exploit in order to seize political power.

It is necessary to recognize candidly, once the political implications are conceded, that Fascism made possible the Lateran Pacts, because fundamentally, and under certain aspects, it pursued a political policy favorable to the Church. As a matter of fact, anticlericalism ceased, Masonry was suppressed, religious teaching was reintroduced into the schools, etc. It is true that Fascism remained laicist and on certain occasions (when the Church sought to vindicate its rights, defending Catholic Action and condemning certain doctrines) controversies and attacks in the press did not fail to arise, but it is also true that it offered to Catholics the possibility, with the elimination of the Masonic incubus, to express themselves without the obstacle of laicist prejudice, even though that of inscription in the Fascist party was imposed. It is also necessary, however, to remember that, as we have already remarked, this Catholic re-emergence in civil, political and cultural life had had its beginnings from the first years of the century, and that the contention of the apologists of Fascism (now taken up by certain neo-Fascists) that it was due to Fascism does not correspond to the truth.

If we now turn to the consideration of these matters from a strictly ideological point of view, we see that in the relations of Church and state, from the beginning of the century to the fall of Fascism, neoghibellinism has grown progressively weaker, even to the point of losing itself in a laicism favorable to concordats and not essentially hostile to the Church. On the other hand, neoguelfism of the Giobertian strain has been made obsolete by the march of events. Fundamentally, history has vindicated Rosmini: the relations between Church and State were reorganized on the new reality of the fact of the unification of Italy and the progress of the times; the Church was guaranteed in her sovereignty and in her religious teaching office, independent of the state, respected both in her doctrine and her spiritual-educative mission of divine origin. At the same time, the Church respected the sovereignty of the Italian state and permitted Catholics to govern themselves according to political methods which seemed to them most efficacious, in such wise as to create peaceful agreements and to avoid an interference which might generate discord and conflicts. For this reason the influence of Rosmini and of what we have called "Rosminianism" in general (both direct and indirect), have been much more powerful than would appear on the surface, since even its earlier adversaries have taken over, without explicit admission, Rosminian ideas. The influence of Gioberti, however, has made itself felt in a curious manner; laicist thought has revaluated him as a philosophical pantheist, a kind of rebellious and progressivist priest, who would have carried his "civil Catholicism" to the point of receiving into the Church the liberal point of view even in its laicist principles, of subordinating the Church to the authority of the state, of limiting her function to a kind of disciplinary action over the masses (the "social function" of religion, in the sense of this expression in Giordano Bruno, one of the masters of Italian Masonry). In fact, Gioberti enjoyed such favor among certain modernists, that Italian "modernism" immediately attached itself to his thought. Laicist thinkers from Spaventa to Gentile and their followers also looked to Gioberti for some of their ideas. At this point it should be kept in mind that in the first years of the century there existed in Italy a "political modernism" (the "Christian Democracy" of Romolo Murri), which was condemned by the Church, but enjoyed the sympathy of both liberal-Masonic and social laicism, a kind of "red Catholicism" as it was defined by Prezzolini.

The influence of Mazzini appears to us to have been secondary. To be sure, he has always remained popular and alive as one of the shapers of the Italian Risorgimento and as the master of the republicans (those who today are called "historical republicans"). But with the extension of the monarchy, with which such republicans as Garibaldi and Crispi collaborated, Mazzinism lost its effectiveness; and even today the party which represents it has slight ideological influence. Italy has not, to be sure, become a Republic through the power of the republican party or of the ideas of Mazzini but as a result of certain contingencies of internal and international politics and even more by the maturation of a republican consciousness through hatred of Fascism to which the King had bound himself. However that may be, the Mazzinian republican ideology is still strictly laicist and not Catholic, convinced as it is that the function of the Church has been exhausted, and that from her there can come no progress for the people.

III. *The Lateran Pacts and the New Constitution of the Italian Republic*

During the succeeding fourteen years of the Fascist regime, Pius XI first and after him Pius XII have had to defend this conquest against attacks coming from Fascism itself and above all from political actions not in conformity with Christianity. With the fall of Fascism and the expulsion of the Nazis from Italy, with the fall of the monarchy and the return of democracy, the new situation, aggravated by the presence of a strong Communist party and of other laicist factions (with the exception of Christian Democracy) made it necessary for the Church to be on her guard to repel the attack and to outmaneuver the tactics of her adversaries. The Lateran Pacts, as a consequence, again became the center of vital discussion and controversy in the sessions of the Constituent Assembly designated to formulate the articles of the new Italian Constitution.

Between 1945 and 1947 there was very nearly a political alignment with respect to the Church: (a) Christian Democracy and Catholic Action were naturally arrayed in defense of the Church and of Christian principles as well as of the Lateran Pacts; (b) the Party of Action (later defunct) was most opposed, extremely anticatholic and anticlerical; (c) the liberals, endowed with greater sensibility, refrained from any antireligious policy and attacked neither the Lateran Pacts nor the Church; (d) the Socialist party reserved its judgment but leaned toward "separation of Church and State"; (e) the attitude of the Communist Party was ambiguous purely for motives of political tactics: it did not believe that the problem could be solved "at the moment" and deferred its solution "to its proper time," that is, when it might be resolved according to the popular will. And everybody knew what "democratic" solutions meant for the Communists; the Catholics in the provinces under Communistic control know it best of all. Nevertheless, it is necessary to distinguish between the "political treaty" and the "Concordat"; with respect to the first, granted historical contingencies, no party, fundamentally, has aligned itself against it, nor is there serious thought of abolishing it and reopening the "Roman Question." To the Concordat, however, there has been opposition from all parties, with the exception of Christian Democracy, and, up to a certain point, the liberals, who have been motivated by political strategy. The rest, laicist and more or less Masonic, if they did not hold for its immediate cancellation, were certainly opposed to making the Concordat a measure for the Constitution, in order finally to arrive at a separation of State and Church on the basis of a presumptive incompatibility between any Concordat and a democratic political constitution.

Thus one arrives (1947) at the debate of the Constituent Assembly over the opportunities of inserting in the new Constitution articles having reference to the Lateran Pacts, religious liberty, liberty of worship and of conscience. The discussion was impassioned and implacable. The laicists were against the Christian Democrats, while the Communists mouthed ambiguities but finally favored the articles for political motives. The nub of the matter, both from the point of view of internal and of international policy, seems to us to have been well-stated in the address of de Gasperi, who asserted forthrightly that it was no part of his purpose to "arrest history" nor "to rivet, by means of this article, our relations, in all forms, to those which prevailed yesterday or those formulated in 1929. The Constitution has the Lateran Pacts as a basic element, but, at the same time, declares them to be modifiable, and says that they are modifiable by a simple parliamentary majority, and not by means of those greater and more solemn guarantees which the Constitution establishes for many matters even less important. The question is not . . . of one or another of the non-essential provisions of the Concordat bound up with historical contingencies, which can be modified without recourse to constitutional revision. . . . We are not concerned consequently with this or with that article which you have criticized and which you can place under your censure. We are concerned with the fundamental question, whether the Republic accepts the offer of religious peace which this Concordat offers." And he added: "We must vote in such wise that we may appeal to the free world of nations, to the world which I know and say watches us. The world which watches us is concerned that there may be created here a constitution of free men; the great Catholic world is concerned that here the Republic may be born in peace and friendship with the Roman Pontiff, who, during the war, vindicated human dignity against tyranny and extended his protective hands to the persecuted of all nations and of all faiths." From a more strictly religious point of view the problem was put into focus by G. La Pira: "if man has an intrinsic religious orientation, if this intrinsic orientation necessarily expresses itself in religious community, a lay State does not exist. There exists a state respectful of this religious orientation and of these associated religious formations, in which it expresses itself . . . ; there is no lay State, there is no agnostic state; we ought not to erect a confessional state, a state, that is, in which civil, political and economic rights derive from a specific confession of faith; we have only to constitute a state which respects this intrinsic religious orientation of the individual and of the collectivity and which conforms to it in all its juridical structure and its social structure."[8]

The fiercest debate waged over Article 7, of which we reproduce

---

[8] Quoted by A. C. Jemolo, *op. cit.*, pp. 710-711; 705.

the definitive text, approved 350 to 149: "The State and the Catholic Church are, each in its proper order, independent and sovereign. Their relations are regulated by the Lateran Pacts. Any modification of the Pacts, bilaterally accepted, does not require the procedure of constitutional revision."

The other articles which are relevant to our argument are:

(1) Art. 3, "All citizens have equal social dignity and are equal before the law, without distinction of sex, race, language, religion, political opinions, personal and social conditions."

(2) Art. 8, "All religious confessions are equally free before the law. Religious confessions other than the Catholic have the right to organize according to their own statutes in so far as these are not in opposition to the Italian juridical order. Their relations with the state are regulated by law on the basis of understandings with their respective representations."

(3) Art. 19, "All have the right of professing freely their own religious faith, in whatever form, individual or associative, to propagandize in its favor and to exercise its worship in private or in public, so long as there is no question of rites which violate good morals."

(4) Art. 20, "The ecclesiastical character and the purpose of religion and worship of an association or institution cannot be the cause of special legislative limitations nor of special fiscal burdens for its constitution, juridical capacity and every form of activity.

Articles 3, 7, and 8 are inserted among the "Fundamental Principles"; articles 19 and 20 among the "rights and duties of citizens." Article 7 introduces the Lateran Pacts into the Constitution; articles 3, 8, 19 and 20 sanction the rights of liberty and of equality, that is, they concern themselves with religious liberty (liberty of conscience and liberty of worship). Nevertheless, on the one hand, the new Italian Constitution "re-affirms and consecrates the principle of religious liberty," and on the other, "especially by means of the reference to (and the consequent approbation of) the Lateran Pacts, reaffirms the character of the Italian state as properly a Catholic State."[9] Even so, there have not been lacking bitter complaints about "religious liberty" and it has been maintained that non-Catholics in Italy are in a position of inferiority and inequality. It is my opinion that in no country with a Catholic majority of

---

[9] A. Piola, *op. cit.*, p. 99.

ninety-seven percent (97%) and a minority of three percent (3%) is there such great liberty for citizens of other confessions nor such equality of rights. For the rest, the principle of equality must be understood in the sense well expressed by an eminent jurist (a liberal and therefore beyond suspicion), G. Ruffini: "After all, an absolute equality of treatment, in the face of such a portentous difference of concrete conditions, would indicate not an operation of practical justice, but simply of abstract justice. And there is strong reason for doubting that it would be an act of *true* justice. For it is clear that to this principle of absolute and abstract justice so solemnly invoked in favor of equality at all costs, there may always and triumphantly be opposed this other principle of a justice at once practical and concrete, that to treat, as the venerable Ahrens used to say, in equal manner unequal juridical relations is as unjust as the unequal treatment of equal juridical relations. And it might also be added, that there is a false sense of equality, which is that of absolute, abstract, mathematical equality, and an equality in a right sense, which is that of relative concrete, juridical equality; for, as Kahl has wisely written, the true principle of equality asserts not: "to each THE SAME, but to each HIS DUE."[10]

During the period from 1945 to the present day: the relations between the Church and the Italian state may be considered normal and tranquil, above all since the time when the extreme left (the Communists and the pro-Communistic socialists) left the government and ranged themselves with the systematic opposition. Whether we consider the time in which all the democratic parties (with the exception of the extreme left and the extreme right) were represented in the government, or the later situation in which the government was composed only of Demo-Christians and historical republicans, there have been no "official" clashes between the Church and State, even though there have been ideological controversies between Catholics and secularists. In this connection, it may be opportune to define more clearly several aspects of the present situation of the Church with respect to the political life of the Republic. Before all else, we may make it clear that Christian Democracy is not a confessional party, even though the greatest part of its membership is composed of Catholics. There are, it must be remembered, Catholics enrolled among or sympathetic with the liberals, the monarchists,

---

[10] G. Ruffini, *Corso di diritto ecclesiastico* (Torino, 1924), p. 423.

etc. Even less is Christian Democracy a "clerical" party, though sustained by the clergy and by the entire ecclesiastical hierarchy. Within this party there are not lacking dissensions and diverse currents, some of which tend in a "laicist" direction. This laicist current is not, of course, anti-Catholic or Masonic, rather, it holds itself apart from all clericalism. Other disagreements of method and of tendency (within, however, the principles of Catholicism and of Christian social doctrine) are to be noted between the progressive "left" and the conservative "right," which latter seems at this time to find its major protagonist in the new president of "Catholic Action," Professor Gedda, as well as in some other doctrinaire currents. This "right" comes close to aligning itself with the monarchists and other rightist movements, concerned as it is with the fact that the so-called democratic parties (which up to this time have cooperated with the Christian Democrats), such as the democratic socialists and the historical republicans, are losing ground to the parties of the right. There is an obvious concern to ally with all solid anti-Communistic forces. There appear to be two courses of action. These may be called respectively the "course of de Gasperi," which seeks to avoid alliances either with the extreme right or the extreme left, confident that its old alliances are still sufficient to confront Communism and to withstand its efforts to gain power; and the "course of the right," which sees in the strengthening of the parties of the right, in the weakening of the minor parties and in the wearing out of Christian Democracy itself, an incipient weakness of the anti-Communist forces and seeks new alliances (to the right) for the party of de Gasperi. In this situation the ecclesiastical hierarchy is essentially concerned: (a) that the anti-Communist forces should not become so weakened and divided by dissensions as to give comfort to Communism; (b) that the Communists should not attain to power; (c) that their doctrines should not conquer new adherents among the masses which are easily moved by propaganda; (d) that there should really and effectively be established a program of social improvement according to Christian principles in such wise as to wrest from the hands of the Communists their most effective weapon and to bring about genuine social justice in favor of the poor and suffering classes; (e) that, whether Communist or not, no party or ruling class hostile to the Church should gain power and be able to disturb the new relations with the Italian state. Consequently, if we may speak of a political policy of the

Church, in the present circumstances, it may be described as above all else *anti-Communistic,* both because Communism denies all the principles of Catholicism and the Church herself and because it denies man, the human person (his values and liberty), whom the Church has always defended against every adversary. It is, moreover, *social* precisely because, according to Christian principles, human brotherhood is necessary, as is the duty of aiding all who are in need or oppressed by poverty, a primary cause of the degradation of human dignity. Finally, it is not *confessional,* but is directed toward all those parties which defend the dignity of man and do not deny the truth and the natural rights of the person and do not oppose the Church and her liberty. Therefore, just as Christian Democracy is not the party of the Church, so the Church is not bound to Christian Democracy or to any other political party. This fact explains why between the Church and Christian Democracy there may be points of agreement (anti-Communism, solution of the social problem according to Christian principles and not according to a confessional program); this also explains why Christian Democracy is able to conduct the government in union with other democratic parties even though these be explicitly laicist, while it cannot work with the extreme left, and why the ecclesiastical hierarchy and Catholic Action do not oppose such alliances. For the rest, the presence in the government of a laicist party such as the Republican, immediately provokes and reenforces anticlericalism; because clericalism is a political phenomenon which has little in common with religion, but rather is actually damaging to it, so much so that many Catholics, precisely because they are more concerned for the Catholic religion than for political conquests, are anticlerical, that is, against clericalism understood in this unhappy sense. Frequently, however, non-Catholics willfully or mistakenly identify "clericalism" with Catholicism itself and with the educative, social and political action of the Church. These critics demand that the Church be completely indifferent to all matters save those pertaining to parishes and seminaries, that she should not defend her principles and her independence from the invasion of the state, that she should counsel Catholics to abstain from political activity, so that the Lay State, the lay family and the lay school can prevail. Obviously they do not consider that should this come about Communism would, in the space of a few months, seize power and that the first to feel its destructive hand would be the non-Communist laicists, because there is no other power in Italy outside that of Catholicism capable of containing Communism. Consequently, the Church today not only defends her own liberty and that of Catholics, but renders possible the liberty of all.

The result of this situation is that today between non-Catholic and non-Communist laicists and the Catholics there has come about a kind of truce and a collaboration on political-social grounds, even an alliance to oppose Communism, to prevent its attainment of power and to save Italian culture, which Catholics and non-Catholics alike realize is threatened by the common adversary. In this truce a double illusion is to be avoided: (a) the illusion that laicism is not anti-Catholic; (b) the illusion that the Church has today accepted doctrines which she opposed yesterday. As to the first, laicism remains faithful to its ideological principles and refrains from opposing the Catholics and Catholicism openly (or even shows respect for the Church and the ecclesiastical hierarchy) only for negative reasons; it does not defend the Church, as the Church, but only as a force incorruptibly opposed to Communism. It remains faithful to its idea of the lay state, which tomorrow, if the Communist danger did not cause it concern, it would uphold with all its force against the Church. As for the second illusion, the Church remains opposed to certain fundamental principles of nineteenth century liberalism because the Church cannot depart from her principles or surrender her religious moral and educative function without denying herself and without generating most perilous confusions.

IV. *The Activity of the Church and of Catholics*

From about 1930, due to a complex of motives which in this place we are not able even to indicate but which are also to be found outside of Italy in the historical conjunction of western civilization at the present moment, the activity of the Church and of Italian Catholics has been and continues to be prodigious in every field. The range extends from a new flowering of culture and philosophy, which in Italy goes back to the first half of the nineteenth century, to the area of social, political and moral action, the religious field always being taken for granted. It is impossible to develop adequately this part of our study (even a substantial volume would not suffice); consequently, we shall limit ourselves to rapid sketches, in such wise as to give a panorama of this remarkable resurgence of initiative and of activity which does honor to Italy and to her great Christian traditions of civilization and culture.

(a) *Activity of a practical character.* The Christian sense of life, and the historical situation conditioned by the rise of the proletariat, have spurred the Church (and not in Italy alone) to the development of an *avantgarde* program of social action which has inspired strenuous efforts. In the orbit of *Catholic Action,* most active in Italy and distinct from every party even though strenuously aligned in the political struggle (for today absenteeism is a fault and every Catholic must assume his responsibilities in the field of action), there have arisen the so-called *Instituti secolari* (lay associations), a kind of third category of Catholic apostolate, between the old religious orders with solemn vows and the Congregations with simple vows. Such Associations, which along with Catholic Action support the ecclesiastic apostolate, unite with the practice of Christian perfection well organized religious activity in such fields as economics, culture, social aid, education, and trade union organizations. Among the congregations there has been a tremendous growth of the *Piccola opera della Divina Providenza* founded by the saintly priest, Don Orione (1872-1940). In 1943 this Congregation had religious houses and 290 programs for the religious instruction and formation of the clergy and of the people, for missions, and for social improvements. In addition it maintained the *Piccolo Cottolengo,* a refuge for the so-called social outcasts. Among the *Instituti secolari* is the Congregation of Saint Paul, founded in 1920, grouped into "cenacles" of men and of women (with the participation of priests) which carries on through the "Home Missions" a fruitful work of social aid, and of cultural and religious renaissance.

The function of these and of other similar institutes are many and convergent: (a) to provide social assistance; (b) to publicize the most urgent problems for the masses (such as a living wage, social aid, unemployment, etc.), according to the directives marked out by Popes Pius XI and XII (*Quadragesimo Anno,* 1931; *Nova impendet,* 1931; *Charitate Christi,* 1932; the Pentecost Discourse (1942) of Pius XII).[11] (c) to halt the progressive alienation of the

---

[11] Such directives are based on the following principles: (a) the extension of private property in both production and consumers' goods to an increasing number so as to decrease social inequalities and overcome poverty; (b) respect of private property, which, however, has a social function; (c) defense

masses, under the influence of the subtle and highly organized propaganda of socialism and Communism, from the practice of religion and from Christian principles.[12] In the realization of these purposes Catholic Action, already mentioned, has been especially effective. The Holy See has sought to unify "Catholic Action" on diocesan bases, but within national and professional frameworks, as a body of lay auxiliaries supporting the specifically pastoral work of the Hierarchy. The Papacy has assigned to it or recognized for it ever widening fields of activity, from the public practice of piety, the provision of recreation and sport for the young, the works of charity, religious instruction, the editing and circulation of papers, even to political action in the true sense, with committees for electoral guidance.[13]

Even political Catholicism (that is, Catholics organized in parties) drew its inspiration from these same directives, indicated by the Pontiffs, even though at times forced, for tactical and opportunistic motives, to enter into mixed alliances, to make concessions and even to accept into their midst heterogeneous elements. Although in Italy there may be found Catholics (of more or less good faith) enrolled in practically every political party, and although Christian Democracy is not a confessional party, and admits non-Catholics to its ranks, nevertheless, the great majority of those enrolled in the party and of its sympathizers are Catholics. But the distinction between it and Catholic Action (which is not a party) and between it and the Church remains clear. The Church cannot attach herself to any party, even if her political sympathies go out to those political currents which affirm the religious and moral principles of Christianity and recognize the rights of the Church herself.[14]

---

and guarantee of the human person, of his dignity and of his fundamental natural rights. It is evident how the social doctrines of the Church, while defending the rights of labor and of the workers, are opposed to the communist ideology, to collectivistic forms of production and of association, to the organization of rights of the human person, to say nothing of Christian principles.

[12] With the diffusion of Marxism in its many forms (English socialism, Russian Communism, etc.), atheism which had always been a mental or practical attitude of individuals, a phenomenon, so to speak, of the "intellectuals," or those who called themselves such, has become a mass phenomenon and a form of social life.

[13] M. Bendiscioli, *op. cit.*, p. 127.

[14] It is no part of our argument to speak of the political parties and consequently of Christian Democracy. But it should be recognized objectively, and

In very recent years, the Church's organization for social aid has become progressively more systematic: the *Conferences of Saint Vincent* now occupy an important position among pastoral activities; the *Pontifical Assistance* for the last several years past has been available wherever there has been a call to relieve poverty or to extend material or spiritual aid; the Institution "La Casa" arose in 1943 with the objective of "restoring the family and its ethical values, and has directed itself above all to the study of the great moral and social problems of the family and toward a well ordered activity in all areas, with the concern of including in its orbit the whole man and the whole family."

Social action has manifested itself in two other directions: (a) material assistance to Catholic workers and to their families by means above all of the Christian Association of Italian Workers (A.C.L.I.); (b) cultural assistance by means of a cultural program adapted to the working class. Each of these programs, of course, includes moral and religious assistance. Two community movements deserve special mention: (a) *Nomadelfia,* begun by the priest Zeno Saltini, for the protection of abandoned children, and from which movement has emerged a community of work and of life; (b) *Regnum Christi* which seeks to achieve community with *our nearest neighbor,* that is, the man in the same house, the same street.

Catholic activity in the field of education has been extensive and intensive. This is a very delicate and complex question; it is well known that the "lay" school, in Italy, as in France, zealously defends the prerogatives it has won. The Church cannot be aloof from the education of youth, for its activity touches upon her own apostolic mission and falls within her right of defending the religious conscience of the faithful. The free, as distinct from the State, school has been effectively defended by insisting that parents have the right to choose the school they wish for their children and to educate them according to the principles of Catholic doctrine. Catholic teachers have formed associations, for example, the Association of Catholic Teachers and the Italian Catholic Association of Teachers in the Secondary Schools. There are also organizations of

---

apart from all other considerations, that Christian Democracy in Italy has been the only political force which has been able to limit Communism and to force it to go on the defensive. In this way it has saved political democracy, has contributed to the safeguarding of Catholicism on the juridical-political terrain and to advancing the nation towards the realization of a concrete social and political democracy.

University youth (the Catholic Italian University Federation; the Catholic Graduates) and various local professional associations of doctors, engineers, lawyers. Each of these associations has a central headquarters (Rome) and sections in various cities, and each has an ecclesiastical director. Further, under the auspices of the Sacred Congregation of Religious there has been founded the Federation of Religious Institutions for Education (F.I.R.E.), "which, by clarifying objectives, studying and undertaking fresh enterprises, examining methods and pooling the common treasure of experience of the various Institutes, is designed to establish, under the direction of the Sacred Congregation, the Apostolate of Religious Educators, in the spirit of their Founders."

B. *Cultural Activity*. In this area, the awakened activity of the last twenty years or so has been truly surprising, especially in the philosophical and juridical sciences, where the best scholarship both scientific and cultural has been the work of Catholics. As evidence one statistical fact regarding the study of philosophy may be illuminating: from 1870 to about 1930 there were in the Italian Universities only about three or four Catholic professors of philosophy. Today, they number nineteen. The merest summary of the recent publications of Catholics in the fields of apologetics and in dogmatics, in biblical and scientific studies and above all in philosophy and on political, juridical, social and economic problems would take far too much space. Nor is it possible to give even a list of names (some of them of international renown) of Catholic writers and artists. But it is possible to indicate the more important cultural institutions, and the journals and reviews of major importance.

Before all others the Catholic University of the Sacred Heart at Milan, whose founder and sustaining force has been Father Gemelli, should be mentioned. Its foundation was a cultural triumph, a national conquest for Italian Catholics and a bold affirmation of the liberty of education. The Catholic University has achieved some notable successes in scientific fields (philosophy, psychology, law, economics, etc.) and in the field of teaching, having contributed to the Italian Universities a number of brilliant professors and numerous teachers to the lower and middle schools. The University has achieved a marriage between the scientific life and the Catholic faith.

In the field of philosophical studies the "Gallarate Center for Christian Philosophical Studies," founded immediately after the war (1945) by the courageous initiative of Professors Felice Battalglia, Augusto Guzzo, Umberto Padovani, M. F. Sciacca and Luigi Stefanini, achieved immediate distinction and in a short time international importance and fame; its animating spirit has been Prof. Carlo Giacon, a priest of the Society of Jesus. The Jesuits of the "Aloisianum" of Gallarate (Varese) have been hosts to the annual Conventions which in the last three years have achieved an international character. The Center has already published six volumes of *Proceedings,* the *Italian Bibliography 1900-1948,* the annual *Italian Bibliography of Philosophy* (the volumes for the years 1949 and 1950 have already been published); and has prepared a monumental *Philosophical Dictionary.* Almost forty university professors (including "liberi docenti") of the philosophical sciences, who represent the most diverse currents of Christian thought (Augustinians, Thomists, Christian existentialists, voluntarists) cooperate in its work and exemplify all that is most alive in philosophy in Italy today. The influence of the Center on contemporary Italian philosophy is decisive and provides for many young scholars their first orientation.

The following also call for mention: (a) The Teaching College of Mary Immaculate at Rome for the higher instruction of Sisters; (b) *The Catholic Encyclopedia,* which is nearing completion and which will prove a valuable instrument of scholarship; (c) the Theological Study Circles for the Laity, among which the Theological Study Center of the Sacred Heart in Florence, under the excellent direction of Father Raniero Sciamannini of the Friars Minor Conventual, is outstanding; as also the "Studium Christi" at Rome, well organized by Don Guidotti of the Congregation of St. Paul; (d) the Civitas Christiana of Assisi, whose tireless promoter is Don Giovannin Rossi; (e) the International Center for Comparative Study and Synthesis, at Rome, founded and directed by Monsignor Raffa. All these centers promote annual cycles of conferences, and conventions, publish books (with the collaboration of various scholars) on themes of current and widely diverse interest, hold courses of lectures and in every sense influence culture and diffuse it among wide sections of professional and laboring groups.

It is impossible to give even a list of the Catholic journals. In addition to the *Osservatore Romano* which is published at Vatican City, there are published in Italy eight Catholic dailies (without party affiliations); one hundred and four Catholic weeklies, many of them diocesan papers; fifty-four central publications of Catholic Action; about eighteen hundred pamphlets edited by various Congregations, religious institutes, confraternities and missions; in all, more than two thousand publications.

The reviews are also numerous. In philosophy there is the *Giornale di Metafisica,* edited with international collaboration and directed by M. F. Sciacca, a review which, in a wide sense, represents the movement of "Christian Spiritualism." This movement may be considered the most advanced position in Italian philosophy; *Rivista di filosofia Neoscolastica,* edited by the professors of the Faculty of Philosophy and Letters of the Catholic University at Milan; *Filosofia,* directed by Augusto Guzzo, with the collaboration of non-Catholic scholars as well, but dominated by the Catholic thought of its director who is one of the outstanding representatives of Christian Spiritualism; *Responsibilita di Sapere,* the organ of the "Centro di comparazione e di sintesi"; *Sapienza,* edited by the Dominican Fathers; *Rivista Rosminiana,* directed by Dante Morando, which, among its many concerns, illustrates, defends and seeks to penetrate the thought of Rosmini; *Rassegna di science filosofiche,* edited by Nicola Petruzzellis. Among reviews of general culture there should be mentioned: *Civiltà Cattolica* of the Jesuit Fathers, always vital and alert; *Humanitas,* edited with international collaboration, the best of the cultural reviews, directed by Giulio Bevilacqua, M.F. Sciacca, Mario Bendiscioli, Mario Marcassan, to which there may be added *Citta di Vita* directed by Raniero Sciammannini, an organ of the "Theological Study Groups for the Laity"; *Studium,* the review of the "Laureati cattolici"; *Vita e Pensiero,* issued by the Catholic University of Milan; *Tabor,* a review of the spiritual life for the laity, directed by Luigi Gedda; *Idea,* which concerns itself with actual problems (especially political and social), and is edited by Monsignor Pietro Barbieri; *Il Regno e La Rocca,* of the "Civitas Christiana" directed by Don Giovanni Rossi; *Letture,* also edited by the Jesuits of Milan; *Ragguaglio Librario,* published by the "Opera Cardinal Ferrari" also centered in Milan. In addition there are reviews for the clergy and those issued by the various Pontifical institutes (Gregorianum, Angelicum, Salesianum, Antonianum, Miscellanea francescana, etc.).

The activity of Catholics is noteworthy also in the field of law; to two generations of laicists, Masons and positivists, there has succeeded a generation predominantly Catholic. The scientific contributions of the Catholic reviews, *Rivista di scienze sociale e politiche* and *Justitia,* as well as the *Rivista Internazionale di Filosofia di diritto* edited by Giorgio Del Vecchio, which also publishes contributions of non-Catholics, are of the highest order.

Italy, today, after the half-century 1870-1920, again has a living Catholic culture, original and active and in many cases of high scientific value. In Italy also the Catholic Church is the most solid bulwark against Communism, the source and the custodian of authentic western culture.

XII

The Church in Spanish Public Life Since 1936*

by Rafael Calvo Serer

I. *The Peculiar National Circumstances*

If one wishes to understand adequately the very special position of the Church in present-day Spain, with its exterior manifestations so distinctly different from those of other European countries, one has to start with the concrete reality of the Spain in which the Church has to function, a reality which is also very different from that which the Church finds elsewhere.

A short time ago there was a meeting in Madrid to study an international Christian order. To this end, various groups of politicians and intellectuals arrived at the Spanish capital; among them was a delegation of French Catholics. With reference to the latter, someone said to the Duke of Maura—a very significant political writer of Liberal-Conservative leanings—that they were making contacts with the Spanish Catholic group interested in these matters. At this point the Duke interrupted forcefully: "Here we are all Catholics; that's what counts for even the most diverse groups, Francoists or Falangists, liberal monarchists or integralists, democrats or totalitarians. That is to say that we in Spain are also Catholics for the reason that Catholicism is the sole element of union, the lack of which makes national existence itself impossible."

Another outstanding personality of Spanish religious life used to justify the very peculiar position of the Church, in the face of the scandal of foreigners, by its persistent and intimate presence throughout all of life. Actually, he explained, Spaniards who give up their contact with the Church are extremely rare: it is possible that the Spaniard's religious practice be minimum and his ignorance

---

* Translated by Walter Langford and William Grupp.

be great, but in any case Baptism, Matrimony and the Last Sacraments are a reality in his individual and family life.

Any observer can verify the truth of what we have just said. This explains the heavily religious atmosphere which contrasts, almost violently, with the secularized atmosphere of Europe, with the lay society of France, with German paganism, with the official, state religion of the English, or even the personal religion of the Italians.

The presence of the Church is a reality in Spanish life, everywhere: in the home and in the school; in the office and in the street; in the factory and in the barracks; in the university and at public functions; in entertainments, in customs and even in sexual relations.

And do not think that this presence is a survival from ancient times, something of an anachronism in modern life, but that in many of its fundamentals it corresponds to that which is the ideal of Christian civilization.

The failing influence which the Catholic Church has had in public life because of the secularization of Western culture—on account of Protestantism and renascent paganism—has been arrested in Spain in a conscious, reflective way, and at the same time, as we are going to see, in struggles which are very far from the calm civil conflicts to which the democratic Anglo-Saxon mentality is so much inclined. Perhaps Americans would have to recall their Civil War, and the English, their struggles to dominate Ireland, if they wish to understand Spanish Catholicism of the present. If in the 19th century and up to a few years ago, the United States and England have had civil conflicts—with killings and bloodshed—for the cotton plantations or the preservation of the Empire, the Spaniards have had them for the defense or the rejection of the Catholic Church.

During the 1800's and even in the last war from 1936 to 1939, the fundamental reason for the profound division of the Spanish people was their relation with the Church. As much because of enmity and hate as because of unity, then, this indisputable reality of the intense presence of the Church in present-day Spanish life is a fact.

II. *The War of 1936 and its Crusading Aspect*

The present relations of Church and State in Spain, and the

present preponderance of the former in public life, stem from the Civil War of 1936. At that time the Church had to ally itself closely with the State. Necessarily this tended to create special circumstances for their subsequent relations.

There is in existence a document of the Spanish Church which allows one to fix the facts exactly: I refer to the *Carta colectiva de los Obispos españoles a los de todo el Mundo con motivo de la guerra de España* (*Collective Letter of the Spanish Bishops to Those of the Whole World Pertaining to the Spanish War*).[1] It is made clear in it how, from the fall of the Monarchy and the forming of the Republic, "since the year 1931 the Spanish Episcopate has given the highest examples of apostolic and civil prudence. Adjusting itself to the tradition of the Church and following the norms of the Holy See, it placed itself resolutely on the side of the constituted powers, with whom it made every effort to collaborate for the common good. And in spite of repeated insults to persons, things and rights of the Church, it did not break its resolve not to alter the rule established some time past by common consent."[2] In this attitude, the letter continues, "the Catholic people supported us."[3] Therefore Spanish Catholics can affirm that they neither provoked the war, nor conspired for its beginning.

With the outbreak of the Civil War, which with reason has been considered "an international struggle on a national battlefield," a series of events take place which force the Spanish Bishops to establish, among others, the following conclusions: "That the Church, in spite of its spirit of peace, and in spite of not having wanted the war nor having collaborated in it, could not be indifferent to the struggle."[4]

The bishops saw clearly the side with which they had to ally themselves. "At the present time, there is in Spain no other hope to reconquer justice and peace and the benefits derived therefrom, than the triumph of the Nationalist Movement. Perhaps today, less than in the beginning of the war, because the opposition, in spite

---

[1] *Carta colectiva del Episcopado espanol* (Collective Letter of the Spanish Episcopate). Published as an appendix in *Por Dios y por España* (For God and For Spain). Pastorals—Pastoral instructions and articles—speeches—messages—Appendix, 1936-1939, by His Eminence, D. Isidoro Gomá y Tomás, Cardinal Archbishop of Toledo, Primate of Spain (Barcelona, 1950), pp. 559-590.

[2] *Ibid.*, p. 563.

[3] *Ibid.*

[4] *Ibid.*, p. 573.

of all the efforts of its statesmen, does not offer any guarantees of political and social stability."[5]

From the attitude of the Church before and during the War we can infer what is desired for the future. "In regard to the future, we can not predict what will happen at the end of the struggle. We do affirm that the War has not been begun to raise an autocratic state over a humbled nation, but so that the national spirit may rise up again with the vigor and Christian liberty of old. We trust in the prudence of statesmen who will be unwilling to accept foreign models for the form of the future Spanish state, but who will keep in mind the demands of internal national life and the trajectory marked by past centuries."[6]

Their recent sad democratic experience makes them condemn any other form of tyranny: "We would be the first to regret that the irresponsible autocracy of a parliament be replaced by the more terrible one of a disordered dictatorship of the nation."[7]

From the petition of pardon for the persecuted which reads "before God and in favor of our martyrs, the ten Bishops and the thousands of priests and Catholics who died . . . ,"[8] one can infer the bloody and fierce behavior of the "reds," which forced the Hierarchy to take this attitude. "Remember our murdered Bishops, so many thousands of priests, religious and excellent laymen who died only because they were the chosen militia of Christ. . . . Not one of them is known to have faltered in the hour of martyrdom."[9]

Actually, the unanimity of Spanish Catholics, in their active or passive resistance to the "red" government, was the undoing of any effort to divide the Church in Spain.

The *Letter* also refers to the "problem of Basque nationalism, so unknown and falsified and which has been made a weapon against the Nationalist Movement. All our admiration for the civic and religious virtues of our Basque brothers. All our charity for the great misfortune which afflicts them, which we consider our own, because it is the misfortune of the country. All our sorrow for the confused reasoning which their leaders have suffered at a serious moment in their history. But all our reproach for having ignored

---

[5] *Ibid.*, p. 574.
[6] *Ibid.*, p. 584.
[7] *Ibid.*, p. 585.
[8] *Ibid.*, p. 588.
[9] *Ibid.*, pp. 588-589.

the voice of the Church, for they give reality to the words of the Pope in his encyclical on Communism, in regard to discords among Catholics of which the agents of destruction take advantage."[10]

This impressive document was signed by all the Spanish bishops, on the first of July 1937, with the exception of Dr. Múgica, Bishop of Vitoria, and Cardinal Vidal y Barraquer, Archbishop of Tarragona, exceptions which correspond exactly to dioceses affected by political problems of separatism, in addition to the Bishop of Orihuela.

As was stated in *Razón y Fe*,[11] a cultural journal of the Spanish Jesuits, the responses in support of the *Carta* from all over the world "are so numerous, so authoritative, that we can well say that they are equivalent to the universal feeling of the entire Hierarchy of the Church. The total number of bishops whose signatures appear on the responses is in excess of 500 . . . we can affirm that the total number of bishops who support the letter today is close to 900."

"To the Pastors of the Church must be added the superiors of the religious orders, who have responded with the same unanimity."[12]

From among the responses, these words of Cardinal Verdier stand out: "Is it not very evident that the titanic struggle which is bloodying the soil of Catholic Spain today is, in reality, the struggle between Christian civilization and the threatening civilization of atheism?"[13]

It is to the point also to read what the English bishops said: "We realized quickly that this is no ordinary civil war in favor of this dynasty or that regime, nor is it, as has been stated falsely, for the benefit of the democracy of the Spanish people. . . . We recognize that the fire on the Spanish peninsula was destined by those who started it to become a universal conflagration, in which Christian civilization was to have been consumed . . ."[14]

And finally, let us recall the response of the American Bishops: "We want you to know that, in common with all the Catholic

---

[10]. *Ibid.*, p. 586.

[11] In *Razón y Fe*, Iberoamerican cultural review, nos. 486-487, Vol. 114 (1938), Burgos, pp. 244 and following.

[12] *Ibid.*, p. 244.

[13] *Ibid.*, p. 245.

[14] *Ibid.*

Bishops of the world, we are on your side, and we thank you for your "Collective Letter," a clear, serene, worthy exposition of the condition of the Church in Spain."[15]

Only bad faith, or voluntary and culpable ignorance, could permit Maritain[16] to say that this war could be licit, but could never be holy, never be a crusade. In view of the documents which we have mentioned, it is impossible to hold this opinion. The ironies of Bernanos in *Les grandes cimitières sous la lune*[17] are not acceptable; it is an unjust vision which makes him consider the Spanish war as "the crusade of the atheist generals."

Victory, total, joyful, full of hope, was gained on the first of April, 1939; a few days later, in the Message which the Pope addressed to Spain on the 16th of April, His Holiness Pius XII said that "the healthy Spanish nation rose in determined defense of the ideals of Christian faith and civilization, deeply rooted in the soil of Spain."[18] This Message was, for the above mentioned magazine, "the unassailable justification of our redeeming movement, the canonization of the character of our Crusade."[19] And it was pointed out that "the theses of the Pope are the same as those of our Episcopate in their *Collective Letter,* those to which almost a thousand Bishops from all over the world subscribed, those which Nationalist Spain defended from the very first. . . ."[20]

Later, the Pope confirmed this appraisal of the war, when he said to the Spanish Military Mission which went to Rome at the head of three thousand Spanish soldiers, "Welcome, leaders, officers and soldiers of Catholic Spain, our beloved sons, who have come to provide an immense comfort to your Father. It comforts us to see in you the long-suffering, brave and loyal defenders of the faith and the culture of your country, who, as we told you in our radio

---

[15] *Ibid.*, p. 246. Cf. *El mundo católico y la Carta Colectiva del Episcopado Español* (The Catholic World and the Collective Letter of the Spanish Episcopate) (Burgos, 1938).

[16] Jacques Maritain: "Considérations françaises sur les choses d'Espagne," (French Thoughts on Spanish Affairs). Published as Preface to Alfred Mendizabal: *Aux origines d'une Tragedie. La Politique éspagnole de 1923 à 1936.* (On the Origins of a Tragedy. Spanish Politics from 1923 to 1936 (Paris, 1947).

[17] Georges Bernanos: *Les grandes cimitières sous la lune* (publ. in English as *A Diary of My Times*) (Paris, 1938).

[18] *Radiomensaje a España* (Radio Message to Spain), in *Discursos y Radiomensajes de Su Santidad Pio XII,* 4 parts in 5 vols. (Madrid, 1946), part I, p. 56.

[19] In *Razón y Fe,* no. 497, 1939, p. 191.

[20] *Ibid.*

message, knew how to sacrifice yourselves heroically in defense of the inalienable rights of God and religion.

"Seeing you before us, covered with glory by your Christian valor. . . ."[21]

The Bishop of Salamanca, Dr. Plá y Deniel, devoted his Pastoral Letter entitled *Las dos Ciudades* (The Two Cities),[22] which he completed after peace was gained with *El triunfo de la Ciudad de Dios y la Resurrección de España* (The Triumph of the City of God and the Resurrection of Spain),[23] to explaining the Crusade aspect of this war which had such extensive repercussions in the consciousness of Catholics, the antithesis of which was in world Communism and even in universal literature[24]—Koestler, Malraux, Hemingway, Stephen Andres. Some years later, in 1943, upon taking possession of the Primate's Chair and giving there his first Pastoral Letter, *La Restauración Cristiana de la Diócesis de Toledo* (The Christian Restoration of the Diocese of Toledo),[25] in reference to his predecessor, Cardinal Gomá, he said of him that he had been the "Defensor Civitatis," expressing in this way the leadership of the Primate in such difficult years.[26] His leadership had caused General Franco to say that Dr. Gomá had been the "man of Spain" in spiritual affairs during the war.

The Cardinal Archbishop of Toledo, who had written the collective declaration, and who put Spanish Catholics on the road toward victory over Communism with bravery and doctrinal certainty, maintained a vigilant attitude in defense of spiritual interests, to which end he presented his *Carta Pastoral sobre el valor de Patria del Catolicismo*,[27] taking issue with attempts to fashion Na-

---

[21]. *A los jefes, oficiales y soldados de la católica España.* (To the Leaders, Officers and Soldiers of Catholic Spain), June 11, 1939; in *Discursos y Radiomensajes,* l.c., p. 179.

[22] *Las dos Ciudades.* (The Two Cities). Pastoral letter directed to his people by the Bishop of Salamanca on September 30, 1936, in *Escritos Pastorales* of His Excellency D. Enrique Plá y Deniel, II (Madrid, 1949), pp. 95-141.

[23] *Escritos Pastorales,* II, pp. 169-284.

[24] I shall deal with this repercussion in my work *La guerra española de 1936, en la literatura universal.* (The Spanish War of 1936, in Universal Literature)

[25] *La restauracion cristiana de la diocesis de Toledo,* (The Christian Restoration of the Diocese of Toledo). Pastoral Letter upon Arrival in the Archdiocese of Toledo; in *Escritos Pastorales,* I, pp. 127-177.

[26] *Ibid.,* p. 131.

[27]. *Catolicismo y Patria.* (Catholicism and Country). Pastoral Letter on the value of Catholicism to the nation which His Eminence the Cardinal Arch-

tionalist Spain without taking into account the Catholicism of the Spaniards. Speaking against these efforts he says: "even though our war, in some of its aspects, has all the characteristics of a Crusade, at least as much as some religious wars of history, certainly much more than has been conceded us in certain foreign Catholic circles, an attempt is made to separate the fact of the war and its consequences from the nation's Catholicism. . . ."[28]

Fortunately, this tendency toward pagan nationalism did not prosper, and the Law of the 9th of November of 1939, re-establishing the budget of 1931 to take care of ecclesiastical obligations, captures the spirit of the episcopal declarations, recognizing the active assistance of the Hierarchy during the War. "The Spanish State, aware that its unity and greatness proceed from the Catholic Faith, the principal source of inspiration for its imperial undertakings, and desirous of displaying its filial attachment to the Catholic Church once more and in a practical way, as well as of repairing at the same time the wicked spoliations out of which the Liberal Governments wrested their patrimony when they carried out that sacrilegious despoilment, which one of our most renowned writers called an immense, systematic Robbery, proposes by this law to render the tribute due our self-sacrificing Spanish clergy, most efficient collaborators in our victorious Crusade. It is, moreover, a just tribute which all of Spain demands and which its government is pleased to proclaim, as an expression of national gratitude for those admirable members of the clergy, vigorous incarnation of the best qualities of the race, who on such an important occasion know how to spiritualize even more the glory of our arms with the example of their heroic virtues, emphasized as never before because of the barbarism of those who, in their hatred for everything truly Spanish and Catholic, found their favorite victims around our altars.

"Therefore, by this law are established the grants which the last general budget of the Monarchy apportioned for ecclesiastical obligations."[29]

---

bishop directed to the clergy and faithful of the Archdiocese on the occasion of Lent. In *Por Dios y por España, op. cit.,* pp. 174-223.

[28] *Ibid.,* p. 176.

[29] *Ley de 9 de noviembre de 1939 restableciendo el presupuesto del Clero.* (Law of November 9, 1939 Reestablishing the Budget for the Clergy). *Boletin Oficial del Estado* (Official State Bulletin), November 15, 1939, no. 319, pp. 6398-6399.

III. *The Church and the Formalizing of the Regime*

In spite of the fact that the New State was being organized with the desire to incorporate Catholic political ideals, it could not achieve a rule agreeable to the Church and to the State. Therefore, on June 7, 1941, Ramón Serrano Súñer, in the name of the government, signed with the Papal Nuncio an "agreement on the manner of exercise of the privilege of presentation," in the ninth article of which it is stated that "Until such time as a new Concordat is concluded, the Spanish Government agrees to observe the provisions contained in the first four articles of the Concordat of 1851."[30]

In 1945, owing to the termination of the Second World War and "its repercussions in Spain," a Pastoral Letter of the Primate Archbishop, Dr. Plá y Deniel, set forth the position of the Church in regard to the development of Spanish politics thus: "even in the case of a friendly agreement between Church and State, which is the case in Spain, there should be no confusion of activity or responsibilities between Church and State."[31]

This Pastoral Letter recalls the previous *Collective Letter,* in which the Episcopate showed itself to be as much the enemy of parliamentary anarchy as of a totalitarian dictatorship, inspired by foreign models and foreign to national tradition.

The attitude of the Primate can not be more explicit in regard to present and future politics: "Fortunately, the *Fuero de los Españoles* (Law of Spaniards), recently approved by Parliament (acting in a consulting capacity until now) and proclaimed by the Chief of State, marks an orientation toward Christian liberty opposed to a state totalitarianism. Let us hope that the practical and complete operation of the *Fuero de los Españoles,* with the rapid promulgation of the laws necessary for the exercise of the rights recognized in it, may soon be a living reality, recognized in Spain, and outside of Spain. Moreover, we believe that the end

---

[30] *Convenio entre el Gobierno español y la Santa Sede acerca del modo del ejercicio del privilegio de presentación* (*Agreement Between the Spanish Government and the Holy See on the Manner of Exercise of the Privilege of Presentation*). Madrid, June 7, 1941. *B.O.,* June 17, 1941, no. 168, p. 4401.

[31]. *Carta Pastoral del Excmo. Sr. Arzobispo de Toledo, Primado de España, a sus fieles diocesanos con motivo del fin de la guerra mundial y su repercusión en España,* (Pastoral Letter of His Excellency the Archbishop of Toledo, Primate of Spain, to the Faithful of his Diocese on the End of the World War and Its Repercussion in Spain) in *Escritos Pastorales,* II, p. 307.

of the World War and international conditions make urgent the complete and definitive ordering of the Spanish State, which necessarily had to be in a formative state during the War (of 1936-39) and Crusade, and for a still longer time, which the dangers and complications of the World War prolonged. The propaganda campaigns against Spain and its Government carried on abroad, as well as what these campaigns have unfortunately achieved, and the dangers they represent, make advisable everywhere a total and definitive setting in order of the Spanish State," so that there may be achieved a "harmonious consolidation of firm authority with historical continuity and of participation on the part of the citizens in the government of the nation."

"This participation can be multiform: as in fact it is in various countries. What is important is that it not be suffrage adulterated either by those who grant it or by those who preside over the election, that we labor conscientiously in such an important matter for the country, with everyone considering and striving for the common good."[32]

And there are still more concrete references to the characteristics of the political plan to be realized immediately, for he asks for the "elimination from the Spanish State of anything which can give even the pretext for suspicions of external forms, even when they are very different in spirit."[33]

The Archbishop of Toledo concluded by insisting that "the formative period" be closed "by establishing firm, unyielding institutional bases conforming to the historical tradition of Spain and to the degree of political education of the Spanish people. Let not the nation be exposed to more aimless wanderings that may lead it into chaos; but let there be opened solid channels for the manifestations of legitimate opinions through natural organs of expression."[34]

Finally he says "that the hour of world peace may also be the hour of total pacification, the hour of spiritual and material peace for Spain, of its new, definitive rule conforming to its historical tradition of sound, just liberties."[35]

In the *Instruction* of the Spanish Archbishops, dated June 3,

---

[32] *Ibid.*, pp. 318-320.
[33] *Ibid.*, p. 321.
[34] *Ibid.*
[35] *Ibid.*, p. 322.

1951, the enemies of these liberties are spoken of. Liberalism is such an enemy in so far as it recognizes "liberties contrary to the common good and to divine or natural right. As the opposite extreme of liberalism, modern totalitarianism concedes all-embracing and unlimited powers to the authority of the state without due respect to the natural, innate rights of the human being, transforming the state from the means necessary to attain the common good of society into the end of society. . . . Any totalitarianism, even a mitigated form, despoils the individual to the benefit of the state."[36]

Between these two documents, in 1947, the popular referendum on the Law of Succession took place. Dr. Plá y Deniel, Cardinal since December of 1945, issued a Pastoral exhorting Catholics to vote "in conscience, weighing your responsibility, upon approving or disapproving the projected Law of Succession for the Chief of State, which is the constitution of a regime."[37] Several Pastorals in the same tone were issued, among them those of the Bishops of Avila, Badajoz, Barcelona, Burgos, Cartagena, Granada, Huesca, Menorca, Oviedo, Sigüenza, Valencia, Mallorca, Tortosa, and Barbastro.[38]

The Bishop of Astorga, don Jesús Mérida, in 1949 issued a Pastoral on the *La Restauración Cristiana del Orden Público* (The Christian Restoration of the Public Order) in which, after analyzing the principles of a Christian political life, he refers to Spain saying "nor is it out of place to proclaim those political-Christian principles and to attempt their effective and total adoption in public life, precisely now when, with its historical personality restored and its position of leadership in defense of Christianity recovered, there is being constructed a new political order born of a Crusade."[39] After pointing out the characteristics and the limits of obedience to legitimate authority, he says: "But noble, discreet and constructive criticism of civil authorities is not opposed to the

---

[36]. *Instruction of the Conference of Bishops on the Duties of Justice and Charity in the Present Circumstances,* June 3, 1951, *Boletín Oficial Eclesiástico del Arzobispado de Toledo,* June 25, 1951, no. 6, pp. 119-120.

[37] *Pastoral Letter. On the Occasion of the Popular Referendum on the Proposed Law Approved by Parliament on the Succession of the Chief of State, Escritos Pastorales,* II, p. 333.

[38] Extracts in *Ecclesia,* Organ of the Central Committee of Spanish Catholic Action, Madrid, July 5, 1947, no. 312, p. (7)-7.

[39] Extracts from *Ecclesia,* May 7, 1949, no. 408, p. (509)-5.

Christian spirit of obedience when, even without becoming sinful, such authorities are certainly or probably less proper and less efficacious for the sound end desired.

"Even more: criticism, understood in its broadest meaning, in so far as it means disagreement in some cases and approval in others, constitutes collaboration on the part of the citizens in the functions of the power of the state and, according to some, is an essential attribute of rational obedience that should be given to the commands of civil authority."[40]

To become familiar with the present state of relations between the Church and the State, the *Instruction* of the Archbishops of 1952 can be read; this document, upon adducing the Law of Succession to the Chief of State, says: "The Catholic State could not but deal with the Church when proposing to pronounce a new law for secondary education; but besides it had been obliged conditionally by the agreements with the Holy See of June 7, 1941 and July 16, 1946, until such time as a new Concordat is reached, not to legislate on any matters of interest to both parties or on those which can be of any interest at all to the Church, without a previous agreement with the Holy See." And the latter "recommended to the Conference of Archbishops that it study the protoplan of the law on secondary education and propose the amendments which it thinks necessary, submitting the definitive plan to the Holy See for approval."[41]

IV. *The Church and Education*

It was possible to avoid the danger which Cardinal Gomá pointed out, thanks to the collaboration of the Church with the State. On the one hand because of the development of school and university legislation; on the other because of the effective presence of the Church in the plan for the political education of youth carried out by the Party.

In both cases, owing to the organization of the Spanish state, and because of the natural influence of the Nazis, up to the time of their reverses in Europe, he could point to a nationalism which

---

[40] *Ibid.*

[41] "The Apostolate of Education and the Church's Rights in It." Instruction of the Conference of Bishops, Toledo, 1952, p. 6.

might enter the conflict with the traditional Catholicism of Spain, for a national morality was opposing the Catholic conscience of the Spanish nationality.

To what point the evil could spread is evident in the scant distribution in Spain of the Encyclical of Pius XII on racism, *Mit brennender Sorge,* and the Pastoral Instruction of the Bishop of Calahorra, in 1942, on the same errors.[42]

The elimination of the threat was achieved, and so, at the height of the Civil War, in 1938, the reform of secondary education was begun, the basic law of which satisfies fully the most severe Catholic demands in the matter. In the Preamble the legislator sets forth the purpose he has: "Classic and humanistic formation is to be accompanied by an eminently Catholic and patriotic content. Catholicism is the very marrow of the history of Spain. Therefore, a solid religious instruction is essential, an instruction which includes Catechism, the Gospels, and Ethics and Liturgy, Church History and an adequate Apologetics, this spiritual formation to be completed with notions on Philosophy and the History of Philosophy."[43]

The direction of our educational policy was, then, directly opposed to that of Nazi, or Fascist, totalitarianism, for it is a question, reads the preamble, "of making evident the moral purity of the Spanish nationality; the superior universalist nature of our traditionally proud spirit, of 'Hispandad', according to the very happy concept of Ramiro de Maeztú, defender and missionary of true civilization, Christianity."[44]

The law had been worked out by the Minister of National Education, Pedro Saínz Rodríguez, with his collaborators Alfonso García Valdecasas, Under-Secretary, and José Pemartín, Head of the National Bureau of Secondary and Higher Education, all of them outstanding Catholic intellectuals and monarchists.

Some years later, in 1951, the Archbishop of Valencia, don Marcelino Olaechea, said of this law, promulgated on September 20, 1938, that "while it is true that it doesn't even speak of the

---

[42] Reference to the Pastoral "in which he combats the errors of modern times," in *Guide for the Church and Spanish Catholic Action* (Madrid), 1943, p. 588.

[43] *Law of September 20, 1938 on the Reform of Secondary Education, B.O.,* September 23, 1938.

[44] *Ibid.*

Church, it consecrates the wholesome liberty of education of non-state institutions, making them equal, if they are recognized—and those that fulfill the legal requirements have been recognized freely—, to the official institutions, as soon as, separating the teaching from the examining function, they submit all their students, official or not, to the same state examination."[45]

In this spirit, the same cabinet group, in 1939, drew up the projected law on university reform, naming in the preliminary article, as one of its directing influences, "patriotic and moral development inspired by religious feeling," just as they also aimed at the "historical revitalization of the Spanish university by its complete compenetration with the ideal of 'Hispanidad', the basis of its original and appropriate life and of its power of universality."[46]

Political changes in this Ministry did not alter the execution of strict collaboration with the Church, and the same tendency can be seen in the University Reform Law of 1943, and the Primary Education Law of July 17, 1945.

In the preamble of the Law of July 29, 1943 on the arrangement of the Spanish university it is decreed that "the state university be Catholic," and that its labors have "dogma and Christian morality and that which Sacred Canons have established in regard to education as supreme guide." For this reason it is stated expressly that the "higher religious culture be the model," since it is wished to attain, in the universities, "the atmosphere of piety which contributes to encouraging spiritual development in all the acts of the life of the student."[47]

Fidelity to pontifical teachings in primary education is expressed also in the Preamble of the Law of 1945, for it is said that "being inspired in the Catholic spirit, consubstantial with Spanish scholastic tradition, it will be adjusted to the principles of dogma and Catholic morality and the pronouncements of the Canon Law

---

[45] *To the Clergy and Faithful of the Diocese. On the French Social Week.* Letter of July 25, 1951 of the Archbishop of Valencia, D. Marcelino Olaechea, *Official Bulletin of the Archbishopric of Valencia,* August 15, 1951, 56th year, no. 2544, p. 288.

[46] *Proposed Law on University Reform.* Order of the National Office of Education of April 25, 1939, published in the *B.O.,* April 27, 1939.

[47] *Law of July 29, 1943 on the Organization of the Spanish University* in *B.O.,* July 31, 1943, no. 212, p. 7408.

in force (Article 5)."[48] About this law the Archbishop of Valencia, in his above mentioned Letter on the liberty of education of July 25, 1951, says "it boasts, with reason, of being based on the Encyclical, *Divini Illius Magistri;* it recognizes the elementary schools of the Church, and the right of the latter to create its own normal schools, whose degrees, besides serving for the Church, will serve, with a comprehensive examination, for teaching in state schools."[49]

In this law of 1945 there is a more advanced step than in the Secondary Education Law of 1938, the recognition of a special personality, superior to that of private institutions, peculiar to the schools of the Church, those established by the Hierarchy as well as those of the religious orders. The Archbishop of Valencia points this out by saying that "schools created and sustained by the orders or congregations approved by the Church for the apostolate of teaching are, without the slightest doubt, schools of the Church."[50]

It was attempted to extend the criterion to university and secondary education. To date there has been expressed in university life only a struggle to establish higher educational activities outside of state controlled activities with full legal capacity.[51] In regard to the projected reform of Secondary education of 1952, the conference of Archbishops has expressed itself in its *Instruction* of September 29, 1952.[52]

Already in 1947, the Pastoral of the Bishop of Astorga on *La Restauración cristiana de la enseñanza* (The Christian Restoration of Education),[53] had considered a Catholic university belonging to

---

[48] *Law of July 17, 1945 on Primary Education,* in *B.O.,* July 18, 1945, no. 199, p. 388.

[49] *Letter* of the Archbishop of Valencia of July 25, 1951, *Official Bulletin* (Valencia), no. 2544, p. 288.

[50] *Ibid.,* p. 289.

[51] *Cf.* E.Guerrero, S.J., "Las Universidades de la Iglesia" (The Universities of the Church) in *Razón y Fe,* no. 579, vol. 133, 1946, pp. 310-328.

[52] Instruction, 1952, p. 6. "The initiative for preparing a new Law for Secondary Education in Spain has been the State's. The Government, on studying the proposal worked out by the Office of Education, submitted to the consideration of the Holy See and the Hierarchy of Spain those extremes which by reason of referring to unofficial education were open to negotiation and agreement with same in regard to the Church's schools, according to the agreement reached in the Agreement of June 7, 1941."

[53] Summary in *Ecclesia,* May 24, 1947, no. 306, p. 16-(576).

the Church to be a necessity in Spain. The principles of the Church in religious matters, says the Bishop of Astorga, are recognized now by Spanish legislation. But there are obstacles to the application of these very principles which must be removed.

So that the Church may enjoy full liberty, to which in matters of education it has the right, the following are necessary: "equality of academic rights of the educational institutions of the Church with official institutions of the same level and dignity; economic support from the State for Church schools and recognition of the value to the public of the courses studied and the degrees conferred in Church schools."[54]

In the often cited Pastoral of 1951, the Archbishop of Valencia recalls that the University law in force recognizes: "the right of the Church to organize its own university, or universities, upon agreement in every case with the State."[55] And, continues don Marcelino Olaechea, "Spain is and proudly proclaims itself to be a Catholic nation, a glory which we owe to the blood of the martyrs and the heroes of the Crusade; and for that reason she makes her own the laws of the Church and has no desire to legislate in matters concerning both Church and State, as in education (agreement of July 16, 1946 between the Holy See and the Spanish government), without a previous agreement with the Church."[56] In fact, as regards the above mentioned agreement, Article X, Paragraph 2, reads as follows: "The Spanish government renews, for this purpose, its pledge to observe the provisions contained in the first four articles of the Concordat of 1851 and not to legislate on matters concerning both Church and State, or on matters which can be of any interest to the Church, without previous agreement with the Holy See."[57]

The problem, then, of the free Catholic university, is one not of legislation, but one of realization. Let us see how the Archbishop of Valencia takes issue with the opposition: "There are those who think that the present higher institutions of culture which the Church has in Spain do not attain the level necessary to be

---

[54] *Ibid.*

[55] *Letter* of the Archbishop of Valencia, *Official Bulletin* (Valencia), no. 2544, p. 288.

[56] *Ibid.*

[57] *Agreement of July 16, 1946 Between the Holy See and the Spanish Government for the Provision of Non-budget Assistance, B.O.,* July, 18, 1946, no. 199, p. 5662.

elevated to university rank; and that the Church might run the risk of loss of prestige.

"It will be a matter of examining each one of the institutions; for the Church does not want odious privileges which lower the scientific value of its degrees recognized by the State, but to have, under the same conditions, the same rank.

"One should consider the fact that the Church in Spain, without having any official economic assistance, with its degrees having no civil value recognized by the State, has succeeded in establishing those worthy Centers of Higher Culture which already have a numerous, select student body and enjoy prestige even abroad.

"To what height will it arrive on the day when, after an agreement with the State, it may establish its faculties or elevate to faculties, by raising their standards, the Centers of Higher Culture?"[58]

This declaration of the objective to be realized can be no more explicit and conclusive: "No one can doubt that the establishment of the Church university, whose degrees will be recognized by the State, is today its most burning desire in matters of education."[59]

Some legislative steps have been taken in this direction. The first was the modification, in 1949, of the law for governing universities, by way of re-establishing free education which had been suppressed in 1943, which provided occasion for a strong hostility in university and Falangist quarters against the plan for a Catholic university.[60] Later, when in the summer of 1950 the legal validity of the engineering degrees of the Instituto Católico de Artes e Industrias, conducted by the Jesuits, was decreed, powerful resistance from the state technical schools, among the professors as well as among the students, prevented the pronouncement of the implementing provisions necessary for said Decree to be put into effect.[61]

---

[58] *Letter* of the Archbishop of Valencia, *Official Bulletin* (Valencia), no. 2544, p. 290-291.

[59] *Ibid.,* p. 291.

[60] *Law of July 16, 1949 by means of which Articles 18 and 58 of the Law for the Organization of the Spanish University of July 29, 1943 are Revised, B.O.,* July 17, 1949, no. 198, pp. 3163-3164. *Cf.* E. Guerrero, S.J., "Hacia una Universidad realmente libre. Reflexiones sobre su necesidad y posibilidad," (*Toward a Really Free University. Reflections on its Necessity and Possibility*), in *Razón y Fe,* no. 622, vol. 140 (1949), pp. 261-282.

[61] *Decree of August 10, 1950 Relative to the Catholic Institute of Arts and Industries of Madrid, B.O.,* August 22, 1950, no. 234, p. 3680.

Negotiations with the Archbishop on the proposed law for secondary education suppose a connection with the doctrine sustained in regard to elementary education. "It would be an error," said the *Instruction* of 1952, "to consider the secondary schools of the Church as private schools, for the division of schools into public and private is by reason of their effective cause or their foundation, and the Church is not a private entity. It is not a mere legal corporation, but a true, perfect society, as the present Spanish state has recognized, for example, in the Preamble to the Elementary Education Law of July 17, 1945. "Perhaps unlike any other law in the world, this law does not hesitate to make use of, sometimes with manifest literalness, the postulates which Pius XI designated as norms of the Christian educative right in his immortal encyclical *Divini illius Magistri*. In conformity with these norms and with the principles of the Canon Law in force, is recognized the right which the Church has in a supereminent way and independent of any worldly power, to offer work for degrees of a supernatural order, and the power, equally with the State, to found schools of any level, primary schools and normal schools, of a public nature, in harmony with the legal nature of the Church as a perfect and sovereign society. Likewise is recognized the prime, inalienable right of the family to educate its children, and, consequently, to choose the teachers. The Church's schools on any level can not be considered private schools."[62]

Following the pattern set by what happened in the University first and later in the technical schools, there was also strong resistance on the part of state education which was expressed in the debate in Parliament on the bill presented by the Government with prior acceptance by the Archbishops.

To these inevitable points of friction can be added that stated by the Archbishop of Valencia, upon dealing with a much debated matter in France in the postwar period, the disbursement of the state budget for education: if the "budget is made up of the contributions of all Spaniards, including those who do not educate their children in a state institution," it is logical to request "a just share in the state's educational budget for the institutions of the Church and of private education," for as long as we do not achieve

---

[62] *Instruction*, 1952, p. 3. In defense of the liberty of education *cf.* José Pemartín: *Professional Studies in Secondary Education and Their Relation to the University Bachelor Degree*, in *Razón y Fe*, no, 577, vol. 133, pp. 108-125.

this, "we will not have achieved the sincere expression of a wholesome liberty of education."[63]

V. *The Hierarchy and the Religious Education of the Falangist Youth*

In 1943, making reference to the exemplary collaboration of all of the youth organizations of Toledo, the Primate said that there was no incompatibility "between political youth groups who also profess the Catholic Faith and the young people of Catholic Action; nor do the latter not have a special mission and apostolate, even in a Catholic state with only one party, for they are able to belong to both youth groups at the same time."[64]

Well then, in the framework of this collaboration, the efforts of the Bishop of Madrid-Alcalá have been decisive in the education of the Falangist youth. It was he who managed from the beginning the *Asesoría de Educación Religiosa y Moral del Frente de Juventudes* (Office of Religious and Moral Education of the Youth Front), from the by-laws of which we shall reproduce article 11, since it has not been a theoretical hope but the guide for real, intense priestly activity. "The sanctifying and liturgical function will be directed principally to the perfection of the supernatural life of the members of the *Frente de Juventudes,* through frequent intercourse with them. Efforts will be made so that all may fulfill the Sunday commandment and receive the holy Sacraments frequently, directing them during the year, without compulsion, to the series of exercises that the parishes and other religious institutions organize."[65]

During these years seminarians and priests have taken active part in the educational activities, with conferences, exercises, lessons, until achieving a wonderful climate of moral purity and religion in the youth, which has been pointed out by the most exact-

---

[63] Letter of the Archbishop of Valencia, *Official Bulletin,* (Valencia), no. 2544, p. 292.

[64] Synthesis of the address delivered by the Archbishop Primate, from the ruins of the Alcazar of Toledo, published in *Ecclesia,* June 19, 1943, no. 101, p. (587)-11.

[65] In Juan Carlos Villacorta: "The Youth Front Favors the Appropriate Religious Formation of the Church," *Arriba,* Organ of the Traditionalist Spanish Falangist Party and of the J.O.N.S., Madrid, November 19, 1952.

ing foreign observers, as can be seen in the article published by Father Bosc, S.J., in *Etudes*[66] in 1948.

The spirit with which they have tried to harmonize this work of political education with the work peculiar to the religious schools, is expressed in circular number 178 of the National Command: "In the mission which the *Frente de Juventudes* has in its trust in regard to Spanish youth and in the work which the religious schools carry on with an important part of the same group, there is, undeniably, a broad, common sphere of activity, namely, the common hope for an integral education; but there are also areas with precise limits in which the spheres of activity become exclusive without any possible fear of confusion. The school is, above all, the center of religious education and cultural and scientific instruction. The *Frente de Juventudes* is, essentially, the crucible of a Spanish way of life served by an exacting political education which, needless to say, is to serve, in its turn, the higher values of dogma and Catholic morality inherent in the Spanish man, and which, in turn, has as necessary and formative instruments physical education and premilitary training. But these areas, under pain of renouncing a truly integral education, can not be either exclusive or excluding."[67]

Numerous testimonials of the Hierarchy testify to the excellence of the carrying out of these rules. The words written by the Bishop of Málaga, in September, 1949, upon a visit to the *Frente de Juventudes* in his diocese serve as an example. "During my brief visit to the camp I was pleasantly impressed by the atmosphere of physical and moral health which one breathes in the camp, the spirit of order and discipline, joined with the spontaneous happiness of the boys and, above all, the effective cultivation of patriotic feelings and Christian piety."[68] Or the words of the Archbishop of Valladolid in October, 1952 to the national delegation of the *Organización juvenil falangista* (Falangist Youth Organization): "I am pleased to inform you that my seminarians are very happy about their stay in the camp of the *Frente de Juventudes of Valladolid*. I spent a delightful afternoon there. My gratitude is profound. The system is fine. May God bless the educational work of the *Frente de Juventudes*."[69]

---

[66] P. Roberto Bosc: "Madrid, Spring 1948," in *Etudes,* Paris, July-August-September, 1948, Vol. 258, pp. 53-67.

[67] In *Arriba,* l.c.

[68] *Ibid.*   [69] *Ibid.*

Finally, in November of the same year, the Archbishop of Valencia wrote to the Head of the Cid Campeador Camp, speaking about his recent visit: "I do not have to tell you that I have received a most excellent impression from this visit as I have from all such visits I have made in previous years to camps of the *Frente de Juventudes*. The education which you give the campers, in the religious and moral field as well as in the patriotic, and in the cultural and physical, is admirable. May the Lord grant that you continue to carry on this great work for our youth for many years; and that He may wish that the latter know how to take advantage of your efforts to the smallest deail."[70]

VI. *The Church and the Press*

Several passages of the discourse delivered by the Pope at the International Congress of the Catholic Press, which took place in Rome in February of 1950, had a profound and immediate repercussion in Spain, as we shall see in texts of the Hierarchy. On that memorable occasion His Holiness uttered words which all those concerned for the manner of achieving the common good should always bear in mind: "In that place where there might appear no manifestation of public opinion, there, above all, where you ought to have examined its real inexistence, regardless of the reason which is given for its muteness or its inexistence, one should see a vice, an illness, an irregularity of social life."[71]

If the press is the organ of expression of this public opinion, wherever a strong, healthy, virtuous press does not exist, either society lacks these conditions, or the political body acts against that society. Pius XII has said it too, in a way that does not permit artful or elusive interpretations: "to drown the voice of the citizens, to reduce it to an enforced silence, is, in the eyes of all Christians, an attempt against the natural right of man, a violation of the order of the world, as it has been established by God."[72]

These words were soon echoed in Spain. The following June the Cardinal Plá y Deniel delivered an *Instrucción Pastoral sobre el*

---

[70] *Ibid.*

[71] *Discourse of His Holiness to the International Congress of Catholic Journalists*, in *Official Ecclesiastical Bulletin of the Archbishopric of Toledo,* March 20, 1950, no. 3, p. 54.

[72] *Ibid.*, p. 54.

"Diá de la Prensa Católica" (Pastoral Instruction on the "Day of the Catholic Press"). In it he invokes the decree of May 3, 1938, of the Minister of Justice, by which the Spanish State recognizes the Church as a perfect society; therefore "it can not be denied the right to have its own press . . . its periodical press for doctrinal and informational purposes."[73]

In view of these remarks the Cardinal's continuation obviously refers to conditions in Spain. "He who reviles or does not even recognize the legitimacy of the Catholic press specifically as such, or wants it arbitrarily subject to the state, in a totalitarianism condemned by His Holiness Pius XII"—in his above mentioned discourse—"therefore is not with the Church, even when he calls himself a Catholic."[74]

Between the extremes of "unchecked libertinism" and "state totalitarianism," the Primate defends "the just median of a responsible freedom of the press, appropriate to a civilized, Christian society, which is the one that defends the Christian *Fuero de los Españoles* (Article 12), which is not an academic program to be binding in future generations, but a law declared basic in the succession of the Chief of State, legalized by a national plebiscite."[75]

An allusion to one of the points of controversy with General Franco is not missing from this Pastoral: "there were several newspapers of the Catholic press in the capital of the nation, and one fails to understand how some have not yet been able to reappear after the Crusade, especially when one succeeded in becoming a press of national influence, of splendid technical form, recognized as such even abroad."[76]

Necessarily, the one who had been the creator and director of that newspaper, don Angel Herrera, the present Bishop of Málaga, in May of 1951 conducted a conference in the Instituto Social León XIII in Madrid on "A Law for the Press," and he had to make reference to the previous Pastoral without a single step having been taken since then according to the spirit so markedly indicated of a "just median."[77]

---

[73] *Pastoral Instruction on the Catholic Press Day* of Cardinal Plá y Deniel, June 16, 1950, in the *Official Ecclesiastical Bulletin of the Archbishopric of Toledo,* June 21, 1950, no. 6, p. 94.

[74] *Ibid.*   [75] *Ibid.*   [76] *Ibid.*

[77] Conference of don Angel Herrera, Bishop of Malaga, on *Relations Between the Church and the State,* extract in *Ecclesia,* May 19, 1951, no. 514, p. (543)-11.

The Archbishop of Valencia again petitioned for a Press Law, upon asking for concrete, effective measures to quiet the discontent of the workers: "if, giving a clear account to the people of these provisions, a healthy, positive criticism were to stem from a well planned Press Law, murmuring, exaggeration and great lies would die and the gigantic efforts which the regime is making would be applauded."[78]

VII. *The Hierarchy and Protestant Activities in Spain*

To understand the theme which has received such very bad publicity in the world press these past few years, in regard to the intolerant attitude or the persecution of Protestants in Spain, one has to keep in mind certain facts which lend to history and recent circumstances very different characteristics from those observed in other countries.

Thus, we can understand the attitude of the conference of Archbishops which in its *Instruction* of May 28, 1948 said: "Spaniards who do not profess the Catholic faith, and above all those who belong officially to some religious profession other than the Catholic are in such an insignificant minority that they can not be considered in a law which serves the social community. If, in Article 6 of the *Fuero de los Españoles,* some element of tolerance toward dissident sects was introduced, it was with foreigners who live in Spain in mind, among whom are people from countries, the majority of whose people is Protestant, or where there are numerous non-Catholic minorities."[79]

Therefore, the doctrine which is applied in Spain is Catholic—for a Catholic nation—where, as we pointed out at the beginning of this work, religious discrepancies are practically nonexistent.

In the *Modus vivendi* of 1941, the Holy See demanded the application of the first four articles of the Concordat of 1851, to which, as we have seen, the Spanish government again bound itself early in 1946; that doctrine is applied in these articles. In the third article it is stated: "His Majesty and his Royal Government will

---

[78] In *Ecclesia,* December 1, 1951, no. 542, p. (607)-11, in which are transcribed at length the conclusions of the exposition of the Archbishop of Valencia on "the results of an investigation made among the workers."

[79] *Instruction of the Conference of Spanish Bishops on Protestant Propaganda in Spain,* Madrid, May 28, 1948, in *Official Ecclesiastical Bulletin of the Archbishopric of Toledo,* June 11, 1948, no. 6, p. 156.

grant, likewise, their powerful protection and support to the Bishops in the event they request it, above all whenever they may have to oppose the will of men who try to pervert the souls of the faithful or corrupt their customs, or whenever they might have to prevent the publication, introduction or circulation of bad or harmful books."[80]

Keeping in mind, then, this legislation, not imposed by the Spanish government, but agreed upon with the Holy See, and in view of the trenchant declaration of the Spanish Archbishops, Prosestant criticism and that of leftist Catholics in Spain are unworthy of any consideration; these Churches should abide by Article 6 of the *Fuero de los Españoles*, drawn up in agreement with the Holy

----

[80] *Concordat Reached with the Holy See on March 16, 1851,* ratified on April 23, 1851. Ordered to be published, observed and put into effect on October 17, 1851. *Gaceta de Madrid,* October 19, 1851, No. 6306. Latin and Spanish text, pp. 1-7. The first four articles are on page 2.

Art. 1: The Roman, apostolic, Catholic Religion, which to the exclusion of any other continues to be the only religion of the Spanish Nation, will always be conserved in the dominions of His Catholic Majesty, with all the rights and prerogatives which it should enjoy according to the law of God and the statutes of sacred canon.

Art. 2: Therefore, instruction in the universities, colleges, seminaries and public or private schools of any level, will conform in every respect to this Catholic religion: and this end will not in any way prevent the Bishops and the other diocesan prelates charged by their ministry from watching over the purity of the doctrine of faith and of the customs, and over the religious education of the youth in the exercise of this trust, even in the public schools.

Art. 3: Nor will said prelates or the other sacred ministers be impeded in any way in the exercise of their functions, nor will anyone molest them under any pretext in so far as it refers to the fulfillment of the duties of their trust; rather will all the authorities of the kingdom be careful to guard them and see to it that they are respected and treated as they should be, according to divine precepts, and that nothing be done to cause them dishonor or contempt. . .

Art. 4: In everything else which pertains to the right and the exercise of ecclesiastical authority and to the ministry of sacred orders, the Bishops and the clergy dependent on them will enjoy all the liberty established by the sacred Canons.

See, the fundamental law, qualified as Christian by the Primate: "The profession and practice of the Catholic religion, which is that of the Spanish State, will enjoy official protection.

"No one will be molested for his religious beliefs, nor in the private practice of his creed. No other ceremonies or external manifestations than those of the Catholic religion will be permitted."[81]

Religious dissidents number .35 per thousand, since in Spain 20,000 inhabitants profess religions other than the Catholic, of which 10,000 are foreigners, in a population of 28,000,000. It was the transgression of the canonical and state legislation by Protestant activities to which Cardinal Segura called attention in his Lenten Pastoral of 1952. In Spain that proselytism disturbs not only religious unity, but also political unity. And religious tolerance is easily used for subversive political activities, prohibited in any civilized state. This is the way one should understand words quoted by the Cardinal, so misunderstood, especially in the United States: certain repressions are necessary when the erroneous conscience does not deserve respect because of entering "into conflict with the righteous conscience and the common good."[82]

VIII. *The Church and the Proletariat*

On March 11, 1951, on the occasion of some union meetings, His Holiness Pius XII addressed a message to the Spanish workers, in which he said: "On this occasion we can not help but address some words of paternal praise to those institutions which you have created and continue to create in large numbers, for the purpose of educating young workers, making of them excellent skilled workers and, at the same time, confirmed Christians. You couldn't do anything better. In the fulfillment of that work we see a promising sign for the future."[83]

The Church has been taking part in these efforts of the unions through ecclesiastical advisors and at the same time apostolic action

---

[81] *Fuero de los Españoles* (*Law of the Spanish People*) B.O., July 18, 1945, no. 199, p. 358.

[82] *Pastoral Letter of the Cardinal Archbishop of Sevilla*, February 20, 1952, in *Official Ecclesiastical Bulletin of the Archbishopric of Sevilla*, March 15, 1952, no. 1617, p. 181.

[83] *Radio Message of His Holiness Pope Pius XII to Spanish Catholic Technicans and Workers*, March 11, 1951, in *Official Ecclesiastical Bulletin of the Archbishopric of Toledo*. April 30, 1951, no. 4, p. 72.

has been increased in the most forsaken centers of the large cities and the industrial regions, which were penetrated by Marxism and anarchism.

Several Pastorals deal with the work of the Church in behalf of laborers. Let us examine some data on the state of this religious action, in anticipation of an overall impression, from Father Florentino del Valle, S.J., in his recent discussion of "Have We Lost the Working Class in Spain?" in which he says: "The conclusion seems to be that, comparing the present with the time previous to 1936, at least as it is reflected in apparently sincere writings and commentaries, a decisive step forward has been taken."[84]

But at the same time it would be well to keep in mind these words of the Archbishop of Valencia written in connection with the conclusions of an inquiry, *Sondeo del alma del trabajador (Exploration of the Worker's Soul)*: "Let us not entertain any illusions. In the political period through which we are passing, we can easily deceive ourselves. I am not a pessimist. But . . . the mass, the great mass of workers, is not with the Church, does not like the Church; perhaps it hates the Church; but it is with management much less, and hates management much more.

"Many workers say that they'll not get very rich burning churches; they'll get richer robbing banks and attacking employers."[85]

So, the religious state of the workers is very closely related to their cultural level and their economic level; therefore, they have to take definite attitudes in regard to the social policy of the State. Here is the judgment of Dr. Olaechea, who is also the founder of a Social Institute in his Archbishopric: "if they would put into our worker's hand, intact, the money they give him plus the money they take away from him and the company for workers' taxes, he would feel happy today . . . he believes that he could eat, dress, lodge himself and bring up his children . . . the legal wage does not cover those necessities, and, therefore, objectively, is not just."[86]

Therefore, the Bishop of Madrid, in his Pastoral of November 27, 1951, sets forth in his exact terms the work undertaken to free

[84] Florentino del Valle, S.J.: "Have We Lost the Working Class in Spain?" in *Razón y Fe,* no. 652, pp. 484-504 and no. 653, pp. 597-611, Vol. 145 (1952).

[85] "Conference of Dr. Olaechea at the Close of the Third Course of Social Orientation in Sevilla," in *Ecclesia,* July 1, 1950, no. 468, p. 24-(24).

[86] In *Ecclesia,* December 1, 1951, no. 542, l.c., p. 12-(608).

Madrid from the shameful spectacle of its miserable suburbs. "The majority of the inhabitants of the suburbs," he says, "certainly not all of the individuals, but certainly the great mass of the people, has degenerated. Their economic misery reduced them to the lowest condition of men; the darkness of their huts, the filth of their rags, the narrowness and muddiness of their streets, the overwhelming anxiety for their daily bread were shrinking their faculties, narrowing their horizons, making them blind to the courses of happiness, creating an atmosphere of tedium, of envy, desperation; the cultivation of the spirit disappeared, replaced by the necessity of living. Religious life was relegated to a very distant position, because of the need to attend to other, more crudely realistic things; soon it came to be hated."[87]

On the basis of this sad, dolorous description is oriented the true road to avoid so many evils: "The streams of gold flooding the extreme sections of Madrid in the way of alms, nothing more, are swallowed up and the suburb continues as before. Money alone can do nothing; because, although it may pave all the streets and construct clean homes and give food to all and light to all, as well, with nothing more than this, nothing has resulted; because soon, by virtue of degeneration, the streets will be dung hills, the homes, stables, the clothes tatters and the food garbage.

"The true solution must be of a type contrary to the existing evil: *regeneration,* and with it the re-education and re-Christianizing in this very order and in ascending gradation. Revaluate the conscience of his human condition, that is, dust off and free his spiritual faculties from their torpor. With these awakened, educate them, put them in serviceable condition, enable the man to utilize them in accord with the ends of the Creator, and, finally Christianize this remade potential human being."[88]

The difficult economic situation through which Spain passed at the end of the war in 1939 is known to all, with its difficulties of reconstruction, aggravated by the Second World War. The Bishops did not fail to raise their voice in defense of the worst victims of hunger at that time. In the Pastoral Letter of 1944, the Bishop of

---

[87] *Pastoral Letter, on the Work of the Church in the Suburbs of Madrid,* November 27, 1951, by the Bishop of Madrid-Alcala, Dr. don Leopoldo Eijo Garay, *Official Bulletin of the Bishopric of Madrid-Alcala,* Madrid, December 1, 1951, p. 522.

[88] *Ibid.,* p. 523.

the Canaries, Dr. Pildain, asked: "and who is the Bishop to meddle in these affairs? Under what pretext are the Church and the Bishop going to interfere (in these problems)? Under what pretext?"[89]

To which he answered, precisely in the name of the Bishop and of the Church.

We can get an idea of the Bishop's energetic defense of the jobless in his diocese from his pronouncement that the State, which has proclaimed as its first duty that of giving work to Spaniards, can find a solution such as that of not applying "with preference, millions from the budget to problems and necessities which in all justice are less worthy of consideration."[90]

And in his Pastoral Letter of 1945, on *Those Who Promote Communism,* he spoke of "the need of a prudent and sober administration," especially in the circumstances in which the authorities can increase "the very grave damages born of the confusion and lamentable mixture of attributes of public authority and economy; and as a notable example, one of the gravest, the loss of prestige of the State, which, free of all party politics and having as its only end the common good and justice, should have been established as the sovereign and supreme arbiter of the ambitions and greeds of men."[91]

For their part, the Bishops of the ecclesiastical province of Granada in October of 1945 issued a Pastoral Letter "on the social question," in which they express their profound concern over the advance of Communism "especially when the revolution surges roaring and threatening over torrents of blood and pyramids of human skeletons."[92] They make specific reference to the problems of their diocese: "the ignorance of the masses, the distance from the towns, poor distribution of land, the hereditary single crop, with no

---

[89] Extracts in *Ecclesia,* September 23, 1944, no. 167, p. (921)-19.

[90] *Ibid.,* p. 20-(922).

[91] This *Lenten Pastoral* is reproduced in *Ecclesia,* nos. 210, July 21, 1945, 211, July 28, 1945, 212, August 4, 1945, 213, August 11, 1945. Citation in no. 212, p. (115)-19. See also the Pastoral Letter of the same Bishop of the Canaries, "What the Catholic Church and Social Justice Demand for the Working Family," Las Palmas de Gran Canaria, June, 1945, published in the *Official Bulletin of the Bishopric of the Canaries,* June, 1945, pp. 63-107.

[92] "Collective Letter of the Bishops of the Ecclesiastical Province of Granada on the Social Question," published in *Ecclesia,* December 15, 1945, no. 231, pp. 5-(509) 9-(512).

variety in products and with no aid from industry; absenteeism, frequent droughts; there is no other course remaining, then, but to hear the voice of God and calm the hunger of our brothers with a flood of justice and charity."[93]

After praising the activity of the State in social legislation, they propose separate associations of workers and employers: "it is fitting that the workers form Catholic institutions and associations, by means of which they may attend to their moral and religious perfection, they may obtain the greatest possible increase in physical, spiritual and monetary benefits, defend their own physical interests and rights with just strength and contribute to the collaboration and harmony of the other classes of society in the restoration of Christian life."[94] The bishops find that "associations of employers and chiefs of industry present more problems; nevertheless, an important role is reserved for them and they will harvest abundant fruits for themselves and for society if they decide to obey pontifical teachings."[95]

On the occasion of the 60th anniversary of *Rerum Novarum* the Bishop of Málaga pointed out the necessity of taking advantage of the social peace of these years: "But, what are we to do? You will ask me. And the answer will always be the same. The contest is yours. It is more important for you than for anyone to break the block of a proletariat, unhappy and quick to organize, upon which society, happy and confident, seeks to establish itself."[96] Don Angel Herrera asks for cooperation "with the Church in the cultural and religious education" of the workers.

To intensify the social apostolate of the priests the *Escuelas Sociales Sacerdotales* of Málaga and Vitoria were created in 1948. From the school in Málaga developed the *Instituto Social Leon XIII* of Madrid, which inaugurated its teaching duties on January 10, 1951.

The *Hermandad Obrera de Acción Católica* (H.O.A.C.), also was organized for the social apostolate. In 1951, on the occasion of the strikes in Barcelona and in the Basque-Navarre region, its National Committee came out in opposition to a campaign against its work, declaring: "First, the HOAC is neither a union nor a polit-

---

[93] *Ibid.,* p. 5-(509).
[94] *Ibid.,* p. 6-(510).
[95] *Ibid.*
[96] In *Ecclesia,* July 7, 1951, no. 521, p. 12-(740).

ical organization, but a Catholic Action group, wholly and exclusively subordinate to the directives of the Hierarchy of the Church.

"Second, because of that, in accord with its character, the HOAC could not intervene nor has it intervened in the preparation or in the realization of any movement for a strike of a political or union nature."[97]

The Bishop of Vitoria also referred to this, at the extraordinary meeting of the HOAC which took place in that city. "Those who believe you are something like a 'party of resistance' to the Spanish political regime are sadly in error. And those who attribute to you criminal purposes of upheaval of your country are sadly in error. . . . I know, too, that your conscience is clear of everything that they have tried to attribute to you in connection with the past conflict, which, as I told you, had all the characteristics of a confused, ugly maneuver against the country and social order."[98]

These words, which reflect positions between the official union organizations and the workers' Catholic Action activities, are a consequence of the close connection already pointed out between the social, the political and the economic. The action of the Church in the social problem requires the action of the State, of all society. This was also stated in the *Instruction* of the Archbishop, dated June 3, 1951, which speaks of the duties of justice and charity in the present difficult political, economic and social circumstances in which those labor conflicts arise. "In the Church, the social question is not insoluble, but neither can She alone solve it; the collaboration of intellectual, economic, and technical forces and the public powers is needed."[99]

With the restoration, in 1949, of the *Semanas Sociales* (Social Weeks)[100]—presided over by the Bishop of Córdoba—which have continued to take place annually, the Hierarchy and Spanish Catho-

---

[97] "Note of the National Commission of the H.O.A.C.," in *Ecclesia*, May 26, 1951, no. 515, p. 18-(578).

[98] "The H.O.A.C. Is not a Union, but a Work of the Church," in *Ecclesia*, July 28, 1951, no. 524, p. (101)-17.

[99] "Instruction of the Conference of Spanish Bishops on the Duties of Justice and Charity in the Present Circumstances," June 3, 1951, *Official Ecclesiastical Bulletin of the Archbishopric of Toledo*, June 25, 1951, no. 6, p. 124.

[100] The following volumes of the Spanish Social Weeks have been published. Week IX, Madrid, 1949: *Toward a More Just Distribution of Wealth*, Madrid, 1950; Week X, Bilbao, 1950. *Present Management Problems*, Madrid, 1951; Week XI, Barcelona, 1951: *Problems of the Middle Class*, Madrid, 1951; Week XII, Zaragoza, 1952: *Labor*, Madrid, 1952.

lics are working to the end of uniting intelligence and wills in the solution of the problems which affect the proletariat most intensely.

IX. *The Church and Higher Culture*

On August 18, 1947, His Holiness Pius XII addressed a letter to the then Minister of Education, Ibáñez Martín, in which he considered the publications of the *Consejo Superior de Investigaciones Científicas* "a legitimate honor of Spanish science, which, with the aid of Providence and the effort of men of good will, tends to approach more everyday the source of wisdom."[101]

Well then, in this organization of higher culture, the Hierarchy of the Church in Spain has always occupied positions of management and scientific direction. We must make special mention of the Bishop of Túy, Fray José López Ortiz, O.S.A., University Professor of the History of Law, vice president of the above mentioned Consejo; the Bishop of Madrid-Alcalá, whom we have mentioned before for his powerful and beneficent influence in the religious training of the youth of the Party. Dr. Eijo presides over the *Instituto de Teología,* and has promoted weeks of theological-biblical studies and of Canon Law studies.

Among the outstanding associates of this lofty scientific organization, we must point out the former Bishop of Vitoria, don Carmelo Ballester, eminent in biblical studies; and the present Bishop of Salamanca, Dr. Barbado Viejo, who directs the *Instituto de Derecho Canónico* (Institute of Canon Law).

The Bishop of Salamanca also presides over the committee of the Pontifical University, under whose auspices is being carried out the gigantic task of the *Biblioteca de Autores Cristianos,* which has published fundamental works of the past and present, presenting copious material of Catholic thought.

In 1940, when he was Bishop of that city, the present Primate, Cardinal Plá y Deniel, achieved the restoration of the Pontifical University of Salamanca, which he endowed with statutes, inspired by the Constitution of Pius XI, on ecclesiastical studies.

Together with this positive work, there has been the vigilant action of the Hierarchy, pointing out dangers and proposing advice

---

[101] "To His Excellency don José Ibáñez Martín, National minister of Education of the Spanish Government," from Castel Gandolfo, August 18, 1947, in *Arbor,* no. 24, Vol. VIII, pp. 329-330.

to avoid them. Therefore, the *Pastoral Instruction* of the Conference of Archbishops of July 1950 says: "there is the frequent, sad case of . . . heterodox or immoral productions finding echo and applause in Catholic writers, orators, and publicists who, because of a certain excessive desire for and pride in impartiality, take pleasure in weaving unconsidered praises of these same writings for their technique or brilliant style; and in our country there has been a popular vogue of the dangerous tendency to cite with praise books and works by militant non-conformists of the present time, while even being silent about Catholic productions although they may be worthy of praise. This means a failure to understand that any praise given in this way, although it may be wrapped in many reserves and be limited to the technical, literary aspect, will always extol the author of the work which has been praised and will be a stimulus in favor of the work."[102]

In regard to moral norms, the *Instruction* asks that they be accepted, "with filial docility; by not reading nor recommending, nor spreading works contrary to the Christian concept of life and the world."[103]

As we have seen above, by virtue of agreements between the Holy See and the Spanish government, these moral and canonical determinations have their support in the legislation and in the action of the government. An example of its application is the policy of censoring books, guided in its practice by the principles of the Church. And this elemental truth has been publicly disavowed by certain intellectuals who, though professing to be Catholics, have distinguished themselves by their criticism of and opposition to the Catholic cultural policy; likewise in these years, those who try to influence national morality through publicity of heterodox authors, violate these principles so clearly expressed by the Hierarchy. The formation for intellectual and political reasons of an opposition on the part of those in power and those out of power easily leads to an opposition on the part of the faithful and the non-faithful against the Voice of the Church, with all the consequences which this brings with it in Spain.

---

[102] "Pastoral Instruction and Norms of Criticism. Propaganda and Publicity of Theatrical and Cinema Works of a Heterodox or Immoral Character," Madrid, July 25, in *Official Ecclesiastical Bulletin of the Archbishopric of Toledo*, September 30, 1950, no. 9, p. 151.

[103] *Ibid.*, p. 162.

The same Cardinal Primate, upon his departure from Salamanca, in March of 1942, spoke clearly on the matter, by virtue of which there can be no voluntary ignorance on this subject among Catholics. "In the midst of our Civil War and Crusade, and precisely because it became necessary to enlist the dangerous labor of many Spanish intellectuals in the aid of the War, we thought it the duty of our episcopal office to issue our Pastoral Letter *Los delitos del Pensamiento y los falsos ídolos intelectuales* (*Crimes against Thought and False Intellectual Idols*), sounding an alert against the unmerited, pernicious and idolatrous respect for writers and intellectuals, only by virtue of the fact they are such, even when they have misused their talent or their writing skill by proposing doctrines destructive of the Faith and frequently of the social order. We feel that, even after the victorious termination of our Crusade, it is still necessary to remind Catholics and Spaniards of these truths and to forewarn them against making an idolatrous fetish of writers whose books and writings have been as contrary to our religion as to the teachings of the great Spanish writers. . . . Because it continues to be necessary not to favor, through respect for a writer's name, books with doctrines dangerous in the religious realm, in the closing days of our Pontificate, we have had to comply with our duty by prohibiting, under the general rules of the Canonical Code, don Miguel Unamuno's book *Del sentimiento trágico de la vida* (*On the Tragic Sense of Life*), republished in the Red zone after his death. We have no personal resentment against its author. . . . But affection for his person can be no impediment to the doctrinal judgment which his book deserves in the eyes of the Church. And since sometimes they like to present him as one of the representatives of the Hispanic spirit, it would be well for those who pretend this to desist, since nearly all the authors which he cites in support of his destructive and truly tragic skepticism are foreigners—English, German and French—, all of whom are most opposed to the true Catholic positive spirit. . . . Nor is a mere literary covering of Quixotism enough to excuse this corrosive skepticism."[104]

X. *Advance or Retreat?*

We have seen the Hierarchy of the Church in Spain through

---

[104] "Our Seven Years of Pontificate in Salamanca." Pastoral Letter of farewell on leaving the diocese of Salamanca. May 24, 1942. In *Pastoral Writings,* Vol. I, pp. 106-107.

various documents such as pastorals, collective letters, decrees and instructions, teaching, admonishing and counselling in all the fundamental problems of public life, stemming from the decisive fact of the Civil War of 1936, recognized by the Episcopate as a Crusade. In the same attitude—a large part of the Spanish people being submissive to this pastoral action—all public life acquires a spiritual tone which contrasts markedly with the secularism, paganism and anti-Catholicism of other countries.

Furthermore, what could be called militant Catholicism, in Catholic Action or in other groups closely related to the Hierarchy, in recent years has shown an intense vitality such as had not been seen in Catholic Spain for two centuries. In education, in politics, in letters, in economy, these effects of a profound religious revival have been manifest.

The balance is, then, favorable, in spite of the faults, errors and the complacency which can derive from the sometimes exaggerated official devoutness. Without any doubt, these faults could be observed more easily in the things rendered to Caesar than in the things of God.

XIII

The Catholic Church in England

by M. A. Fitzsimons

The members of the Catholic Church in England form a minority, generally without decisive influence on the national life, a minority which remained aloof from some of the formative movements of English history and, withal, a creative minority reflecting some of the divisions[1] of English life. In 1951 the number of Catholics in England and Wales was roughly estimated to be about 2,700,000 out of a population of 43,595,000.[2] While this number

---

[1] This essay draws heavily upon two volumes: *Catholicism in England* (Second edition, London, 1948) by Archbishop David Mathew, a work which becomes less analytical and more allusive and impressionistic as it approaches the present; *The English Catholics, 1850-1950,* edited by Bishop Beck (London, 1950), an unusually frank series of essays commemorating the centenary of the reestablishment of the hierarchy in England and Wales. As a number of the essays will be separately mentioned later, only two essays by Father Philip Hughes, "The Coming Century" and "The English Catholics in 1850" may be cited as of particular interest here.

The Tablet is valuable for ecclesiastical history as are the principal Catholic newspapers, the *Herald,* the *Times* and the *Universe.* None of them is of great value in revealing the social history of the largest part of the Catholic minority. For other general accounts see the essays by Christopher Hollis and Father Philip Hughes in the second supplement (1950) to the *Catholic Encyclopedia.* Christopher Dawson's reflections in a review article on the Centennial volume are extremely valuable, "The English Catholics, 1850-1950," *The Dublin Review* (4th Quarter, 1950), pp. 1-12.

[2] It is generally recognized that the figures in the *Catholic Directory* are based on the roughest estimates, and, on the whole, the figures tend to be too low. The Co-adjutor Bishop of Brentwood, George Beck, has pointed out that about 10% of newly born English children are baptized as Catholics, and that about 11% of the British armed forces were Catholic. A Gallup Poll (in 1946) estimated the Catholic population of England and Wales at 8.7% of the population. After giving other evidence, Bishop Beck suggested that the total Catholic population may be as much as five million. "Today and Tomorrow" in *The English Catholics: 1850-1950.* Dr. Zybszewski in *The Tablet,* March 6, 1948 and Robert L. Carson in *The Clergy Review,* XXXII (1949), 21-30, reach an estimate of 4,000,000.

is not large, and the growth of the English Catholic community is not numerically striking, the Church does appear to be thriving in numbers, when a comparison is made with the extraordinary decline of attendance at the Anglican Church. But the materialism and indifferentism which have made such heavy inroads on the churches of the Establisment and of non-conformism have also caused losses to the Church. Although the Protestant outlook from which English national sentiment developed once made conversion appear as heresy to the nation, this view has largely lost strength. The succeeding indifference, however, provides its own obstacles to serious religious practice.

A small group of English people formed the heroic core of English Catholicism, remaining steadfast in their faith through long years of persecution and longer periods of misrepresentation and isolation. The expediently ambiguous religious settlement of Queen Elizabeth prevailed in England through the power of the Queen's government, which dexterously sought to identify Catholicism with foreign influence, disloyalty and treason. Her government, indeed, developed a modern touch in creating martyrs and attempting to deny them the dignity of martyrdom.[3] The tortuousness of Elizabethan treason trials arose from the desire of her government to prove overt acts of treason against priests and laymen who, often enough, had been apprehended for religion's sake. Later occasions, the Gunpowder Plot and the marriage of Charles I to a Catholic Princess, served to confirm English antipathy to the foreign religion of Catholicism, which in England is called "Roman Catholicism." Among religious and indifferent English people there is still a tendency to consider Catholicism as a typical form of extremism,—the usual mark of enemies to English interests abroad.

These old English Catholics were long debarred from the universities, the professions and until 1829 from the political life of their country. While the eighteenth century saw a dwindling of Protestant feeling and a readiness on the part of Whig aristocrats such as Charles James Fox to support the removal of disabilities from Catholics, two other developments intervened before Catholics achieved political equality. The first was a favorable change in

---

[3] Materials for the study of Recusant History are published by the Catholic Record Society, *The Month,* and in a recently inaugurated series, edited by A. F. Allison and D. Rogers, *Biographical Studies* (Bognor Regis: Arundel Press, 1951).

England's attitude to Catholicism during her own struggle with the French Revolution and Napoleon.[4] The second and decisive event was the Act of Union (1800) which brought Irish members to the English House of Commons. The later election of the Catholic, Daniel O'Connell, to the House of Commons finally compelled the British government to support Catholic political emancipation (1829) in order to avert revolution in Ireland. This mingling of the affairs of the English and Irish Catholics is a constant point in the history of English Catholicism.

By 1850, when conversions had already become numerous, the total of English Catholics was over one-half million in a population of nearly 18,000,000. The old English Catholics were already being swelled by the two other principal elements of the Catholic minority, converts and immigrant Irish, the latter and their descendants representing the largest part of the Catholic Church in England today. The old Catholics, largely a politically quietist minority, were mainly connected with the English landed interest, a doomed cause in the industrial and commercial triumph of nineteenth century England. They had preserved their faith by maintaining chaplains and missions[5] at home, by supporting schools abroad and later at home, but in spite of foreign schools, travel and domestic persecution they were deeply attached to English ways and grateful for the sheltered time of toleration which the nineteenth century had brought.

In many respects Father John Lingard (the title Father would have annoyed him) represented their outlook. John Lingard (1771-1851) in his truly great *History of England* aimed to make Catholicism respectable in the eyes of his Protestant countrymen through the removal of their prejudices by a work of scholarship. In itself this was no mean tribute to his belief in their good sense and justice. He grew anxious when the Church in the time of the later Cardinal Wiseman (died 1865) became aggressive in its preaching and witness. Constantly he mistrusted the introduction of what he termed continental and Italian devotions. His background had made him perhaps too sensitive to Protestant sensibilities. Nonethe-

---

[4] At one moment there were as many as 19 bishops and nearly 5000 refugee priests in England. David Mathew, *Catholicism in England* (2nd edition), p. 163.

[5] The Catholic Churches founded in England were called missions to distinguish them from the long established parish churches of the continent and elsewhere.

less his mordant criticism of Victorian Gothic—he believed rood-screens played a part in causing the Reformation—and of the mis-apprehensions of those who looked for an early union of the Anglican Church with Rome reveal a powerful and penetrating mind.[6]

The reenforcement of the old Catholics by converts, beginning notably with the converts of the Oxford Movement, is the most widely known story in the history of English Catholicism. The zeal and brilliance of the converts still foster an exaggerated estimate of the Church's flourishing estate in England. From the converts have come the greatest member of the modern hierarchy, Cardinal Manning, the subtle intellect of Newman, and the most famous of recent English Catholic apologists and scholars, G. K. Chesterton and Christopher Dawson. Their fervor and training enabled them to become the leaders and spokesmen of a minority, once held down by persecution and more recently by poverty and lack of opportunity. It is necessary to emphasize this explanation of the prominence of the convert, because it is sometimes made a reproach to Catholicism in England that it can gain brilliant converts but cannot produce great minds from its own ranks. As a reproach, this ignores the history of the Catholic minority in England, for the herding of the Irish in the cities meant that "the future roots of the Church in England had to be planted in the slums."[7]

Many of the quiescent old Catholics were troubled by the stir of the conversions, and, of course, the Oxford Movement, which had died out before the end of the eighteen fifties, did eventually sharpen Anglican hostility to Rome and intensify a sense of difference. In part, this sense was based on the Anglican compromise, which permitted High Churchmen to emphasize the Catholic character of the Anglican Church and enabled the Low Churchmen to emphasize its Protestant character. In part, too, it was based on fear, and clergymen with high ideas about the Church sometimes were anxiously asked if they were moving towards Rome.

Nicholas Wiseman (1802-1865), later the leader of the restored hierarchy, welcomed the Oxford converts with the most gen-

---

[6] "I do not believe that Dr. Wiseman means by unity the same thing as his Protestant friends. He means an unity of submission, they of equality. I do not conceive that they will give up their English service or anything else." Lingard quoted in Denis Gwynn "Lingard and Cardinal Wiseman," *The Clergy Review*, XXXV (June, 1951), 377.

[7] Shane Leslie reviewing *The English Catholics* in *The Month*, new series, V (1951), 62.

erous enthusiasm. But Wiseman was not an old English Catholic. The future Cardinal, deeply romantic in imagination, born in Spain of Irish parents, and with long experience of the cosmopolitanism of Rome, saw in the Oxford Movement the imminence of England's return to the Church, and Newman's "Second Spring" moved him to tears. He watched Newman's progress towards the Church with deep sympathy. To Ambrose Phillips he wrote: "Let us have an influx of new blood; let us have even but a small number of such men as write in the Tracts, so imbued with the spirit of the early Church, so desirous to revive the image of the ancient fathers. . . . I will willingly yield to them place and honour, if God's good service require it."[8] Wiseman was responsible for the ordination of Manning but a few weeks after his reception into the Church.

In general, however, by the end of the nineteenth century the old Catholics, who abandoning their quietism entered the Army, the civil service, the professions, and the converts had become cohesive and, as a rule, with some extraordinary exceptions such as Manning, removed in their social and political outlook from the major numerical element of the Catholic Church in England, the Irish immigrants. This division of Catholics in England into a well-educated group (largely English and overwhelmingly Conservative) and a working class (very largely Labour) follows the general division of England. But in the case of the Catholics, the Labour group is mainly Irish by descent.

The Irish had begun coming to England during the eighteenth century and their numbers assumed the proportions of a steady stream before the Irish Famine (1846) precipitated a flood. Through these people Catholicism became involved in the industrial transformation of England. These immigrants, with little skill beyond their energy, poured into London, Bristol, Liverpool, over the industrial midlands, and to the Tyneside area. By 1851 the number of Irish-born residents in England and Wales was 519,959 out of a population of eighteen million. These immigrants, predominantly Catholic, continued to come to England through the century, although the scale of the movement diminished and, of course, a number of them later moved on to the United States, Canada and Australia.

---

[8] Quoted by Denis Gwynn in "The Paradox of Wiseman," *The Clergy Review*, XXXIV (1950), 196.

This multiplication of the Catholic population added to the missionary task of converting England to Catholicism, the onerous duty of providing churches and schools for a numerous foreign element which further underlined in English eyes the non-English aspects of the Catholic Church.[9] The English Bishop, Bernard Ward, memorably estimated the part of the Irish in the history of the English Catholic Church. "It was the influx of Irish in 1846 and the following years, which made our congregations what they are, and led to the multiplication of missions. . . . The English Catholics relied for the building of their Churches almost solely on the donations of the few hereditary Catholics and others of the upper classes; after the great Irish immigration it became possible to build from the pennies of the poor. Many missions owe their very existence, including serviceable churches and schools, to the large Irish congregations. If any proof be wanted of the importance of the immigration it is only necessary to cast one's eye on those parts of England, as, for example, East Anglia, whither the Irish hardly penetrated, and to see the desolate state of those counties so far as the Catholic religion is concerned. Even in Lancashire and the northern counties generally, where the numbers of English Catholics was far greater than in other parts of the country, the congregations were largely increased and many missions established due in many cases in great measure to the influx of Irish immigrants."[10]

In 1850 occurred the reestablishment of a regular English hierarchy, the decisive step in the forward movement of Catholicism during those years. It was expected that the action would arouse some Protestant antagonism but the Catholic leaders were inclined to put their trust in the basic tolerance of their countrymen. The opposition against the "Papal Aggression" proved to be surprisingly sharp, and Wiseman, the new Cardinal Archbishop, had fomented it by the jubilant tone of his pastoral "from the Flaminian Gate." Wiseman's jubilation may partly be explained by the fact that in

---

[9] Manning in 1887 wrote that he at first worked for the English people and "then have spent my life in working for the Irish occupation in England. But that occupation is the Catholic Church in all the amplitude of faith, grace, and authority." Quoted by Denis Gwynn, "Manning and Ireland," p. 111 in *Manning: Anglican and Catholic,* edited by Rev. John Fitzsimons (London, 1951).

[10] Ward, *The Sequel to Catholic Emancipation,* quoted by Denis Gwynn in "The Flight from the Cities," *The Clergy Review,* XVII (1939), 474-475.

being called to Rome at this time he had believed that he was to receive a post in Rome and was sadly leaving England forever. The "No Popery" agitation was headed by Lord John Russell, who, in abandoning the toleration traditional for many a Whig Peer, confessed that he was more indignant than alarmed.[11] The result of the agitation was the Ecclesiastical Titles Bill (1851) which menaced the new hierarchy with fines and loss of property, an act of spite, which remained unenforced and was repealed under Gladstone (1871). Wiseman's trust in the English people, expressed in his many lectures and in *An Appeal to the English People* and Newman's *The Present Position of Catholics* contributed to the immediate nullification of the public effect of Russell's action.

The English Catholics had long been governed by missionary bishops, Vicars Apostolic, whose number as a preliminary to the new arrangement was raised to eight in 1840. The Papal Brief, *Universalis Ecclesiae,* which reestablished the hierarchy, following up "a work so well commenced," created the metropolitan see of Westminster and twelve other dioceses.[12] This establishment of ordinary Church government was designed to end the numerous and bitter disputes which the unusual regime of the Church in England fostered, and to recognize and abet the Second Spring of English Catholicism. The "restoration" was also an act of faith, for the dearth of clergy and suitable bishops caused many misgivings. All the more was it an act of faith, if one considers the troubled state of Rome at the time. Characteristically, for England was a missionary land, many of the negotiations in Rome about the establishment of the hierarchy were conducted by that energetic and much travelled Benedictine, William Bernard Ullathorne who had served as vicar-general in Australia and became the first bishop of Birmingham. In creating the hierarchy some of the English vicars urged that a few ancient titles be used to avoid any appearance of recognizing the validity and continuity of Anglican orders. But Rome

---

[11] *Punch,* which was extremely unfriendly to Catholicism, published a cartoon, which showed Russell running away after having chalked "No Popery" on Wiseman's door.

[12] Subsequently a number of other dioceses were created. In 1911 Liverpool and Birmingham were made Archepiscopal sees and in 1916 Cardiff was made the See of a Welsh Province. Until 1908 the Catholic Church in England and Wales, as missionary lands, was under Propaganda, so that it may be said that the establishment of the hierarchy in 1850 did not bring England wholly under the Common law of the Church.

was unwilling to stir up legal disputes with the English government, and no old titles were used.

In the year following the establishment of the hierarchy the census, the only English census to make a reckoning of church attendance, revealed that a very substantial number of the English people did not trouble to attend church, notably, the Church of England. This religious indifference, which was to increase greatly during the following century, provided and still provides a major problem for the Catholic Church in England.

The new hierarchy slowly developed its organization. With the shortage of priests, even with European and Irish recruits, the bishops could not afford any large curia and organization.[13] Many difficulties persisted from the extraordinary organization of the past. The privileges of religious orders which had undertaken missionary work often conflicted with the plans and the authority of the bishops. In general these quarrels were decided in favor of the bishops. But as a mark of England's missionary status, it may be mentioned that in the eighteen-eighties the Benedictines themselves went through a controversy over the proper sphere of action in the country. Dom Edmund Gord, who led a group of Downside monks in an endeavor to turn the Benedictines away from their missionary activity and back to a more properly monastic life, won his cause when Leo XIII issued the Bulls *Religiosus Ordo* and *Diu Quidem.* The flourishing state of the community at Downside and Benedictine schools and scholarship at the Universities bear witness to the value of this papal decision.

Moreover, though the Archbishop of Westminster and the bishops and laity acted together on a number of national issues, the chief center of activity and development was the parish. This was inevitable in the fundamental work of providing churches and elementary schools for a population mainly in concentrated groups amidst the industrial squalor of England. The Irish at first were largely in the mining and the factory areas, and associated with shipping and army life. A downtrodden and alien group living in slums, made more horrible by the prevalence of drunkenness, often

---

[13] Cardinal Vaughan established a central seminary at Oscott but his successor at Westminister, Archbishop Bourne turned back to the practice of diocesan seminaries. Vaughan's policy did not run counter to the Council of Trent, for Vaughan argued that only a central seminary could make efficient use of available resources and talent.

developed a sense of community, a social milieu, which helped to preserve their faith. The era of church and school building may be summarized in the following figures (which are approximations) :[14]

	Schools	Pupils	Churches and Chapels	Priests (including) religious orders)
1850	..	41,382	600	800
1870	350	101,556	1000	2000
1900	1050	..	1500	3000
1920	1639	290,185	1900	3929
1940	1990	438,513	2500	5839
1951	2080	529,812	2825	6684

In all this the essential unit was the parish. Yet for many activities, for example, for the provision of secondary schools, organization and direction of a wider scope was necessary. This parochial limitation has also been responsible for the few achievements of Catholic Action.

By the beginning of the twentieth century Protestant feeling against the Church had greatly diminished and Catholics were to be found in most fields of activity. There was a merging of the Catholics in the national life,[15] although the Irish problem continued until after the First World War. During the long archepiscopate of Cardinal Francis Bourne, the progress of the Church was quiet rather than spectacular. But, in the retrospect of contemporary problems, what appeared originally as a time of growth and consolidation, now seems to be a time of lost opportunities.

The major activities of the Church may be called defensive. They were attempts to reach, provide for and maintain the Catholic minority in England. In 1895, however, the hierarchy permitted Catholics to attend Oxford and Cambridge. Originally Catholics had been debarred by the universities from attendance. When it became possible for them to do so, the Catholic ecclesiastical authorities hesitated and then in effect forbade Catholics to attend the principal universities. But Cardinal Manning's effort to establish a

---

[14] The increase of schools by 1920 is to be explained by the fact that the secondary schools are included in the figure.

[15] See the admirable essay by Denis Gwynn "Growth of the Catholic Community," *The English Catholics*, 410-441.

Catholic university was a failure. Thus, it was not until Oxford and Cambridge were beginning to lose their religious character, that Catholics finally were allowed to enter them. Even to this day the results of this earlier development are apparent. Catholics eagerly cherish this opportunity of being associated with English national life and on the whole are mistrustful of any move towards a Catholic university on the grounds that they could not create a university comparable to the established ones. There have, however, been few successful efforts to provide courses in philosophy and theology to act as a guiding influence, but chaplaincies at Oxford, Cambridge and elsewhere were established. But students privileged to hear the Sunday sermons of Monsignor Ronald Knox at Oxford will always be grateful for a provision which could bear such happy fruit.[16]

The English Catholic minority, notably the converts, has been remarkably active in the field of letters and journalism. The number of Catholic English periodicals is surprisingly large. These range from the three weekly newspapers, *Universe, Catholic Herald* and *Catholic Times,* and the weekly journal, *The Tablet* to *The Month* and *The Dublin Review.*

The Dominican monthly, *Blackfriars,* founded in 1920 by Bede Jarrett, O.P., and published at Oxford, carries on in a strikingly successful way the original Dominican mission to the clerks. Devoted to the works of the mind, it is probably the only magazine in English which, breaking through the isolation cell of terminology and jargon of the confined specialist, makes the vitality, breadth and relevance of Thomism intelligible to men of general education. *The Downside Review,* founded by Gasquet in 1882, a Benedictine publication, deals mainly with theology, philosophy, biblical studies and monastic history.

In the mid-nineteenth century, the Catholics, as a rule, had run against such national views and policies as British approval of the seizure of the papal states. In the nineteen thirties, the influential Catholics generally supported the appeasement policy with warmth, and particularly seconded Prime Minister Chamberlain's efforts to

---

[16] See the articles by H. O. Evennett, "Catholics and the Universities," *The English Catholics,* pp. 291-321; by A. H. Armstrong, "Catholics and the University" and by Monsignor Gordon Wheeler, "University Apostolate," *Blackfriars,* XXXII (1951), 334-339, and XXXIII (1952), 289-292.

reach an understanding with Mussolini.[17] When war came, the Catholics gave the most ardent support to the war effort.[18] It was during this period that the Catholics, through the Sword of the Spirit, made a considerable momentary impress on the national life. The Catholic Primate at the time, Archbishop Arthur Hinsley, found a ready response among his countrymen to his appeals.

When in 1935 he arrived at Westminster, he strikingly said: "If we must talk of policy, our home policy is Catholic Action and our foreign policy is missionary action." When war began, his views also struck home: "I declare that for me neutrality of heart is impossible in this struggle. I see it as a great conflict between light and darkness."

London had become the refuge of many European Catholics as the governments-in-exile were established, and Cardinal Hinsley saw in this concentration an opportunity to rally Christians to an informed struggle against the paganism of the totalitarian countries, against the eroding elements in the national life and for a peace based on Christian principles. On December 21, 1940, the movement which the Cardinal described as "Catholic Action in the crisis of the war,"[19] found a most striking expression in a proclamation, which included the Five Points of the Pope's Peace Program

---

[17] When Barbara Ward reproached some of her fellow Catholics for their past sympathies with Italian Fascism, Robert Sencourt replied that in 1940 "they were working in close touch with the Foreign Office in an attempt to counter German propaganda and keep Italy out of the war. By showing their friendship to Italy they not only delayed Mussolini's fatal mistake, but they deprived it of much of its venom." Unlike many others, Sencourt had no second thoughts on Fascism, which, he believed, had been favorable for the Church, necessary for Italy and even for Britain in its contemporary extremity. *Catholic Herald*, Jan. 4, 1946.

[18] It is melancholy to reflect on the unheeded advice of *The Tablet*, July 5, 1941: "But we have to be prepared from now on, if the Soviet Armies fight as well as we hope they will, for a revival of the old attempts to confound irreconcilable opposites in one popular anti-Fascist front."

[19] *The Tablet*, Jan. 4, 1941. Christopher Dawson, its lay leader, defined the purposes of *The Sword of the Spirit* as designed "to deal with the particular issues raised for Christians by the present war; and above all, the need for national unity and defence of human liberty and the principles of justice and international order for which the British Commonwealth of Nations claims to be fighting. These principles are not peculiar to Catholics, or even to Christians, they belong to the natural law. Nevertheless, it is, above all, in the tradition of Christian Western Culture that they have been realized and where they are denied, there is no room for a Christian state, whether monarchist or democratic." *The Tablet*, Jan. 11, 1941.

(1939), signed by the Anglican Archbishops of Canterbury and York, the Moderator of the Free Churches and by Cardinal Hinsley. But the movement's serious influence did not survive the war, and, indeed, the controversy over the schools question in 1943-1944 and after the passage of the Butler Education Act (1944).

In this controversy the English Catholics were and are acutely conscious of their minority status in what they call "post-Christian" England. They even appealed to the minority treaties and the United Nations Declaration of the Rights of Man. From this sense of minority status in a religiously indifferent England stemmed the discussion of the principal problems which have beset the Catholic Church in England since the war: the School Question, the leakage and social policy in the age of the Welfare State.

As long as the Anglican and Non-Conformist Churches were seriously concerned about doctrine, the Catholic insistence on Church schools did not remove them from general sympathy and policies. Thus, Cardinal Manning argued that the Catholics did not seek to be separated from a national educational system.[20] He could argue so because the Anglicans and the Non-Conformists were also interested in religious education, and, thus, a system of secular education did not enjoy general favor at all.[21]

Until 1870 Catholic schools founded by voluntary effort could receive grants from the government and these grants were an important support of Church schools until 1902. But the provision of schools by the Churches was insufficient, and when in 1870 the government empowered locally elected boards to provide schools out of local taxation the great threat of tax-supported non-denominational schools appeared.[22] The resulting dual system of local and

---

[20] A. C. F. Beales, "The Struggle for the Schools," p. 374, in *The English Catholics, 1850-1950.*

[21] Non-Conformist mistrust of the Anglican schools caused opposition to tax support for voluntary schools. This is an almost classic example of religious divisions making possible the triumph of secularism, for the government in 1870 provided that schools supported by a local rate should have only general, strictly non-doctrinal religious instruction. Later developments have witnessed the general (excluding the Catholics) acceptance of this principle. Ironically, this policy (now known as the agreed syllabus) which is designed to give religious training to the young appears to further the decline of religious practice in England. Santayana wrote aptly in this connection: "The attempt to speak without speaking any particular language is not more hopeless than the attempt to have a religion that shall be no religion in particular."

[22] Although Manning had anticipated difficulties over the educational bill, the English bishops in 1870 were all away at the Vatican Council.

voluntary schools was anathema to the secularist Radicals of the Liberal Party.[23] Government grants made elementary education free in 1891 but this did not lessen the burden of providing, maintaining and staffing schools. In 1902 a Unionist government with Irish support gave rate assistance to the Voluntary (including the Catholic) schools. The sites and buildings and repairs were paid for by the Churches but thereafter Church schools were to be maintained by Local Educational Authorities, who had a veto over teachers appointed by the School Managers (representing the religious interests and the Local Educational Authority).

Compared with American and French arrangements this settlement was generous but did not meet the Catholic claim that the parent and not the state had the supreme right in educating the child. As Manning wrote to John Morley: "I believe that the English people ought to educate themselves with such State aid as individuals require.[24] Both Cardinals Manning and Vaughan sought general support for this principle of parental right and denominational instruction. The principle has been consistently repeated by Cardinals Bourne, Hinsley and Griffin. In 1929 the Hierarchy declared that it is no part of the normal function of the State to teach and that "the teacher is always acting *in loco parentis,* never *in loco civitatis,* though the State, to safeguard its citizenship, may take reasonable care to see that teachers are efficient."

In this emphasis the Catholic Church has been fighting a losing battle in England, for the decline of the Protestant Churches[25] has deprived the Catholics of general Christian support for denominational schools and emphasizes the new minority status of the English Catholics in a secular, post-Christian society. The English

---

[23] The Liberals generally appealed to the Irish workers, both as Irish and workers. But on the question of education the Liberals under Radical and Non-Conformist influence favored secular schools. The Conservative Party, which the old Catholics and converts mainly favored, was more favorable to the Catholic schools but also was devoted to the Anglican Church and hostile to the Irish cause. Nonetheless, the Irish Catholics consistently supported the Catholic educational claim.

[24] Quoted by Gordon Wheeler, "The Archdiocese of Westminster," p. 159 in *The English Catholics, 1850-1950.*

[25] Although thousands of non-Catholic Church schools had been handed over to public authorities in the first half of the twentieth century, not a single Catholic school had been surrendered up to 1944.

H. O. Evennett, *The Catholic Schools of England and Wales,* (Cambridge [Eng.], 1944), p. 22.

Catholics pressed their case vigorously in the wartime discussions of a new education program. The Butler Act (1944), however, has been presented as the greatest concession which will be made to the Catholics, and has created a grave financial crisis for their schools. This settlement which involved the reorganization and extension of secondary education did not do away with the Voluntary schools but offered only 50% of the costs necessary to repair or replace them. If the Church schools raised 50% of these costs—and the repair and reorganization costs were high—they would continue to receive public money to maintain them. The government sadly underestimated these costs for the Church schools, which are now estimated to be about £60,000,000. Moreover, the war years, in particular, witnessed a considerable redistribution of the Catholic population and thus made necessary the building of many new schools, to the cost of which the government, as a rule, will not contribute at all. The protests of the hierarchy and of Catholic organizations and the campaign of the *Sword of the Spirit* on the subject failed and, indeed, Mr. Butler's act did probably represent the largest concessions that could be made at the time.

In 1949 the Bishops, against the wishes of the government which considers the settlement final,[26] proposed that Catholic schools be leased to Local Educational Authorities, who would be allowed to appoint the teachers on condition that the latter be religiously acceptable to the Church authorities.

The particular difficulty is that the Catholics have relatively few secondary schools. Of course, many secondary schools would have been possible only at the cost of sacrificing the building of churches (such was the general practice before 1870 and such again is the policy of the hierarchy today).[27] At any rate the Catholic secondary schools for boys are few and their fees meant that the bulk of the Catholic population could not attend them. In this the Catholics repeated, though on a more extreme scale, the general educational pattern of England. The Catholic secondary schools were to a large

---

[26] The two Labour Ministers of Education, Ellen Wilkinson and George Tomlinson, as well as their Conservative successor, have administered the act with great fairness.

[27] Archbishop Masterson (Birmingham) said in June: "The Hierarchy are putting schools before everything else. We have, of definite intention, put first the provision of schools for our children. . . . Where we can we use the schools as churches until circumstances allow us to erect a permanent church." *The Universe*, June 15, 1951.

extent the work of religious orders, whose importance in the field is best revealed by the fact that the number of secondary schools for girls, provided by nuns, far exceeds those for boys.

The social and political division of the Catholics in England have prevented the formulation of generally acceptable social and political programs. The English Catholics have acted together on such fundamental matters as the schools question and legislation on the family and divorce. Conflicts about social teaching are not unknown in the United States and France. But the differences in social outlook between *The Tablet* and the organ of the Young Christian Workers is unusually wide. The difference reflects the basic contrast between the largely conservative English Catholics and the Catholic working class, mainly Irish in origin.[28]

It is noteworthy that *The English Catholics,* the volume commemorating the centenary of restoration of the hierarchy, contains no chapter on the social thought and action of the English Catholics. An article on "The Care of the Poor" provides interesting material on a necessary work of salvage but does not remedy an omission, made inevitable by the recent history of English Catholic social action.[29]

The work of Manning was continued by the Catholic Social Guild (1909),[30] which emphasized study programs and recently has been rather anti-Labour Party, and the Catholic Workers College

---

[28] The differences of national origin are being obscured. Richard O'Sullivan, who was educated in Ireland, contributes regularly to *The Tablet.* In *Etudes* (July, 1946) Raymond Jouve, however, noted: "Five-sixths of the English Catholics belong to the working class and to the Labour Party. But the Catholic press does not reflect in any way the worker's point of view. Therein lies an anomaly which is very difficult for the foreigner to understand." Quoted in *Blackfriars,* XXX (1949), 202.

[29] This deficiency is all the more remarkable in view of the early leadership of Cardinal Manning. Moreover, in the twenties Georgiana McEntee found in the beginnings of English Catholic social action a subject for a useful book, The *Social Catholic Movement in Great Britain* (New York, 1927).

[30] After 1918 the Catholic Social Guild carried on valuable educational work in yearly summer schools and in the thirties helped to establish Colleges of Social Studies in Leeds, Liverpool, and Manchester. But Archbishop Hinsley noted in his Pastoral Letter for Advent, 1937 that the efficiency of diocesan guilds and societies "is often seriously impaired by an unhappy circumstance. They do not attract from the general body adequate membership, and, in particular, those Catholics who by reason of their position and education are best fitted to be leaders among the laity do not always give to these organizations a support which is commensurate with their influence and opportunities." *Brotherhood in Christ* (Oxford, 1937), pp. 8-9.

(1921) at Oxford. The latter seeks to prepare workers, as Catholics, for effective leadership in the trade unions. But the brave work of the Workers College reaches very few people.

The paucity of social thought may partly be explained by the fact that those brilliant apologists for Catholicism, G. K. Chesterton, Hilaire Belloc and Father Vincent McNabb went into the dazzlingly blind alley of distributism. This protean social viewpoint, ranging from an advocacy of extending property-holding to a return to a green and peasant England along with a condemnation of Capitalism and Socialism, has inspired a few community experiments, which failed, and ultimately has exercised no influence on English social thinking and action.

The distributists even dignified their position with the name sociology and, sometimes, Catholic sociology.[31] Now in its most sweeping form distributism conjured away social problems and the necessity for political action by looking forward to a universality of conviction and moral reform. On almost all levels it was a program of individuals and not of political action. The distributists proclaimed that the industrial capitalist ship was doomed, and, while waiting for the sinking and subsequent salvage by the few survivors, their social program amounted to little more than *sauve qui peut*. The theory provided the means for witty and amateurish denunciations of the money-power and capitalism, and of most social legislation as forging further chains of slavery.[32] The distributists have been negative, and, by and large, their journalistic influence was thrown to the Conservative Party.[33]

---

[31] The present writer has been impressed by "agrarian" criticism of the centralizing and potentially tyrannical tendencies within industrial capitalism. The English distributists, however, limited themselves to criticism and proposals of distant solutions. Failing a dictatorship and planned reorganization of a distributist state, which would have horrified distributists, what was to be done immediately and for the next twenty years?

[32] A good example of this all or nothing attitude of the distributists may be found in *The Catholic Times*. When the Coalition Government was considering the establishment of Family Allowances, *The Catholic Times*, April 24, 1942, was critical, and, calling for a family wage, argued that, if Britain was to have security, there must be a return to the land!

[33] When Dom Aelred Graham referred to the "unimpeachable High Toryism of *The Tablet*" the latter's editor, Douglas Woodruff, disavowed "High Toryism" in favor of "High Whiggery." The editor of *The Tablet* favored the Conservative Party, because it is anti-Socialist, but not Conservatism. "I think it is reasonable to have more hopes of the Conservative than of the Labour Party coming to understand and accept the Catholic social philosophy we try to expound, of

Whereas this theoretical alienation and practical Conservatism have characterized *The Dublin Review* and *The Tablet,* the Hierarchy has called for sweeping social and moral reform. The Joint Pastoral of the Bishops of England and Wales, read in the churches on June 21, 1942, contained the following points. A living wage, sufficient for comfort and savings, should be the first charge on industry. A minimum family wage should be sufficient for husband, wife and three or four children, and if the employer can not meet the requirement, it should be met by pooling within an industry or, in default of this, by the state. Coordination of each industry should replace cutthroat competition, and workers and employers should unite to secure the best conditions of work and fairest division of output. Minimum housing conditions should include sufficient bedrooms, sanitation and a bathroom for each family. The manufacture and sale of contraceptives and obscene books should be banned. Religious education should be available for every child, and the measures necessary to that end should not mean that the general education of the child would suffer. The Pastoral, also, denounced the enormous inequalities in the distribution of England's wealth, and, pointing to wartime price and profit controls, observed that there should be no practical difficulty in solving the main problems of economics. "The national interest in matters of profits and prices does not differ in peace time from what it is in war time. The same means, the same men and materials are available in peace time no less than in war. It is the purpose only that is wanting, the common force of mind and will that is lacking. . . . There must be a renewal of the Christian spirit of brotherhood which the last few generations of scientific prosperity and "get rich quick" has gone far to kill." Noting that "the teaching of the Church [*Rerum Novarum*] has had little effect on the life of our country," the Bishops stated that the purpose of the Pastoral was "to awaken Catholics to a sense of danger and to spur them to face the perils that threaten society."[34]

The Tablet's comments on the publication of the Joint Pastoral went far towards emasculating it. Subsequently, its editors

the plural society and subsidiary functions, and voluntary association, of the family unit and of personal responsibility, of diffused ownership; this last item has, at length, reached the party programme." *Blackfriars,* XXX (1929), 204-205. The last hopeful point, which is most unlikely to amount to anything, is characteristic and revealing.

[34] *Catholic Times,* June 26, 1942.

explained their position: "No one who watches the development of religious activities in Great Britain can fail to note the danger that the central Christian criticism of modern society may be overlaid and lost through a concentration of attention on matters which are important in their own sphere, but are not important by comparison with the great debate about what kind of doctrine of human nature should be accepted as providing the basis of society. . . . From many a social policy sermon nowadays the hearer would conclude that no one can be expected to think about religious truth until he has a much more secure and adequate income than has, in sober fact, ever been the lot of the vast majority of Christians since the foundation of the Church."[35]

To criticism of the gulf between his views and those of a large part of his fellow Catholics *The Tablet's* editor, Woodruff replies that "the Glasgow and Liverpool Irish are not voting to express any Catholic social philosophy." The opposition to Woodruff's self-conscious minority position is well represented by the chaplain of the Young Christian Workers, Father John Fitzsimons, who echoes Ozanam's *Passons aux barbares:* "It is no good standing on the outside with a penny catechism in one hand and a book of apologetics in the other, hoping to influence a historical evolution. By being in, and of, this human tide, we can make some attempt to direct it."[36]

The Young Christian Workers movement, derived from Canon Cardijn's *Jocist* movement, is a zealous form of Catholic Action among the industrial classes. The Archbishop of Westminster, Cardinal Griffin, in praising the practicality of its approach, stated his judgment of the back-to-the-land proposal: "I would not say that it was not practical; it is not facing up to the position here in England. . . . It is no use looking forward to wonderful schemes in fifty years' time."[37]

---

[35] "First Things and Secondary," *The Tablet,* Nov. 21, 1942; the account of the Pastoral is in *The Tablet,* June 27, 1942. Later, Douglas Woodruff wrote: "In proportion as the Catholics at all economic levels become politically conscious as Catholics, they will become alive to the primary importance of preserving their personal liberty in matters so intimate to themselves and their families as education, health, employment, savings." *Blackfriars,* XXX (May 1949), 210.

[36] Speech at Liverpool, *Catholic Herald,* February 1, 1946.

[37] Speech at Brighton, *Catholic Herald,* Aug. 13, 1948. In his allocution at Westminster, Jan. 18, 1944, Archbishop Griffin reaffirmed his support of adequate housing and family allowances. *The Month,* CLXXX (1944), 2.

By and large, though the English Catholics have been confirmed in their awareness of minority status, there is, happily, little disposition to retreat to defensive and isolated positions. The religious indifferentism,[38] which is well revealed in Rowntree and Lavers, *English Life and Leisure* (1950) and so vividly portrayed by such novelists as Evelyn Waugh and Graham Greene, surrounds the Catholic youth with a multitude of distractions and inducements to forget his religion. This unfavorable social milieu is primarily responsible for the leakage problem. The magnitude of this loss was forcefully stated by an RAF Chaplain, Father Francis Ripley: "The leakage in England and Wales during the last century has more than nullified the increase in the Catholic population from any cause. . . . The effects of migration from Eire, the gaining of converts, the higher Catholic birth rate, have all been rendered null and void. It is obvious that if the Catholic population only increases at the same rate as the total population, the country will never be converted."[39]

In the past, the leakage occurred in part because Catholics, far away from Church and priest, gradually abandoned their religion. Even this problem remains, and was dramatized in a mission campaign (1948), which visited every village and hamlet in Oxfordshire, in an effort to reach lapsed Catholics and to accustom non-Catholics to the sight of priests living in villages.[40]

The Catholic response to this challenge of a post-Christian society has taken many forms: the struggle for the schools; literary, scholarly and apologetic activity; new kinds of radio religious programs; the workers' apostolate, and many others. Above all, it must be emphasized that the problem is clearly visualized: "The great task of the future is, therefore, to increase the internal coherence and the external activity of the Catholic Community as a Christian minority in a secularized mass society."[41]

---

[38] Edgar Ashby, a veteran member of the Catholic Evidence Guild, noticed the contrast between thirty years ago when most of his audience believed in heaven, hell and God, and today's crowds who "are completely indifferent to God or actively hostile to all religious ideas and practice." *Universe,* Jan. 5, 1940.

[39] *Catholic Herald,* Jan. 25, 1946. A valuable study of lapse of religious practice among the English youth was made by the Young Christian Workers and published in the magazine *New Life* (1951).

[40] *Catholic Herald,* May 21, 1948.

[41] Christopher Dawson, "The English Catholics: 1850-1950," *The Dublin Review* (Fourth Quarter, 1950), 11.

XIV

The Catholic Church in the United States

by Thomas T. McAvoy, C.S.C.

Because of the growth and prosperity in the nineteenth century of the Catholic minority in the United States some European Catholics, particularly those who favored democratic political institutions, had begun to argue during the 1890's that European Catholicism should imitate certain policies of American Catholics.[1] In this country Archbishop John Ireland of St. Paul, Cardinal James Gibbons of Baltimore, Bishop John J. Keane of the Catholic University of America, and Monsignor Denis O'Connell, the rector of Cardinal Gibbons' titular church in Rome, were the leaders of a group of progressive American clergymen who also felt that European Catholicism should attempt to copy at least the American Catholic cooperation with democratic institutions and participation in the social reforms of the age. At the same time Archbishop Ireland, Cardinal Gibbons and their friends had achieved such general acceptance in American public life by these same policies that they were encouraged to believe that the country might soon see a notable popular movement into the Catholic Church.

In Europe the admirers of American Catholicism met defeat at the hands of European conservatives who accused them of certain ascetical and doctrinal heresies under the name of Americanism, particularly as found in the French adaptation of Father Walter Elliott's biography of Father Isaac Hecker. They induced Pope Leo

---

[1] The latest treatment of the episode of Americanism is contained in the autobiography of Abbe Felix Klein, *Une Hérésie Fantome, L'Américanisme* (Paris, 1949) which is volume 3 of his 7 volume *La Route du petit morvandiau*. I have discussed the problem in the *Review of Politics*, V (July, 1943), 275-301, and in *The Catholic Historical Review*, XXXI (July, 1945), 133-153.

XIII to condemn this Americanism in an Apostolic Letter, *Testem Benevolentiae,* on January 22, 1899. Archbishop John Ireland and Cardinal Gibbons denied that the condemned heresies existed in this country, but other American bishops asserted that they did exist. The European defenders of Americanism were silenced and the movement to spread the ideals of American Catholicism received a definite check. Four years after the condemnation, Archbishop Ireland, feeling that the appointment of Monsignor Denis O'Connell to the rectorship of the Catholic University in 1903 evidenced a more friendly feeling toward American Catholicism in Rome, wrote exultingly to Monsignor O'Connell "Viva L'Americanismo! Viva sempre."[2] But the Americanist movement as such was dead, and as the American leaders of the movement passed away Europe heard less of American Catholicism, while American Catholics became less interested in introducing American Catholic practices into Europe. As a result, even a half century later it can be said that most European Catholics do not yet understand the particular character of American Catholicism. In America, during these same first decades of the twentieth century, despite a continuing growth of the Catholic population, there was also a decline in the public acceptance of Catholic leaders and a fading of the hope for an early conversion of the United States to Catholicism.

The death of such figures as Archbishop Ireland, Cardinal Gibbons and Bishop John Lancaster Spalding, who were international as well as national figures, and the lack of similar figures among their successors played an important part in the change. Even the international character of the two intervening World Wars, with the resulting exchanges between the old and the new world and the interdenominational cooperation in patriotic activities in this country during the war time, did little to check the development of critical attitudes towards American Catholicism.[3] European Catholics still

---

[2] Letter of Archbishop John Ireland to Denis O'Connell, St. Paul, January 14, 1903, Richmond Diocesan Archives. Quoted in Peter E. Hogan's *The Catholic University of America, 1896-1903* (Washington, 1949), which treats of the reaction of the Americanist controversy on the University.

[3] Among recent European criticisms of American Catholicism are, that of Georges Escoulin, "Le Catholicisme aux Etats Unis," in *Le Monde,* Jan. 10, 11, 12, 1950; of Erik von Kuehnelt-Leddihn, "American Catholics Revisited," in *The Tablet* (London), April 22, 1950; "Eine Laie" 's "Kirchliches Leben in Amerika" in *Schweizer Rundschau* (Einsiedeln), March, 1946, pp. 887-95; and Luigi d'Apollonia's "Die Kirche in den Vereinigten Staaten von Amerika" in the same periodical (July, 1950), pp. 201-8. Denis W. Brogan, a former

question the "American" in American Catholicism and non-Catholic Americans still object to its Catholicism.

The European critic persists in looking for European traditions in American Catholicism and the non-Catholic American persists in judging Catholics by American non-Catholic standards. And American Catholics themselves, disturbed by this criticism and very anxious to prove their loyalty to both the Church and to the country, have added to the confusion by failing to make clear that American Catholicism is both American and Catholic at the same time, and that the particular characteristics of American Catholicism deserve to be studied and evaluated for what they have to offer toward the solution of many problems of the present crisis.

European critics accustomed to official churches have continued to point to the lack of official recognition of Catholicism in American public life, to the limitation of Catholic cultural institutions, especially to the paucity and poverty of Catholic universities, and to the lack of Catholic leadership in politics and in literature. American critics continue to attack Catholic insistence on the age-old doctrines and moral practices, especially when applied to the movies, to the press, and to such legal questions as divorce laws and laws regulating the dissemination of certain types of literature. In both lines of criticism, moreover, there is an ill-defined belief that American Catholicism functions through a secret clerically dominated organization, national in scope, which is so powerful because it is so secret. It is the fear of this mythical organization which greatly disturbs these critics, and American Catholics think the suggestion so absurd that they have failed properly to demonstrate their own freedom in social and political matters.

Stated simply, the greatest cause for misunderstanding American Catholicism probably is the paradox that despite the remarkable national conformity in faith and practice in the Catholic minority

Catholic and an English critic of America, has given an estimate of American Catholicism in "The Catholic Church in America," *Harper's* (May, 1950) CC (no. 1200), pp. 40-50. American non-Catholic criticism has been frequent in *The Churchman, The Christian Century, The Nation* and *The New Republic*. The recent book of Paul Blanshard, *American Freedom and Catholic Power* (Boston, 1949), was a financially successful journalistic venture. The superficial consultation of many Catholic sources by Blanshard caused many unwary readers to believe this a scholarly study. However, these quotations from Catholic sources are carefully chosen merely to implement his unproved presupposition of a secret organized national Catholic power. There are many errors in these quotations and in his footnotes.

that minority has no real national organization. Of like importance is another paradox that the strength of American Catholicism lies in its acceptance of the American tradition of disestablishment[4]—incorrectly called separation of Church and State—and the resultant concentration of its material forces on religious or socio-religious activities. Further, as a result of these two paradoxes of a mysterious religious uniformity without a national political organization it is difficult, if not impossible, to speak of a national Catholic attitude on any political or social matter.

To say that American Catholicism has no national organization calls attention to the most important characteristic of the Church in this country: its almost absolute division into diocesan units with the individual bishop in almost absolute control of the institutions and the faithful of his diocese. It is true that several dioceses are usually united into a province presided over by an archbishop and that several bishops in an area do at times agree on common policies in public affairs, but the governing unit is the bishop and his diocese. Of course the supremacy of the bishop in his diocese is not peculiar to the United States; but it is peculiar to the United States that there is practically no direct relation between the civil and political divisions or governments and the diocesan limits. On the national scale the primatial see, Baltimore, has no real authority in other dioceses. Nor is the Apostolic Delegate, even when he acts

---

[4] I have chosen the word "disestablishment" because I think it best expresses the actual law. The phrase "separation of Church and State" was the more common phrase for the relationship during the nineteenth century but did not have the connotation of absolute separation given to it in some recent writings on the school question. Thomas Jefferson insisted on a "wall of separation" but the speeches of the Congressmen who framed the First Amendment imply a different intention. The word "separation" is not in the First Amendment. The best Catholic approach to the problem has been the essays of Father John Courtney Murray, S.J., in which he claims the purpose of the Constitution is the establishment of religious freedom and that the words "separation of Church and State" must be understood in that sense. Cf. his articles in *America*, LXXVI, 261-3 and 541-5 and LXXVIII, 627-9 and 683-6, and in *Theological Studies*, VI, 229-86. An older statement of great clarity is that of Dudley G. Wooten "Church and State in the United States" in *Catholic Builders of the Nation*, 5 vols. (Boston, 1923) I, 61-89. Note also Richard J. Gabel's *Public Funds for Church and Private Schools*, (Washington, 1937). James M. O'Neill, *Religion and Education under the Constitution* (New York, 1949) discusses the question of Federal aid to education and the relations of Church and State. Dean Anson Phelps Stokes, *Church and State in the United States*, contains much valuable material on the topic but this material is used to bolster his own belief in absolute separation instead of being edited objectively.

in the name of the Pope, in any sense the head of a national organization. In discussing American Catholicism, once the critic goes outside the general doctrines and practices of the Church, there is little uniformity in these dioceses or their bishops. Some of these bishops, such as Cardinal Samuel Stritch of Chicago, have prosperous dioceses, others like Bishop Bernard Espelage of Gallup, New Mexico, very poor ones; some like Archbishop Richard Cushing of Boston govern large Catholic populations in predominantly Catholic communities, others like Bishop Vincent Waters of Raleigh are endeavoring to shepherd a scattered flock where Catholics are few. Some bishops, like Cardinal Francis Spellman of New York are very active in public affairs, others confine themselves mostly to ecclesiastical functions. Some like Archbishop Robert Lucey of San Antonio are progressive in political and social ideas, others should be classified as conservative. The fact that they are uniformly devoted to the spiritual life of the Church in matters of essential faith and morals makes the contrasts among them in personal, social and even political matters quite evident to the close observer.

Historically speaking, during the nineteenth century there were a series of national synods and councils held in Baltimore[5] which decreed certain common practices about public services, clerical garb, and American customs, but there has been no national council for over sixty-five years. For many years after the latest Plenary Council of Baltimore, in 1884, there was an annual meeting of Archbishops and today there is an annual meeting of the hierarchy in Washington, but the decisions of these meetings are of counsel only. At the direction of the annual meeting of Archbishops in 1917 a National Catholic War Council, administered by a committee of bishops, attempted to unite the various Catholic war activities during World War I. In 1919, after the war,[6] there was formed at the suggestion of Pope Benedict XV the National Catholic Welfare Council for the unification of Catholic activity in the country. But even this in 1922 significantly changed its name at

---

[5] The best general accounts of these councils is Peter K. Guilday, *A History of the Councils of Baltimore*, (New York, 1932).

[6] The most authentic account of the formation of the National Catholic War Council is that by the late Archbishop Austin Dowling, "The National Catholic Welfare Conference" in *The American Ecclesiastical Review*, LXXIX, 337-54. The story of the action by which the Council became a conference is implied in the issues of the *N.C.W.C. Bulletin* in 1922, but the full story is not yet in print.

papal insistence to the National Catholic Welfare Conference and announced that its decisions were of counsel and not binding on the individual bishops. The National Catholic Welfare Conference functions in any diocese only where it has the sanction of the local bishop.

The same can be said of all other national organizations in comparable matters, even of the Catholic University of America in Washington, D. C. Catholic educational, scholarly or literary organizations, despite their support from colleges and seminaries in various parts of the country, have failed to attain great importance because of the lack of any organized national support. Likewise, despite the existence of the National Catholic Press Association and the Press Department of the N.C.W.C., there is no really national Catholic press. Only the Jesuit periodical, *America,* claims to be a national Catholic publication and that claim is based on a country-wide appeal and not on any national authority or official recognition.

Crossing the diocesan limits are many religious communities of priests, Brothers, or Sisters, such as the Jesuits, the Dominicans, the Franciscans, the Christian Brothers, the Sisters of Charity, and the like, but their religious institutions, even when belonging to orders exempt from direct episcopal control, are for practical purposes and in their relations with the Catholic world under diocesan supervision. Add to these diocesan divisions the fact that the Catholic population consists of widely differing national stocks and of all strata of society and one can easily understand the paradox, from the viewpoint of non-Catholics, of the practical unanimity of these same people on so many points of belief and moral practices.

Aside from the Catholic acceptance of the basic doctrines, such as are contained in the Baltimore Catechism,[7] the explanation for this uniformity lies in the quite uniform training of the Catholic clergy and, as a result of that training, in a uniform insistence by the individual bishops and their parochial clergy on the essential Catholic religious practices. There are, indeed, a variety of religious practices such as processions, novenas and congresses used to stimulate piety, but in these there is great liberty of choice so long as

---

[7] Although there are several editions of the Baltimore Catechism, they are essentially that published in Baltimore in 1885 under the title *A Catechism of Christian Doctrine, Prepared and Enjoined by order of the Third Council of Baltimore.*

there is in them fidelity to certain minimum requirements in re-vealed dogmas and basic moral principles. There are also some common qualities of American Catholicism which stem from the common rather than from the accidental qualities of Catholicism. One important quality found uniformly throughout American Catholic history has been an unyielding loyalty to the Pope. Like-wise, the generally practical character of American Catholicity, with insistence on the Sunday Mass, the recitation of the Rosary, the observance of Friday abstinence, and the like, while not connected with any national organization is an acknowledged characteristic of American Catholic life arising from this uniform training of the clergy. Some observers have claimed that this practical character of American Catholicism is the product of the puritanism dominant in American Protestantism. Some leaders of liturgical movements have been scornful of this simple but practical piety, yet the litur-gical movement of recent years has been acceptable to American Catholics only in so far as it is a development fully consonant with this practical character of the piety of most of the American faithful.

Contributing directly to this practical and parochial character of American Catholicism and its concentration on spiritual matters is the Catholic minority's acceptance of the disestablishment of reli-gion under the Constitution. The Catholic Church in the United States, unlike the churches throughout most of Europe, has no offi-cial political or civic function.[8] The President, the Governor of a State, or a mayor may choose to ask a clergyman to assist at a civic function, but the cleric has no right to do so by law. Cardinal Spellman in defending the rights of Catholic parochial schools spoke as a Cardinal and Archbishop but could not thereby exercise any civil authority. There have frequently been Catholic clergymen who have exercised political influence by reason of personal leader-ship, such as that exercised by Father Charles Coughlin in the early 1930's, or by reason of their spiritual authority in moral matters over the consciences of their subjects, as in the episcopal opposition to the laws about birth control information in Massachusetts. In some cases where political units have been coterminus with diocesan or parochial limits some clerical authority has been able to transpose personal spiritual power into a semblance of political authority but

---

[8] D. W. Brogan has brought out this lack of an establishment in the United States quite clearly in his article in *Harper's* mentioned above.

that authority, except in serious moral matters, has no binding power on the consciences of the individual Catholic.

The actual independence of the bishop in the United States arises almost as much from his independence in political and civil matters as from his spiritual supremacy. There is more than simple civil liberty in the independence of the Catholic bishop. This independence was made secure against lay interference nearly a hundred years ago in the notable controversies over trusteeism. For a brief time some laymen, chiefly trustees of church property, attempted to step into the gap left by the lack of state control and by disestablishment and claim rights to choose pastors and to control church property. But on the direction of the Pope and by the decision of the Councils of Baltimore, the ownership and control of Catholic church property in the United States has been vested in the individual bishop.

The individual bishop may be wise or he may be imprudent, his chief interest may be in establishing schools or he may be primarily interested in other phases of his pastoral work. The progress of the diocese will generally depend upon his decisions. Thus in estimating the present status of the Catholic Church in the United States, the British, French, or German travelers who visited only the larger cities or only the chief railway or air stations of the country have frequently been misled into faulty generalizations about American Catholicism because they generalized the conditions of a few cities. Outside of essential spiritual matters there is no notable basis for their generalizations. What may be true in social matters of the city diocese or the industrial diocese is frequently not true of the rural or agricultural diocese, and the German Catholics in the Middle West may hold the same attitudes on political matters as the Irish Catholics in the eastern dioceses but for entirely different reasons.

From the viewpoint of the historian it would be impolitic to try to estimate the character of each of the present 125 sees and their occupants. Nevertheless, abstracting from this basic fact of diocesan individualism in accidental matters and rigid uniformity in essential matters, certain incomplete generalizations can be made and some explanations can be given for situations that are puzzling to those who try to evaluate American Catholicism by European or non-Catholic American standards.

One must begin a study of American Catholic opinion with certain data that have little to do with either diocesan or organizational questions. The first fact that must be remembered is that the American Catholic minority is approximately eighty-five per cent urban,[9] that it has an even higher percentage of persons of non-English ancestry in its congregations, that about ninety per cent of those Catholics of English-speaking ancestry are of Irish origin or ancestry. Further, considering the urban concentration of American Catholics it is not surprising to find Catholics influential in political matters in the larger urban centers where numbers can be brought to bear through the ballot box, or that they have considerable influence in those labor organizations which thrive chiefly in urban surroundings. The work of the Catholic Trade Union Schools, for instance, has been chiefly to train up Catholic leadership among these workers. Neither is it surprising that along with millions of other urban workers the mass of Catholics have little economic security, but are dependent upon earned wages and that like all urban groups, despite Catholic doctrines on marriage and the family, they tend to die out. Some Catholics have risen from the ranks of the workers to positions of economic security in our urban groups, but most Catholic cultural and social leadership in the United States has come from the non-urban families who either now or a generation ago had the economic security more easily attained and maintained in non-urban America. There are also Catholics of wealth in the United States but they are not numerous in proportion to the Catholic population. This is very important in evaluating Catholic influence in those activities in which large funds are required. In those activities where generations of cultural pursuits are presupposed it is important to realize that the Catholic minority has not had many families with long traditions of American cultural leadership. In this connection it must be borne in mind that, with the exception of the early English Catholic group in

---

[9] The Census for Religious Bodies for 1946 was never published because Congress failed to make the necessary appropriation. The lack of religious statistics is embarrassing in any discussion of the relative membership of church bodies in the United States. The Catholic population in the United States has been variously estimated as from nineteen millions to thirty-five millions. The higher figure is based upon Catholic percentages in the armed forces during World War II. The figure given by the *Census of Religious Bodies,* 1936 (Washington, 1941) vol. 2, pt. 2, 528-9, is 19,914,937 of which 80.6 were classed as urban and 19.4 as rural. In *Catholic Rural Life Objectives* (Second Series, St. Paul, 1936) there are two notable essays on this topic: John F. Noll, "American Catholics in Agriculture," pp. 7-18, and O. E. Baker, "Will More or Fewer People Live on the Land?", pp. 57-71.

Maryland, the Germans exiled during the Kulturkampf, and the recent refugees from Nazism and Communism, most Catholics in the United States have come to this country for economic reasons, fleeing from peasantry and poverty in Europe. Most of them, by reason of their lower economic status in Europe, were not learned in the culture of their fatherlands, and this fact coupled in so many cases with the handicap of learning a new language and new cultural traditions has kept them from high cultural attainments during their first generations in this country. Generally, however, these handicaps have deepened their loyalty to the Church and to the Catholic clergy who have been sympathetic with their economic and social problems and anxious to protect them in the process of Americanization.

The process of Americanization, nevertheless, has been generally so prompt as to arouse criticism from European Catholics and from American clergymen of European origin who fear the influence of a culture so dominantly non-Catholic as that of the United States. Such leaders as Archbishop Ireland and Cardinal Gibbons, who favored rather giving Europe American ideas, as early as the 1890's[10] won the battle against any attempt to make European nationalism permanent in American Catholic life. Actually the more important factors drawing the Catholic immigrant toward Americanization have been the freedom of the new citizen and the abundance of material wealth, particularly in the comparatively high wages of the American worker. The Catholic immigrant has usually joined the local political group that welcomed him first, and has cooperated socially with the first group that recognized him as an American. But in religious matters he has remained faithful to the same type of parochial and diocesan organization he had known in the old country and now found also in the Church in America. Sometimes these foreign groups have formed enclaves in the larger diocesan group, even at times forming separate national churches, but eventually as the younger members became English-speaking these national divisions have tended to disappear in the general diocesan order. It is an observable fact, however, that the children of the immigrants are frequently more vocal than their parents in

---

[10] Allen S. Will, *Life of Cardinal Gibbons*, 2 vols. (New York, 1922), I, 497-516, gives an account of this controversy over national churches and Americanization. The life of Cardinal Gibbons by Father John T. Ellis had not appeared when this was written.

expressing ancestral national prejudices in public affairs because they feel more secure as Americans against charges of being aliens.

Aside from these observable general truths, in practically every diocese a definite diocesan church pattern has developed according to the executive ability of the individual bishop and the material wealth of his flock. Freed from political and civil attachments, the American bishop has been able to concentrate on the essential spiritual needs of his diocese. Churches and chapels, some frame, some red brick, some magnificent gothic and romanesque buildings, have sprung up over the country. Parish schools taught by religious Sisters and Brothers have been attached to these churches, at least where the number of Catholics attending a church and the available resources have made them practical. In some of the larger cities where the large number of Catholics is out of proportion to their wealth and in rural communities where Catholics are scarce, these schools have not always been established. In the Middle West and in some other localities there are central Catholic high schools offering Catholic religious education to those within reach. There are also many Catholic academies scattered throughout the country maintained by religious communities where the clientele is a bit more select, and where the support is obtained directly from the pupils. Diocesan charity organizations seek to coordinate the aid to the poor and the unfortunate. Homes for children exist in nearly every Catholic diocese and Catholic hospitals and homes for the infirm and the aged have been set up in considerable number. In Chicago, New York and many other urban centers church youth organizations and social centers for adults have been attempted. The theme of all this effort is to bring the Catholic Faith and the Sacraments to every Catholic child, and religious comfort to the unfortunate. The value of this investment in physical properties alone is enormous, and leads occasionally to sly remarks in the press about the wealth of the Church, but it is not mobile wealth; in fact, the maintenance cost is enormous—at times making beggars of the clergy in charge.

The very fact that in this diocesan setup all the energy and wealth is consumed in local charitable and religious effort has been criticized. Nevertheless, the critic who fails to observe the great moral force in the nation exerted by this concentration of free religious energy through these activities misses the greatest contribution of the Catholic Church to the nation. One might even say that this spiritual and moral ministration is the chief work so far of the

Catholic Church in the United States. It has kept millions of American citizens going to church regularly and kept them instructed in Christian doctrine and morals. The major handicap in this work, in a country boasting disestablishment, is financial. Perhaps too much money has been spent on some church building or spent unwisely, but had this wasted money been spent on less expensive structure or spent with less waste, the material wealth of Catholics could scarcely provide many more of these religious institutions or create a stronger moral force.

The critic looking for proportionate Catholic influence in politics or society has been disappointed. The influence in public affairs of this investment in church institutions is generally slight, at least directly, except that the Americanization process adopted by the bishops, particularly in the parochial schools, has added a simple insistence on loyalty to the country to the spiritual ministrations of the Catholic Church and school. Unfortunately, also, the bishops after this effort have had practically no funds left for higher education or for social and cultural endeavors which would give the Catholic Church the civic leadership expected by many of her critics. At the same time the abstinence of the Catholic clergy themselves from political and social effort has further handicapped the production of Catholic civic leadership among the laity by creating a notion that Catholicism cannot cooperate in such public affairs.

In the absence of a national organization or a real national university, leadership in the Catholic Church in the United States has for the most part devolved upon the individual bishop. There have been few bishops with the flair for civic leadership possessed by Archbishop Ireland or Cardinal Gibbons; and the Catholic bishop who has attempted to be partisan in political matters is a rare exception. Generally speaking, the personal politics of American bishops and priests has been mostly the politics of their individual parents or family, and in public most Catholic clergymen have adhered to the American policy of disestablishment so completely as to express no party preference. So also the participation in public and social enterprise by Catholic clergymen has depended individually upon the personality of the bishop or priest, and the fear of appearing to direct non-religious enterprises has been a strongly restraining factor.

As a part of the diocesan organization in this country, at one

369

time nearly every bishop endeavored to maintain his own seminary for the training of priests and, where possible, a diocesan college for the same purpose. Most of these diocesan colleges have proved too costly and have disappeared or have been taken over by religious communities. Among the Catholic colleges for men the most numerous are those operated in large cities where a concentrated Catholic population makes attendance easier. The chief exceptions are the boarding colleges of Notre Dame conducted by the Fathers of Holy Cross, Providence College by the Dominicans, Georgetown and Holy Cross by the Jesuits, and Villanova by the Augustinians. In recent decades many colleges for women have been maintained by communities of Sisters. Catholic medical schools are not numerous because of the great expense involved in furnishing the technical equipment, but there are a few Catholic law schools. Although several Catholic colleges are designated as universities, the most important graduate work so far has been done at the Catholic University, Notre Dame, St. Louis and Fordham. But here again the financial burden of graduate work has been forbidding in many fields. With the exception of the Catholic University these colleges and universities have little or no connection with diocesan activities and have no national plans. Consequently, each institution goes more or less each its own way, doing the best it can for its own students and hoping to produce the much-needed Catholic leadership. These colleges and universities have not yet risen to the point in facilities where they can handle all the aspiring Catholic leaders, and a high percentage of Catholics who have achieved political or civic prominence have had very little training in Catholic institutions. Of the younger Catholic men of prominence there is a growing number of Catholic college graduates, although it is scarcely possible that the limited facilities of Catholic institutions of higher education will ever be able to care for a proper percentage of scholars in the Catholic population.

Under these conditions Catholic leadership in the United States has been scattered and without plan. Some general leadership such as that of Cardinal Spellman of New York, Archbishop Cushing of Boston, Archbishop Lucey of San Antonio, Bishop Francis Haas of Grand Rapids, and Bishop John Francis Noll of Fort Wayne is attributable to their own zeal and sense of public service. The same can be said of the leadership of such Catholic laymen as former Postmaster General Frank Walker, Joseph Scott, Carlton J. Hayes,

James Farley, Thomas Braniff, Joseph Kennedy and other Catholic laymen prominent in the political or business world; their leadership, beyond official position, has come from individual effort. The Catholic colleges, unable financially to give their faculties leisure for research and travel, have not furnished many leaders either in research or in education. American Catholics are proud of Msgr. John A. Ryan and of Governor Alfred E. Smith but they have not provided a philosopher of the calibre of Jacques Maritain, a theologian like Father Jean Danielou, or a historian like Christopher Dawson. In industrial and technical fields a few Catholics have achieved prominence, but few Catholics are found in those families which have traditionally dominated the financial and commercial concerns of the country. In the field of literature and the fine arts there have been a few Catholics of prominence but there can scarcely be said to be an American Catholic literature or school of fine arts. There are many Catholics working in the secular press but there is really no national Catholic Press. There are numerous diocesan papers some of which have a limited circulation outside the diocese but most of them serve chiefly as bulletin boards for diocesan decrees and for records of diocesan social activity. Some, such as the *Brooklyn Tablet,* the *Los Angeles Tidings,* and the Chicago *New World,* achieve some importance by reason of their editorials. The national editions of *Our Sunday Visitor* and the *Denver Register* lack this editorial quality. The late daily *Sun Herald* of Kansas City was a quixotic effort, a delicate flower wasting its fragrance on desert air. Scarcely any one of these papers could demand support by virtue of its literary excellence or its strong editorial opinion. Attempts to establish a national Catholic daily have been futile, chiefly because there is no national Catholic opinion on most public questions. *America* and *Commonweal,* the latter edited by laymen, attempt to view the national picture from a Catholic viewpoint, but in the divided status of Catholic political and social opinion they can express little more than the opinion of their editorial councils. The monthly magazines, such as *The Catholic World, Sign* and *The American Ecclesiastical Review,* cater to a limited clientele. Most of the other Catholic periodicals are devotional or attached to mission interests. Of the scholarly publications, the *Review of Politics, Thought,* and the *Thomist* have attained the best support but none has a circulation proportionate to the Catholic population of the country.

The question arises naturally, considering this absence of national organization, as to how Catholics can hope to do their share in the great crisis of the present day. American Catholics have always furnished their share of soldiers and sailors in the armed services in time of war, but have not been represented in the policy making groups. European Catholics accepting American leadership in world affairs look for Catholics to do their share; the American non-Catholics likewise expect a leadership proportionate to the Catholic population. American Catholics themselves, in their embarrassment over the lack of a strong national Catholic opinion on public affairs, have tended to underestimate the present contribution of the Catholic body to the national welfare.

The first phase of national Catholic activity must be the existing fidelity of the Church to her great spiritual work, despite the unromantic and parochial quality of that work. This is perhaps the strongest contribution it or any other religious institution can make against that secularism and materialism which is the forerunner of communism and national decay. In other fields of religious activity this work with the lower classes must continue. Diocesan organizations would miss the point of the great conflict with communism if they slackened in their zeal for the spiritual and material welfare of the poorer classes and the urban workers to pursue the more spectacular or softer work among social and political leaders. The formative years of the Catholic minority are passed. The early problems of Americanization and of the erection of the physical plant are nearly solved. Continued fidelity of the diocesan organizations to their work will, without doubt, eventually produce leadership on the higher level. In early periods of the Church in the United States whenever one group of immigrants was ready to achieve higher standards, the Catholic group has been burdened with newer immigrations of impoverished Catholics. The recent refugees from Europe are not so numerous as to cause a new decline and a more rapid progress can be expected. Nevertheless, that is not the only handicap hindering the efforts of Catholic people to rise to new heights in public service: it is not so easy today for the poor or less privileged to rise in the economic and social scale. Conditions, however, are not yet static, and properly organized effort and sacrifice towards the higher ideals can be fruitful. There are now thousands more Catholic men and women on the college and university level. These as individuals are already beginning to be noticeable in public life. For the rest, the hope lies in the few functioning Catholic organizations which can claim supra-diocesan character.

About the only national lay organization is the Knights of Columbus, with its 700,000 members. It is largely a social and an insurance society. While the Knights have fostered several worthwhile projects in some dioceses they have missed the point of the diocesan organization of the Church.[11] In the beginning of World War I and in several apologetical adventures the Knights have begun movements which have been national in scope, but they have had to yield their leadership to clerical organizations. Outside of the N.C.W.C., the chief Catholic organization claiming to be national is the National Catholic Educational Association.[12] Even though it has lost much of the brilliant leadership that characterized its earlier years it is a potent public organization. The Association has great influence over the teaching communities and diocesan directors of schools and has been a great aid in meeting advanced technical standards. While its regulations are only counsels, its membership is representative of all sections of the country and all kinds of Catholic cultural activity. Yet it has not concerned itself with public affairs, national or international, except where education is directly concerned. The Catholic Theological Association, the Catholic Philosophical Association, the Catholic Historical Association, the Catholic Library Association, the Canon Law Society, and the Catholic Hospital Association do not have nationally representative membership but have done much to foster high ideals in American Catholic colleges and university faculties. The Catholic University of America,[13] as its name implies, was intended to be a national institution, beginning first with a theological graduate school. It has not been successful in either aim because of the opposition of some of the bishops who wished to establish their own

---

[11] There is no satisfactory account of this Catholic lay organization which has attempted some national action in the World Wars and in combating the extremes of anti-Catholic propaganda. Rev. Arthur J. Riley has been appointed official historian to prepare an authoritative history of the Order.

[12] The story of the foundation and the early activities of the Catholic Educational Association is to be found in the annual *Bulletin of the National Catholic Educational Association,* 1904.

[13] John T. Ellis, *The Formative Years of the Catholic University of America* (Washington, 1946), has given the circumstances of the formation of this University.

theological schools and because of the controversies over nationalism which afflicted its early years and alienated much support. In those departments of the University where funds have been available the Washington institution has achieved real scholarship, but so long as the support of the University is diocesan the future of the University is dependent upon the support of the bishops; and that has not been sufficient either in finances or in students and faculty to make it a strong institution.

The void left by the lack of a great Catholic university has in many respects been filled by the National Catholic Welfare Conference.[14] Formed originally to meet the national Catholic problems resulting from World War I and to guide Catholics in the reconstruction after that war, the Conference has been the chief national force in American Catholicism even when directly opposed by some of the bishops. The executive committee, ordinarily headed by an Archbishop, is elected by the bishops at their annual meeting, and its individual officers may not hold office permanently. The pastorals and statements issued in its name come closest to being an official statement of the American Catholic hierarchy. But by constitutional limitations its decrees, except in so far as they are restatements of papal or conciliar definitions, are only of counsel to the individual bishops. These pastorals are now issued each year and the frequency has tended to lessen their importance. Yet the pastoral of 1919 dealing with the reconstruction of the social order, the pastoral of 1940 on the Church and the social order with an advanced statement of the same problem after the depression, and the pastoral of 1947 on Secularism, stand out as important documents pointing the way for Catholic national leadership, and they have had weighty influence on the Church throughout the country.

Beneath the executive committee in the N.C.W.C. are various departments which have carried on much of the research and leadership that might have been expected from the universities. The most notable of these departments were the Social Action Department and the Press Department. Under the directors of the Social Action Department and under the leadership of Fathers John A. Ryan, Raymond A. McGowan, John S. Cronin, and George G. Higgins, the pastoral of 1919 and the Social Encyclicals of Popes

---

[14] The most official source for the activities of the N.C.W.C. and of the annual letters of the hierarchy is in the periodical *Catholic Action* (1930-   ) formerly *The N.C.W.C. Bulletin* (1919-1929).

Leo XIII, Pius XI and Pius XII have been carried to the Catholic people, and Americanization work has been supervised and fostered among Catholic immigrants. By establishing a school for social workers, by promoting conferences between labor and business, by articles in the press and by lectures, this department has, besides its extensive social work, to a great extent offset the lack of strong graduate departments of economics in Catholic universities. The Department of the Press has never had any real power over the diocesan weeklies, but by setting up the N.C.W.C. Press Service, it has furnished reliable Catholic news to these papers and fostered a higher ideal in content and format. The Department of Education did yeoman service after World War I in urging Catholic youth to go through high school and to enter college, and under Monsignor Frederick J. Hochwalt it is very active in defending the rights of the Catholic parochial school and in promoting high standards in Catholic education. The Legal Department has labored most faithfully in supplying the Federal Government with information on legal topics in which religion is concerned and in supplying to bishops and parochial schools the legal advice necessary to protect their rights. But its activities have had to be negative because of the Catholic acceptance of disestablishment.

This national work of the N.C.W.C., limited as it may be, completes the picture of the Catholic minority in the United States. As has been pointed out, this minority has lacked any consistent public policy in political and civic matters because it has accepted constitutional disestablishment of religion and has placed its religious leadership in diocesan organization. Only on such issues as atheistic communism and secularism, which touch the basic faith and practice common to all Catholics, can there be said to be national Catholic unity in public affairs. The strong moral power in the Catholic minority and the practical qualities of American Catholicism are the direct products of the freedom of the American bishops to concentrate on the spiritual welfare of their flocks. Yet the prevailing use of the material wealth in building churches and elementary schools and in Catholic charitable and social institutions has limited and handicapped the formation of Catholic universities and a strong Catholic press. At the same time the abstinence of the bishops from the field of politics has made the neglect of the universities and the press more evident. There is no clear statement of an American Catholic opinion on world politics or even on the ethical aspects of American foreign policy. This is not as bad as it might seem. The practical character of American Catholicism and its concentration on the religious welfare of the ordinary citizen are sound American traditions as well as sound Catholic doctrine.

The growth of Catholic colleges, the development of research in Catholic universities, has begun already to give the solid religious faith of the Catholic multitude a small voice which must eventually be more representative of more than thirty millions of practicing Catholics. Whether that voice will ever try to dictate to its non-Catholic brethren is a question occasionally expressed in the non-Catholic press. There is no better evidence that American Catholics have no real desire to dictate to their non-Catholic brethren than their concentration on diocesan and parochial services. There is, however, a desire among many Catholics to have a proportionate share in determining American public opinion. The acceptance of disestablishment does not in any way disfranchise Catholics or bar them from a full practice of their Catholic faith. Neither should it prevent them from leadership in American public life. So long as the Catholic voice in public affairs is faithful to the present principles of American Catholic faith and practice, Catholic public leadership will always be welcomed by the freedom loving American people, and such a Catholic voice will give a welcome tone to the Voice of America among the common people of the whole world.

XV

The Catholic Church and the American Social Question

by Aaron I. Abell

"The ending of the Great War has brought peace. But the only safeguard of peace is social justice and a contented people." These simple statements in the "Foreword" to the famous Bishops' Program of Social Reconstruction, issued in February, 1919, struck a new note in the social teachings of the Catholic Church in America, namely, the realization—still faint perhaps—that the maintenance of world peace was becoming a great Christian problem in the solution of which social reform must play a conspicuous part. Alertly-minded Catholics have more and more realized, especially in the two decades of world-wide depression, international anarchy and global war after 1930, that efforts in behalf of social justice and world peace must go hand in hand. This conviction is voiced, either expressly or by implication, in the many weighty pronouncements of the American Bishops on the social question since World War I. The bearing of movements for social betterment on the cause of international peace has been thoroughly explored by the Catholic Association for International Peace which was formed in 1927 by persons vitally interested in the Catholic social movement as well as in a juridically directed system of world organization.

World peace has been, however, only one, and not the most important, motivating factor in the American Catholic social movement.[1] The evils of the industrial system, notably the vast dispari-

---

[1] The literature on the American Catholic social movement, though still scanty, is growing. Several monographs have exhaustively treated significant aspects of the subject which is also touched upon in numerous biographies and scholarly articles. In three articles the author has discussed the general nature and scope of the movement to 1920: "The Reception of Leo XIII's Labor Encyclical in America, 1891-1919," *Review of Politics*, VII (October, 1945),

ties in personal incomes, the tyranny and arrogance of employers in their dealings with employees and consumers and the violence and potential subversiveness of the armies of labor,—these are the basic and inner factors that account for the Church's effort in the United States as elsewhere to apply its age-old principles of justice and charity to the economic and social order. By far the most impelling of the external factors influencing the Church has been the impact of the American environment which as a form of nationality and a way of life has confronted the Catholic Church with a new and unique experience. In order to survive and to prosper the Catholic Church in both its lay and clerical manifestations discerned at the outset that it must understand and esteem the ideals of American nationality and harmonize its working forces with these ideals. From the days of Bishop John Carroll in the early Republic to the present, the Church authorities have been at great pains to avoid prolonged and irreconcilable conflicts between Catholic opinion and American traditions and customs. Though Catholics have objected to some of the applications of the American religio-political system, in education notably, they have warmly approved the system itself, including the principle of religious liberty as a natural civil right— though not of course as a natural right in the strictly moral sense. This American Catholic attitude was called prominently to the world's attention by Alexis de Tocqueville whose *Democracy in America*, written in the early 1830's, is unsurpassed as a commentary on American institutions in their early making. The Catholic de Tocqueville was amazed to find that the million American Catholics of that day were the most republican and democratic element in the country's population and at the same time, of all Catholics in the world, the most loyal and obedient to the Church. He could find no ecclesiastics—he conversed with all the leading ones—who did not believe fervently in the principle of separation of church and state and attribute the prosperity and growing influence of the Church to religious liberty.[2]

Two factors served to strengthen Catholic support of this type of political liberalism after 1840: the influx of converts from the

---

464-495; "Origins of Catholic Social Reform in the United States: Ideological Aspects, *ibid.*, XI (July, 1949), 294-309; "The Catholic Church and Social Problems in the World War I Era," *Mid-America*, XXX (July, 1948), 139-151.

[2] *Democracy in America*, edited by Phillips Bradley (New York, 1945,), I, pp. 300-302.

country's social and intellectual elite and the rise of a nativist movement directed against the inroad of immigrants whose evil deeds
and shortcomings were attributed to the alleged un-Christian, anti-
republican and morally debasing influence of "Popery," the religion
of nearly all the Irish and of a good part of the German newcomers. In order to enhance the power of the first factor and to check
that of the second one, leading Catholics in the quarter century
after 1845 elaborated a theory of political and social liberalism. The
two most noted theorists were converts, the philosopher Orestes A.
Brownson and the missionary Isaac T. Hecker. Life-long friends,
Brownson and Hecker entered the Church in 1844, sobered but not
disillusioned by their active careers amid the social and intellectual
upheavals of the day. Among other things, Brownson had been one
of the major architects of the Transcendentalist philosophy on its
social side and "Isaac the Seeker" was deeply and incurably affected
by that upsurge in American thought. Both men harbored the conviction that the claims of the Catholic Church, if properly presented,
must be irresistible to the great body of Americans, however diverse
their religious and social backgrounds. The conversion of America
to Catholicism was the romance and passion of Hecker's life. Year
in and year out he demonstrated that the Catholic faith met all
the needs of the soul, was grounded on reason, made room for the
natural virtues of the robust American and accepted and guaranteed the cherished American liberties, including religious liberty.
In the course of probing American civilization in all its aspects,
Brownson defended religious liberty repeatedly and at length, con-
cluding that separation of church and state need not and in fact
did not imply religious indifference or mitigate against the claim of
the Catholic Church to be the one and the only true church of
Christ. Religious liberty as a full civil right was applicable, he contended, not only to the United States but to the whole Catholic
world, in principle if not everywhere and immediately in practice.

In the very nature of the case, devotion to religious liberty has
been the test of American Catholic patriotism, on which Catholics
have relied to disarm opposition and to win converts in appreciable
numbers. To be sure, the Church at no time naively depended, for
protection and progress, upon patriotism alone; it was obliged of
necessity in an age of advancing industrialism to pay special attention to the moral and temporal needs of the urban poor, mostly
immigrants, who made up the great bulk of its membership. Even

379

so, the Church's charity and social service have been inspired in no small degree by the core idea of Americanism, namely, to win recruits from the non-Catholic population and to make Catholicism an integral and vitally important factor in American civilization. As an Americanizer preoccupied with the religious condition of the cultivated classes, Brownson believed that religious welfare work among immigrants would indirectly result in accessions from the native stock. Thus he pointed out in 1857, when Catholic social work was still in its infancy, that "the proper training of Catholic children, the correction of the vice of intemperance, and other immoralities, prevalent in a portion of our Catholic population . . . would do more for the conversion of non-Catholics than all the books and reviews we can write, all the journals we can edit, or efforts we can make expressly for their conversion, for it would prove to them, what they now doubt, the practical moral efficiency of our religion. We must provide first for our own spiritual wants," he continued, "get our population all right, and then we may turn our attention with confidence and success to those who are without."[3]

In this spirit of uniting missionary endeavor and Americanization, Catholics launched during the third quarter of the century a crusade for urban welfare, the beneficent results of which helped to save many from physical extermination as well as from spiritual and moral ruin. The varied efforts in behalf of neglected children and the victims of the drink curse yielded perhaps the most satisfying results.[4] In the development of Catholic charities, which noticeably softened the old animosities toward the Church, Father Hecker and his fellow priests in the Congregation of St. Paul the Apostle played a conspicuous if not a decisive part. Hecker's views, now apparently vindicated, deeply influenced the new generation of Catholic leaders—priests, laymen and a coterie of eminent prelates, among them James Cardinal Gibbons of Baltimore and Archbishop John Ireland of St. Paul. Fully alive to the insidious and subtle character of the period's irreligion, these men rather than attempting

[3] "Aspirations of Nature," *Brownson's Quarterly Review*, New York Series, II (October, 1857), pp. 495-496.

[4] Richard H. Clarke, "Catholic Protectories and Reformatories," *American Catholic Quarterly Review*, XX (July, 1895), pp. 607-640; James J. Green, "The Organization of the Catholic Total Abstinence Union in America, 1866-1884," American Catholic Historical Society of Philadelphia, *Records*, LXI (June, 1950), pp. 71-97.

to isolate Catholics from the deadly plague urged them to overcome the enemy by applying the Church's teachings to the difficult problems of the age.

The seeming success of the Americanization policy, extended to all phases of the nation's and the Church's life after 1880, served to precipitate a crisis in world Catholicism. The growing number of European Catholics, wishing to put the Church on the side of democracy and modern progress, pointed to America as an object-lesson. Toward the end of the century they unwisely made of the Reverend Walter Elliott's *Life of Father Hecker* an instrument of their propaganda, for anti-Americanists in Europe argued plausibly that Father Hecker was not the saint his followers claimed him to be but a heretic and that the spread of his teachings would destroy the Church. After the controversy had raged for months with mounting bitterness and fury Pope Leo XIII early in 1899 condemned the obvious heresies allegedly contained in the Hecker biography, in a letter *Testem Benevolentiae* to Cardinal Gibbons.[5] Although the condemnation ended the attempt to Americanize the Universal Church, it did not retard but rather accelerated the Catholic social movement in the United States.

The core idea in Americanism has also, to a degree, guided the Church in its dealings with the problems of industry and labor. In the United States the Catholic population, until recently almost wholly a wage-earning group, kept pace numerically with the progress of the economic revolution which transformed the country after the Civil War from a predominantly agricultural to a predominantly industrial one. Restive under the restraints and hardships imposed by triumphant capitalism, Catholic workers sympathized with radical labor movements and frequently participated in their violent manifestations. From the outset they constituted a good half of the trade union membership and furnished much of its leadership. In the face of some opposition and much suspicion on the part of the clergy, the loyalty of Catholic workers to the labor movement continued unimpaired. At least one distinguished prelate, James Roosevelt Bayley, Archbishop of Baltimore, wished to suppress the movement, publicly endorsing in 1874 the recently founded Irish Catholic Benevolent Union because it "extends itself and exerts

---

[5] Thomas T. McAvoy, C.S.C., "Americanism, Fact and Fiction," *Catholic Historical Review*, XXXI (July, 1945), pp. 133-153; Vincent F. Holden, C.S.P., "A Myth in 'L'Americanisme'," *ibid.*, pp. 154-170.

a proper influence guarding . . . from what is worse than secret societies—that is, the miserable associations called labor organizations. Their idea is communistic," he opined, "and no Catholic with any idea of the spirit of his religion will encourage them." Labor unions had done more harm than good, he thought, and it had become a question "not of opposition to capital, but to government itself."[6] Catholic workingmen did not view the matter in this light and Bayley exerted no influence upon them except possibly to confirm the apprehension of many of them that their religious leaders were on the side of capital. With few exceptions the Catholic newspapers ignored the Archbishop's warnings and continued to report favorably the activities of organized labor. The Boston *Pilot,* rather than Bayley, accurately reflected Catholic opinion when it insisted that "strikes are necessary for the protection of the laboring class" and that organized labor should force employers to relinquish some of their tyrannical powers, notably the power arbitrarily to discharge workers.[7]

Many Catholic spokesmen, while recognizing that workingmen must organize in order to survive, feared that even non-socialist trade unions would wean Catholic members away from their faith, and for this reason as well as for others urged them after 1875 to become farmers on the rapidly disappearing frontier.[8] Earlier the Catholic jurist T. Wharton Collens, who with Jesse H. Jones and other Protestants organized the Christian Labor Union to win religious support for the labor movement, suggested that the Catholic solution of the labor question might be communities modeled on the historic Paraguay Missions.[9] But in the crisis which followed the two condemnations of the Knights of Labor by Rome at the instance of the Archbishop of Quebec, the American hierarchy all

---

[6] *Pilot,* October 31, 1874. For similar views, urging missionary and charitable effort as a means of counteracting "tyrannical" trade unions, see Rt. Rev. Francis S. Chatard, "Catholic Societies," *American Catholic Quarterly Review,* IV (April, 1879), pp. 212-221 and John Gilmary Shea, "The Rapid Increase of the Dangerous Classes in the United States," *ibid.,* pp. 240-268.

[7] "Strikes and Their Results," February 28, 1880; "The Power of Discharge Must Be Taken from Employers," *ibid.,* July 3, 1880.

[8] Bishop John Lancaster Spalding, *The Religious Mission of the Irish Race and the Catholic Colonization* (New York, 1880), p. 205; M. F. S., "The Labor Question," *American Catholic Quarterly Review,* III (October, 1878), pp. 721-746.

[9] "Views of the Labor Movement," *Catholic World,* X (March, 1870), pp. 784-798.

but unanimously supported Cardinal Gibbons in his successful efforts in 1887 to secure a suspension of the unhappy ruling.[10] Once dubious bishops now favored trade unionism in order to counteract the widely current assumption that the official Church was unfriendly to the poor. Much of the distrust of the Church in labor circles stemmed from the penalties imposed on Father Edward McGlynn by his religious superior, Michael A. Corrigan, Archbishop of New York. An ardent believer in the justice of Henry George's crusade for the confiscation of land rents, McGlynn with a large Catholic following supported the reformer in his campaign for the mayoralty of New York in 1886. When called to account for his alleged communism, he refused to disavow his "anti-poverty" views, whereupon he was suspended from the exercise of his priestly functions and finally excommunicated.[11]

As an alternative to McGlynn's economic radicalism trade unionism gained in favor among the more conservative Catholics. They did not succeed, however, in putting an end to Father McGlynn's agitation. Partly for prudential reasons and partly because McGlynn toned down his statements, Monsignor Francis Satolli, the Pope's representative, lifted the sentence of excommunication in 1893, asserting "there is nothing" in his opinion "contrary to the faith and teachings of the Church." When McGlynn passed from the scene at the turn of the century, numerous Catholics with a few insurgent priests at their head turned to socialism, which was now taking on the character of an aggressive, well-organized movement. The Catholic press of the period carried many letters and communications from Catholics who could see no wrong, only good, in socialism. This suggests the continuing presence of economic radicalism in the Catholic body. The role of Catholics in politics points to the same conclusion. With one or two exceptions the Catholic press supported the populist Bryan against the conservative McKinley in the so-called campaign of education in 1896—a campaign of education with fifteen million dollars, as Bishop Spalding caustically observed. The era of reform preceding World War I found most Catholics on the side of radical Progressivism as represented by

---

[10] Henry J. Browne, *The Catholic Church and the Knights of Labor* (Washington, D.C., 1949), p. 242.

[11] For an excellent discussion of the McGlynn-Corrigan conflict to 1889, see James J. Green, "First Impact of the Henry George Agitation on Catholics in the United States," a master's essay at the University of Notre Dame, 1948.

Bryan, Roosevelt and Wilson. More recently they have been the backbone of successive New Deal administrations.

Until recent years the attitude of the Church on the labor question assumed an apparently negative form which may be defined as ecclesiastico-social liberalism. Until well into the twentieth century the Church as such was not called upon to initiate measures for social justice; Catholics, still mostly workingmen, needed no stimulus from their religious guides. Rather the role of the Church was to caution, to restrain and to inculcate right principles while leaving their application to Catholics themselves. Though the church authorities were alive to the dangers to faith in the labor movement, they were, for the most part, confident that they could keep it under control, if only they could convince the workers that the Church opposed the excesses of the movement but not the movement itself. In his famous letter that persuaded Rome to lift its condemnation of the Knights of Labor, Cardinal Gibbons counseled ecclesiastical authority "to acknowledge frankly what is true and just" in the cause of workers "in order to deter them from what is false and criminal, and thus to turn into a legitimate, peaceable and beneficent contest what might easily, by a course of repulsive severity, become for the masses of our people a dread volcanic force like unto that which society fears and the Church deplores in Europe." In this spirit the Church in America seemed content so long as atheism and revolutionary socialism were kept in check. Leading Catholics learned to refrain from any word or deed which might conceivably be interpreted as unfriendly to the cause of labor; the occasional layman or cleric who acted differently was promptly repudiated. The same fate was meted out to the few persons who dared suggest that American Catholics follow the example of Catholics in continental Europe and French Canada by organizing Catholic trade unions apart from the regular ones. Such a course, it was strongly argued, would divide the labor movement and in the end deliver it into the hands of the irreligious socialists. The conclusion seems warranted that the Catholic Church in the United States by its sympathy for a labor movement aiming at legitimate ends through not improper means and by refraining from any demand directly to lead the movement, displayed an economic liberalism unique in the history of organized religions.

To this result the theory of Americanism measurably contributed. The church authorities feared a dangerous revival of popular persecution if they interfered unduly with the liberty of Catholics to participate in social reform movements. Gibbons was well aware of this fact, pointing out in his letter defending the liberty of Catholics to join the Knights of Labor that the "accusation of being un-American—that is to say, alien to our national spirit—is the most powerful weapon which the enemies of the Church can employ against her." Considerations such as these defeated the efforts of Archbishop Corrigan to have Henry George's *Progress and Poverty* placed on the Index of Prohibited Books and secured Father McGlynn's restoration. The charges against Father McGlynn, "as they are understood by the American people," the Brooklyn priest, Sylvester Malone, wrote Leo XIII in 1886, "raise the question of the right of the citizens to express his views on all questions that are non-essential" (not involving faith and morals).[12] Cardinal Gibbons explained with his usual insight that the Church's teachings on socialism and private property were not directly involved in the controversy and that the fate of the single tax must rest with the whole people judging its expediency and justice as freely as any other public policy. To forbid Catholics to participate in the discussion and decision, wrote the *Catholic Standard* of Philadelphia, would be to acknowledge "the truth of the accusation of our enemies that Catholics are not and cannot be truly loyal to the civil authorities of their country."[13]

If Americanism meant liberty for Catholics in the social movement, the doctrine also lent itself to the cause of conservatism and restraint. Thus Archbishop Ireland in justifying his open denunciation of the Pullman strike of 1894 reminded Gibbons that the Church "must be kept before the American people as the great prop of social order and law—all the more so that Catholics are numerous in strikes and riots. Socialistic ideas have gone into our people," he complained, "and into many of our priests. We have been siding with labor in its grievances; the unthinking ones transgress the golden mean, and rush into war against property."[14] Ireland fully believed that immigrant workingmen were naturally law-abiding, but being only half-Americanized could not distinguish between liberty and

---

[12] Sylvester L. Malone (Ed.), *Memorial of the Golden Jubilee of the Reverend Sylvester Malone* (Brooklyn, 1895), pp. 61-62.

[13] Quoted in the single-tax organ, *The Standard*, December 21, 1891.

[14] Ireland to Gibbons, July 21, 1894, Baltimore Cathedral Archives, 93 J 4, ALS 4 p.

license and were easily led into evil ways by designing demagogues who cared nothing for the welfare of the country and its working people. One remedy was to revive that genuine Catholic patriotism which originated in Maryland and had always centered in the great Archbishopric of Baltimore. Ireland ceaselessly preached the economic virtues—thrift, temperance, education—urging Catholics to make the best of their opportunities to acquire property and social standing. His advice was not unheeded by the millions who fell under the spell of his magnetic influence.

Ireland's social philosophy, really a Catholic version of the Old Puritan individualism, mirrored, no doubt, the needs and aspirations of a large part of the Catholic body. But no form of social liberalism, it was increasingly realized, could fully solve the Church's problems in the twentieth century. If the hands-off policy had not entirely outlived its usefulness, it needed to be supplemented by a greater degree of positive teaching and organization under the direct supervision of the Church for social justice and related ends. Only as the Church made social action an integral part of its religious mission could it deal adequately with the situation presented by the enlarging number of wealthy Catholics and overcome their natural resistance to the demands of the poor for better living conditions. As for the workers themselves, now promised an earthly paradise by organized socialism, they needed to be shown the Christian alternatives in the way of effective and permissible programs of social reform and encouraged to strive for their attainment. The realization of these ends required systematic study and organization as did also the religious needs of the new class of immigrants.

With the so-called "new" immigrants—mostly Italians, Magyars and Slavs—the methods which had sufficed to keep the Irish and Germans loyally attached to the Church proved unsatisfactory. Constituting a majority of total immigrants after 1896, the new immigrants came at an average rate of about six hundred thousand a year until the outbreak of World War I. Although they were overwhelmingly Catholic by tradition and inclination, they were sadly deficient in clergy of their respective nationalities, and, having been accustomed in Europe to state support of their church, they were slow to establish and maintain religious institutions in the land of their adoption. The newcomers presented the Church with a vast missionary problem not easily or quickly solved. Experience demonstrated, however, that the task was best approached through native

American priests speaking the immigrant's language and sympathetic with his traditions and aspirations. It was also found that effective work often necessitated use of the bodily aids of the new social service—kindergartens, clubs and social settlements. In diverse ways informed of and inspired to meet the religious needs of the new immigrant, the Church gained most from the conventions and Apostolic Mission House of the Catholic Missionary Union, formed in 1896 by the Reverend Walter Elliott to systematize religious work among non-Catholics, and from the activities of the Church Extension Society, the creation in 1905 of the Reverend (later Bishop) Francis C. Kelley. Under its auspices were held two magnificent American Catholic missionary congresses, in 1908 and 1913, which mirrored the new religious and social scene.[15]

Happily the Church by this time was in a position to carry forward the program of the missionary organizations. The oldest and most powerful groups in the Church, the Catholics of Irish and German descent, whose dissension and rivalry had impeded social reform during the 1880s and 1890s, were now in agreement on a policy of steady, though "unforced," Americanization of all immigrant peoples. Esteemed from the beginning for their devotion to Catholic institutions, notably the parochial school, German Catholics as early as 1855 had federated their benevolent societies into the American Roman Catholic Central Verein, and thereafter had kept in close touch with the well-organized Catholic social movement in Germany, the work of Emmanuel von Ketteler, the distinguished Archbishop of Mainz, and his followers in the German Catholic congresses and other organizations. Inasmuch as Ketteler had formulated his social teachings expressly to counteract Marxian socialism which seemed dangerous in the United States also after 1900, American Catholics turned to him for inspiration, relying

---

[15] See especially Reverend William Stang, "The First National Congress of Missionaries to Non-Catholics," *American Ecclesiastical Review*, XXV (October, 1901), pp. 331-338; John T. McNicholas, O.P., "The Need of American Priests for the Italian Missions," *ibid.*, XXXIX (December, 1908), pp. 677-687; Rev. Roderick A. McEachen, "The Apostolate of the Immigrants," The Catholic Missionary Union, *The Mission Movement in America* (Washington, D.C., 1906), pp. 93-99; Rev. Francis C. Kelley, "Church Extension," in Francis C. Kelley (Ed.), *The First American Catholic Missionary Congress* (Chicago, 1909), pp. 95-110; Bishop Peter J. Muldoon, "Immigration to and the Immigrants in the United States," in Second American Catholic Missionary Congress, *Official Report, 1913* (Chicago, 1914), pp. 132-146; Andrew Shipman, "Emigration," *ibid.*, pp. 154-171.

less than formerly on French and English leaders, notably Count Albert de Mun and Cardinal Henry E. Manning.

As for the Germans themselves, Ketteler's work helped inspire the formation in 1887 of the German-American Union of Priests whose purpose, in cooperation with the Central Verein, was to prepare Catholics of German descent to play a conspicuous role in the American Catholic social movement.[16]. For a decade or more, however, the social program was abandoned in favor of contests against alleged "Irish" supremacy in the Church and the vigorous Americanization crusade of Archbishop Ireland and other "liberal" Catholics.[17] The heavy German immigration during the 1880s encouraged these attitudes. By the same token the sharp decline in accessions from Germany after 1895 and the irresistible lure of American ways and speech led to a renewal of interest in social questions. Thus German-American Catholics were numerous and influential in the American Federation of Catholic Societies, formed in 1901 to defend Catholic interests, promote racial harmony and fight socialism. In 1908 the Central Verein established a bureau for the promotion of social education and began publishing a German-English magazine, Central-Blatt and Social Justice, devoted exclusively to social advancement. Besides social education the Verein supported trade unionism and in lesser degree political reform and scientific charity. These objectives were presently worked into the much larger and increasingly representative American Federation of Catholic Societies which in 1910 formulated in specific terms a notably constructive program and set up a Social Service Commission the following year.[18]

In this organizational endeavor the leading figure was the Reverend Peter E. Dietz, who for two decades after his ordination in 1904 devoted his entire energies to the social question. He went as the first fraternal delegate from the American Federation of Catholic Societies to the American Federation of Labor, founded the Militia of Christ to bring the Church and the labor movement into more harmonious relations, served as secretary of the Social Service

---

[16] Northwestern Chronicle, September 25, 1891; ibid., September 20, 1895; "German Roman Catholics," Christian Union, October 3, 1891.

[17] John J. Meng, "Cahenslyism: the First Stage, 1883-1891," Catholic Historical Review, XXXI (January, 1946), pp. 389-413, and "Cahenslyism: the Second Chapter, 1891-1910," ibid., XXXII (October, 1946), pp. 302-340.

[18] A. I. Abell, "The Reception of Leo XIII's Labor Encyclical in America, 1891-1919," loc. cit., pp. 486-487, 490-491.

Commission, edited various journals, and organized and headed a social training and labor school. Dietz' incessant activity was directed to the main purpose of saving and enlarging the Catholic labor movement that had taken shape in the earlier days of Cardinal Gibbons. To this end he fought extremists. On the one hand, he beat back the inroads of socialism on the Catholic body; on the other, he tried to enlighten conservative and cautious Catholics who exaggerated socialist strength in the labor movement and seemed indifferent to social welfare.[19]

More explicitly than Dietz, the Reverend John A. Ryan laid bare the motivation and strategy of the enlarging Catholic social movement. Ryan had grown to manhood in the Middle West amid Populist influences, and with the aid and encouragement of Archbishop Ireland, his religious superior, attained great academic distinction. His first book, *A Living Wage* (New York, 1906), was hailed as "the first attempt in the English language to elaborate a Roman Catholic system of political economy." While Father Dietz seemed satisfied with "pure and simple" trade unionism, Ryan urged industrial democracy in the form of worker participation in management and ownership as a more effective answer to socialism.[20] He pointed out that socialism was a three-fold thing: it was a philosophy, a party and agitational movement, and an economic system. With the first two there could be no compromise: the philosophy was materialistic, and "the great majority of Catholics who remain long in the Socialist movement cease to practice their religion." But the economics of socialism was another matter. Essential Economic Socialism or Semi-Socialism, as he called it, did not fall "under the condemnation of either the moral law or the Church"; socialism of that type permitted all that the moral law called for, namely, "that the rights and opportunities of private ownership be sufficiently extensive to safeguard individual and social welfare." Ryan himself never favored economic socialism: he thought it neither desirable nor practicable. But the Catholic "who can see no adequate remedy for present industrial ills except in some moderate form of economic socialism, has a right," he insisted,

---

[19] Mary Harrita Fox in her *Peter E. Dietz, Labor Priest,* (University of Notre Dame Press, Notre Dame, Ind., 1953), treats all aspects of Dietz's stormy career.
[20] See Morris Hillquit and John A. Ryan, *Socialism—Promise of Menace?* (New York, 1914) and its review by William English Walling in *American Journal of Sociology,* XX (January, 1915), pp. 534-537.

"to as much moral freedom as other Catholics with respect to other theories and practices."[21] Socialism, he untiringly reiterated, was the spearhead of the broad movement for economic democracy—a movement which "shows, even in our country," he said, "a strong tendency to become secular, if not anti-Christian." Should the clergy remain unable or unwilling "to understand, appreciate and sympathetically direct the aspirations of economic democracy, it will inevitably," he warned, "become more and more unchristian, and pervert all too rapidly a larger and larger portion of our Catholic population."[22]

The truth of this analysis was recognized by an ever-growing number of Catholics, including the men and women who directed the Church's manifold charities. Alarmed at the growth of social discontent which stemmed, they believed, from bad industrial conditions, they organized in 1910 the National Conference of Catholic Charities. Though its primary purpose was "to take advantage of the ripest wisdom in relief and preventive work and to serve as a bond of union for the innumerable charity organizations," the Conference determined to correlate its charity with justice, affirming that it "aims to be the attorney for the poor in modern society, to present their point of view and to direct them unto the days when social justice may secure to them their rights." In keeping with this high purpose the Conference in the years that followed championed protective labor legislation, persuaded Catholics to expand and improve the old and to adopt the new forms of charity, and encouraged the growth of a trained personnel for Catholic social service. To provide the necessary training, schools of philanthropy and social service appeared on the scene. The first of these schools opened in Boston in 1913; by the end of the decade a half-dozen or more flourished in various parts of the country. The Boston school functioned alongside the Catholic charities of the city, while most of the others were university enterprises, notably the excellent ones at Loyola University, Chicago, and Fordham University, New York. The Loyola school was founded by the Reverend Frederic Siedenburg whose brilliant career in the social movement followed several years of study in Europe.

---

[21] "May a Catholic Be a Socialist?" *Catholic Fortnightly Review,* XVI (July 1, 1909), p. 393.
[22] "The Church and the Workingman," *Catholic World, LXXXIX* (September, 1909), pp. 781-782.

Perhaps the best results in the field of social training were scored by Father Dietz whose school, the American Academy of Christian Democracy for Women, as he called it, was widely acclaimed. Sharing in the growing conviction that successful social work required a trained personnel, he opened his institution in 1915 at Hot Springs, North Carolina, relocating in Cincinnati once the experiment demonstrated its usefulness. In the eight years of its existence, the school provided its hundreds of graduates with a most satisfactory social education which enabled them to assume positions of leadership in almost every major Catholic community. Gradually Dietz's school developed into a labor college, the first in the English-speaking Catholic world.

The graduates of the social service schools facilitated the vast expansion in Catholic social work which occurred after 1910. Within a decade charity agencies doubled in number, institutions of the new philanthropy making up nearly all the increase. The number of social settlements increased from about twenty to a hundred or more, while other forms of the new charity, for example, child-caring devices and boarding homes for working women, also multiplied many fold. The various industrial schools, day nurseries and kindergartens, already established, broadened the scope of their work. Lay women, through hundreds of clubs, leagues or guilds, some of which were national in extent, were mainly responsible for these efforts at social betterment. By the end of the decade Catholics had come to regard social service as a religious vocation. So great was the interest that in the early twenties some immigrant groups and their friends organized to promote "institutional" methods of church work, these methods being esteemed the American way of securing religious results.

As the new charities multiplied, means of coordination on the local level became increasingly imperative. Beginning in Pittsburgh in 1910, bureaus of Catholic charities were organized in over thirty heavily Catholic communities by the end of World War I. On the genesis of these bodies the National Conference of Catholic Charities and the federated Catholic societies exerted a decisive influence. While their primary task was to supervise and correlate Catholic charities, a good half of the bureaus employed full-time social workers for family case work. Only a few bureaus were strong enough to cover the whole field of Catholic relief. The prevailing practice restricted the bureaus to Catholic cases involving religious or moral problems, the more normal cases being left to secular agencies.

Catholic social service steadily advanced in spite of the resistance it met from many priests and a large part of the Catholic press. Objection centered on the professional social worker who in some quarters was considered "as a sort of cold-blooded mercenary." Many Catholics were slow to realize that the specialist had become necessary, that for the performance of the new tasks the Church could not rely entirely upon lay volunteers or members of religious orders. This was a most serious difficulty—the psychological inability of many to understand how a person could legitimately earn a money income helping others. The extent and character of the opposition alarmed and distressed social workers; one of their number, Margaret Tucker, widely known settlement leader and teacher in Dietz's school, suggested a compromise system, namely, the semi-cloistered deaconess institution. This arrangement, she felt, would allay suspicion that the social worker was motivated by worldly considerations without impairing her lay freedom and usefulness.

Her plan was not widely adopted, partly because the nation's entry into World War I called for social action which only lay folk could perform. To this end, the Hierarchy itself, in August, 1917, assumed general oversight of Catholic war-time social service by creating the National Catholic War Council, whose Administrative Committee was headed by Bishop Peter J. Muldoon, the chairman of the now virtually defunct Social Service Commission. The Council was the Catholic counterpart of the War-Time Commission of the Federal Council of Churches and the Jewish Welfare Board, and with them derived its main financial support from the various war drive funds. With ample means at its disposal the National Catholic War Council through its Committee on Special War Activities expanded and coordinated existing social agencies and created new ones for the purpose of securing the spiritual welfare of the service man and his family and of maintaining patriotic morale in the major cities. Besides establishing two playgrounds and twenty-one welfare houses in Allied countries, the Council built and operated twelve visitors' houses in connection with army camps, founded twenty-two clubs and subsidized hundreds of others for the use of service men, opened fifteen Catholic hospitals to the free after-care of discharged veterans and their families and set up two rehabilitation schools, thirty-nine employment bureaus and fifteen workingmen's clubs. By early 1920 when its activities terminated the Council had also established twenty-eight settlement or community centers to the end that the discontent stirred up by the war and its aftermath might be turned from "radicalism and anarchy" "into the ways of American liberty and freedom."

The Council was deeply concerned, in fact, with Americanization, launching a country-wide Civic Education Program aimed primarily at the millions of immigrants "who have had," it was regretfully said, "no instruction in democracy or any experience in its operation." The oversight of the campaign was entrusted to Dr. John A. Lapp, an expert in the fields of vocational education and labor legislation. For the use of students and lecturers he prepared two text-books, *The Fundamentals of Citizenship,* and *Co-Builders of Our America,* which in the judgment of some non-Catholic educators were the best of their kind. While Lapp and his associates in the Council urged all immigrants to seek speedy naturalization, they avoided the usual attempts at forcing the English language and American ways upon the foreign-born. Nor did they teach that true patriotism meant blind devotion to the nation apart from the great ideals of truth, justice and human brotherhood. "We hold," they emphasized, "that no plan short of complete social justice should be held as a goal in programs for good citizenship or Americanization."[23]

The Council acted on this conviction when in February, 1919, it issued the Bishops' Program of Social Reconstruction. Although in two places the undesirability of socialism was alluded to, the document exposed the flaws in the existing system and advanced a dozen remedies, some of which seemed far-reaching at the time. Thus the Program called for social insurance against unemployment, sickness, invalidism, and old age; a federal child labor law; the legal enforcement of labor's right to organize; public housing for the working classes; progressive taxation of inheritances, incomes and excess profits; stringent regulation of public utility rates; government competition with monopolies if necessary to secure effective control; worker participation in management; and cooperative productive societies and co-partnership arrangements in order to enable the majority of wage earners to "become owners, or at least in part, of the instruments of production."[24] These were indeed far-reaching

---

[23] See A. I. Abell, "The Catholic Church and Social Problems in the World War I Era," *loc. cit.,* for Catholic Social Service, 1910-1920.

[24] John A. Ryan, *Social Reconstruction* (New York, 1920), p. 235.

proposals—for the reform, of course, not the overthrow, of the existing order. Compared to the "voluntarism" of Samuel Gompers and the ruling groups in the American Federation of Labor, the Bishop's Program of Social Reconstruction was truly radical. It epitomized in fact the aspirations of the democratic, non-communist left-wing of the post-war American labor movement. On one issue, namely, the legal enforcement of labor's right to organize, the Bishops' Program displayed uniqueness and prophecy. The Catholic bishops were the first important group to suggest legislation for the positive encouragement of trade unionism and collective bargaining. Neither wing of the labor movement recognized the possibilities of the proposal until the economic crisis of the late twenties and the thirties. Then it speedily became an article in labor's faith and finally as a result of the New Deal labor laws and court decisions, avowed public policy.

Besides promoting more or less directly the triple program of industrial reform, civic education and social service, the National Catholic War Council sought to co-ordinate all the working forces of the Church to these and other ends. Its peace-time successor, the National Catholic Welfare Council, formed late in 1919, continued the task, working through five bureaus one of which was the Department of Social Action, headed by Muldoon and directed by Ryan and Lapp. Fearing that the Council would prove an agency of undue centralization, many Catholics, including several bishops, for a time opposed it and wished for its suppression by the Holy See. Actually, experience was to show that the creation of the new body (National Catholic Welfare Conference after 1922) meant, as its friends contended, the unification rather than the centralization of Catholic effort. From its origin to the present the Conference has untiringly labored not to dominate or suppress but to aid and facilitate the working plans of all Catholic social agencies.

The Conference's industrial program rather than its procedure and methods accounted for the serious opposition encountered during the early 1920s. When in the idealistic afterglow of World War I the Church launched its new social program, the progressive elements of the country, still in partial control of the federal government and enjoying public favor, confidently expected that economic democracy would be the basis of the forthcoming peace and reconstruction. Soon, however, the reform impulse lost its force and frenzied reaction gripped the country, in the course of which the recent gains of union labor were wiped out and the whole structure of pre-war social legislation imperiled. The clumsy preparations of Bolshevist zealots for a communist revolution in America frightened many people who lent a ready ear to the clever propaganda of business and other conservative groups that all reformers were *Bolsheviki* in disguise or the naive and witless abetters of violent revolution. The more active Catholic champions of social justice were thus branded, and one of them, Father Dietz, was forced to close his Cincinnati labor school even though it had demonstrated its capacity to promote social peace in the community. The reactionaries struck at Ryan and his group by claiming that the Bishops' Program of Social Reconstruction lacked authoritative status, being merely the personal opinion of the men who had formulated it.[25]

Happily the bishops ignored this assault and continued to support the Bishops' Program—their own creation—and the agencies set up to win the country's approval, notably the Social Action Department. With the experienced Bishop Muldoon as chairman, Ryan as director and the Reverend Raymond A. McGowan as assistant director, the Department fearlessly, if cautiously, applied the Church's social teachings to the current situation, insisting at the crest of the "Red scare" that the reduction of wages and the drive against labor unions violated social justice. When with the revival of business after 1922 hysteria gave way to smug satisfaction in the social field, the Department repeatedly warned that economic conditions were unsound "so long as productivity was high and the income of the masses, including that of the farmers, low."[26] In addition to the usual means for communication, such as books, pamphlets, lectures and study clubs, the Social Action Department developed "a traveling school of social thought" in the Catholic Conference on Industrial Problems, formed in 1922, whose many national and regional meetings freely discussed the findings of experts on all controversial economic questions and presented hundreds of thousands of people with an opportunity to learn, often for the first time, of Catholic social doctrine and its relevance to present-day issues.

---

[25] "Anonymous Critics of the Bishop's Reconstruction Program," (editorial), *Catholic Charities Review*, III (June, 1919), pp. 163-165; John Hearley, "Plutocracy Ascends the Pulpit," *ibid.*, V (April, 1921), pp. 116-118.

[26] Rev. R. A. McGowan, "Catholic Work in the United States for Social Justice," *Catholic Action*, XVIII (May, 1936), pp. 5-11, an excellent survey of social thought and action as viewed by the Social Action Department.

The rising interest in social service reached its climax during the 1920s and the 1930s, when many priests, nuns and lay folk prepared themselves for teaching or administrative careers in applied sociology. The steadily increasing number of diocesan social service bureaus made it easier for the Church to participate in community fund drives as well as to extend its influence over foreign-born peoples, many of whom it had been unable to reach during the immigrant invasion of pre-war years.[27] With immigration now virtually ended by federal law, the Church at last had a chance in its parish-extension work to make performance equal aspiration. Inasmuch as immigration could be no longer a source of the Church's growth, far-seeing Catholic leaders urged that the necessary steps be taken to expand Catholicism in the rural areas. The country, it was urged, provided the better environment for the nourishment and exercise of the Christian life, and by its higher birth rate would compensate the Church for its inevitable decline in cities which without rural accessions were unable to reproduce themselves. These views were personified by the Reverend (later Bishop) Edwin V. O'Hara who after a brilliant career in the field of labor legislation secured in 1921 the establishment of a Rural Life Bureau in the National Catholic Welfare Conference, experimented successfully with church extension in an Oregon rural parish and in 1923 launched the National Catholic Rural Life Conference. Besides serving to "de-urbanize" Catholic attitudes, the rural crusade has many victories to its credit in the way of church extension and social betterment.[28]

The rural movement might well have become the Church's primary social interest had economic conditions remained normal and stable. But world-wide depression during the 1930s, entailing unemployment and indescribable misery for millions of human beings, focused attention on the industrial system, the causes of its breakdown and the search for reform and stabilization. More thoroughly and extensively than in any previous decade, Catholics by thought and action worked to usher in a better economic order.[29] They were encouraged to redouble their efforts by Pope

[27] Rev. John O'Grady, "New Perspectives in Charity," *Commonweal*, X (October 30, 1929), pp. 668-670.

[28] Raymond Philip Witte, S.M., *Twenty Five Years of Crusading. A History of the National Catholic Rural Life Conference* (Des Moines, 1948).

[29] For a general discussion of Catholic social action since World War I, see M. Clara Ann Gatzemeier, O.S.F., "The Reception of the Papal Labor

Pius XI's encyclical, *Quadragesimo anno* on the reconstruction of the social order, issued in 1931 to commemorate the 40th anniversary of Pope Leo's *Rerum novarum* and to bring the Church's economic teachings to bear more directly on the new situation. Co-operation among organized occupational groups, especially between employers and employees, was the best method, Pope Pius thought, of securing justice and peace in the industrial world. The government should assist and supervise but not dictate to the occupational groups. In this way society could work and plan for social justice without plunging humanity into some form of totalitarian despotism.

The encyclical teachings were widely publicized, notably by Charles E. Coughlin of Royal Oaks, Michigan, "the radio priest," whose attentive audience comprised a large part of the entire nation during the early 1930s. Father Coughlin was more interested, however, in monetary inflation and banking control than in the creation of a modernized guild system. His popularity declined when the New Deal refused to adopt his proposals and when he subscribed increasingly to ideas and techniques of Fascist lineage. From the beginning Monsignor Ryan and others noted that the Coughlin remedies were out of line at essential points with official Catholic pronouncements. As spokesmen for the National Catholic Welfare Conference, Ryan and McGowan believed that the Roosevelt measures, notably the NIRA, were steps, though only steps, in the right direction. In this sense they approved and supported the New Deal while continuing to issue statements and pamphlets, multiply conferences on industrial problems and promote study and discussion conventions, among them two social action congresses of national scope in 1938 and 1939.

New forces entered and fructified Catholic social action during the 1930s. Of these the most important was the Catholic Worker movement, begun in 1933 by Peter Maurin, a French-born itinerant social philosopher, and Dorothy Day, social worker recently converted from communism. Miss Day and her numerous followers lived among the exploited and unemployed poor in the industrial quarters of the great cities. In their Houses of Hospitality the Catholic Workers entertained and helped the poor in a most informal, personal and Christ-like manner. The Workers reached "the people through voluntary poverty (going without luxuries in order

---

Encyclicals in America since 1919," a master's thesis at the University of Notre Dame, 1947.

to have the essentials) and through the works of mercy (mutual aid and philosophy of labor.)"[30]

From the outset, the Catholic Workers were in active sympathy with the growing labor movement, publicizing bad working conditions, joining and organizing unions, and on picket lines and in less dramatic ways helping wage-earners secure justifiable objectives. In order to systematize these activities, Catholic Workers in New York, led by John C. Cort, formed in 1937 the Association of Catholic Trade Unionists which by the end of the decade had several active chapters in the larger cities. At the Catholic Social Congress of 1939 the various chapters federated. Inspiring ACTU and its work was the admonition in *Quadragesimo anno* that "side by side with . . . trade unions there must always be associations which aim at giving their members a thorough religious and moral training, that these in turn may impart to the labor unions to which they belong the upright spirit which should direct their entire conduct." Thus orientated, ACTU has been strikingly successful in helping fight communism, racketeering and undemocratic abuses within the unions. Though in no sense a Catholic clique in the labor movement, as Professor Philip Taft has shown,[31] the accusation that it was such prompted the Chicago chapter, the Catholic Labor Alliance, to open its membership to non-unionists and persons of all faiths who subscribe to the labor teachings of recent popes.[32]

In the long run the greatest influence will come from the Catholic labor schools, the first of which in the recent period was established in 1937 by the Association of Catholic Trade Unionists in connection with Fordham University. Similar schools rapidly multiplied, opened and maintained by many different groups in the Church and offering workers—and others too—systematic instruction in labor ethics, labor history, parliamentary practice and various phases of labor-management relations. According to a recent compilation by the Reverend George C. Higgins, assistant director of the Social Action Department, there are nearly a hundred labor schools regularly engaged in the task of preparing Catholic work-

---

[30] Dorothy Day, *House of Hospitality* (New York, 1939), p. 275.

[31] "The Association of Catholic Trade Unionists," *Industrial and Labor Relations Review,* II (January, 1949), pp. 210-218.

[32] Raymond J. Maly, "The Catholic Labor Alliance. A Laboratory Test of Catholic Social Action," a master's thesis, University of Notre Dame, 1950, pp. 16, 18-22.

ingmen to take an active and morally responsible part in the organized labor movement.[33]

Few deny that Catholic performance in the social field, especially in recent years, has been impressive. Even from persons whose antipathy to Catholicism is intense and frenzied come grudging tributes to the zeal and effectiveness of the Church's battle for social justice. Thus James Hastings Nichols of the Federated Theological Faculty of the University of Chicago states that since World War I Catholic social action has been "second to none in America" and that "on the whole, and due primarily to its sociological location among the urban poor, the Catholic record for social democracy probably outweighed the Protestant."[34] The Catholic contribution, now evident to all, is not the result of recent efforts alone; it is rather the culmination of a movement that began a century ago. In its origins and first stages of development, social reform was largely a by-product of an Americanization program, then the great need of the Church. In the recent past the Catholic social movement has been preoccupied with the problems created by a horrifying economic crisis. In the atomic age of today and tomorrow Catholic social action may well serve the cause of world order: "The only safeguard of peace is social justice and a contented people."

---

[33] "Appendix," to Gatzemeier, *op. cit.*, pp. 112-113.
[34] *Democracy and the Churches* (Philadelphia, 1951), pp. 131, 251.

XVI

The Church in Latin America

by Peter Masten Dunne, S.J.

The title of this chapter might well serve as the title of a book. Within the compass of a few pages a thorough study cannot be made, in view of the fact (among other things) that Latin America comprises twenty nations. Each one of these governments has had its dealings or troubles with the Church or churchmen. For each one a history could be written. In this church question, however, as in other things, there are certain common denominators. These may with profit be called to the attention of Anglo-American scholars and students who are interested in the subject.

In approaching other peoples and other situations the people of our country have often been naive and unintelligent. Witness our repeated blunders in international diplomacy. We have made a fetish of democracy, thinking that it is the only possible form of desirable government and thinking (yet more naively) that all nations should adopt this form immediately and be able to administer it with success equal to our own. We forget that there is required a sufficient amount of experience, cohesion, education, and civic virtue if democracy is to succeed. We forget that there are people who lack some or all of these social requisites and that with them democracy cannot now function successfully. Most countries are not ready for it yet, but can be educated to it if and when this becomes desirable.

In the century and a quarter since the end of the wars of independence, revolt and dictatorship have been the rule in Latin America rather than the exception. There are legions of citizens in those countries, and among these are many churchmen, who do not believe in the democratic form of government because they do not believe it can work well with them. In this they are backed by the record of history. Experience, cohesion, education, and civic virtue —one or all of these have been found wanting in the past in all of the nations of Latin America without exception. In many instances these qualities are found wanting in the present. In the midst of this situation are the Church and churchmen.

Since we cannot understand Catholicism in Latin America as it is today without certain indications of the historical background, it will not be amiss to adumbrate some important parts of the past. Only slight reflection will be required to realize how different have been the historical background and development of the Church in the United States.[1] The blend of Church and state in the Catholic governments of western Europe was nowhere so complete as it was in Spain. The system had its roots in the Middle Ages. In the code of Alfonso the Wise of Castille (1252-1284), called the *Siete Partidas,* the King assumed to himself, at least with the acquiescence of Rome, the patronage over churches built in lands conquered from the Moors. As the conquest proceeded to its completion in 1492 the patronage of the King over church affairs was materially extended. Before the discovery and conquest of the New World Pope Sixtus IV (1471-1484) augmented appreciably the power of the Crown over the administration of the Church—a move which he later regretted—by conceding to Ferdinand and Isabella in 1478 complete authority over the Inquisition. Henceforth this powerful institution was used not only as a tribunal for the preservation of orthodoxy, but also as an instrument to round out the absolutism of the Crown. "Both these rulers insisted on papal recognition of their own candidates for episcopal sees, sometimes readily granted, sometimes wrung from the Pope by threats against the Holy See." What more natural than that when Portugal in Africa, and Spain in America, began to develop their overseas dominions, this control over the Church would be extended beyond the shores of Europe. The Spanish Borgia Pope, Alexander VI (1492-1503) and Julius II (1503-1513) granted to the Spanish kings practically complete control over the Church in America. This *patronato real* developed to full-blown maturity during the long reign of that great caesaro-papist, King Philip II (1556-1598), who even in Spain,

---

[1] Richard Pattee gives a good summary of the differences which have existed in the development of the Church in the United States. *Cf. El Catolicismo en Estados Unidos* (Mexico, 1945), pp. 530 f.

but more so in America, was both king and pope. He was not, however, another Henry VIII, who in England carried Erastianism to its extreme limits, and who was "the pope, the whole pope, and something more than the pope," to quote the distinguished Bishop Stubbs of the Church of England. Philip II was exceedingly conscientious and had at heart the best interests of religion.

Governing the colonies through the Council of the Indies, as did his successors, he ruled over the Church in every phase of its organization and activities. No priest or missionary could embark for America without approval of the Government. If new dioceses had to be created and episcopal appointments to be made for them, the direction came from Madrid and not from Rome. When new religious orders, such as the Jesuits, went over to the New World, permission and regulation concerning the building and placement of their houses and churches issued from the Crown. When the Jesuits in Cartagena (of St. Peter Claver fame) built their house so that it was buttressed on the side by the protecting wall of the town Philip II ordered it removed, though later a compromise was agreed to. The ecclesiastical tithes in every bishopric and in every parish were minutely regulated, so much going to the bishop, so much to the canons of his cathedral, so much to the parish priest, so much to the King.[2] Finally, with the consent of the Holy See, the Government took upon itself the heavy responsibility of the spread of the Faith, through the conversion of the Indian. It had the right to sanction the extension of missionary activity. Other prerogatives usurped by the Crown were the reviewing of decrees of ecclesiastical councils and synods; the *exequatur* as applied to papal bulls, decrees, and ordinations; in short, intervention in the affairs of the colonial church in all matters short of dogma. The intimate union of Church and state is indicated by the fact that in colonial Mexico, of sixty-six viceroys, eleven were at the same time both viceroy and bishop.

One more instance may serve as an illustration of the King's power over the Church in America during colonial times. As St. Teresa in the ecclesiastical difficulties over the progress of her reform appealed to King Philip II, so did the Governor of the far-flung

---

[2] For a scholarly account of the organization of the tithes in the diocese of Oaxaca in Mexico, cf. Woodrow Borah, "The Collection of the Tithes in the Bishopric of Oaxaca in the Sixteenth Century," *Hispanic American Historical Review,* XXI (August, 1941), 361-409.

province of Nueva Vizcaya in northern Mexico, Luis de Valdés, appeal to King Philip IV. The occasion of the appeal was a difficulty of the missions, which were so necessary to the well-being of his province. During the 1640's the third Bishop of Durango, Francisco de Quintanilla Evía y Valdés, showed himself unfriendly to the regular clergy, the Franciscans and Jesuits, who had missions in his diocese. Wanting to replace the regulars with his own men, he did so for several mission establishments. The Governor penned a protest to the King under date of December 13, 1642. The diocesan clergy could not successfully manage the missions, said he, and besides the Bishop did not have enough priests to man them. The Governor won his case, orders came from Spain to reinstate the regulars, and the Bishop was transferred to another diocese.[3]

All of this was well and good while the kings and their Council of the Indies remained zealous and efficient. But in the course of three centuries of Spain's national as well as colonial government a general decline and decadence set in. And when the Church is intimately linked with the state, the decline of one affects the other. During the seventeenth and eighteenth centuries conditions grew persistently worse and civic virtue both in Spain and in the colonies diminished. The best men were not sent across the waters as clerics, bishops became remiss in the administration of their dioceses and in the disciplining of their clergy, and there are many indications that this laxity also crept into some of the religious orders, or at least into some of their communities. A bishop in Guatemala built special apartments, a wing of the convent, for one of the nuns who was apparently his mistress; a convent of nuns in Baia in Brazil had food carried in to them, each one for herself; they had their servants and slaves and were visited by young men of questionable character; a highly placed churchman in Botogá complained shortly after independence in a letter to the Holy See of the scandalous immorality existing in a monastery of the regular clergy.[4]

---

[3] Peter Masten Dunne, *Early Jesuit Missions in Tarahumara* (University of California Press, 1948), pp. 84 ff.

[4] On the corruption of part of the clergy in Bogotá half a century after independence, see an authentically documented study: Cary Shaw, Jr., "Church and State in Colombia as observed by American Diplomats, 1834-1906," *Hispanic American Historical Review*, XXI (November, 1941), 577-613. Cf. especially p. 590 where Father Vicente Bernal's letter to the Pope is given. Dr. Bailey W. Diffie who details these matters in *Latin American Civilization* (London, 1945), as for instance in Chapter XXXII dealing with conditions in

Then came independence with its wars and revolutions, marches and counter-marches, victories and defeats, extending over a period of fifteen years. In 1808 Charles IV was removed from Spain's throne and replaced by Joseph Bonaparte. By their repudiation of this government the *criollos* of the colonies were led ultimately to declare complete independence. In the meantime bishops died or fled to Spain, and the King was prisoner in France. Who was going to look after ecclesiastical matters? Nobody in high authority. Result: by 1825 in Greater Colombia alone eleven sees were vacant, while in Mexico the hierarchy became all but extinct. Similar conditions existed for the most part in other religions. After Napoleon's defeat Ferdinand VII was restored to the Spanish throne, but the colonies, in continued and open revolt, began soon to win decisive victories, while the Riego Revolution in Spain made Ferdinand a prisoner of the Liberals. A year after the King had been restored to his throne by French arms, his colonies in South America finally defeated his last forces in the Peruvian battles of Junín and Ayachucho and were free (1824). Ferdinand VII, reactionary, stubborn, and cruel, had no armies to win them back even if England and the United States (the latter through the Monroe Doctrine) had not stood in the way.

But Ferdinand would not face realities. He not only refused to admit the loss of his American colonies, including Mexico after 1821, but he clung with stubborn, and we can say, stupid tenacity, to his old privileges of the *patronato real,* so that whenever the Papacy made any move to apply a remedy to the deplorable condition of the Church in Latin America the King of Spain fumed and threatened and held over the head of the popes the time-worn bluff of schism. The popes of this period were on their part linked rather with the forces of reaction and they were not sufficiently forthright and realistic in their attitudes, not sufficiently strong be-

---

colonial Brazil, thinks that Catholic and non-Catholic historians will never agree on this question of ecclesiastical laxity or abuse in Latin America. But where the factual record is at hand agreement *must* be reached. In the past both groups have been at fault. Non-Catholics have generalized upon these abuses and have written of them with animus, a practice which has been offensive and unscientific. Catholic historians have assumed an apologetic attitude which has been as irritating as it is unscientific, and sometimes they have denied the facts because of lack of proper knowledge and scholarship, or what is worse because of lack of candor. Timid souls thought the truth would do harm. If both correct these attitudes agreement will be reached on the record. Later Dr. Diffie appears to have admitted this in a letter to the writer.

fore the threats of the Spanish King. Because of Spanish pressure Pius VII (1800-1823) made the mistake in 1816 of writing to the American hierarchy and urging them to exhort their people to resume their loyalty to the unspeakable Ferdinand; and Leo XII (1823-1829), the very year that independence in America was completely won (1824), did the same. These documents pointed to the non-existent virtues of the Spanish King. Yet Leo XII, apparently realizing the adverse effect such a gesture would have upon the American patriots, tried to counter it by the deletion of the clause for direct political exhortation (which the Spanish ambassador vainly tried to have inserted) and by his personal letters to such American bishops as Lasso de la Vega of Colombia and to Guadalupe Victoria, President of Mexico. Leo XII and his predecessors should have acted independently of Ferdinand, but diplomatic practice prevented such action and Spanish threats and intimidations frightened the popes. Diplomatically the Holy See was placed in a difficult position by the intransigence of Spain.[5] Finally, Gregory XVI (1831-1846), though an arch-reactionary in Europe, dealt with ecclesiastical matters in America as he saw fit. After Ferdinand VII's death (1833), and with Spain divided by civil war, the Papacy tried to heal the wounds of Latin American Catholicism through the establishment of a nunciature for Brazil.

Meanwhile, as we can well surmise, the conditions of the Church and her prestige were declining among the nations of Latin America that had just won their independence. With the disorders of the revolutions, the wars for independence, and the dearth of bishops, the laxities of later colonial times grew worse. Moreover, each particular government, though unstable and dictator-ridden (with the exception of Brazil and Chile) insisted on exercising all the privileges of patronage which had been enjoyed by the Spanish kings, so that the *patronato real* was now changed into the *patronato nacional*. Greater Colombia in 1824 passed a Church-State law called the *Ley de Patronato* according to which the state governed the Church: congress was empowered to reorganize dioceses and erect new ones, to summon ecclesiastical councils, to regulate tithes and parochial fees, to grant or refuse the *exequatur*

---

[5] For a scholarly exposition of papal attitudes and policies during the post-Napoleonic period, cf. William J. Coleman, *The First Apostolic Delegation in Rio de Janeiro and its Influence in Spanish America* (The Catholic University of America Press, 1950), Ch. I.

to papal bulls and briefs, to organize and administer missions among the Indians, and to enact whatever legislation was thought beneficial to the Church. Similar laws were created for the United Provinces of La Plata in the famous *Memorial Ajustado*. Bernardo O'Higgins, head of the Chilean state (1818-1823), Irishman and good Catholic, exiled the recalcitrant Spaniard, José Santiago Rodríguez y Zorilla, Bishop of Santiago, while Bernardino Rivadavia, president of the United Provinces (Argentina, 1824-1827), wanted to purge the Church in Buenos Aires, which for years had been without a bishop and which suffered a partly corrupted clergy. He abolished the tithes and ecclesiastical courts (phases of which were fast becoming outmoded), repressed religious houses and limited their number, and regulated the age which was to be required by law for the pronouncement of religious vows.[6]

There appeared now, as it had earlier in Europe, another phenomenon—anti-clericalism, often the fruit of a Latin Masonry violently opposed to the Church.[7] This movement was blended with a political liberalism which was at times acutely fanatical and unrealistically doctrinaire. On the other hand there was the irritating ultra-conservatism of many Catholics led by the higher clergy. Both sides had, or thought they had, their reasons, while the extremism of the Spanish character precluded compromise.

These struggles, often more political than religious, time and again disrupted the internal peace of almost every nation, led to frequent changes of government, to new constitutions, and sometimes, as in Mexico, to deadly civil wars. Then arose the *caudillo* or dictator, sometimes disreputable, like Melgarejo in Bolivia (1864-1870) and Blanco in Venezuela (1873-1888), sometimes more respectable though tyrannical like Rosas in Argentina (1835-1852). Dictator Blanco, a Mason of high degree, dealt the Church a mortal blow in Venezuela from which she has scarcely recovered. Rosas and Melgarejo,—like Francia and the two López, father and son, in Paraguay—"ran" the Church. Rosas had his portrait hung

---

[6] For a survey of these developments, cf. John Francis Bannon and Peter Masten Dunne, *Latin America: An Historical Survey* (Milwaukee, 1947), Chs. 17 and 19. For a more complete study see J. Lloyd Mecham, *Church and State in Latin America* (University of North Carolina Press, 1934).

[7] The Masons, however, must be credited with an important share of the success of the movement for independence. English and North American Masons, by and large, have not shown that acute antagonism against the Church which has characterized Latin Masonry.

in the sacred edifices and honored in ecclesiastical processions; and he enacted one good regulation; sermons should be short! Melgarejo decreed that bishops should remain in their dioceses, while here as elsewhere the excessive number of holy days was reduced. García Moreno of Ecuador (1860-1875) elevated the Church to the highest prestige and power, making the country almost a theocracy. But when he was assassinated through the persuasions of the infuriated liberals there came the inevitable reaction. In almost every case the Church was under the thumb of the *caudillo*. Some Latin American countries, such as Nicaragua and the Dominican Republic, even up to the present time have not been able to shake themselves free from the tyranny of dictatorship. Others, like Argentina, apparently with the consent of Congress and a large section of the population, accept a seeming dictatorship.

Such, historically, have been the problems which the Church in Latin America has had to face in the past and which have affected to a large extent its present condition. Shortcomings there are, of course, both of laity and clergy, but such are common to every group of mortals. The imperfect human element is always there. The ecclesiastical group, though most often morally superior to the secular (as it should be), is nevertheless human, so that in every region and in every age of the church's history members of the group have exhibited faults and failings. But why dwell on these with regard to the Church in Latin America? They are known and admitted and they find their explanation in human nature and in history's evolution.

In every Latin American country the faith is still alive and strong in a large portion of the population. This is remarkable in view of the difficulties that historically have had to be encountered. One reason is that the grass roots of all the nations have been Catholic. This is proven by the attitude of each government at the beginning of independence. All without exception recognized Catholicism as the official religion, while some, like Mexico and Peru, excluded every other cult. When Argentina framed the constitution by which she still lives, the instrument stated in part that "the federal government supports the Roman, Catholic, Apostolic Church," while both the president and the vice-president are "required . . . to belong to the Roman, Catholic, Apostolic faith." Argentines are proud of their official Catholicism and boast of it to the North American Catholic. Freedom of religion, which always prevailed in such countries as Brazil and Argentina, has been later introduced by statute or by practice into every country. When by decree of the present Argentine government (October, 1943) the teaching of religion was made obligatory in the public school system, those not of the Catholic faith were exempted from attendance at such instruction. Monsignor Gustavo J. Franceshi, intellectual leader in Buenos Aires, in an article in *Criterio* proclaimed at that time the principle of freedom of religion as did likewise an editorial in the Catholic and conservative *El Pueblo.*

While union of Church and state had been the rule (and it often meant domination of the Church by the state), eventually Brazil, Chile, Uruguay, Mexico, Cuba, Guatemala, El Salvador, and Honduras adopted regimes of separation. This has usually proved to be wholesome. The Catholic leaders of Uruguay, lay and cleric, form an activated and energetic group. They have had to fight for and they have won liberties of which former anti-clerical groups would deprive them. The same can be said of Mexico, where even vicious governmental antagonism or persecution has but seemed to invigorate the living Catholic stock. Two famous Concordats with the Holy See crystallized union in Ecuador (1862) and in Colombia (1887). In Ecuador came the inevitable anti-clerical reaction after the assassination of the ardent Catholic dictator, García Moreno, in 1875. But in Colombia Catholicism still thrives under the more liberal statutes of the Concordat drawn up during the pontificate of Pope Leo XIII (1878-1903). Concordats with the Holy See were also made by the government of Haiti, Guatemala, Nicaragua, and Costa Rica. Nevertheless, in the Central American countries, with the exception of the last mentioned, dictators have tended to lord it over the Church as well as the state. Churchmen, more or less openly and often with good reason, have linked themselves with the conservative regimes so that difficulties for the Church have been created whenever "Liberal" or radical groups came into power.

Among the difficulties which beset the Church in Latin America, two in particular deserve our attention: the inadequate number of priests and the Protestant propaganda of evangelicals from the United States.

Always, it seems, there exists a shortage of priests and nuns. This is the case today even in the United States, where vocations are supposed to be plentiful.

408

In Brazil the shortage of priests is very serious. "In 1944 the population of the country was approximately forty-one million. To administer to this large number of alleged Catholics there were not more than five thousand priests. The number is calamitously inadequate. Wide regions of the country's interior are entirely neglected spiritually."[8] There are districts in southern Mexico where the Indians of the ancient Maya tribe have not seen a priest for decades and decades. But they carry on in their own way, intermingling, like many other Indian tribes in a dozen countries, their ancient superstitions with Catholic prayers and ritual. Today, in the isolated villages throughout Mexico, many an old colonial church stands empty and without benefit of clergy. The men, of course, seldom if ever enter it, but the women keep it swept and garnished and go thither for quiet prayer. Over the wide pampas of the Argentine, the people could not attend services if they would, for churches are practically non-existent and communications are bad.

It was this problem that suggested the title of Father J. Considine's book: *Call for Forty Thousand*.[9] In his estimation the figures show that forty thousand additional priests are needed in Latin America to care properly for the population. According to his tables there are only 23,480 priests for a supposedly Catholic population of 140,147,153. These figures are striking when we compare them with conditions in the United States. Here in 1945 there were more than twice the number of priests to care for a Catholic population only one-sixth as great; there were, in round numbers, 47,000 priests to care for 22,000,000 Catholics.

This lack of priests and of priestly vocations in Latin America was noted by the group of Catholics who attended the Second Inter-American Week of Catholic Action, which held its meeting at Havana, Cuba, early in 1949. Statistics which were released through the National Catholic News Service showed that in Colombia there is one priest for every 1,397 nominal Catholics; in Chile one for every 2,622; in Costa Rica and Venezuela one for every 5,000; in Peru one for every 6,000; in Bolivia one for every 8,750;

---

[8] Peter Masten Dunne, S.J., *A Padre Views South America* (Milwaukee, 1945), pp. 132 f.

[9] Father Considine, M.M., was official visitor to the Maryknoll missions of Latin America. His book (New York, 1946) is as sympathetic as it is enlightening.

in Panama one for every 10,000. The conditions which these figures indicate become striking if we again compare the conditions in Canada and the United States. In Canada there is one priest for every 630 Catholics; in the United States there is one for every 453. The Catholic Action Congress of Havana alleged two reasons for the situation: religious ignorance on the part of Catholics, and the failure of Catholic educators to provide for the religious formation of youth. The Congress stressed the need of a parochial school system and of such catechetical instruction as is sponsored by the Confraternity of Christian Doctrine.[10]

As for Protestants they have but scratched the surface. In the entire Latin American population of some one hundred and forty million there are only three or four million Protestants. To be sure, since the closing of Far Eastern fields during World War II, and even before that time, the numbers of Protestant ministers and of converts have increased. The Presbyterians have been in Colombia since 1856, yet up to 1930 they had made only 663 proselytes. Evidently the country was not turning Presbyterian! However, later years tell a different story. In one parish alone in the province of Antiochía five thousand persons became Presbyterian within a decade, and by the middle of the forties ten different centers were able to count 600 converts a year. The Christian Missionary Alliance has been in South America since 1900. During the years up to 1930 seven ministers had each made six converts. But in the following thirteen years nine pastors netted 569 proselytes. In Colombia the Protestant Sunday schools have advanced in numbers from a figure of 1,958 in 1930 to 2,532 in 1943. The Committee for Cooperation in Latin America financed these activities in Colombia under the slogan "Educational Advance in South America." In Brazil the Baptists have been active since 1882. Ninety-nine pastors, assisted by 283 native catechists, were working there in 1943, and had made some 60,000 converts.[11]

Much bad blood has been created by these activities. These North American Protestants have money; they are practical and energetic. In places where the Protestant works the Catholic clergy is often sold short. Certain types of Protestant ministers use meth-

---

[10] *America*, LXXX (Feb. 26, 1949), 561.

[11] Dunne, *A Padre Views South America*, pp. 268 f. and Ch. 21, *passim*, "Politics and Religion."

ods which are offensive to laity and clergy alike, and which in themselves are an indication of an aggressive bad taste. Granted that large portions of Latin males reveal "basic indifference" to their Catholicism, yet they are at least in name Catholic and their culture is Catholic. The Latin American has an instinctive dislike for North American aggressive methods issuing from a Protestant and "materialistic" civilization. This refined Ariel neither admires nor can be attracted to the Caliban of the North. The Blessed Virgin has been insulted in gatherings organized by the Protestant ministers, the popes have been cried down, and points of Catholic worship or devotion have been labeled superstitious. Many a United States ambassador to Latin America has been embarrassed by these insulting activities on the part of the more ignorant Protestant ministers, while many Catholics, clergy and laity, have been convinced, erroneously of course, that these zealots were financed by the United States government.

During the past decade the Catholic press has been loud in the expression of its alarm and anger. The Catholic daily of Buenos Aires, *El Pueblo,* came out with these headlines: "An Endeavor to Conquer Peru for Heretical Opinions" and "A Growing Danger to the Catholic Nations of America." The *Revista Xaveriana* of Bogotá, in its issues of February and March, 1944, published well-documented articles on the growth of Protestantism in the country since 1931. One was entitled: "Protestant Sabotage of the Good Neighbor Policy." An Argentine Jesuit, Hernán Benítez, asserted in a public gathering in Buenos Aires that the two great dangers to Argentina today are Russian Communism and Protestant invasion from the United States. Father Leonardo Castellani, Jesuit Seminary professor, writing in the learned *Estudios,* organ of the Catholic University of Chile, declared: "The most dangerous poison of our times lies in the religious attitude and activity of the non-Catholic Anglo-Saxons which in torrents enters into Argentina today with Yankee cultural influence."[12]

Non-Catholics in South America have been amazed at the effrontery of some of the sects. Horace W. Jones, Englishman and school teacher in Florida, Uruguay, protested vigorously when a Protestant meeting was being organized and timed to coincide with the religious procession through the plaza in celebration of the

---

[12] *Ibid.,* p. 272.

Fast of Corpus Christi. The place of meeting was the same plaza. Mr. Jones was invited to participate in the meeting. He refused, and pointed out to the ministers the odious quality of such procedure. John W. White, non-Catholic and for years resident in Argentina, expatiated upon the ill effects of such methods in his book entitled *Our Good Neighbor Hurdle* (Milwaukee, 1943). Many of his fellow Protestants resented his book and many of them were petty about it, averring that he had been subsidized by the Catholics. A Methodist of Buenos Aires wrote that the book should be dubbed: "Facts and Fancies About the Good Neighbor Policy." George P. Howard in his *Religious Liberty in Latin America* (Westminster Press, 1944), professed to establish his prior opinion, namely, that ever so many leaders in Latin America do not resent the presence of Protestants but rather welcome this manifestation of religious liberty. The following year Wade Crawford Barclay indicated in his *Greater Good Neighbor Policy* (Willett-Clark, 1945), what the larger lines of religious toleration can be. These works, moderate in context and irenic in intention, remain somewhat one-sided, as one supposes this kind of book is bound to be.

Catholics could learn from the Protestants more practical methods of reaching the people and attracting them to centers and to activities where church social life will be pleasing and enjoyable. Protestants, of course, should amend their insulting or offensive tactics, such as handing out their propaganda at the doors of Catholic churches while the people are issuing from Mass. Some of the Protestants who pursue such practices are mere ignorant zealots; others (really not Protestants) are the fanatical "Jehovah's Witnesses."

It would be untruthful to generalize on such activities. Evidences of genuine good will must also be recognized. For example, certain North American Protestants administering a school in Guayaquil, Ecuador (a town the directing couple selected as the fittest place for personal sacrifice and well-doing), invited the Maryknoll missionary fathers resident there to come and give courses in religion. The Episcopalians are always proper. The Presbyterians in Colombia were given orders from their superiors not to indulge in offensive propaganda or any other activity which would offend Catholics. The Baptists in Rio de Janeiro administer their excellent school in a manner that is inoffensive to the Catholic civilians. But, if Catholics only knew it, Protestant activity in Latin America can be a blessing in disguise if it acts as a stimulant to increased activity.

The national background in Latin America and the national traditions are Catholic. In San José, Costa Rica, every Sunday morning the official city band plays before the cathedral church, and just before the late Mass its members in uniform march in to the tune of their music and continue playing during certain portions of the Holy Sacrifice. On the high altar, opposite the bishop's throne, is the dais of the president of the republic. Large crowds gather on festal occasions at the quasi-national shrines: Guadalupe in Mexico, Our Lady of Luján in Argentina and in Uruguay, Our Lady of Quinche in Ecuador, Our Lady of Copacabana in Bolivia, Our Lady of Caacupé in Paraguay. Crowds will always gather on special church festivities which assume a sort of official state character.

Late in 1950 there was celebrated the Fifth National Eucharistic Congress in Rosario in Argentina. Evita Perón was much in evidence, distributing graces and favors. The papal delegate, Cardinal Ernesto Rufini, marched in procession dispensing benedictions, his long train held from the dust of the streets by a boy. Great crowds gathered. Similarly in Caracas, capital of Venezuela, each Lent there is a Communion Sunday for the men. Crowds gather in the public plaza, a dozen priests distribute Holy Communion, and the cadets of the army, standing at attention, receive.

On the feast of the Immaculate Conception (December 8, 1950) in Cuenca, Ecuador, there took place one of those flamboyant ecclesiastical celebrations of which the Spaniards and the Hispanic-Americans are so fond. It was the coronation of Mary Auxiliatrix. There was a procession in which cadets marched to the beat of drums and the students of the Colegio San Borja carried an image of the Madonna (to which are attributed miraculous powers). The populace looked on, crowded against the walls of the narrow streets—the poor Indian with his usual stolidity, young men in festive mood. Forty thousand people assembled at the stadium where the Salesian Bishop Domingo Comín, after reading a papal bull sent for the occasion, crowned the Madonna. The crown, valued at 500,000 Ecuadorean sucres, was of gold, adorned with 467 diamonds, 110 pearls, 45 emeralds and other precious stones. "Very notable was the reception of Holy Communion by

413

the men and students."[13] When Our Lady of Quinche is taken from her little village and carried through the streets of Quito the city puts on one of its biggest shows and everybody turns out. A decade ago the people spent fifty thousand dollars for a new crown for her. In Chile, December, 1950, Cardinal Caro Rodriguez celebrated the seventieth anniversary of his ordination to the priesthood. There was a great procession in Santiago, army officers filed along followed by churchmen, while the President of the Republic, Gabriel González Videla, offered his official felicitations.

The impression among the clergy is that in many Latin American countries the condition of the Church is much improved. The hierarchy in Bolivia as in Venezuela has been intent on bettering the quality of the clergy. In Argentina there has been noted an improvement ever since the Eucharistic Congress of 1934. Catholic Action in Argentina, the *Acción Católica Argentina,* has become a notable youth movement in the nation. It is growing lustily. Whereas in 1934 during the Eucharistic Congress only six hundred young men were in attendance, nine years later at its sixth convention held in Mendoza at the foot of the Andes the meetings reached a fine total of eight thousand. A glance through the ecclesiastical guide of the Argentine will reveal an activated and energetic Catholicism.[14] In Chile where formerly a man was seldom seen at Mass, now it is not an uncommon sight. The Catholics of Uruguay, having to battle anti-clerical legislation and to fight even to retain the crucifix in their schools, are a vigorous and devoted group. Colombia has once again since 1946 enjoyed a sympathetic conservative regime.

Missionaries from the United States have for decades aided in the invigoration of Latin American Catholicism. Late in the 1920's the North American Redemptorist Provincial of Baltimore sent two of his men to Brazil to labor for souls in "green hell." By 1946 this Baltimore Province supported the vice-province of Campo Grande in Brazil which numbered twelve communities. The Redemptorists of the St. Louis Province went to Brazil in 1943 and by 1946 had established four houses of the Order. The Fathers of the Holy Cross have opened a school in Santiago, Chile, and North American nuns have done the same. The religious of the Sacred

---

[13] *Latinamerica,* III (April, 1951), 165.
[14] *Guia Eclesiástica de la República Argentina* (Buenos Aires, 1943), *passim.*

Heart have sent American nuns to their school in Vigna del Mar just outside Valparaiso. The Maryknoll fathers and nuns have for some years been doing magnificent work in Chile, Peru, Bolivia, and Ecuador, while groups of Franciscan missionaries from the north have long been working in the interior of Brazil. Outstanding in certain parts of South America are the industrial schools of the Salesians, the most practical native group of the Continent.

Catholicism is considered a power in Latin America. If an ambassador or other important representative from the north is a Catholic, Latin Americans are always proud of the fact and it facilitates his personal or official relations. For instance, in Rio de Janeiro it is more difficult for a Protestant to be accepted in the higher social circles of the Capital. Then, if we go on to compare Catholicism in the south with Protestantism in the United States (where only a slight minority either of men or women attend service regularly and are active) the scales incline decisively in favor of the Catholicism of the south.

Thus it is that North American missionaries have been able to aid the Latin American Church in solving the problems which history has bequeathed her. But over and above this the Latin American clergy themselves are harkening to the splendid leadership offered by the Holy Father. The hierarchy in Colombia, aided by members of the regular clergy, have launched upon an energetic program of social betterment. The bishops of many dioceses are zealous for a good and solid education of their clergy. But many of these bishops are poor. As North American manpower is needed in the missions, so North American dollars are required for the building and good support of seminaries. Within the last two years the Bishop of Puerto Montt in Chile and the Bishop of Yucatán have appealed to the North American clergy for financial aid. Pope Pius XII, in his last selection of cardinals, picked out for the honor such Latin American leaders as had shown themselves active and energetic in the improvement of social conditions. One of these was the Bishop of Rosario in Argentina, now Cardinal Antonio Caggiano, chief inspirer of the above-mentioned Argentine Catholic Action group. Another was the Archbishop of Santiago, Chile, now Cardinal Caro Rodríguez. It is he who cooperated with President Juan Antonia Ríos in energizing the Popular Front government of the President which included the Latin American Workers Federation. The Cardinal's action was aimed at devising ways and means for the elevation of the Chilean worker. Thus the innate vitality of Catholicism is gradually solving the problems (it must necessarily be a slow process) with which the Latin American Church found herself confronted during the initial period of independence.

Contributors

JOHN COURTNEY MURRAY, S.J., of Woodstock Seminary is the editor of *Theological Studies*.

EDWARD L. HESTON, C.S.C., PH.D., S.T.D., J.C.D., is Procurator General of the Congregation of Holy Cross.

MONSIGNOR HARRY KOENIG of Mundelein Seminary, long-time student of papal pronouncements on peace, has edited *Principles for Peace*.

OSKAR BAUHOFER is a Swiss student of religious history and political philosophy.

YVES R. SIMON, who is a member of the Committee on Social Thought of the University of Chicago, is the author of *The Philosophy of Democratic Government*.

HEINRICH ROMMEN of Georgetown University is the author of *The State in Catholic Thought* and *The Natural Law*.

KARL THIEME is a German educator and student of religious sociology, living in Switzerland.

G. NAIDENOFF, S.J., is a student of missionary problems.

OTTO ROEGELE is the editor of *Rheinischer Merkur*.

ADRIEN DANSETTE, French historian, has written *Histoire religieuse de la France contemporaine*.

MICHELE F. SCIACCA of the University of Genoa is an editor of the *Giornale di Metafisica*.

RAFAEL CALVO SERER, a Spanish critic, is the editor of *Arbor*.

THOMAS T. MCAVOY, C.S.C., of the University of Notre Dame, is the author of many studies on American Church history.

AARON I. ABELL of the University of Notre Dame is the author of *The Urban Impact on American Protestantism*.

PETER MASTEN DUNNE, S.J., of the University of San Francisco, has written numerous works on the history of Latin America.

Index

INDEX

Jugoslavia, 196

Ketteler, Archbishop von, 207, 387-388
Knights of Columbus, 373
Knights of Labor, 382-385
Kulturkampf, 206

La Farge, S.J., Father J., 162
Lateran Treaty, 59-60, 285-289
Legates, 41
Leo XII, 405
Leo XIII, 20, 25, 27, 28-29, 31, 37-38, 48, 49, 50, 51, 74, 88-90, 102, 110n, 237-238, 283, 381
Leuba, J.-L., 165, 170
Liberalism, 2, 21, 23, 24-26, 92-94, 118-119, 238, 277-279, 281-283, 378

McNicholas, Archbishop John, 145
Manning, Cardinal Edward, 343, 347-348, 350-351
Maritain, J., 111, 178, 250, 310
Maurras, Charles, 247-249
Mindszenty, Cardinal, 196
Modernism, 241-246
Mussolini, 59, 60, 62, 65

National Catholic Educational Association, 373
National Catholic Welfare Conference, 222, 362-363, 374-375, 394-396
National Conference of Catholic Charities, 391-392
Nazism, 4, 60-61, 208-211, 227
Newman, Cardinal, 343
Niemoeller, Martin, 157, 158, 161, 162-164
North Atlantic Treaty Organization, 67
Notre Dame, University of, 370
Nuncios (Apostolic), 41

O'Hara, Archbishop John, 180
Orthodox Church, 198-199
L'Osservator Romano, 66-67, 284-285, 302

Papocaesarism, 129
patronato nacional, 405-407
patronato real, 401-406
Pétain, Marshal, 251
Pilot (Boston), 382
Pius VI, 88, 98
Pius VII, 1, 405
Pius IX, 20, 278-279

Pius X, 51, 52, 89, 100, 111n, 237, 248, 273-274
Pius XI, 4, 41, 57-62, 246, 249, 286-287, 397
Pius XII, 44, 46, 47, 61-68, 80, 111n, 182, 185, 189, 310, 325, 329, 335
Poland, 184, 198
Popular Republican Movement, 255-256
Pontifical Ecclesiastical Academy, 45-46
Proudhon, P.-J., 93, 105

Quadragesimo anno, 151, 397-398

Rerum Novarum, 151, 240, 283, 355, 397
Roosevelt, Franklin D., 64
Rosmini, Antonio, 277-280, 289
Rousseau, Jean-Jacques, 75-76, 84-86, 92-93
Rumania, 197
Ryan, Monsignor John A., 371, 374, 389-390, 394

Sacred Congregation for Extraordinary Ecclesiastical Affairs, 45
Sacred Congregation for the Oriental Church, 45
Sacred Consistorial Congregation, 45
St. Louis, University of, 370
Saint-Simon, 93-94
Schools, 224-225, 235, 252-254, 316-323, 347, 350-352, 368, 370, 375
Separation of Church and State, 31, 236-237, 254, 260, 361
Sillon, 100, 240-241
socialism, 282-283, 383, 384, 385, 386, 389-390, 393
Social Movement (Catholic), 223-224, 238-240, 246-247, 298-300, 329-335, 353-356
Spanish Civil War, 266, 306-311
Spellman, Cardinal Francis, 362, 370
Stepinac, Archbishop, 196
Suarez, 109
Sword of the Spirit, 349-350
Syllabus, 278-279

Tametsi, 50
Thomas Aquinas, St., 96-97, 103, 104-105, 107, 128-129, 145, 150-151
Thomism, 244, 250, 348
de Tocqueville, Alexis, 378
totalitarianism, 79, 86, 122

Ultramontanism, 233

INDEX

Printed at Ave Maria Press